Daily Truth
for
Godly Youth

365 Practical Devotionals
for
Teens and Adults

•Howard Bean•

Christian Light Publications, Inc.
Harrisonburg, VA 22802

DAILY TRUTH FOR GODLY YOUTH

Christian Light Publications, Inc.
Harrisonburg, Virginia 22802

Printed in the United States of America

Fourth Printing, 2013

Cover Photo: © Jupiter Images/Liquid Library
Cover Design: David W. Miller

ISBN: 978-0-87813-640-7

Dedication

I dedicate this book to the four children
God has given to my wife, Barbara, and me:
Esther, Brenda, Karen, and Richard

Our experiences with them have taught me volumes about youth—their problems, their energy, their idealism, their challenges, their commitment to God, and their desire to know God's will.

I thank God that each one has received Christ as Saviour and Sovereign, and is actively serving Him in the church and missions. They have been a stimulus to me in my commitment to Christ, in my devotional life, and in my reaching out to others.

Acknowledgments

- I'm thankful to my wife, Barbara, for her helpful suggestions and typing skills.

- I appreciate Howard Lichty's permission to use his seven articles in the series called "Worship the Creator."

- I'm also grateful to a couple of young people—my daughter Karen, and Juliann Ropp—who read the manuscript, encouraged me, and made helpful suggestions.

- And thanks to Leon Yoder and the personnel at Christian Light Publications for lending their editing, typesetting, and publishing skills to the manuscript.

- Most of all I am thankful to God. May He receive glory as the lives of youth are shaped by His truth.

Books by Howard Bean

Devotionals for teens and adults

Daily Truth for Godly Youth

Daily Strength for Growing Youth

Devotionals and stories for families

Fruitful Families: Cultivating Spiritual Fruit

Worshipful Families: Marveling at God's Awesome Creation

Devotionals for courting couples

Keepsakes: Courtship Meditations and Memories

Handbook for Christian Leaders

A Good Minister: How to Preach, Pastor, and Serve Effectively

Contents

How to Use This Book

The quality of a Christian's spiritual life is usually reflected in his devotional life. This book has been written with the goal to help you think about Biblical truth and apply it to your life.

I hope you will read the Scripture passage thoughtfully. To encourage you to look for things about God and for applications to your life, a space is provided at the bottom of each page for brief comments. With the heading "About God" jot one or more things that the passage indicates about God the Father, Jesus, or the Holy Ghost. With the heading "To Do," write things stated or implied in the passage that you should put into practice in your Christian life. This may include things to say, attitudes to have, and guidelines to aspire to as well as actions to do.

For example, for January 1, here is what you might write:

About God:

Is a master.
Is in heaven.

To Do:

Be just.
Pray, watch, thanks.
Pray for missionaries.
Walk wisely.
Speak with grace.
Make good use of time.

Sometimes you will have only one item (or maybe none) under one of the categories; sometimes you may have more than there is space for. Or maybe you'd rather enter your thoughts in a separate notebook or journal. The important thing is to be looking for something that will stimulate you to read purposefully.

Your jottings can be drawn from the Scripture verse, the Bible reading, or the verses given in the devotional. Feel free to highlight and underline in the devotional book.

Sharing something from the Bible reading or the meditation with a friend or family member will reinforce the truth in your mind as well as encourage another person. Also, you will find it helpful to check whether or not you did the things in yesterday's **To Do**.

Not only can this book be used on a daily basis, it can also be referred to for Biblical instruction on a variety of topics which are developed in a seven-day series. For instance, if you want to know more about God's guidance, go to the devotionals on January 8-14, or for thoughts on the snares of a technological age, check out September 24-30. These meditations can also be used for group devotionals with youth groups or in a classroom.

—Howard Bean

Redeem the Time

"Remember now thy Creator in the days of thy youth." —Ecclesiastes 12:1

Read Colossians 4:1-6

How do you feel about the new year? Excited? Nostalgic? Regretful? Enthusiastic? Determined?

Some people feel uneasy when they think about the passage of time. For instance, once a group of young people decided to visit a novelty shop. One girl was interested in an hourglass to add to her collection of antiques. The store clerk demonstrated one of these old timepieces. The group stood and watched for several minutes as the tiny trickle of sand moved from the top to the bottom.

"I don't think I want it after all," the girl said abruptly. "It makes me feel creepy to watch it—the sands keep trickling away—and you can't stop them. It makes me feel like I'm getting old. Let's get out of here."

Moses thought about the passage of time. He prayed, "So teach us to number our days, that we may apply our hearts unto wisdom" (Psalm 90:12). How can we apply our hearts to wisdom? By applying such Bible teachings as these: "Seek ye the LORD while he may be found" (Isaiah 55:6). "Be still, and know that I am God" (Psalm 46:10). "Love the LORD thy God with all thine heart" (Deuteronomy 6:5). "Believe on the Lord Jesus Christ" (Acts 16:31).

A Christian's goal is to be "redeeming the time" (Ephesians 5:16). This means making good use of time and not wasting opportunities. Each person has twenty-four hours in a day. Our days are like identical suitcases—they are all the same size, but some people pack more into them than others.

But as you seek to redeem the time, don't forget to keep your life in balance in this rat-race age. Christians are to experience everlasting life, not exhausting life.

The following words appear on the door of a grandfather clock in Chester Cathedral in England: "When as a child I laughed and wept, time crept. When as a youth, I dreamed and talked, time walked. When I became a full-grown man, time ran. And later, as I older grew, time flew. Soon I shall find while traveling, time gone."

Determine to make good use of each day this year. Before you kill time, remember that it has no resurrection.

As an unknown poet wrote:

I have only just a minute—
Only sixty seconds in it,
Have to take it, can't refuse it,
But it's up to me to use it.

I must suffer if I lose it,
Give account if I abuse it,
Just a tiny little minute,
But eternity is in it.

About God:

To Do:

January 2

I Am Resolved

"Study to shew thyself approved unto God." —2 Timothy 2:15

Read 1 Timothy 6:11-20

Pluck a hair from your head. Now look at its width. At the time of the judges there were seven hundred left-handed slingers who could strike within a hair's breadth of their target. Check it out in Judges 20:16. How well can *you* aim? Your aim might not be so exact, but it's important that you have an aim in life.

Imagine a game of basketball with no hoop, a game of hockey without any goals, or a game of baseball with no bases. Clearly, the "game of life" needs a goal.

Jesus had a goal in life. And He had perfect aim. He said, "I do always those things that please him" (John 8:29).

The marksmen of Israel were resolved to hit their target. Players in an athletic contest are resolved to win. Jesus was resolved to do His Father's will. Put a check mark beside the aims that you, by God's grace, are resolved to do.

- I will have a time of Bible reading and prayer every day.
- I will have a grateful spirit and regularly give words of thanks to God, to my family members, and to all who contribute to my life.
- I will respect those in authority such as my dad and mom.
- I will say "No" to temptation and avoid places of temptation as much as possible.
- I will witness for Jesus and not be ashamed of Him or of His words (see Mark 8:38).
- I will yield myself to the Holy Spirit and ask to be filled with Him.
- I will forgive those who say nasty things about me.
- I will eat in moderation and keep recreational activities in balance.
- I will show kindness and forbearance, beginning at home.
- I will have a pure, godly thought life.
- I will be friendly to all in my youth group and avoid being exclusive.
- I will follow the example of Christ.

About God: **To Do:**

Abhor Sin

"Ye that love the LORD, hate evil: he preserveth the souls of his saints; he delivereth them out of the hand of the wicked." —Psalm 97:10

Read 2 Corinthians 6:14–7:1

I heard of a public school in Oregon that had a problem with some of its adolescent girls. After applying lipstick, they would press their lips against the restroom mirrors, leaving dozens of little prints.

The principal asked the girls to meet with her and the custodian in the restroom. "These lip prints are making a major problem for our custodian," she said. "He needs to clean the mirrors every day." Turning to the custodian, she said, "Would you please demonstrate for us what is involved in cleaning these mirrors?"

The custodian solemnly took out his long-handled brush, dipped it into the toilet, and began scrubbing the mirror. There were no more lip prints on the mirrors after that!

"Abhor that which is evil" (Romans 12:9). Sin needs to be as abhorrent to us as the toilet brush was to the girls. God is holy and cannot tolerate sin. If, therefore, we become part of God's family and God dwells in us, we will desire to be holy and we will "touch not the unclean thing" (2 Corinthians 6:17).

Praise God that He is able to cleanse us from the sins of the past. We are given a clean slate. But we personally have a responsibility to cooperate with God in turning from sin. We need to see sin from heaven's standpoint: Sin is repulsive, vile, abhorrent, loathsome, deadly, obnoxious, disgusting, and damning. If we see sin as it really is, we will be compelled to follow the injunction of 2 Corinthians 7:1, "Let us cleanse ourselves from all filthiness of the flesh and spirit."

Let's have the attitude of young Joseph when a woman repeatedly tried to entice him with sexual sin. He identified sin for what it was and asked rhetorically, "How then can I do this great wickedness, and sin against God?" (Genesis 39:9).

Let's have the aim of Daniel who, when faced by peer pressure, "purposed in his heart that he would not defile himself" (Daniel 1:8).

Let's have the aspiration of the psalmist who said, "Thy word have I hid in mine heart, that I might not sin against thee" (Psalm 119:11).

About God: **To Do:**

January 4

Pressing Toward Heaven

"My soul thirsteth for God, for the living God: when shall I come and appear before God?" —Psalm 42:2

Read Philippians 3:8–16

Perhaps one of your goals this year is to lose weight. I read of an obese woman who went to an exercise and diet clinic. First, the supervisor went to a mirror and drew on it a silhouette of the shape that the overweight woman wanted to achieve. The woman was significantly larger than the outline. The supervisor said, "Our goal is for you to fit this shape." So the woman dieted. She exercised. Each week she stood in front of the mirror. Her size decreased, but she was still too big. She exercised longer and dieted more strictly. Finally, one day she stood in front of the mirror and discovered that she was conformed to the outline on the mirror!

Paul longed to be conformed to Christ. His goal was to attain heaven through faith in Christ and growth in Christlikeness. This involved ten specific goals:

1. Win Christ (v. 8). To know Christ now and be with Him forever is the best reward possible.
2. Be found in Christ (v. 9). As Paul had faith in Christ, he had peace with God, and the fruit of righteousness grew in him.
3. Know Christ (v. 10). By living with someone, we get to know that person better; so it is with Christ.
4. Know the power of His resurrection (v. 10). This power not only will raise a person from the dead in the future, but will also raise a Christian to victory over sin in the present.
5. Know the fellowship of His sufferings (v. 10). Christ took up the cross—Christ's followers must too.
6. Be made conformable to His death (v. 10). Christ denied Himself and submitted to God's will concerning Calvary. We need to deny self and say, "Not my will, but thine, be done," even if it means physical death.
7. Attain unto the resurrection of the saints (v. 11). Someday Paul's dead, decapitated body will be restored, transformed to new life, and rise to glory.
8. Apprehend (v. 12). Paul still had maturing to do in Christ. Paul still wasn't perfect or fully developed, so he continued taking hold of Christlikeness, for which Christ had taken hold of Paul.
9. Forget hurtful things (v. 13). Paul didn't dwell on past sins, such as his persecution of the church, but determined to do God's will in the present and the future.
10. Press toward the mark (v. 14). His target was Christlikeness and being in the eternal presence of Christ.

About God: **To Do:**

Grow Up Into Him

"But grow in grace, and in the knowledge of our Lord and Saviour Jesus Christ." —2 Peter 3:18

Read Ephesians 4:1-15

One warm, sunny day in spring, Dan D. Line began to compare himself with the other dandelions. As he looked at his relatives and neighbors, he thought to himself, *I believe I'm one of the tallest. At least I'm no smaller than the rest. My leaves are nice and green, my stem is slender and straight, and my head is as full as any. In fact, I think I'm above average. Good for me. I see I have every reason to be proud of my growth.*

Wisely, Dad D. Longlegs told him, "Take your eyes off the other dandelions. Look up, not around. Look at that hundred-foot pine tree. Do you still feel so big?"

People commonly have the same faulty viewpoint as Dan D. Line. "They measuring themselves by themselves, and comparing themselves among themselves, are not wise" (2 Corinthians 10:12). Instead of looking around at other people with whom to compare our maturity, we should look up to Jesus and see our actual smallness in Christian maturity.

You should aim to "let this mind be in you, which was also in Christ Jesus" (Philippians 2:5).

There are seven areas of growth indicated in Ephesians 4:1-3, especially in regards to working for the Lord on the job.

"I therefore, the prisoner of the Lord, beseech you that ye walk worthy of the vocation wherewith ye are called, with all lowliness and meekness, with longsuffering, forbearing one another in love; endeavouring to keep the unity of the Spirit in the bond of peace" (Ephesians 4:1-3).

1. *Submission to God's will.* Paul was mainly a prisoner *of the Lord,* not of Nero. Paul recognized that it was God's will that he be a prisoner. This was the basic underlying reason for his imprisonment.
2. *Responsibility.* God has called us. Keep this in mind. Please Him.
3. *Lowliness.* Many young people grow small by trying to be big.
4. *Meekness.* While on the job for the Lord, we can expect to be mistreated. Respond meekly, without retaliation or hatred.
5. *Longsuffering.* If you have ever worked with others, you know patience is essential.
6. *Forbearance.* Love puts up with things that may annoy or "bug" us about other people.
7. *Effort.* Peace and unity don't just happen. They are the result of an attitude that yields to the Spirit, to fellow Christians, and to those in authority.

About God: **To Do:**

January 6

Be a Witness

"We pray you in Christ's stead, be ye reconciled to God."
—2 Corinthians 5:20

Read Acts 18:1-11

I heard a young man challenge his fellow youth, "Be a booster cable for Jesus." This idea of being like a jumper cable sparked in me a few thoughts about transmitting the Gospel.

First, like a jumper cable, you have to be connected to the source of power. Therefore, have a good grip on Jesus. He is "the life" (John 14:6).

Sometimes when I've used battery cables, I didn't get a good, tight connection on the battery terminal, and the power didn't flow through. Sometimes I've used cables with clamps that were rusty and corroded—again, no electrical current. Likewise, I need to be firmly connected to Jesus without the corrosion and dirt of sin.

Second, like a jumper cable, which helps a dead battery, you must make contact with the one in need. Therefore, you need to touch the lives of those who are dead spiritually.

Jumper cables can be used at work, at home, at church, while traveling, or anywhere in your neighborhood. So the Christian can make contact with Christ's power on the job, in the congregation, among neighbors, on vacation, and in one's home. In the early church, "They that were scattered abroad went every where preaching the word" (Acts 8:4).

Third, like a jumper cable, you need to have both a positive and a negative component. Your life needs to correspond to Romans 12:9: "Abhor that which is evil; cleave to that which is good."

Fourth, as with a battery, you dare not confuse the positive and negative. If you attach the negative cable to the positive terminal and the positive cable to the negative terminal, sparks will fly and damage may result. Isaiah 5:20 says, "Woe unto them that call evil good, and good evil."

No matter what the issue is—gambling, same-sex marriages, abortion, premarital sex, divorce and remarriage—our life and teaching need to correspond to God's Word.

Fifth, like a jumper cable, you must be available to meet the need. A jumper cable that stays on the store shelf or in a sealed package in the car trunk isn't going to be helpful. So the Christian needs to be ready to put people in touch with God. Be like Paul who said, "So, as much as in me is, I am ready to preach the gospel" (Romans 1:15).

About God: **To Do:**

Serve One Another

"Even as the Son of man came not to be ministered unto, but to minister, and to give his life a ransom for many." —Matthew 20:28

Read Philippians 2:1-11

"Hey, Ryan, you hit that ball way out of bounds." A group of youth was playing volleyball.

"Just watch me next time," Ryan yelled back.

The next time Ryan smashed the ball into the net.

"Hey, Ryan, you really ought to work on your serve."

So should many Christians. Do you need to improve the way you serve—others, I mean, not a volleyball? Considering the wonderful example of Jesus will help us improve our serve.

"Would you be willing to teach the intermediate class this year?" the pastor asked a young man. "It is a real opportunity to serve the Lord."

"Well, I don't know. I would be the regular teacher, wouldn't I? I really don't think I will. You see, it's just that I don't like to be tied down."

"Hmmm." The pastor thought a moment. "Think of Jesus—how He served. He was not just *tied down*; He was *nailed down*. Aren't you willing to be tied down for Him?"

We may think we are doing a lot for the Lord, serving others, until we think of what He has done for us, as shown in the daily reading.

In what ways is Christ our Perfect Example in service?

1. He was humble and lowly.
2. He was obedient.
3. He was unselfish.
4. He did not act through strife or vainglory.
5. He put the welfare of others ahead of His own, to the extent that He died for all.
6. He loved sincerely and fervently.
7. He identified with the problems of men.
8. He lived for the glory of God.

What a challenge to be like Christ! Our attitude (mind) should be like Christ's—through our service, our humility, and our obedience.

Just think of Him: God the Son, mighty and majestic, holy and high, taking on the form of man. *Thought it not robbery* means He didn't cling to His heavenly rights. Instead, He put aside His heavenly glory and dignity (*"made himself of no reputation"*) and became as a servant or slave. He obeyed God and served us, laying down His life to give us real life.

He who stooped so low is now exalted to the highest by God. Let us also exalt Him by kneeling before Him in worship, love, and thanksgiving, and by openly testifying that He is our Lord and Saviour.

About God: **To Do:**

God Wants to Guide You

"Thou in thy mercy hast led forth the people which thou hast redeemed: thou hast guided them in thy strength unto thy holy habitation." —Exodus 15:13

Read Exodus 33:12-17

My favorite Bible verses as a youth were these: "Trust in the LORD with all thine heart; and lean not unto thine own understanding. In all thy ways acknowledge him, and he shall direct thy paths" (Proverbs 3:5, 6). Such trust is not blind because it is *in the Lord.* He knows and He cares.

- What should be my occupation?
- Where should I go into VS?
- Should I get more education or training?
- Does God want me to be single or married?
- Should I extend my time of VS?
- Should I change jobs?
- Should I begin courtship?
- Should I keep living at home or get an apartment?
- Which congregation should I attend and support?
- Should I buy a different vehicle? New or used?
- How shall I use my time this weekend?

Many questions and discussions face us throughout our lives. We are thankful God delights in guiding His child. "For this God is our God for ever and ever: he will be our guide even unto death" (Psalm 48:14). Like a shepherd, "He maketh me to lie down in green pastures: he leadeth me beside the still waters" (Psalm 23:2).

He is willing to guide us very intimately. "Direct thy paths" sounds specific and personal. True, God gives general guidance. For example, seek ye first the kingdom of God. Do all things for the glory of God. Don't marry an unbeliever. Honor thy father and mother. Keep thyself pure.

But I believe He also gives direct direction—what job to have, where to live as a single person, whom to marry. "The steps of a good man are ordered by the LORD: and he delighteth in his way" (Psalm 37:23).

Young person, trust in the *Lord.* Don't trust in horoscopes, clairvoyants, and fortune-tellers. On August 31, 1997, Princess Diana of England died after a violent auto crash. A psychic that she and her companion, Dodi al-Fayed, had consulted nineteen days earlier had said nothing about this upcoming tragedy. Instead, during their almost two hours with the woman psychic, the couple evidently had received a very encouraging prediction.

Only God knows the future, and He wants to direct your life. Be yielded to Him. He who makes God first will find God with him to the last.

About God: **To Do:**

Ways God Has Guided

"I will instruct thee and teach thee in the way which thou shalt go: I will guide thee with mine eye." —Psalm 32:8

Read Joshua 7:6-15

God has used a variety of ways to guide people in both the Old and New Testaments. When Joshua prayed, God showed him the reason for the disaster at Ai and what to do about it, as indicated in the daily reading. In Joseph's experience in his teens and twenties, God used adverse circumstances. This included such things as the envy of his brothers, slavery, a false accusation by his boss's wife, jail time, and bad weather.

Moses encountered a burning bush and received direction from God's voice. Eliezer found a wife for Isaac, using a combination of a prayer, a sign, and a confirmation. Nehemiah "found written in the law" instructions for worship (Nehemiah 8:14).

In the New Testament we read of the wise men who were guided by a star and by the prophecy of Micah 5:2. Joseph was instructed in a dream to marry his betrothed, to flee to Egypt, and later to return to Galilee. Mary and Joseph were directed by government decrees to go to Bethlehem where Jesus was born.

Peter had a message from God in a vision (while the soup was warming) which was confirmed by a delegation from Cornelius (Acts 10:9-23). The leaders of the early church cast lots to find God's will for leadership. At the Jerusalem Conference, they used Scriptures, personal experiences, and what seemed good to the Holy Ghost and the brotherhood to find direction.

One day my nine-year-old daughter, Brenda, asked, "How can a person know if God is calling her to do something or to go someplace? Is it instinct or what?"

"No, it's not instinct," I said. "However, circumstances can help you. For example, you might hear people talk of their experience in Guatemala. You might think, *I would really like to go and help them.* You might think of going as a teacher or nurse or housekeeper. Then, after that, perhaps someone might ask you, 'Have you ever thought of going into mission work?' "

Now, almost twenty years later, I came across my notes of this long-forgotten conversation. They're especially interesting because Brenda has been involved in a mission in Guatemala for several years and will continue there as long as the Lord so leads. It reminds me that God can use ordinary conversation among ordinary people to give guidance.

About God: **To Do:**

God Guides Through the Bible

"Thou shalt guide me with thy counsel." —Psalm 73:24

Read 2 Timothy 3:14–4:4

A young man was considering courtship. He took three identical slips of plain paper. On one, he wrote the name of a girl he really liked. On the second, he wrote the name of another girl. The third, he left blank. Then he turned the names facedown and mixed them thoroughly with his eyes closed. After prayer, he drew one slip. It had on it the name of the girl he liked.

To be sure, he made it two out of three. The second time he drew the blank slip; the third time he got the special girl's name again. So he concluded he should court her. He went to talk to her. She was not as convinced as he was.

For the next several days, let's consider how God guides Christians today. The basic way God directs us is by the teachings of the Bible. He has written to tell us how to please Him, how to be happy, and how to attain heaven.

Jesus said, "Search the Scriptures" (John 5:39). They show much of God's will clearly. Get fully acquainted with the Bible, and you will automatically understand God's will. For example, the Bible tells us to repent, believe in Jesus, tell the truth, love, don't hate, be pure, show kindness, don't marry an unbeliever, obey your authorities, and work honestly. Jesus said, "Ye do err, not knowing the Scriptures" (Matthew 22:29).

As A. W. Tozer put it, "If God gives you a watch, are you honoring Him more by asking Him what time it is or by simply consulting the watch?"

Everything we need to know for a spiritually successful life and a safe passage to the Celestial City is found in the Bible. This is quite different from a statement found in a collection called *365 Stupidest Things Ever Said:* "If you bought our course, 'How to Fly in Six Easy Lessons,' we apologize for any inconvenience caused by our failure to include the last chapter, 'How to Land Your Plane Safely.' Send us your name and address and we will send you the last chapter posthaste. Requests by estates will be honored."

Not so with the Lord's instruction manual. Don't be foolish and try to fly through life without thinking where you are headed and what will happen upon landing on your deathbed. Follow the Scriptures, "which are able to make thee wise" (2 Timothy 3:15).

About God: **To Do:**

God Guides Through Prayer

"For every one that asketh receiveth; and he that seeketh findeth; and to him that knocketh it shall be opened." —Matthew 7:8

Read Genesis 24:10-37

For daily guidance some consult the stars—but the Christian consults the Maker of the stars. Do you need some direction? "Ask, and it shall be given you." Do you need to find some answers? "Seek, and ye shall find." Are you waiting for something to open up? "Knock, and it shall be opened unto you."

An aircraft pilot was following a busy two-lane highway and observing the traffic below. He noticed a car whose driver was trying to pass a large transport truck. Despite repeated attempts, the driver was unable to pass because of hills and curves and oncoming traffic. The pilot, able to see several miles down the highway, said to himself, "If only the driver could communicate with me, I could tell him when and where it is safe to pass."

God, our heavenly Pilot, has provided a means of communication through prayer. He sees beyond the hills and curves in our lives. He is eager to tell us how to travel down the highway of life. If we ask Him, we will find the guidance we seek.

Examples abound in the Scriptures of people who longed for God's guidance. Eliezer prayed for very specific guidance as he sought a wife for his master's son. Moses needed God's directions for leading the Israelites out of Egypt and through the wilderness. Solomon felt like a little child with a huge responsibility when he asked God for an understanding heart to decide what was right. The psalmist said, "Teach me thy way, O LORD, and lead me in a plain path, because of mine enemies" (Psalm 27:11). Before ordaining a replacement for Judas, the apostles prayed and said, "Thou, Lord, which knowest the hearts of all men, shew whether of these two thou hast chosen" (Acts 1:24).

The important thing while praying for God's leading is to have the attitude "whatever God reveals, I will do." As John 7:17 says, "Whoever has the will to do the will of God shall know" (*New English Bible*). I must be willing to do it before I know it.

About God: **To Do:**

January 12

God Guides Through His Spirit

"Praying always with all prayer and supplication in the Spirit."
—Ephesians 6:18

Read Acts 8:26-40

Jesus said of the Spirit, "He will guide you into all truth" (John 16:13). If we want to know God's will for the future, we need to follow God's will in the present. The Holy Spirit will not guide someone away from the truth. Jesus said in John 17:17, "Thy word is truth." Therefore, if we want to be led by God, we must be obedient to God's Word.

The Spirit generally gives direction through the Scriptures (which He wrote). He will not guide contrary to the guidance that He has already given. Like a compass that always points north, the Spirit will always point the same direction as the Bible.

We need to try (test) the spirits (1 John 4:1) because many false spirits are gone out into the world. In addition, we often must distinguish between our wish and His will.

Sometimes the Spirit impresses a believer with an inner compulsion—for example, that we should witness to an acquaintance or a sense that danger is near. Isaiah 30:21 says, "And thine ears shall hear a word behind thee, saying, This is the way, walk ye in it, when ye turn to the right hand, and when ye turn to the left." But impressions always need to be subject to the Bible. Any action not in harmony with the *Word* of God cannot be in harmony with the *will* of God.

The Spirit will lead those who are surrendered to God's plan. An unsuccessful life is the result of an unsurrendered will. Be assured—if God sends you on a stony path, He will provide you with sturdy shoes.

The Spirit led Philip into the desert where he met an Ethiopian who was seeking God's will. This Ethiopian had been to Jerusalem to worship God. Now, as he was reading the Bible, his heart was open to a godly counselor. He illustrates the verse: "The steps of a good man are ordered by the LORD" (Psalm 37:23). This good man was living up to what light he had, and God rewarded him by leading him to Jesus.

The way to see farther ahead is to go ahead in the will of God as far as you can see.

About God: **To Do:**

God Guides Through Godly Counselors

"Where no counsel is, the people fall: but in the multitude of counsellors there is safety." —Proverbs 11:14

Read 1 Samuel 20:1-17

Often God's will has become clear to me after talking with several other Christians. God gives each of us someone with whom to counsel. A young person who disregards the advice of godly parents is taking the road to heartache. Even Jesus "came to Nazareth, and was subject unto [His parents]" (Luke 2:51).

Friends can help us know what to do as is shown by the daily reading. The brotherhood is a great source of collective wisdom. To go contrary to your congregation's teaching and counsel is to place yourself in great peril.

I have found much of God's guidance to me to be cumulative. As a youth I read George Mueller's way of discerning God's will and I still find it very helpful. He wrote:

1. I seek at the beginning to get my heart into such a state that it has no will for its own in regard to a given matter. Nine-tenths of the trouble with people is just here. Nine-tenths of the difficulties are overcome when our hearts are ready to do the Lord's will, whatever it may be. When one is truly in this state, it is usually but a little way to the knowledge of what His will is.
2. Having done this, I do not leave the result to feeling or a simple impression. If I do so, I make myself liable to great delusions.
3. I see the will of the Spirit of God through, or in connection with, the Word of God. The Spirit and the Word must be combined. If I look to the Spirit alone without the Word, I lay myself open to great delusions also. If the Holy Spirit guides us at all, He will do it according to the Scriptures and never contrary to them.
4. Next, I take into consideration providential circumstances. These often plainly indicate God's will in connection with His Word and Spirit.
5. I ask God in prayer to reveal His will to me aright.
6. Thus, through prayer to God, the study of the Word, and reflection, I come to a deliberate judgment according to the best of my ability and knowledge; and if my mind is thus at peace and continues so after two or more petitions, I proceed accordingly. In trivial matters, and in transactions involving most important issues, I have found this method always effective.

About God: **To Do:**

January 14

God Guides Through Circumstances

"A door was opened unto me of the Lord." —2 Corinthians 2:12

Read Judges 6:33-40

As Joseph looked back over his teenage years, he saw God's direction through circumstances. He told his brothers who had thrown him into a pit, sold him as a slave, and lied about him to their dad, "Ye thought evil against me; but God meant it unto good, to bring to pass, as it is this day, to save much people alive" (Genesis 50:20).

Not only are the *steps* of a good man ordered of the Lord, but also the *stops*. David Livingstone was stopped from going to China as he had planned initially. Then the door opened to go to Africa.

A young man once considered taking training for a certain profession, which would have meant living away from home. But his parents needed him to care for some of their health needs. While he was pondering what to do, he read 1 Timothy 5:8, "But if any provide not for his own, and specially for those of his own house, he hath denied the faith, and is worse than an infidel." He decided that due to circumstances, the Lord wanted him to stay in his home community.

Sometimes we make tentative plans, but then God closes the door. Don't attempt to go through closed doors.

What about "the fleece"? Gideon asked God for a sign to confirm His leading. First, he asked God to put dew on a fleece but to keep dew off the surrounding area. The next morning, he wrung a bowl of water from the fleece, but all around the fleece it was dry.

Should we likewise ask God to show us His will by supernatural means? The "fleece" is not commanded. It should definitely not be used if the principle of Scripture is clear. If it is used, it should be used sparingly. Zacharias asked for a sign to confirm the promised birth of a son in his old age; he became mute until his son was born. Asking for a supernatural sign is debatable. But applying the principles of the supernatural Scriptures is always wise.

About God: **To Do:**

Devoting Oneself to Devotions

"I cried with my whole heart; hear me, O LORD: I will keep thy statutes." —Psalm 119:145

Read Psalm 19

When a backslidden person returns to the Lord, it's very common for the person to say, "I began straying from the Lord when I neglected my devotional life." Bible reading, prayer, meditation, and fellowship with God are vital to a healthy, victorious Christian life. An anonymous poet wrote:

Begin the day with God,
Kneel down to Him in prayer;
Lift up thy heart to His abode;
And seek His love to share.

Open the Book of God
And read a portion there,
That it may hallow all thy thoughts
And sweeten all thy care.

Go through the day with God,
Whate'er thy work may be;
Where e'er thou art—at home, abroad
He is still near to thee.

Conclude the day with God:
Thy sins to Him confess,
Trust in the Lord's atoning blood,
And plead His righteousness.

William Borden, known as Borden of Yale, said, "I have only missed my morning watch once or twice this term. . . . I can easily believe that it is next in importance to accepting Christ. For I know that when I don't wait upon God in prayer and Bible study, things go wrong."

Sometimes personal devotions are easy and delightful as we enter the closet (Matthew 6:6), humming "I Love to Steal Awhile Away"; other times devotions take a lot of discipline. If personal devotions is a habit (but not a rut), it will more likely happen daily. Devotional life, like muscle, develops with exercise.

My brother-in-law has made his devotional life a priority. His rule is, "No Bible, no breakfast."

When to have personal devotions varies with people. For many Christians, morning is best. Even if you are busy getting ready for school or work, give some time to communing with God. You wouldn't go to work or school with a dirty face. Why face the public with the face of your soul unwashed?

But others find evening is best because it is more relaxed. Hudson Taylor said, "Whatever is your best time in the day, give that to communion with God."

About God: **To Do:**

January 16

Milk, Please

"I have esteemed the words of his mouth more than my necessary food."
— Job 23:12

Read 1 Peter 2:1-12

I love a glass of cold milk, especially if complemented by a chocolate chip cookie. I have heard that milk is "the most nearly perfect food," containing proteins, carbohydrates, fats, minerals, and vitamins—all the nutrients for healthy bodies. The Bible is the perfect food, containing comfort, correction, cleansing, and teaching.

In order to grow, our souls must feed on the Bible, which is compared to milk in 1 Peter 2:2: "As newborn babes, desire the sincere milk of the word, that ye may grow thereby." In what ways is the Bible like milk?

World Book reports that children who drink milk grow faster than those on similar diets who do not drink milk. In our private time with the Lord we may have helpful devotional books, study guides, and resource material, but we will not grow as we should unless we drink the pure milk of God.

The encyclopedia also states that milk is one of the easiest foods for the body to digest. I thank God that the Bible is delicious and digestible, not only for saints of forty years but also for babes in Christ who have recently found the Saviour.

Milk is called a "protective" food because it makes up deficiencies in the diet. Bible reading accompanied by prayer also protects and strengthens the child of God in his areas of weakness. In addition, it also has some antidote-like properties when taken after accidental ingestion of certain toxic substances.

Each person in the U.S. consumes an average of 560 pounds of dairy products a year. That sounds like a lot. No doubt you appreciate the Bible, yet don't you feel you could profit from more Bible reading and meditation?

Even when you are busy, don't neglect to drink in the truths of God's Word. F. B. Meyer said, "We may measure our growth in grace by the growth of our love for private Bible study." R.A. Torrey stressed, "There's nothing more important for the development of the spiritual life of the Christian than regular systematic Bible study." Another writer wisely says, "Turn to the Bible each day, no matter how you feel. It's not primarily a shelf of medicines for emergencies; it is daily food for daily needs."

Personally, I love milk. If you want to be a growing, vibrant Christian, you must love the Scriptures.

About God: **To Do:**

Priority of Prayer

"And in the morning, rising up a great while before day, he went out, and departed into a solitary place, and there prayed." —Mark 1:35

Read Ephesians 1:15-23

Fanny Crosby, author of eight thousand songs, never attempted to write a hymn without kneeling down in prayer. Composer William Doane once sent her a tune and wanted words put to it. Somehow, she couldn't seem to write—suitable words evaded her. Then she remembered she hadn't especially prayed. Rising from prayer, she dictated as fast as her assistant could write, "Jesus, Keep Me Near the Cross."

Is prayer important to you? It is to God. Jesus said we ought to have personal private fellowship with the Father. "When thou prayest, enter into thy closet, and when thou hast shut thy door, pray to thy Father which is in secret; and thy Father which seeth in secret shall reward thee openly" (Matthew 6:6). The fact that the Father will reveal openly tells me that one's private prayer life or lack of it will show in one's life. The Apostle Paul, writing to Timothy, knew the importance of prayer. "I exhort therefore, that, *first of all,* supplications, prayers, intercessions, and giving of thanks, be made for all men" (1 Timothy 2:1). Prayer needs to have priority. That's why Jesus would go to a solitary place to pray early.

Tertullian, an early church leader in Northern Africa, wrote, "Prayer is the wall of faith. It is her arms and missiles against the foe, who keeps watch over us on all sides. And so we never walk unarmed." As for how loudly we pray, he wrote, "The sounds of our voice, likewise, should be subdued. For, if we are to be heard for our noise, what large windpipes we would need! But God is the hearer—not of the *voice*—but of the *heart.* . . . What superior advantage will those who pray too loudly gain—except that they annoy their neighbors?"

Pray or you may be deceived as Joshua was when he failed to ask the counsel of the Lord and was severely misled by the Gibeonite fakes. Pray or you will sin as Peter did when he slept instead of praying and shortly after denied Jesus. Pray or you will lack power as did the disciples of Jesus when they failed to heal a demon-possessed boy. Jesus explained, "This kind goeth not out but by prayer and fasting" (Matthew 17:21).

Therefore, give prayer priority. Our ability to stay with God in the prayer closet is the measure of our ability to stay with God when we are outside of it.

About God: **To Do:**

Worship

"O come, let us worship and bow down." —Psalm 95:6

Read Exodus 3:1-17

There is an old story about a man who dreamed that an angel escorted him to church one Sunday. There he saw the keyboard musician playing vigorously and the praise team singing with enthusiasm. But the man heard no sound. The congregation was singing, but the sound was totally muted. When the minister rose to speak, his lips moved, but nothing could be heard. In amazement, the man turned to his escort for an explanation.

"That is the way it sounds to us in heaven," said the angel. "You hear nothing because there is nothing to hear. These people are engaged in the form of worship, but their thoughts are on other things, and their hearts are far away."

That is the way it can be in personal devotional life. Yes, the Bible chapter is read, and the person drops to his knees, but his thoughts are far away. Haven't you sometimes read a portion of the Bible, but after you have finished, you really couldn't say what it was about?

Worship means devoting one's attention to the worth of someone or something because one considers it worthy. The word *worship* comes from the old English word *worthship*. For the Christian, worship is declaring God's worth to God. In the Lord's Prayer, Jesus taught the disciples to begin worship with "Hallowed be thy name." Worship involves recognition of God's attributes, a response of awe, an expression of praise, a pondering and meditating upon His truth, a heart of gratitude, and an attitude of love and devotion.

In fact, worship should extend into daily life. We should worship not only with our lips, but also with our lives.

I find it interesting that the main word for worship in the Old Testament is the Hebrew word meaning "to prostrate oneself, to bow down in awe and submission." This concept is illustrated by Moses at the burning bush.

In the New Testament the most common word for worship means "to come forward to kiss." Through Jesus Christ we come to God in love as our friend, or as a child calling Him "Daddy" (Abba, Father).

Our worship should combine both elements: submissive reverence and loving friendship.

About God: **To Do:**

Purposes of Prayer

"In every thing by prayer and supplication with thanksgiving let your requests be made known unto God." —Philippians 4:6

Read Daniel 9:1-23

Prayer has at least six purposes:

1. *To exalt God.* Psalm 95:6 says, "O come, let us worship and bow down: let us kneel before the LORD our maker." Spurgeon advised, "Wash your face every morning in a bath of praise."

2. *To confess.* Psalm 32:5 says, "I acknowledged my sin unto thee, and mine iniquity have I not hid. I said, I will confess my transgressions unto the LORD."

3. *To receive guidance.* Psalm 25:5 says, "Lead me in thy truth, and teach me: for thou art the God of my salvation; on thee do I wait all the day."

4. *To obtain help.* Hebrews 4:16 says, "Let us therefore come boldly unto the throne of grace, that we may obtain mercy, and find grace to help in time of need." My wife and I have often been on a very limited budget. Once we tackled a major plumbing project in an attempt to save money. Neither of us had any experience in plumbing. After about 24 hours of cutting copper pipes and soldering them, there were still a discouraging number of leaks. Although I cannot say I had great faith, we prayed. Then we soldered a little more, and the leaks all stopped.

5. *To intercede.* Paul told his friends, "Brethren, pray for us."

6. *To request.* Hymnwriter Fanny Crosby commonly prayed about material things and money matters. One time she was short of money and desperately needed a certain sum. Although she had no idea where it could come from, she simply prayed for the money.

A few minutes later, while she paced back and forth to get into the mood for writing another hymn, a knock sounded at the door. A stranger who admired her hymn writing came in and they chatted awhile. Then as the stranger gave her a parting handshake, he placed some money in her hand. It was the exact amount she needed. Rising from a prayer of thanks, she wrote the words to the song, "All the Way My Saviour Leads Me."

She said, "I have no way of accounting for this, except to believe that God put it into the heart of this good man to bring the money. My first thought was that it is so wonderful the way the Lord leads me, I immediately wrote the poem."

Prayer is not the last extremity—it's the first necessity.

About God:

To Do:

Coughing and Praying

"Praying always with all prayer and supplication in the Spirit."
—Ephesians 6:18

Read Luke 18:1-14

"Pray without ceasing." It's a Bible command—concise, but perhaps not altogether clear. I for one have wondered how to literally obey the instruction of 1 Thessalonians 5:17.

Does it mean praying for twenty-four hours a day nonstop? Would a tape recording of my spoken voice be a good application of this verse? How about a prayer chain involving all members of the congregation? Just what is meant by *praying without ceasing*?

My understanding of the phrase has been broadened by discovering that during Roman times the Greek word translated "without ceasing" was used in describing a cough. A praying person is something like a coughing person.

- Even someone who coughs all day does not give one long, continuous cough. Rather, he coughs at intervals. In the same way, a Christian isn't involved in one long, drawn-out prayer, but prays whenever he needs to or is prompted to.
- You wouldn't say a person with a cough has stopped coughing just because at a given moment he is not coughing. Likewise, though a child of God isn't constantly on his knees or engaged in conscious prayer, you wouldn't say he has stopped praying.
- Our bodies may unexpectedly feel the need to cough; our spirits may suddenly sense the need to pray. A person with a cough may cough frequently—hardly a good thing. A person walking with God will pray frequently—definitely a good thing. The spirit of prayer will prevail without ceasing. Thus a devotional time can continue through the day.

Opportunities abound to pray frequently, especially of the "open eyes" type. For instance, a woman ironing clothes was thinking about lines—clotheslines, phone lines, fishing lines, etc. She thought, "Why not a prayer line?" So she strung a short rope across one corner of her kitchen where she irons and hung cards on it with the names of people she knew needed prayer. Now as she irons, she prays for each person by name. Not surprisingly, news has spread, and she gets regular requests to "hang me on your prayer line."

About God: **To Do:**

Hide It in Your Heart

"Thy word have I hid in mine heart, that I might not sin against thee."
—Psalm 119:11

Read Deuteronomy 11:13-21

One Sunday evening our congregation had an emphasis on Bible memory. The devotional leader began by quoting Colossians 3. The congregation was then invited to quote verses, chapters, or books of the Bible. Some were short passages, others long. It was a blessing to hear an octogenarian quote Hebrews 1, a fourteen-year-old quote Matthew 5, and others between those ages quote other chapters. We ran out of time. The brother who was planning to say the entire Book of Philippians by memory did not have the opportunity.

Perhaps your congregation would like to devote an evening to Bible memorization. At the least, you personally can give attention to this difficult but rewarding task.

You or your congregation could recite at least one verse by memory from each of the 66 books of the Bible. Your Sunday school teacher could assign portions of a book such as Ephesians or James to various pupils and have the entire book recited in a service.

I remember when our congregation studied Acts in a series of midweek meetings, volunteers were asked to recite the chapter studied on a particular evening. I remember my mother learned and quoted Acts 2 with four days' notice.

Somehow, I have always found memory work to be difficult. (Maybe that's the way most people feel, which would explain why little memorization is done.) In group efforts I seem to stumble and stutter around while others sail smoothly along. But I keep plugging away, trying to add a few more verses—at least to replace the verses previously learned, which fade with time. The verses I know best are those I learned shortly after becoming a Christian, while bumping around on the seat of an Allis-Chalmers tractor. I wrote several verses on a card, stuffed it into my back pocket, and then pulled it out and memorized the verses while doing fieldwork.

Memorizing Bible verses takes a lot of time. Yet knowing Scripture by heart is very valuable. How? It comforts in time of trouble. It is an aid to victory: "Thy word have I hid in mine heart, that I might not sin against thee" (Psalm 119:11). It helps in witnessing and personal work. It is useful in teaching. And it's tremendous for meditation (Psalm 1:2).

Yes, *hide* the Word in your heart. But the blessings of your efforts need not be *hidden*.

About God: **To Do:**

We All Die

"There is no man that hath power over the spirit to retain the spirit; neither hath he power in the day of death." —Ecclesiastes 8:8

Read Psalm 49:1-15

Harold Lee Duncan was mowing his lawn. His wife and two children were watching. Suddenly Duncan grabbed his left side, staggered a few steps, collapsed, and then died. A half-inch piece of wire, no bigger than a piece of pencil lead, had been hurled into his heart by the lawnmower.

A twenty-four-year-old newspaper reporter, Jost Lemann, put a bottle on top of his head and asked another man to shoot it off. J. Poetschke took aim with a .38 caliber pistol, pulled the trigger, and missed. The bullet penetrated Lemann's head. He died on the spot, and the "William Tell" episode ended in tragedy.

Carlos Umbos was fishing in Pampanga, in the Philippines. According to the police, Umbos yawned, and a fish jumped in and became stuck in his throat. He choked to death before the fish could be pulled out.

Mario Cianca entered a funeral parlor and saw a man rise with a satisfied smile from a coffin. Cianca died of shock. Pedro Fernandez, owner of the parlor, had been measuring the coffin for a client about his own size. The shock of what Cianca thought he saw was too much for him.

In contrast with the above deaths, most people die of old age or illness—cancer, cardiovascular disease, malaria, typhoid fever, tuberculosis, etc.

Whether we are old or young, death is an appointment no one will miss, apart from the Second Coming of Christ. The old *will* die soon, and the young *may* die soon.

The young often feel immune to death. A fourteen-year-old girl was trapped in a car in a fiery wreck. No one could get close to the flames. "Get me out of here!" she screamed. "I'm too young to die!" But she wasn't too young.

Death is final. Second Samuel 14:14 says, "For we must needs die, and are as water spilt on the ground, which cannot be gathered up again." As the daily reading says, both wise men and the fool die and leave their wealth to others.

In addition, the Judgment follows death. "It is appointed unto men once to die, but after this the judgment" (Hebrews 9:27).

Really, how we die does not matter—whether by common or unusual means. The important thing is that one is right with God and ready to die.

About God: **To Do:**

Advantages of Living in Sin

"Good understanding giveth favour: but the way of trangressors is hard."
—Proverbs 13:15

Read Hebrews 11:23-29

Living a sinful life has its advantages:
- Sensual pleasures.
- Living without self-denial.
- Being perfectly in style.
- Popularity with the crowd.
- Being your own boss (supposedly).
- Feeling right at home in bars, theaters, and most other places (probably not revival meetings).
- Adulterers even have the approval of some church leaders.

Yes, living in sin has its advantages. But they are very, very, very, very short-lived. Then eternity! Suppose a person without a parachute were to jump from a plane a mile high. What a view! It would be the thrill of a lifetime. But think of the tragedy at the end of that plunge. Think, too, of the spiritual tragedy at the conclusion of the life of one who has plunged into sin.

Living in sin has its disadvantages. They are overwhelming—eternally overwhelming—disadvantages. Even prior to death, one could cite a guilty conscience, a lack of abiding peace, insecurity, unhappiness from the consequences of sin, and fear of death. The way of the transgressor is hard, the Bible says. The way of the transgressor also leads to everlasting damnation. The rich man in hell was reminded of the pleasures he had enjoyed. After his death, they were of absolutely no consequence. Moses had eternal perspectives, as shown in the daily reading.

Multitudes are captivated and enslaved by the allurement of sin.
- Pray that their eyes may see eternal values.
- Speak that their ears may hear of everlasting judgment.
- Love that their hearts may be touched by the Saviour's love.
- Live that their minds may be turned to Jesus Christ.

About God: **To Do:**

January 24

There Is a Way Out

"I am the door: by me if any man enter in, he shall be saved, and shall go in and out, and find pasture." —John 10:9

Read John 14:1-19

Mankind feels trapped, cornered, frustrated, beset by guilt from the past, harried by problems in the present, and tormented by worry about the future. The human race tries to find a way out.

Money says—*buy your way out.* If only you would have a thousand more or a million more, all would be well. But trust in riches is shortsighted, and the relief provided by wealth is, at best, temporary.

Philosophy says—*think your way out.* Use reasoning and logic to inquire into the mysteries of life. Take your pick of the "answers." As one "church" advertises in a local newspaper, "Invent your own theology." But God says, "Beware lest any man spoil you through philosophy and vain deceit" (Colossians 2:8). Philosophy is not the remedy.

Alcohol says—*drink your way out.* A six-pack, a bottle of champagne, a night at the tavern—these are ways to drown your troubles and find a way of relief. But alcohol only "irrigates" the troubles and increases the bitter reaping of sin. As Ben Franklin said, "No man ever drank lard into his tub, or flour into his sack, nor meal into his barrel, nor happiness into his head, nor God into his heart."

The drug scene says—*hallucinate your way out.* Snort, sniff, swallow, needle, or smoke yourself into a world of elevated moods, brilliant lights, and euphoric sensations—along with downers, despair, addiction, and anguish. Drugs are not the answer.

Psychiatry says—*talk your way out.* Relive your childhood memories on the psychiatrist's couch. Rehearse your hurts and fears. Review your week with a psychologist. But just talking is not the answer.

And the list goes on. Television says—*fantasize your way out.* New Agers say—*meditate your way out.* Industry says—*work your way out.* Science says—*invent your way out.* Politicians says—*spend your way out.*

Satan says, "THERE IS NO WAY OUT." Life is hopeless, give up in despair. End it all.

But Jesus says, "I AM THE WAY OUT." In answer to the question, how can we know the way, Jesus said, "I am the way, the truth, and the life" (John 14:6). He is the way out of sin and guilt. He is the way out of aimlessness and frustration. He is the way out of despair.

He is the way out of this sin-cursed earth into the mansions of glory!

About God: **To Do:**

Present Blessings of the Christian

"Ye rejoice with joy unspeakable and full of glory." —1 Peter 1:8

Read Ephesians 1:1-14

An Oklahoma native was once asked, "How did Christ save you? You say you are saved. What do you mean?"

The old Indian took some dry leaves and placed them in a little circle. Then he took a worm, put it inside the circle, and set fire to the leaves all around the circle. As the fire burned, the caterpillar crawled first in one direction, and then in another, trying to find a way out. It turned this way and that, but there was no escape. Finally the worm curled up to die.

The native then reached down, picked up the worm and placed it outside the circle and safe from the fire. He said, "That's what Jesus did for me. I was perishing. I had no peace and no hope. Jesus lifted me up and saved me."

The daily reading mentions wonderful "spiritual blessings in heavenly places in Christ."

- *Grace* (v. 2). Grace basically means God's favor for us. Christ was born for us. He died for us. He intercedes for us. He is preparing heaven for us, and He is coming for us.
- *Peace* (v. 2). "There is no peace, saith my God, to the wicked" (Isaiah 57:21). But Jesus said, "My peace I give unto you" (John 14:27).
- *Adoption* (v. 5). An adopted child has been chosen. God has chosen those who choose Him. They become part of His family.
- *Acceptance* (v. 6). We all have a deep need to be accepted. We find fulfillment for that need within the family of God.
- *Redemption* (v. 7). To be redeemed is to be purchased. The ransom price was the blood of Christ.
- *Forgiveness* (v. 7). We owed a debt we could not pay; He paid a debt He did not owe. When I became a Christian, I was ecstatic as it dawned on me that all my sins were totally gone. Forgiveness means God buries our sins and does not mark the grave.
- *Knowledge of God's will* (v. 9). By looking into the Bible and looking unto Jesus, we know what God wants us to be and to do.
- *Inheritance* (v. 11). The ultimate inheritance will be celestial property. Though now we have a cross, there we'll have a crown. The cross of Christ is the only ladder tall enough to reach heaven.

About God: **To Do:**

January 26

God Wants All to Be Saved

"For God so loved the world, that he gave his only begotten Son, that whosoever believeth in him should not perish, but have everlasting life." —John 3:16

Read Revelation 22:1-17

Ike Miller was the terror of a North England mining district. Evangelistic services were being held, and many miners were listening to the Gospel. Ike Miller had said he would break up the meeting. One evening he came into the service and took a seat near the front. Henry Moorhouse, the young preacher, was preaching on the love of Christ.

The preacher and all his fellow workers were afraid Ike would create a disturbance. Unknown to them, a disturbance *was* created. It was in the depths of Ike's soul. As he listened to the message of a Saviour's love, his proud heart was broken. The light of the Gospel shone in.

When the meeting was over, Ike left for his home. Several older Christians surrounded the young evangelist and told him he had missed a great opportunity. They thought that a warning of judgment should have been sounded, not a winsome message of love. "What does he care about the love of Christ?" they asked.

"I'm really sorry I did not preach to him correctly," said young Moorhouse. "I did so much want to help him."

Little did those well-meaning men know of the power of the Gospel.

Ike Miller reached his home, where he had ofttimes been a terror.

"Home so early?" his wife cried, as he entered. She came forward to meet him, hoping to shelter their children, who had fled into a corner. Then, to her astonishment, she saw he was not drunk but perfectly sober. Even more astonishing, he put his arms around her and kissed her.

"Lass," Ike said, "God has brought your husband back to you." Taking up his children, he said, "My little boy and girl, God has brought your father back to you. Now let us all pray."

The Apostle Paul writes about "God our Saviour; who will have all men to be saved, and to come unto the knowledge of the truth" (1 Timothy 2:3, 4). Jesus said that there is joy among the angels when a sinner repents and comes to God.

God is not willing that any should perish (2 Peter 3:9). As the daily reading indicates, whosoever *will* may find salvation in Christ.

About God: **To Do:**

Reality of Hell

"The wicked shall be turned into hell, and all the nations that forget God." —Psalm 9:17

Read Luke 16:19-31

Floyd tossed and turned in bed. The words of the preacher's text burrowed deeper into his mind: "The wicked shall be turned into hell" (Psalm 9:17). Floyd felt bad inside. He was fearful. "There are just two groups in God's eyes—the wicked and the forgiven," Floyd recalled the preacher saying. "There is no middle ground."

"I'm not really what you'd call wicked, am I?" Floyd said to himself. "But I've never asked God's forgiveness." Deep down he knew he was a sinner. "I don't want to be turned into hell."

Wisely, Floyd was concerned about his soul and his destiny. The rich man told about in the daily reading evidently lived only for the present.

Hell is a real place. Jesus talked more about it than nearly anything else. He spoke more of hell than of heaven. He advised us to make preparations so we don't go there. What kind of place is hell?

- *A place of pain.* The rich sinner was "in torments" (v. 23). He longed for a drop of water on his tongue (v. 24). Jesus described hell like it is.
- *A place of separation.* Abraham in paradise was "afar off" (v. 23), and there was "a great gulf" (v. 26) between the godly and the ungodly. The rich man was alone. Many scoffers have the mistaken idea that their buddies will be with them. But the person in hell won't have company; he will be isolated.
- *A place of justice.* The rich selfish man enjoyed his food, clothes, and status on earth (v. 25). Now in hell, all pleasures are gone.
- *A place of weeping.* Jesus said, "There shall be weeping and gnashing of teeth, when ye shall see Abraham, and Isaac, and Jacob, and all the prophets, in the kingdom of God, and you yourselves thrust out" (Luke 13:28).
- *A place of darkness.* Matthew 8:12 calls it "outer darkness." God is light. The absence of God is darkness.

In view of the reality and terror of hell, we should "flee from the wrath to come" (Luke 3:7) and run to Jesus. "For God sent not his Son into the world to condemn the world; but that the world through him might be saved" (John 3:17).

God doesn't want anyone to choose to go to hell. Choose Christ, who will take you to heaven.

About God: **To Do:**

January 28

Procrastination Is Dangerous

"The harvest is past, the summer is ended, and we are not saved." —Jeremiah 8:20

Read Matthew 25:1-13

Live as though every day were your last—and someday you will be right. To put off repenting of sin and receiving Jesus as Saviour is perilous.

I know from personal experience that it's easy to put off accepting Christ. Unfortunately, I did it for several years. But such delay is extremely dangerous. It can harden the heart, deaden the conscience, and confuse the mind. Hebrews 3:15 says, "To day if ye will hear his voice, harden not your hearts."

One of the most successful wiles of the devil is to encourage someone to wait awhile. Felix, a Roman ruler, was under conviction from Paul's testimony. "And as he reasoned of righteousness, temperance, and judgment to come, Felix trembled, and answered, Go thy way for this time; when I have a convenient season, I will call for thee" (Acts 24:25).

I rejected the call of the Holy Spirit so many times that after a while I didn't feel much conviction any more. Later, when I began to think seriously about becoming a Christian, I didn't know if I still could. I worried that by saying "No" to the Holy Spirit time after time, I may have committed the unpardonable sin. However, through godly counsel based on the Bible, I came to realize as long as I desired to become a Christian, felt sorrow for my sins, and wanted to be rid of them, the Holy Spirit had not abandoned me, but was still working in my heart. I'm so glad I decided to place my faith in Christ and was granted salvation.

Truly, if you haven't received Christ, now is the day to receive Him. "Behold, now is the accepted time; behold, now is the day of salvation" (2 Corinthians 6:2). Proverbs 29:1 warns, "He, that being often reproved hardeneth his neck, shall suddenly be destroyed, and that without remedy."

You can come to Jesus only when the Father draws you. John 6:44 says, "No man can come to me, except the Father which hath sent me draw him: and I will raise him up at the last day."

How long you will live is uncertain. David said, "There is but a step between me and death" (1 Samuel 20:3). All it takes is a drunk driver, a brain aneurysm, or a terrorist attack.

Don't delay. Come to Christ today.

About God:

To Do:

Admit

"Therefore we conclude that a man is justified by faith without the deeds of the law." —Romans 3:28

Read Romans 2:1-25

Once a duke visited a galley ship. It was powered by the arms of convicts suffering their punishment at sea instead of in prison. The duke went around asking different galley slaves why they were there. One blamed others; the next said the judge was bribed; other convicts made other excuses.

But one said, "Sir, I deserve to be here. I stole money. No one is at fault but myself. I'm guilty."

"You scoundrel, you!" said the duke after a moment of thought. "What are you doing here with all these honest men? Get out of their company at once!" And the slave was set at liberty.

Admitting that I have sinned, am a sinner by nature, and am desperately in need of forgiveness is the key to my freedom too. It is not by acknowledging that I have transgressed that I am declared righteous; instead, that righteousness comes from God through faith in Jesus Christ. But confessing that I have sinned is an important first step toward repentance and saving faith.

Sin is very deceptive. It can be so hard to identify in oneself. And it is hard to acknowledge sin openly. This can lead to the sin of self-righteousness—seldom confessed but often experienced.

The Jews were quick and outspoken in condemning (judging) the Gentiles for their sins mentioned in the previous verses (Romans 1:21-31). But to paraphrase Paul's point from the daily reading: "You Jews are equally guilty of sin before God. You who condemn others, you are condemned yourself. And you Jews had more light, more knowledge of God's will."

Sometimes young people, having been taught to be good boys and girls, having gone to Christian schools, having been instructed at home and at church, do not really see themselves without Christ as guilty and condemned in God's sight. Like the Jews of Paul's day, they are in the grips of self-righteousness.

True, some may seem to be greater sinners than others. But all without Christ are sinking in the quicksand of sin. What matters it if some are deeper than others—all need to be rescued. If you recognize yourself as a sinner in need of deliverance and forgiveness, won't you reach out your hand to Christ today? Only He can save you from the quicksand of iniquity.

About God: **To Do:**

January 30

Accept the Pardon

"Who is a God like unto thee, that pardoneth iniquity . . . ? he delighteth in mercy." —Micah 7:18

Read Isaiah 55

George Wilson had a decision to make. Because he was a murderer, he faced the death penalty in Pennsylvania. But U. S. President Andrew Jackson had offered him a pardon. Would he accept the pardon or refuse it? Incredibly, he refused the pardon and chose to die.

Pardon was offered, but since it was rejected, it didn't apply to Mr. Wilson. Chief Justice John Marshall gave the following decision: "A pardon is a paper, the value of which depends upon its acceptance by the person implicated. It is hardly to be supposed that one under sentence of death would refuse to accept a pardon, but if it is refused, it is no pardon. George Wilson must be hanged!" And he was hanged.

You have a decision to make. The choice that faces you is like the choice that confronted George Wilson. Because you are a sinner, you face the death penalty—eternally. But God offers you a pardon. However, for that pardon to take effect, you must accept it.

Tragically, many young people are following the foolish example of George Wilson and spurning their pardons. The result is given in John 3:36: "He that believeth not the Son shall not see life; but the wrath of God abideth on him."

As the daily reading indicates, God wants us to seek the Lord. If you will call upon Him, forsake sin, and return to God, God will apply His pardon. These verses show God's part and man's part in salvation; that is, man must cooperate with God by yielding totally to Him. It is within our power to *seek* salvation; it is within God's power to *supply* salvation.

Take warning. Don't delay! Choose today!

God will remove and forget your sins. "I am he that blotteth out thy transgressions for mine own sake, and will not remember thy sins" (Isaiah 43:25). Not one sin will remain to condemn us to hell. Claim the promise of 1 John 1:9: "If we confess our sins, he is faithful and just to forgive us our sins, and to cleanse us from all unrighteousness."

About God: **To Do:**

Be Cleansed by Jesus' Blood

"The blood of Jesus Christ his Son cleanseth us from all sin." —1 John 1:7

Read Romans 5:1-17

Jesus' blood is essential to salvation. "Without shedding of blood is no remission. Now . . . hath he appeared to put away sin by the sacrifice of himself" (Hebrews 9:22, 26).

What does Jesus' blood do?

1. *It gives peace.* The daily reading says we experience peace with God through Jesus (v. 1). And Colossians 1:20 refers to Jesus as "having made peace through the blood of his cross."
2. *It justifies.* Verse 9 indicates that we are "now justified by his blood."

   When a plague would strike Athens, Greece, a man would come forward and offer himself as a sacrifice to atone for the sins of the people. After prayer and confession, he was taken outside and stoned. It was believed that as blood oozed from his wounds, atonement was made for their sins.

   Over ninety percent of ancient societies had some concept or practice of blood sacrifice. The Aztecs of Mexico offered over twenty thousand human sacrifices to their gods every year. Every day in ancient Egypt's City of the Sun, three men were sacrificed after having been scrutinized to ensure that they were unblemished. In Tahiti, early European travelers saw a tree from which thousands of human sacrifices had hung.

   The Old Testament records numerous animal sacrifices, pointing to the Lamb of God who would be crucified to redeem all nations and kindreds and tribes and people.
3. *It redeems.* Jesus' blood is the ransom price to release us from our "kidnapped" status as slaves to Satan. I thank God that He has "delivered us from the power of darkness, and hath translated us into the kingdom of his dear Son: in whom we have redemption through his blood, even the forgiveness of sins" (Colossians 1:13, 14).
4. *It brings us nigh.* Sin separates us from God. But Jesus' blood brings us together by removing our sins. Ephesians 2:13 tells us, "But now in Christ Jesus ye who sometimes were far off are made nigh by the blood of Christ."
5. *It makes us clean.* Glory is ascribed to Jesus who "loved us, and washed us from our sins in his own blood" (Revelation 1:5). What can wash away your sin? Nothing but the blood of Jesus.

Jesus' blood meets man's deepest need. By His breath, God gave man natural life. By His blood, God gave man eternal life.

About God: **To Do:**

February 1

Repent

"But now commandeth all men every where to repent." —Acts 17:30

Read Acts 9:1-22

Africaner was a Hottentot outlaw in Mamaqualand. He and his men were the terror of South Africa. The governor at Cape Town offered a large reward for him—dead or alive.

A missionary, Robert Moffat, felt directed by God to go to Africaner's tribe. He was warned, "You'll not come back alive! Africaner will use your skull as a drinking cup!"

With his trust in God, the brave missionary preached the Gospel to those needy folk. Who was his first convert? Africaner! Later Moffat took him to Cape Town. When the governor saw that the notorious destroyer was changed into a humble Christian man, he said, "What a miracle! This is the eighth wonder of the world."

Folks no doubt thought the same of Saul. God's work in him was a wonderful miracle. In the same remarkable way, God can transform each of us—from death to life. Praise God!

Without Christ, each person is traveling on a dead-end road—literally, spiritually, and figuratively. Literally, we die and turn to dust. Spiritually, without Christ we face eternal death at the end of life's road. Figuratively, a non-Christian is dead in trespasses and sins.

God's life-giving command is, "Make a U-turn." In other words, "Repent." You need a change of direction—so that you are walking in God's will, living in the Spirit, and traveling toward heaven.

Repentance is crucial to a right relationship with God. When Jesus began His ministry, He said, "Repent: for the kingdom of heaven is at hand" (Matthew 4:17). When John the Baptist began his ministry, he said, "Repent ye: for the kingdom of heaven is at hand" (Matthew 3:1, 2). What did Peter say on the day of Pentecost in his first sermon as a Christian? "Then Peter said unto them, Repent, and be baptized every one of you in the name of Jesus Christ for the remission of sins, and ye shall receive the gift of the Holy Ghost" (Acts 2:38).

Repentance literally means a change of mind. A group of Christian Indians in Guatemala describe repentance this way: "It pains my heart." Sorrow for sin is a vital part of repentance. A group of Christians in West Africa describe repentance as: "It hurts so much I want to quit it." Repentance means a heart broken for sin and from sin.

About God: **To Do:**

Believe in Jesus

"And as Moses lifted up the serpent in the wilderness, even so must the Son of man be lifted up." —John 3:14

Read John 5:19-29

When John Paton, the first missionary to the cannibals of the South Sea Islands, was translating the New Testament into their language, he was stumped by the word *faith.* He didn't know a native word which adequately expressed its meaning.

One day a runner came into his tent out of breath and, with an exclamation, sank down on his bamboo couch. Paton leaped to his feet shouting, "That's it! That's it!" He asked the native for the word that referred to the way he had cast his weight upon the couch.

Paton said, "That's what faith in Christ is: it means to cast yourself upon Jesus Christ for reconciliation, for forgiveness, for redemption, for peace, and for everlasting life."

Faith is often misunderstood. It is more than saying, "I believe," which is only a mental assent. Saving faith is committing oneself wholly to Jesus.

Faith in Christ is essential for salvation. Our daily reading gives a tremendous promise for time and eternity. "He that heareth my word, and believeth on him that sent me, hath everlasting life, and shall not come into condemnation; but is passed from death unto life" (v. 24). John 3:36 puts things very clearly, "He that believeth on the Son hath everlasting life: and he that believeth not the Son shall not see life; but the wrath of God abideth on him."

When the Philippian jailer (shaken both physically and emotionally) asked, "What must I do to be saved?" Paul answered, "Believe on the Lord Jesus Christ, and thou shalt be saved, and thy house" (Acts 16:31).

Paul certainly emphasized faith. But the faith he refers to is not merely professed—a raised hand to indicate acceptance of Jesus Christ with no intention of changing conduct, speech, or attitude. True faith is a belief which brings the life into a pattern of obedience to God.

Our faith is centered in Jesus—the Christ, the Lord, the Promised One through David, the Son of God, the Resurrected One. Praise His name!

About God: **To Do:**

February 3

Confess

"Whosoever therefore shall be ashamed of me and of my words in this adulterous and sinful generation; of him also shall the Son of man be ashamed, when he cometh in the glory of his Father with the holy angels." —Mark 8:38

Read Psalm 32

A newspaper carried a headline "Guilty Plea Sets Inmate Free." The article told of a man who admitted his guilt after being in prison for eight years. He had made a deal with the state attorney's office. The time he had already served satisfied his sentence. By confessing his wrong, he was set free.

Before a sinner can be set free, he needs to confess his sin. Proverbs 28:13 says, "He that covereth his sins shall not prosper: but whoso confesseth and forsaketh them shall have mercy." The prodigal son became free from slavery in the far country by saying, "Father, I have sinned against heaven, and in thy sight" (Luke 15:21). The confession of evil works is the beginning of good works.

David testified of the blessing of confession after his heinous sins of lust, adultery, prevarication, and murder. In Psalm 32 he tells first of the misery of guilt. Then he said, "I will confess my transgressions unto the LORD; and thou forgavest the iniquity of my sin" (v. 5). The Bible makes a wonderful promise in 1 John 1:9: "If we confess our sins, he is faithful and just to forgive us."

Where sin is not strictly private, confession should be made to others, at least to the extent that the sin is known. James 5:16 says, "Confess your faults one to another, and pray one for another, that ye may be healed."

Not only must a person confess sin—a person must confess Christ. This means to publicly identify with Christ and live openly for Him. Matthew 10:32, 33 says, "Whosoever therefore shall confess me before men, him will I confess also before my Father which is in heaven. But whosoever shall deny me before men, him will I also deny before my Father which is in heaven." It seems so foolish and unreasonable for any Christian to be ashamed of Christ, but it can easily happen.

Romans 10:9 clearly states the connection between salvation and confession of Christ. "That if thou shalt confess with thy mouth the Lord Jesus, and shalt believe in thine heart that God hath raised him from the dead, thou shalt be saved." Thousands of Christians have chosen to be martyred rather than deny Christ. All but one of the twelve apostles experienced a violent death. Justin Martyr of the second century was beheaded because he refused to deny Christ and sacrifice to pagan gods.

About God:

To Do:

Follow Jesus

"My sheep hear my voice, and I know them, and they follow me."
—John 10:27

Read Luke 14:15-33

It is imperative to repent of sin, believe in Jesus, confess sin, make restitution, and confess Christ. This all takes cooperation with the Holy Spirit, as Titus 3:4, 5 says: "But after that the kindness and love of God our Saviour toward man appeared, not by works of righteousness which we have done, but according to his mercy he saved us, by the washing of regeneration, and renewing of the Holy Ghost."

But also of vital importance is a daily following of Jesus. A sheep that belongs to Christ follows the Shepherd. Jesus tells His followers to "take up his cross daily, and follow me" (Luke 9:23). This means a definite difference from the way a non-Christian lives.

According to an article in *Christianity Today,* "Survey data show that most Americans believe you cannot tell a born-again Christian from non-believers because there is no difference in the way they live. The only distinction, they say, is that Christians are more religious, more fanatical, or more close-minded. There is no widespread sense that the religious experience of Christians has changed the fabric of our thinking or the nature of our lifestyles."

Christians need to realize that faith and personal action are Siamese twins. They are joined together. They are inseparable.

James 2:17 says, "Faith, if it hath not works, is dead, being alone." The marginal reading says, "by itself." Yet works are not the means of our salvation either. Ephesians 2:8, 9 says, "By grace are ye saved through faith . . . not of works, lest any man should boast."

Consider a comparison to salt. The two chemical components of salt, sodium and chlorine, are deadly. If we ingest either of these poisons, we would die. But if they are combined, they form sodium chloride, which is our common table salt. Not only does it give flavor to our food, it is a necessity for health and life. So also, faith and works properly joined together are necessary for life and give flavor to our witness.

Even Martin Luther, with his emphasis on faith, wrote at one point, "Faith is a living, busy, active, powerful thing: it is impossible for it not to do us good continually. It never asks whether good works are to be done, but has done them before there is time to ask the question, and it is always doing them."

About God: **To Do:**

Busy Bones

"All my bones shall say, LORD, who is like unto thee, which deliverest the poor from him that is too strong for him, yea, the poor and the needy from him that spoileth him?" —Psalm 35:10

Read Proverbs 3:1-15

Bones are always busy. They make red and white blood cells twenty-four hours a day, seven days a week. Every minute an astounding number of red blood cells die—about 180 million of them, according to a *Reader's Digest* article. It is up to your bones to replace them with more healthy cells—otherwise, you will become weak from anemia and eventually face death. This marvelous manufacturing takes place in the marrow of the bone, making your bones among the busiest parts of your body.

Job tells of a healthy person whose "bones are moistened with marrow" (Job 21:24). And wise Solomon recognized the importance of bone marrow (although probably not in a medical sense) as he wrote that fearing the Lord and departing from evil would be "marrow to thy bones" (Proverbs 3:8).

Besides making red blood cells, your busy bones have other very important manufacturing responsibilities. For instance, they also make white blood cells. These cells act like soldiers in that they attack and kill harmful cells which invade the body.

If you ever cut yourself, your survival depends on your bones in still another way. Your bones produce platelets in the blood. These platelets are essential for blood clotting so you don't bleed to death.

If you are a lazybones, sitting in your recliner or lying in bed most of the day, the idea gets through to your bones that you have no need for strong bones, causing some of the calcium to be removed. Part of taking good care of your body to the glory of God is good exercise. The Bible says that "bodily exercise profiteth" (1 Timothy 4:8), but also tells us that compared to spiritual exercise, it is not nearly as important. People who fail to exercise are much more likely to have broken bones in their later years.

Drinking milk when young is very important in avoiding problems like osteoporosis, which is a weakening of the bones, especially as a person grows older. Proverbs 16:24 says, "Pleasant words are as an honeycomb, sweet to the soul, and health to the bones."

There are many marvelous mysteries of the work of the bones and how they grow. As Ecclesiastes 11:5 points out, "Thou knowest not . . . how the bones do grow." Truly we should thank God for the development and formation of the bones—from the bottom of our hearts and probably from the depths of our bones as well.

About God: **To Do:**

Focusing on the Eye

"Thine eyes shall see the king in his beauty:
they shall behold the land that is very far off." —Isaiah 33:17

Read Mark 8:22-37

"The hearing ear, and the seeing eye, the LORD hath made even both of them" (Proverbs 20:12). Let's focus on a few aspects of the eye that clearly show the wise design of the Creator.

The eye is *sensitive*. No scientific instrument is as sensitive to light as your eye. Its sensitivity in the dark increases several thousand times to the point that it can detect light from trillions of miles away—the stars.

The eye is *hardworking*. It is estimated that the eye can handle over a million simultaneous messages at one time. I'm glad my eyes work hard, moving on an average day about one hundred thousand times (especially in focusing), and gathering about eighty percent of the knowledge I absorb.

The eye is *unbelievably rapid*. Each eye can send a billion impulses per second to the brain.

The eye is *complex*. The retina, for example, has about 137 million receptor cells. Under a microscope most of them look like rods, which are for black and white. There are also about seven million "cones" for deciphering color. Let's say an airplane's light passes your line of vision as you gaze at the night sky. The faint light bleaches *rhodopsin*, a pigment in the retina at the back of the eye. The bleaching process generates a very little bit of electricity—too small for a mosquito to feel. This slight flow of electricity flows into the optic nerve and moves to the brain at three hundred miles per hour. Altogether it takes about two thousandths of a second until the brain says that it is an airplane's light.

The eye is *automatic* in many respects. Look up from reading this article and then find your place again. How amazing is automatic focusing! Consider the moisture automatically provided for the eye, the way the eyelids wipe cleanly, the way the excessive moisture from the eye is drained into a nostril. (Crying, of course, is a flood situation.)

Psalm 139:14 expresses it very well. "I will praise thee; for I am fearfully and wonderfully made: marvellous are thy works."

The human body alone is ample proof of the Designer. George Gallup, a well-known pollster, has said that he could prove God's existence statistically. "Take the human body alone—the chance that all the functions of the individual could just happen, is a statistical monstrosity."

About God: **To Do:**

February 7

Marvels of Your Hands

"And he led them out as far as to Bethany, and he lifted up his hands, and blessed them." —Luke 24:50

Read Matthew 8:1-15

Taking a spoonful of soup seems simple, but more than thirty joints and fifty muscles are involved. Just describing their movements and interaction would be a complex project. Such coordination of the hand with arm and shoulder muscles and joints is a marvel.

God's hand designed our hands in wonderful ways. Psalm 143:5 says, in reference to God, that it is good to "muse on the work of thy hands." One of these "works" is the magnificently engineered human hand, made up of muscle, fat, bone, ligament, tendon, and very sensitive fibers.

Although the hand is packed with bones—eight in the wrist, five in the palm, and fourteen in the fingers, it can move freely. Ligaments—cords of stringy material—hold our bones together at the joints. Tendons—tough fibers that connect the hand and wrist bones to the muscles that operate them—control movement of the fingers. Herein is another marvel: the muscles that operate the fingers are basically in the forearm, not the fingers, else our fingers would look like sausages.

Another marvel is how water gets out of the hand by means of 2,000 sweat glands per square inch, but when you wash the dishes, water doesn't get in.

The hand's ability to perform a wide range of complex movements is another indication of its divine design. The palm can be up or down. The hand can rotate to turn things. The hand can reach all parts of the body except part of the back. The hand can push or pull things. It can do so close to the body or at arm's length.

Although it is good to have clean hands physically, it is more important to have clean hands morally. In order to receive the blessing from the Lord, we should have clean hands and a pure heart (Psalm 24:4, 5).

Let's use the hands God has given us to help others. Peter met a lame man and took him by the right *hand* and helped him up (Acts 3:7). The virtuous woman works willingly with her *hands* (Proverbs 31:13) and stretches out her *hands* to the poor and needy (Proverbs 31:20). Like Jesus, use your hands to bless children.

And finally, let God hold your hand. "For I the LORD thy God will hold thy right hand, saying unto thee, Fear not; I will help thee" (Isaiah 41:13).

About God: **To Do:**

Wonderfully Made: The Brain

"For who hath known the mind of the Lord, that he may instruct him? But we have the mind of Christ." —1 Corinthians 2:16

Read Philippians 1:25–2:5

It is hardly proper to compare your brain to a computer because the human brain is so much more complex and versatile. The brain has about ten billion neuron cells, each connected to hundreds of other cells. The amount of memory is stupendous. Scientists estimate that after seventy years of activity, the brain may contain as many as fifteen trillion separate pieces of information.

The brain has been described as the most marvelous and mysterious object in the universe. It stores all the information it receives, but you can't recall nearly all of it. God designed it with the capacity to hold more information than the millions of books in the Library of Congress.

Interestingly, although the brain informs you of pain, when the brain itself is cut, there is no pain.

The brain houses the mind. Philippians 2:1-5 tells us of three attitudes of mind that a Christian should have. First, be likeminded with the believers. Verse 2 says, "Be likeminded, having the same love, being of one accord, of one mind." This likemindedness will be demonstrated in our goals, our love to Christ, and our obedience to the Scriptures.

Second, have lowliness of mind. As verse 3 says, "Let nothing be done through strife or vainglory; but in lowliness of mind let each esteem other better than themselves." This phrase did not occur in the Greek language until the New Testament was written. It refers to an attitude that Colossians 3:12 calls "humbleness of mind." Lowliness of mind will be demonstrated by a servant attitude, by courteously saying, "You first," and by giving honor to another.

Third, have the unselfish, meek, compassionate mind of Christ. As verse 5 says, "Let this mind be in you, which was also in Christ Jesus." Therefore, ask yourself often, "How would Jesus respond? What would be His attitude?"

We should care for our brain. Alcohol, narcotics, and other sinful abuse can destroy those cells. Incidentally, the more you use your brain, the more cells you retain. Therefore, use your brain to God's glory. That's truly using your brain.

About God: **To Do:**

February 9

Your Wonderful Muscles

"Finally, my brethren, be strong in the Lord, and in the power of his might." —Ephesians 6:10

Read 2 Timothy 2:1-15

I am often amazed at the muscles I have. Now, I'm not boasting. I am just profoundly thankful that God has given me muscles to enable me to move.

When I do something as "simple" as walking, I can marvel at the miracle of muscle movement and coordination. Although there are about three hundred main muscles on each side of the body, there are hundreds of thousands of small individual "muscle-cell engines." With each step, about one hundred thousand of these engines are at work.

Whether I am rebounding a basketball, washing dishes (rarely), or scratching my nose with my forefinger, the workings of a hydrogen bomb are dwarfed by my muscle action. This muscle action, though commonplace, is yet so mysterious that it baffles scientists.

We may think our muscles are tough. However, the working or contractile part of a muscle is a soft jelly. How this jelly contracts to raise a thousand times its own weight is an enigma and a marvel.

About half of the body is muscle. Muscles are needed for walking and other limb movements. They propel food along the digestive system. They provide most of our internal heat. They bring us into the world in the first place, and life ends when the heart muscle, having beat some two to three billion times, falters and stops.

Muscles need a balanced diet—proteins for muscle repair and carbohydrates for muscle fuel. But muscles can also be starved through lack of exercise. Think of a well-nourished hospital patient who gets out of bed too weak to walk. In an inactive adult, the tiny capillaries which nourish the muscles of an active person collapse and go out of business. Exercise alone can open them up. Muscles also need rest—that's one reason why our Creator has blessed us with sleep.

As our daily reading indicates, a Christian is to develop and demonstrate strength like a soldier. This takes the grace of Jesus (v. 1). It means facing tough situations (v. 3). It means a single aim (v. 4). It takes effort for excellence (v. 5).

How wonderful that the Lord has designed our bodies! Let's use our muscles in loving service to God. "And thou shalt love the Lord thy God . . . with all thy *strength*" (Mark 12:30).

About God: **To Do:**

Marvelous Functions of Skin

"And I will lay sinews upon you, and will bring up flesh upon you, and cover you with skin, and put breath in you, and ye shall live; and ye shall know that I am the LORD.*" —Ezekiel 37:6

Read 1 Timothy 4:1-11

God has given each of us a wonderful gift in the form of skin—about 25 pounds (made mostly of fats and water) if you weigh one hundred fifty pounds. And the Creator has given skin the capacity to replace itself. Skin cells formed in the inner skin gradually push their way outward. As millions of skin cells daily are washed or brushed away, the newly formed cells keep appearing on the surface. The cells you now see on the surface of your skin are about 27 days old. Thus you have about thirteen new skins per year.

If you think of your skin as merely something to be bathed, scratched, and perfumed, you ought to realize and give thanks for the many functions the skin performs. Consider its range of jobs:

1. *Security Guard.* The skin repels and kills germs. As a solid wall of defense, it lets waste materials pass outward from the body through pores, yet keeps out dirt and enemy organisms. Your body is covered with countless bacteria waiting for a suitable opportunity to invade your body, but they cannot enter unless the skin is broken.
2. *Thermostat.* The blood vessels of the skin help keep your body at one temperature.
3. *Air conditioner.* If your temperature rises more than a few degrees, you die. How wise and wonderful that our Creator provided a way for our bodies to cool off. About two million sweat glands, tightly coiled little tubes, are buried in the skin. Although they are very tiny, the glands in your body would form a line totaling six miles. A person exerting himself on a hot day may lose over ten pounds of water.
4. *Leather jacket.* Skin is tough. It is flexible. It is adaptable—it thickens under rubbing or pressure. The skin cells say, in effect, "There's something pressing hard, trying to get in. Let's build a wall and keep it out." A *callous* or *corn* results.

It's not too serious for the skin to become calloused, but it is very serious when the heart becomes calloused. The daily reading warns against those who speak "lies in hypocrisy; having their conscience seared with a hot iron." Acts 28:27 says, "For the heart of this people is waxed *gross* [hardened and calloused—*Amplified*]. It is dangerous to reject the call and work of the Spirit as was the case of the unbelieving Jews.

About God: **To Do:**

February 11

More Marvelous Functions of Skin

*"Thou hast clothed me with skin and flesh,
and hast fenced me with bones and sinews." —Job 10:11*

Read John 20:19-28

God made us all "skinny"! And as He continues to keep us alive, He continues to make us "skinny"—that is, covered with skin. (My dictionary says *skinny* means "of or like the skin" as well as its common meaning of "very lean or thin." Here are some more functions of the skin:

1. *Sunshade.* The skin protects the delicate cells of internal organs against the ultraviolet rays which, in heavy doses, are deadly. Thank God too, that the blanket of ozone gas God placed forty miles above the earth blocks most of the dangerous rays.
2. *Thermometer.* Your skin tells you if you are hot or cold. When you are chilled, your cold receptors inform your brain. Your muscles then go to work making you shiver to stimulate circulation.
3. *Insulator.* Like a thermos, the skin can keep the hot in and the cold out, or vice versa.
4. *Stockroom.* The skin stores such things as salt, gland chemicals, water, and sugar.
5. *Pollster.* Your skin gathers information about things the skin cells contact. It is continually taking a poll of what its environment is like. The sense of touch is a remarkable capacity God has given our bodies.
6. *I. D. Card.* Your fingerprint is never the duplicate of another. Although skin from one part of your body may be successfully transplanted to another part, it will only survive temporarily on another person's skin (unless the other person is an identical twin.)

Someday my body will die (unless Christ returns first), and my skin will decay and disappear. As Job looked to his living Redeemer who shall stand in the latter day upon the earth, he said, "And though after my skin worms destroy this body, yet in my flesh shall I see God" (Job 19:26). Job was confident that, although after death his skin and body would be destroyed, God would raise his body again at the resurrection.

It seems to me the believer's resurrected body will have skin also, for the Lord Jesus "shall change our vile body, that it may be fashioned like unto his glorious body" (Philippians 3:21). Jesus' resurrected body apparently had skin, since He showed the nail prints to Thomas.

About God: **To Do:**

Know Christ as Saviour and Example

"Neither is there salvation in any other: for there is none other name under heaven given among men, whereby we must be saved." —Acts 4:12

Read Luke 8:26-40

In order to serve the Lord, you must first become alive in Christ. One would hardly expect a dead person to be of service. Jesus said, "Ye must be born again." You must become a new person in Christ. This means repenting of sin, forsaking it, and showing your faith in Christ by following His way and His teachings.

The daily reading tells of a man whose life was transformed by Christ. Jesus told him to return to his home community and serve Him there by sharing the Gospel.

As a Christian, you will desire to have the attitudes of Christ as you seek to share His love in Christian service. When I was a youth, my pastor told a story in a sermon that made a deep impression on me. It taught me to prepare for Christian service by developing certain attitudes and habits:

At three o'clock one wintry morning, a missionary candidate climbed the steps to the examiner's home. He was shown into the study, where he waited until eight o'clock for an interview.

Upon arriving, the old minister proceeded to ask questions.

"Can you spell?"

"Yes, sir," was the reply.

"All right—spell *baker*."

"Baker—b-a-k-e-r."

"Fine. Now do you know anything about numbers?" the examiner inquired.

"Yes, sir—something."

"How much is two times two?"

"Four," replied the youth.

"That's splendid," returned the old man. "I believe you have passed. I'll see the board tomorrow."

At the board meeting the man submitted his account of the interview. "He has all the qualifications of a missionary," he began.

"First, I tested him on self-denial. I told him to be at my house at three o'clock in the morning. He left a warm bed and came out in the cold without a word of complaint. Second, I tried him out on promptness. He appeared on time. Third, I examined him on patience. I made him wait five hours to see me, after telling him to come at three. Fourth, I tested him on temper. He failed to show any sign of it; he didn't even question my delay. Fifth, I tried his humility. I asked him questions that a seven-year-old could answer, and he showed no indignation. So you see, I believe this young man meets the requirements. He will be the missionary we need."

How would you have rated?

About God: **To Do:**

February 13

Know the Bible

"Study to shew thyself approved unto God, a workman that needeth not to be ashamed, rightly dividing the word of truth." —2 Timothy 2:15

Read 2 Timothy 3:10-17

Menno Simons emphasized the importance of the Bible. "Therefore I admonish all beloved brethren, yea, I pray you by the mercy of God our Lord Jesus Christ, to give heed to the Word of God, and not to forsake Christ, with the eye of faith and you have heard His voice, saying, this is the true way, walk upon it, go neither to the right hand nor to the left."

Hudson Taylor, missionary to China, in his fortieth year of ministry was in the presence of a friend when he closed his Bible and said, "For the fortieth time I have finished reading the Bible." Taylor's tenacity to stay in the Bible explains why God used him in such a significant manner.

In preparing for an occupation, a worker needs to get to know his tools: a computer operator, a keyboard; a surgeon, a scalpel; a mechanic, his wrenches; a dentist, his drill. In Christian service, a Christian needs to know his primary tool, the Bible. Other tools I use a lot are *Nave's Topical Bible, Strong's Exhaustive Concordance,* a parallel Bible, and a Bible dictionary.

Not only is reading the Bible good preparation for service, but memorizing it also is excellent. True, it does take great self-discipline and effort, but it is worth it. It helps you to be "throughly furnished" (v. 17).

Knowing the Bible helps you to avoid deception and error. Jesus said, "Ye do err, not knowing the scriptures" (Matthew 22:29).

Know the Bible to the extent that you let it mold and shape your life—especially in those areas which run counter to your nature.

A man from East Asia acquired a beautiful microscope. He found it fascinating to use. One day he examined a tiny bit of his dinner rice with the microscope. To his horror he discovered that there were actually tiny living creatures in it.

It was part of his religion not to eat any animal life. What could he do? He was not only fond of his rice, but it was also the staple item of his daily food.

He thought he saw only one way out of it. He would destroy the instrument that had pointed out the distasteful fact, and so he dashed the microscope to pieces.

But when God's Word reveals truth that contradicts your thinking, change your thinking.

About God: **To Do:**

Understand and Demonstrate Humility

"Let this mind be in you, which was also in Christ Jesus." —Philippians 2:5

Read Matthew 20:20-34

A well-known minister was asked to come to a large Japanese city where Kagawa, recognized as a great Christian, worked for the Lord in the slums. Kagawa, clad in poor clothing like the destitute he served, met the important speaker at the train station. However, the preacher mistook Kagawa for a porter and commanded, "Here, fellow, carry my bags. I'm looking for Kagawa." So Kagawa quietly carried the luggage.

God hates pride. God honors humility. Eliphaz rightly said, "He shall save the humble person" (Job 22:29). No garment is more becoming to a Christian than the cloak of humility (1 Peter 5:5). It never goes out of style.

But how is humility expressed? A humble person exalts God and thinks rightly about himself. He responds with thanksgiving and praise to God as he views his abilities, assets, achievements, and appearance, all of which have their source in God. He thinks not more highly of himself than he ought (Romans 12:3) nor less highly than he ought of others (Romans 12:16). A humble person serves, as typified in the feetwashing ordinance.

But there are counterfeit expressions of humility. Consider a few:

"I'm not good at giving a topic," says a capable young man, hoping his listener will disagree. One lady repeatedly told her pastor what a sinful and wicked woman she was. One day he stunned her by saying, "Yes, so I've been told." Indignantly she demanded, "Who told you I was a wicked woman?" He replied, "You did!"

"You lead the singing tonight. You can sing better than I can," says a good singer to a poor singer. Rather than deprecate the gifts and abilities the Lord has given us, we should serve Him gladly for His glory.

"Oh, I couldn't do that," says the person, adding to himself, *What if I made a mistake!* Self-acceptance and a willingness to do our best and leave the rest in the hands of God harmonizes with humility. Phillips Brooks said, "The true way to be humble is not to stoop until you are smaller than yourself but to stand at your real height against some higher nature that will show you what the real smallness of your greatness is."

The daily reading gives Christ's example of humble service in contrast to the expectations of the ambitious disciples. Certainly, true humility *attracts*. Lack of humility *subtracts*. And artificial humility *detracts*.

About God: **To Do:**

Be Salt

"Ye are the salt of the earth: but if the salt have lost his savour, wherewith shall it be salted? it is thenceforth good for nothing, but to be cast out, and to be trodden under foot of men." —Matthew 5:13

Read Genesis 18:16-33

Considering that there are over fourteen thousand uses of salt, how are Christians like salt?

1. *Salt preserves.* My dad put salt on meat after butchering and put salt on hay in a haymow to keep the hay from overheating. We should help preserve society from the rot of sin. This is probably the main truth that Jesus had in mind when He referred to salt.

   Christians should be free from alcoholism and divorce. They should be honest in business and have stable homes. Proverbs 14:34 says, "Righteousness exalteth a nation: but sin is a reproach to any people."

   According to our daily reading, had there been a few more righteous people in Sodom, God's judgment would have been averted. Not one life was lost in the shipwreck at Melita; mostly, I think, because of Paul's presence on board.

2. *Salt flavors.* It is different from the food it is put into—that's why it is valuable. We should have an encouraging effect on others, bringing out the meaning of life—Christ. Our lives should say, "O taste and see that the LORD is good" (Psalm 34:8).

3. *Salt creates thirst.* Our lives should point others to Jesus, who said, "If any man thirst, let him come unto me, and drink" (John 7:37).

4. *Salt burns a wound.* Godly living and speaking, such as Stephen showed, may result in unbelievers being "cut to the heart" (Acts 7:54). When a Christian appears on the scene, the language often changes. Sometimes, a listener may get belligerent toward the truth.

5. *Salt is a healing agent.* In our role as peacemakers, we are to help heal divisions and disputes. "Let your speech be alway with grace, seasoned with salt" (Colossians 4:6).

6. *Salt is sprinkled.* Christians need to be sprinkled around a community (and the world). Is God calling you to get out of the salt shaker?

About God: **To Do:**

I'm Gonna Let It Shine

"Ye shine as lights in the world; holding forth the word of life; that I may rejoice in the day of Christ, that I have not run in vain, neither laboured in vain." —Philippians 2:15, 16

Read Matthew 5:14-26

How are Christians like light?

1. *Light dispels darkness.* Our influence in reflecting Jesus the Saviour should help dispel the darkness of sin. Second Corinthians 4:6 says, "For God, who commanded the light to shine out of darkness, hath shined in our hearts, to give the light of the knowledge of the glory of God in the face of Jesus Christ."
2. *Light is conspicuous.* A city on a hill, as were most cities in Palestine, including Jerusalem, was very noticeable. A Christian is noticeably different in speech, appearance, conduct, and interests. John the Baptist "was a burning and a shining light" (John 5:35).
3. *A light should serve its purpose.* For this reason headlights on a car are not placed under the seat or inside the muffler. Christians should let their lights shine so that men will glorify God.
4. *Light enables sight.* In a Christian's life, the good work of the fruit of the Spirit should be seen by the unbelievers to show them what sort of life pleases God. Don't hide your light under a bushel of materialism or a blanket of pleasure-seeking.
5. *A light is useful as it shines steadily, quietly, and brightly.* So it is with the Christian. A living Christ within makes a steady light without.

Hudson Taylor told of a Chinese pastor who always instructed new converts to witness as soon as possible. Once, upon meeting a young convert, the pastor inquired, "Brother, how long have you been saved?"

The man answered that he had been saved for about three months.

"And how many have you won to the Saviour?"

"Oh, I'm only a learner," the convert responded.

Shaking his head in disapproval, the pastor said, "Young man, the Lord doesn't expect you to be a full-fledged preacher, but He does expect you to be a faithful witness. Tell me, when does a candle begin to shine—when it's already half burned up?"

"No, as soon as it's lit," came the reply.

"That's right, so let your light shine right away."

About God: **To Do:**

February 17

Be Consistent

"And why beholdest thou the mote that is in thy brother's eye, but considerest not the beam that is in thine own eye?" —Matthew 7:3

Read Judges 16:1-21

In Hawaii, a man was beaten into a coma by his anger-management counselor and died a few days later. What a tragedy! Miguel Gonzales, 32, had been ordered to attend the anger-management class for assaulting his girlfriend. Gonzales had come to a session drunk and had begun disrupting it. The counselor then punched him, knocked him to the ground, and continued beating him, causing his death.

My mind went to Romans 2:21. "Thou therefore which teachest another, teachest thou not thyself?" We need to be very careful lest our lives form an inappropriate irony. Due to the weakness of human nature, an incongruity may worm its way into our experience. As I look into the lives of Bible characters and observe twenty-first-century lives (including my own), sometimes I see things that don't fit what one would expect or desire.

Consider a few examples: Samson was an extremely strong man physically, but morally he was a pushover for Satan, as seen in our daily reading. Simon Peter was the first of the disciples to confess Christ as the Son of God (Matthew 16:16), yet, when under pressure, he denied ever knowing Him. Moses, renowned for his meekness, became agitated in the face of the Israelites' murmuring for water, and struck the rock twice instead of speaking to it as God had commanded.

Jesus' life did not show any tragic incongruities. He said, "I do always those things that please him" (John 8:29). He is "the same yesterday, and to day, and for ever" (Hebrews 13:8).

An old church officer was asked if he was a Christian. He answered honestly, "In spots."

And how are we doing? Are our lives incongruous with the Gospel? As the songwriter put it, "So let our lives and lips express the holy Gospel we profess. So let our walks and virtues shine, to prove the doctrine all divine."

One of the best ways for a young person to prepare for future Christian service is by living consistently. Of course, consistency also leaves a powerful testimony in the present.

About God: **To Do:**

Be Willing to Die

"For I am now ready to be offered, and the time of my departure is at hand."
—2 Timothy 4:6

Read Philippians 1:12-24

For five years, a professor in Texas asked freshmen, "Is there anything you would be willing to die for?" For five years every student gave the same answer: "No." In the sixth year one student wrote, "I would be willing to die for my family."

How would my students at winter Bible school answer? I wondered. So before discussing Paul's attitude toward death in my Philippians class, I asked my 26 students the question posed by the Texas professor. I was glad that all 26 students replied, "Yes." Here are some of their responses:

"I would be willing to die for Christ's sake and also perhaps for my family or a close friend."

"I found this a real heart-searching question. The faithful men before us were willing to give their lives for Christ, and suffer much reproach for His name. I hope that, if necessary, I would be willing to suffer, or even die, for my Saviour."

"I would die for my father, mother, and sister, my church and my pastor, my Lord and my Saviour."

"Yes, I would be willing to die for my faith regardless whether a gun would be pointed at my head, or if I would face a slow torturous death. Also I would give my life to help someone who is drowning or in any other peril. I can say with Paul in Philippians 1:21, 'For to me to live is Christ, and to die is gain.' "

"Yes, I do feel that I would be willing and gladly die for the cause of Christ. What better way to die than this! I also think that if my life was free from guilt of sin as far as I knew, and I felt ready to meet my God, I would gladly die, so that my fellowman may yet have the chance to accept Christ and be saved."

"I would be willing to die if it would bring my three brothers and their families to Christ."

"Christ has done so much for me. He saves, loves, and keeps me, besides other blessings."

"If I would be given the choice of living for Christ and what I believe the Bible teaches, or dying, I believe I can truthfully say I would be willing to die. If your faith isn't worth dying for, it is not worth living for either."

About God: **To Do:**

The Green Sickness

"Charity envieth not." —1 Corinthians 13:4

Read Genesis 37:1-11

You may have experienced this sickness of the soul quite often. You may have contracted it when a fellow student received a higher grade in math than you did. It may have infected your mind when you heard someone tell a peer, "You have the loveliest voice in the youth group." Or you may have turned green when a good friend partially abandoned you in order to be better friends with someone else.

Envy—or "the green sickness," as Shakespeare called it—is a common spiritual problem. It is also an ancient problem.

Joseph's brothers were infected with this contagion. When they saw their father Jacob favoring their brother Joseph, "his brethren envied him" (Genesis 37:11). After Joseph received a special coat from his dad, "they hated him, and could not speak peaceably unto him" (Genesis 37:4).

Cain had a bad dose of this malady. When he saw that God had accepted the offering of his brother Abel, an envious hatred filled his heart. The result? "Cain talked with Abel his brother: and it came to pass, when they were in the field, that Cain rose up against Abel his brother, and slew him" (Genesis 4:8).

Korah, Dathan, and Abiram envied the prominence of Moses and Aaron in Israel. "And they gathered themselves together against Moses and against Aaron, and said unto them, Ye take too much upon you, seeing all the congregation are holy, every one of them, and the LORD is among them: wherefore then lift ye up yourselves above the congregation of the LORD?" (Numbers 16:3).

For your social and spiritual health, avoid the green sickness. It is a cancer that can kill a friendship, weaken a marriage, decimate a church, wreak havoc in a place of employment, and destroy good relations among siblings. It is truly a deadly sin.

Do you have an infection of envy? Let the sunlight of love kill all the germs of the green disease.

About God: **To Do:**

Put Away Envy

"Fret not thyself because of evildoers, neither be thou envious against the workers of iniquity." —Psalm 37:1

Read Galatians 5:19-26; 6:1-4

What should you do with the feeling that you get when:

- Your cousin buys a late-model car while you bounce around in an old clunker?
- A job opportunity you wanted is given to a fellow graduate?
- Your classmate is chosen to be valedictorian of the graduating class?
- You are not picked first at the youth baseball game?
- You overhear a Sunday school class member being given credit that you wish you had received?
- You sense that your brother is more popular than you are?

You should put the feeling of envy away. First Peter 2:1 tells us that we should be "laying aside all malice, and . . . envies." This is in the context of the brotherhood. In the context of sinners, Proverbs 23:17 says, "Let not thine heart envy sinners: but be thou in the fear of the LORD all the day long."

Envy is a sense of discontent regarding another's advantage, success, or possessions. Thomas Aquinas said, "It is sadness at another's good." It includes a grim satisfaction at the troubles that overtake a rival. It is a "mental cancer," according to one woman seeking a cure for it.

Although the terms *jealousy* and *envy* are often used interchangeably, there is a slight difference. An envious person longs to have what another has. A jealous person *has* something (such as wealth, popularity, or success) but feels threatened that a rival will surpass him.

For example, an envious person wants to have a special friendship with Michael or Stephanie, while a jealous person feels anger and rejection when Michael or Stephanie develops a special friendship with someone else. Joseph's brothers were envious of the favoritism shown to him, and Saul was jealous of David's rise in popularity. Envy has empty hands desiring to get; jealousy has full hands desiring to keep.

Do you have a twinge of envy or jealousy in your heart? "Let us not be desirous of vain glory, provoking one another, envying one another" (Galatians 5:26).

About God:

To Do:

February 21

Warning Signs of Envy

"A sound heart is the life of the flesh: but envy the rottenness of the bones." —Proverbs 14:30

Read Numbers 12

Envy or jealousy is especially a problem for very talented individuals. Although it seems strange, it is often true that the most gifted people find it very difficult to praise or applaud others who slightly surpass them in their field. It seems so illogical that a highly competent person should experience feelings of sadness, anger, and regret simply because a rival does a little better.

The leaders of the city of Florence, Italy, asked Italy's most prominent artist, Leonardo da Vinci, to submit sketches for the artwork in a grand hall of a public building. One of the leaders had heard of a young, little-known artist called Michelangelo. They told him also to submit some sketches.

Da Vinci's sketches were very good. But when the city leaders saw those of Michelangelo, they were enthusiastic. "Leonardo is getting old," a city leader said.

When da Vinci heard that the leaders liked Michelangelo's work more than his own, he became jealous. His remaining years were clouded by gloom and unhappiness.

When I cannot applaud a friend's success and wish him well, I know I have a problem with envy. Few people have the strength to honor a peer's success without envy. Without jealousy I should be able to praise another person for work well done.

Another warning signal concerns one's speech. If I criticize another's work or if I make snide remarks, I know I need to search my heart. I need to watch out for unkind thoughts and a "it-serves-him-right" mentality. And what is *my* motive if I cast doubt on another's motive?

Still another red flag that may indicate envy is the tendency to acknowledge some ability, yet point out a deficiency. For example: "She's a good singer, but did you ever see her art? Her dogs look more like horses." "He's a good dairyman, but did you ever see his plowing?" "She's pretty, but she needs to lose a few pounds."

Check your life for danger signs that envy has edged its way into your heart. Thank God for the success of others. Praise others. Pray for the continued achievement of others.

About God: **To Do:**

Envy Leads to Every Evil Work

"But if ye have bitter envying and strife in your hearts, glory not, and lie not against the truth." —James 3:14

Read Daniel 6:1-17

Where might envy lead you? Into all kinds of sin and trouble. As James 3:16 says, "For where envying and strife is, there is confusion and every evil work."

Envy may lead to hatred. So it was with Cain. "We should love one another. Not as Cain, who was of that wicked one, and slew his brother. And wherefore slew he him? Because his own works were evil, and his brother's righteous" (1 John 3:11, 12).

Envy may lead to manipulation. So it was with the princes and presidents of Babylon at the time of Daniel. Upon seeing Daniel promoted above them, they schemed to get Daniel into trouble with the king.

Envy may lead to stubbornness and unreasonableness. So it was with the elder brother who refused to join the celebration of his repentant, returned brother. Have you felt a twinge of envy when a person who has been saved from a life of obvious sin is asked to give his testimony?

Envy may lead to violence. So it was with the unbelieving Jews at Thessalonica. They wanted to hurt the Apostle Paul when they were "moved with envy" (Acts 17:5). Every year, people are murdered because one man is jealous of the attention given to another man by a woman he is fond of.

Envy may lead to critical speech. So it was with Moses' siblings. His brother, Aaron, and his sister, Miriam, resented the idea of God speaking through their younger brother. "And they said, Hath the LORD indeed spoken only by Moses? hath he not spoken also by us?" (Numbers 12:2). Many faultfinding, unkind words among family members have their roots in the soil of envy.

Envy may lead to pouting. So it was with King Ahab. After Naboth, in obedience to God's commandment, refused to sell Ahab some land, Ahab "laid him down upon his bed, and turned away his face, and would eat no bread" (1 Kings 21:4). Envy takes the joy and contentment out of living.

Do you want to avoid every evil work? Don't let envy get rooted in your life.

About God:

To Do:

February 23

Envy Puts Others Down

"For we ourselves also were sometimes foolish, disobedient, deceived, serving divers lusts and pleasures, living in malice and envy, hateful, and hating one another." —Titus 3:3

Read Luke 15:20-32

I've been told that if you have more than one crab in a bucket, you don't need a lid on it. When one crab tries to climb out, the other crabs pull it down. "Who is able to stand before envy?" Proverbs 27:4 asks rhetorically.

Envy put Christ down in the grave. When the Jewish leaders wanted Jesus killed, Pilate "knew that for envy they had delivered him" (Matthew 27:18). So they yelled, "Away with Him! Crucify Him!" Truly, "jealousy is cruel as the grave" (Song of Solomon 8:6). Many of us aren't prepared to accept success—at least not someone else's.

Envy put Joseph down in the pit, awaiting death. His brothers disliked him intensely after he told them he dreamed that he would be promoted above them. So "they conspired against him to slay him. And they said one to another, Behold, this dreamer cometh. Come now therefore, and let us slay him, and cast him into some pit, and we will say, Some evil beast hath devoured him: and we shall see what will become of his dreams" (Genesis 37:18-20).

When attention was given to the penitent prodigal son, the elder brother became envious. He pulled attention away from his brother by being stubborn, argumentative, angry, and critical. His words to his father oozed with envy: "Lo, these many years do I serve thee, neither transgressed I at any time thy commandment: and yet thou never gavest me a kid, that I might make merry with my friends: but as soon as this thy son was come, which hath devoured thy living with harlots, thou hast killed for him the fatted calf" (Luke 15:29, 30). Frequently, envy provides the mud that is thrown at others.

Some of the older generation's criticism of the younger generation is tinged with envy. And envy is often the mother of gossip.

If you find yourself thinking negatively about others, sharing unfavorable reports about others, or putting people down, take a look at your heart. Envy may be lurking there. By God's grace, put it away.

About God: **To Do:**

Envy Brings Trouble to Oneself

"For ye are yet carnal: for whereas there is among you envying, and strife, and divisions, are ye not carnal, and walk as men?" —1 Corinthians 3:3

Read Esther 5:7-14; 7:1-10

In Greece an athlete killed himself for envy. His fellow citizens had erected a statue in honor of another athlete, a champion. The first athlete was bitterly disappointed. In his envy, he vowed to destroy his rival's statue. Every night he would creep through the dark and chisel at the base of the statue to undermine its foundation and make it fall. At last he succeeded. It did fall—but it fell on him. He was a victim of his own envy. Unfortunately, he didn't know the words of Job 5:2, "For wrath killeth the foolish man, and envy slayeth the silly one."

"A sound heart is the life of the flesh: but envy the rottenness of the bones" (Proverbs 14:30). When you feel yourself turning green with envy, you are ripe for trouble. It can cause chronic fatigue, irritability, and poor mental attitudes. Or to use another analogy, envy is like a carelessly thrown boomerang. It can return and hurt the person who threw it.

Haman was jealous of his position. He saw the Jew Mordecai as a threat to his power and prestige. He concocted a plot to get rid of Mordecai by destroying all the Jews (talk about overkill). The end result was the end of Haman—hanging on a gallows.

Envy causes spiritual disaster. In Asaph's case, an envious attitude almost led him to commit spiritual suicide. He gave this testimony. "But as for me, my feet were almost gone; my steps had well nigh slipped. For I was envious at the foolish, when I saw the prosperity of the wicked" (Psalm 73:2, 3). But then, fortunately, he recognized his perspective by coming before God. He testifies, "Until I went into the sanctuary of God; then understood I their end" (Psalm 73:17). Envy always involves a lack of proper vision and perspective

Avoid envy and you will avoid much trouble. Envy shoots at others but wounds herself.

About God: **To Do:**

February 25

Envy Poisons Interpersonal Relations

"Let us walk honestly, as in the day; not in rioting and drunkenness, not in chambering and wantonness, not in strife and envying." —Romans 13:13

Read Genesis 26:12-33

In the days of the Crusades, Richard, the King of England, and Philip, the King of France, were good friends and comrades when they first went to the Holy Land. However, in their battles against the Turks, it became evident that Richard was the more courageous of the two. The soldiers watching the two leaders nicknamed Richard "the Lion-hearted."

Philip became envious. He objected to Richard's strategies. He refused to cooperate. He returned to France, quite upset. Later, Philip invaded the territory of Richard the Lion-hearted and fought against him.

Similarly, King Saul and David were good friends and comrades in battle. Saul was a great warrior. But David was a greater warrior. The women recognized this and sang, "Saul hath slain his thousands, and David his ten thousands" (1 Samuel 18:7). Saul was poisoned with envy. His life illustrates the idea that there are many roads to hate, but envy is the shortest one of all. "Saul was very wroth, and the saying displeased him; and he said, They have ascribed unto David ten thousands, and to me they have ascribed but thousands: and what can he have more but the kingdom? And Saul eyed David from that day and forward" (1 Samuel 18:8, 9).

On the very next day, Saul tried to nail David to the wall by throwing his spear at him. This happened twice, and each time David dodged the spear. He went into hiding, and Saul demoted him. Saul wasted his life trying to capture and kill the man he envied. Being overcome with envy is like running into the ocean: the deeper you go in, the harder it is to get out.

When Laban heard of his nephew's success in animal husbandry, his countenance was not toward Jacob as before (Genesis 31:2). You see, love looks through a telescope, but envy looks through a microscope. When the Philistines saw Isaac's success, they also absorbed the poison. They proceeded to fill in the wells of water upon which Isaac's flocks and herds depended.

Envy spoiled relations between leaders (Saul), relatives (Laban), and neighbors (the Philistines). Have you allowed envy to interfere with your relations between you and your peers, your relatives, or your neighbors? Let the antidotes of love and prayer purge your life of this poison.

About God:

To Do:

Have I the Right Awareness?

"Blessed are the poor in spirit:
for theirs is the kingdom of heaven." —Matthew 5:3

Read James 4:1-10

The Beatitudes that Jesus spoke in the Sermon on the Mount are "Be-attitudes"—attitudes demonstrating what followers of Christ should be.

To be prosperous, you must be poor, Jesus says in the first beatitude. *Blessed* means "spiritually prosperous or happy." Jesus said, "Blessed are the poor in spirit: for theirs is the kingdom of heaven" (Matthew 5:3). Thus, to be spiritually prosperous, you need to sense your spiritual poverty. If your financial assets consisted of only dirty, useless rags, how rich would you be? By nature we all are spiritual paupers. "All have sinned, and come short of the glory of God" (Romans 3:23) and "All our righteousnesses are as filthy rags" (Isaiah 64:6). We become prosperous only by receiving the riches of Christ's grace.

The Pharisees were not poor in spirit. They were full of pride and self-righteousness. They wouldn't admit their poverty and need. Before we can be filled, we need to be emptied. Acknowledging our need of God and His pardon opens the door to His bountiful blessing.

Possibly, you used to be poor in spirit. But after being a Christian for several years, you think of yourself as important and successful due to your abilities and hard work. You think of God as being handy, but not essential. We don't say it aloud, but our attitude suggests that we can handle life quite all right by ourselves. We forget that Jesus said, "Without me ye can do nothing" (John 15:5).

Are you truly poor in spirit, depending on God, humbly acknowledging your daily need? Or have you become self-sufficient, proud, independent, and full of self?

TESTS:

- Do I take credit for myself, or do I thank God, realizing my dependence upon Him?
- Do I ask His blessing and direction, or do I just forge ahead?
- Do I love the praise of men more than the praise of God?
- Is my spiritual life on autopilot, or is Jesus at the controls?

About God: **To Do:**

February 27

Have I the Right Sorrow?

"Blessed are they that mourn:
for they shall be comforted." —Matthew 5:4

Read Psalm 32

The story is told of a man in the Orient who was caught for stealing. He was put into the stocks in a public place. A friend came along and saw him with his neck in the large wooden collar.

"What have you done to get this punishment?" he asked in astonishment.

The thief answered, "I was just walking along the street when I saw a grass rope on the ground. Knowing that a grass rope isn't of much value, I picked it up and brought it to my home; so I got into this trouble."

"But what's wrong with picking up a grass rope?"

"Well," replied the thief, "it happened to be tied to something that came along with it."

"And what was that?" asked his friend.

"A very small ox."

To *mourn* (which precedes blessing) means "to be sorry about one's sin"—so sorry that one abandons it.

We don't have the right sorrow for sin if we defend it, minimize it, or justify it. We don't have the right regret for sin if we joke about it.

We have the right sorrow only if we are broken, contrite, and repentant. This means we will confess, forsake, and hate sin.

When David sinned, he was not immediately mournful, but then he came to his senses, thanks partly to Nathan. Then David said, "Have mercy upon me, O God. For I acknowledge my transgressions: and my sin is ever before me. Against thee, thee only, have I sinned, and done this evil in thy sight: that thou mightest be justified when thou speakest, and be clear when thou judgest" (Psalm 51:1, 3, 4).

TESTS:

- Have I shed tears or at least felt very bad about my sin?
- Do I have an aversion to sin?
- Am I mellow and open to God's Spirit?
- Am I approachable when friends, family members, or pastors confront me about questionable areas of my life?

About God: **To Do:**

Have I the Right Response?

*"Blessed are the meek:
for they shall inherit the earth."* —Matthew 5:5

Read Psalm 37:1-11

A godly senior citizen had an acquaintance who hated him to the extent that he did everything possible to make the old man's life miserable. For a long time the elderly Christian did nothing in response. But finally, it was too much. The Christian announced he was going to retaliate by *killing* his tormenter. When his enemy heard this, he was greatly amused, saying that he couldn't wait to see what this harmless relic would try to do.

At every opportunity, the elderly saint showed his adversary kindness and returned good for evil. This caused a mixture of merriment and consternation to the non-Christian.

One day the godly man risked his life to save his enemy's wife from drowning. When the rescuer and his enemy met, the ungodly man had a different attitude. "You have done what you said you would do. You've killed me—or at least you've killed the man that I was. Now, what can I do for you?"

That Christian senior citizen demonstrated an attitude of meekness by responding in a gentle, non-retaliatory way. This concept of gentleness and meekness was rarely heard of before the Christian era. In fact the word meaning *gentleman* was not known. It is not our nature to be mild, submissive, controlled, and meek. Rather, our tendency is to be stubborn, revengeful, and bitter.

The word *meek* relates to being tamed like an animal that is useful and controlled. In order to be useful and pleasing to God, we need to be controlled by Him.

Jesus said, "I am meek" (Matthew 11:29). His meekness was very noticeable during His trial—silent in the face of false accusation, calm when mocked and humiliated, and nonresistant when bruised and beaten.

Tests:

- Are my temper and tongue tamed?
- Do I accept times of adversity, or do I bitterly complain and accuse God?
- Do I defend my rights and try to get even?
- Am I receptive to criticism?

About God:

To Do:

March 1

Have I the Right Appetite?

"Blessed are they which do hunger and thirst after righteousness: for they shall be filled. —Matthew 5:6

Read Psalm 81:10-16

When our son was young, he said he had three stomachs: a first-course stomach, a dessert stomach, and a snack stomach. This explained why he always had room for cookies and ice cream even though there were lots of vegetables left on his plate. Likewise, even though his piecrust was still on his dessert plate, he still had room for candy or potato chips.

You may have an ingenious explanation for lacking an appetite for righteousness. But if you want to be blessed, you need to have a hunger for the right things.

Your appetite for righteousness (right relationship with God, right living, right attitudes) may be stunted by several things. It may be you have a love of pleasure, as did Demas, who, "having loved this present world," abandoned Paul (2 Timothy 4:10). It may be secret sin, such as jealousy, an unforgiving attitude, worry, or impure thoughts. It may be self-righteousness and pride, being so full of self that there's no hunger for God.

Tests:

- Do I have an appetite for Bible reading? "Desire the sincere milk of the word, that ye may grow thereby" (1 Peter 2:2).
- Do I have an appetite for worship? "Not forsaking the assembling of ourselves together, as the manner of some is" (Hebrews 10:25).
- Do I have an appetite for prayer? "Praying always with all prayer and supplication in the Spirit" (Ephesians 6:18).
- Do I have a hunger for heaven as did Paul? "Having a desire to depart, and to be with Christ; which is far better" (Philippians 1:23).

About God: **To Do:**

Do I Have the Right Spirit?

"Blessed are the merciful: for they shall obtain mercy."
—Matthew 5:7

Read Philemon 1-21

A native of South Africa was falsely accused by a white settler of stealing a horse. The white man, a non-Christian, ignored his explanation and proceeded to punish the native to serve as a warning to other natives. So he tied the native to a tree and cut off his right hand. Months later the white man was overtaken by darkness and storm far from his cabin. Seeking shelter in a native hut, he was given food and a place to sleep. When he awoke, a tall African was standing over him. As their eyes met, the native held up his arm without any hand. The white man realized that his time had come. He knew the natives in the area were cruel and revengeful. He waited, expecting each moment to be his last. Slowly the right arm dropped, and the native said: "This is my cabin and you are in my power. You have maimed me for life; but I am a Christian, and I forgive you."

Doing good to those who hatefully mistreat you is Jesus' command. It is not natural for unregenerate man, but is normal and necessary for the follower of Jesus.

Being merciful involves our attitude toward other people. We show mercy as we forgive those who wrong us and hurt us. We show mercy as we have compassion for those in need and extend a helping hand. We show mercy as we demonstrate forbearance toward family members who borrow our clothes, take the biggest slice of pizza, or hog the computer. We show mercy as we are kind and understanding toward those with physical and mental handicaps.

Tests:

- Do I give others the benefit of the doubt?
- Do I hope something nasty happens to someone who has wronged me?
- Do I get upset when someone "cuts in front of me" literally on the highway—or on the road of life?
- Do I freely forgive, or do I say, "Pay me what thou owest"?

About God: **To Do:**

March 3

Do I Have the Right Devotion?

"Blessed are the pure in heart: for they shall see God."
—Matthew 5:8

Read Luke 11:33-42

A fellow wrote to the girl of his dreams, "Darling, I would climb the highest mountain, swim the widest stream, cross the burning desert, or die at the stake for you.

"P. S. See you Saturday—if it doesn't rain."

God wants sincerity and purity. It starts with the heart, the root of life. One's life dare not be clean on the outside only while harboring dirt on the inside. God detests the superficial and demands the genuine.

Although the basic thought of being pure in heart is not referring to moral purity, having a right devotion will maintain sexual purity. The Christian's thoughts need to be pure (Philippians 4:8). His words must be pure, letting "no corrupt communication proceed out of [his] mouth" (Ephesians 4:29). His appearance must promote purity by "modest apparel" (1 Timothy 2:9). His deeds must be pure. "But fornication, and all uncleanness, or covetousness, let it not be once named among you, as becometh saints" (Ephesians 5:3).

Tests:

- Is my love genuine? Is it without dissimulation (Romans 12:9)?
- Is my giving and praying sincere or to be "seen of men" (Matthew 6:1-5)?
- Is my worship pure, or am I described by the words of Jesus, "This people draweth nigh unto me with their mouth, and honoureth me with their lips; but their heart is far from me" (Matthew 15:8)?
- Are my work habits the same whether the foreman is watching me or not? Employees should work consistently, "not with eyeservice, as menpleasers; but as the servants of Christ, doing the will of God from the heart" (Ephesians 6:6).

About God:

To Do:

Do I Have the Right Cause?

"Blessed are the peacemakers: for they shall be called the children of God." —Matthew 5:9

Read Acts 9:23-31

A new Christian said, "My wife and I used to bicker from the time we awoke in the morning till we went to bed at night. But since we have found peace with God, our home is a heaven on earth."

Peacemaking is the right cause. Making peace with God by surrendering to Him is the foundation for peacemaking among people. "Therefore being justified by faith, we have peace with God through our Lord Jesus Christ" (Romans 5:1).

After being at peace vertically, we can begin working at making peace horizontally. We can do this in three areas:

First, be at peace with others. Make confession to those you have hurt. Ask for forgiveness. Make restitution. Show that your attitude is different. "If it be possible, as much as lieth in you, live peaceably with all men" (Romans 12:18).

Second, encourage others to find God's peace. Witness to them. Pray for them. Befriend them. Invite them to church. Be an example to them.

Third, attempt to restore strained, broken relationships. Be a reconciler. Bring people together to talk. Don't be a gossip. If two people don't appreciate each other, you can repeat the rare, kind, and appreciative comment that one may make about the other. Be like Paul who made efforts to reconcile Onesimus to his master, Philemon.

Tests:

- Am I truly at peace with God?
- Am I at peace with my parents, my siblings, my co-workers, and my acquaintances?
- Am I urging others to find peace with God by repentance of sins and faith in Jesus Christ?
- Am I open to opportunities to reconcile people who are at odds with each other?

About God: **To Do:**

Respect Stabilizes Society

"Honor all men. Love the brotherhood. Fear God. Honour the king." —1 Peter 2:17

Read Romans 13:1-14

Do I need to obey traffic laws? Is it all right to evade some taxes? What about hunting and fishing regulations that aren't to my liking?

The Bible is clear that God has set up civil authorities, and His children need to obey them. Here is my paraphrase of verses 1 and 2 of today's reading: "Everybody needs to obey civil authorities. All authority comes from God and is put into place by God. If anybody resists a government authority, he is really resisting God—and will be punished."

When I was in my late teens, I found out what can quickly happen if civil authority is removed and society feels free to act without fear of punishment.

The entire police force of Montreal, then Canada's largest city, went on strike. During the first sixteen hours, the absence of law enforcement was fun. Motorists drove merrily through red lights, ignored no-parking signs, and ignored speed limits. But soon the atmosphere changed. No police meant no fear of getting caught; criminal activity mushroomed. Near noon, four heavily armed men boldly and easily robbed a bank of $28,000. Sixty more armed robberies followed. Gangs of looters used bricks and sledge hammers to break into 150 stores, stealing more than half a million dollars worth of merchandise. One man was murdered, property was wrecked, and the fires of arson raged. Montreal and observers around the world saw graphically God's wisdom in establishing government.

In the aftermath of Hurricane Katrina, which devastated New Orleans in 2005, there was little law and order. As a result, there was much looting, misconduct, and violence.

Without respect for civil authorities, society experiences anarchy and chaos. When government breaks down, such as during civil war, very sad and tragic events occur. This happened in Russia during the Communist Revolution in 1917, and Mennonites suffered tremendously because of it. They were subject to robberies, rapes, murders, and terrors of every sort. It happens also after practically any victory in war, when men have had no direct accountability for their behavior.

Even a government that is anti-God and totalitarian is better than no government. My son visited large cities in communist China. He felt very safe, much safer than in America, walking or biking throughout the city, even at night. There was respect for authority and fear of punishment (often severe).

About God: **To Do:**

Respect for Authority Pleases God

"As the Father gave me commandment, even so I do." —John 14:31

Read Numbers 16:1-21

As a young person, one of the best ways to please your heavenly Father is to respect the authority of your earthly father and mother. The life of Jesus Himself teaches us this. Luke 2:51, 52 tells us that Jesus as a young man "went down with them, and came to Nazareth, and was subject unto them . . . and Jesus increased . . . in favour with God."

Jesus was under authority. The centurion who wanted Jesus to heal his servant recognized this, saying to Jesus, "For I *also* am a man set under authority" (Luke 7:8).

Jesus recognized His Father's authority. He said, "For I came down from heaven, not to do mine own will, but the will of him that sent me" (John 6:38). He also said, "I have kept my Father's commandments" (John 15:10). And in John 8:29, Jesus said, "I do always those things that please him."

God's displeasure and condemnation is directed against those who "despise dominion," that is, those who reject authority (Jude 8). This was vividly demonstrated in today's Scripture reading about Korah and company. The rebels complained that Moses exercised too much authority. "Ye take too much upon you, seeing all the congregation are holy, every one of them, and the LORD is among them: wherefore then lift ye up yourselves above the congregation of the LORD?" (v. 3). They failed to recognize that the authority was delegated by God. The Lord then took them down (literally) for complaining that Moses had lifted himself up.

As we come under God's authority and the authorities He has set over us, we can anticipate the words, "Well done, thou good and faithful servant."

Respect for authority also pleases our earthly authorities. As Hebrews 13:17 says, "Obey them that have the rule over you, and submit yourselves: for they watch for your souls, as they that must give account, that they may do it with joy, and not with grief: for that is unprofitable for you."

Church leaders, missionaries, teachers, and parents unite to say, "I have no greater joy than to hear that my children walk in truth" (3 John 4).

About God: **To Do:**

Respect Promotes Protection

"Honour thy father and mother . . . that it may be well with thee, and thou mayest live long on the earth." —Ephesians 6:2, 3

Read Proverbs 4:1-22

I like the story of the little boy pedaling his tricycle furiously around the block. A police officer watched him go around again and again.

"Why are you going around and around the block?" he asked the little boy.

"I'm running away from home," he said.

"Then why do you keep going around the block again and again?"

"Because my mom said I'm not allowed to cross the street."

In childhood, respect for authority often keeps a person safe. As such, it is valuable to children and to parents. I used to tell my young children stories of children who were spared injury because of prompt obedience. For example, a boy in Germany wandered onto the railroad track near his home. His mother, coming out onto the porch, saw the boy and also saw a train coming around the curve. She shouted to her son, "Lie down flat." He dropped immediately between the rails. He lay there as the train thundered over him. When the train was gone, the boy ran to his mother.

In youth, obedience to parents can spare a young person much spiritual danger as well as physical jeopardy. If Dad says, "You need to get rid of those CDs," or if Mom says, "That jacket needs to be returned to the store," obedience is for our spiritual safety. Does not God protect those young people who submit to their parents?

The wise writer of Proverbs puts it beautifully, "My son, keep thy father's commandment, and forsake not the law of thy mother: bind them continually upon thine heart, and tie them about thy neck. When thou goest, it shall lead thee; when thou sleepest, it shall keep thee; and when thou awakest, it shall talk with thee. For the commandment is a lamp; and the law is light; and reproofs of instruction are the way of life" (Proverbs 6:20-23).

In adulthood, there are also blessings in recognizing authority—God's smile of approval, a good example for youth, and spiritual safety. One reason a Christian woman is to cover her head (1 Corinthians 11:1-16) is "because of the angels." Perhaps this relates to authority—the angels are under authority, and we should be too.

About God: **To Do:**

Respect Contributes to Liberty

"If the Son therefore shall make you free, ye shall be free indeed."
—John 8:36

Read Luke 15:3-24

As a fish stays in its element, water, it experiences freedom of movement and life. If you see a trout on land, acting like a kangaroo, or see it soaring through the air like a hawk, you know it has problems and will soon lose its freedom and life.

A Christian who removes himself from under the authority of God, direct or delegated, will experience a loss of liberty.

The prodigal son wanted freedom to spend, to sin, and to live as he liked. But the result was anything but freedom. In the end he longed to come back under the authority of his dad—even if it meant becoming a hired servant—in order to have greater liberty.

Samson disrespected parental counsel about whom to marry. His rejection of authority ultimately led him to prison in fetters.

Second Peter 2:19 warns of sinful persons. "While they promise them liberty, they themselves are the servants of corruption: for of whom a man is overcome, of the same is he brought in bondage."

People who have a valid driver's license enjoy a lot of freedom. I can drive on eight-lane highways in cities or on dirt roads in the country. I can drive on the east coast or along the west coast. However, if I seriously violate the rules of the road, I may have my liberty to drive restricted or removed. But as long as I follow the rules and submit to traffic authorities, I have remarkable freedom of movement.

Prior to the Oklahoma City bombing in 1995, Terry Nichols sent a letter to government officials. In his letter, Terry wrote that he was not subject to the laws of the U. S. government, which he called a "fraudulent, usurping octopus." Terry was convicted of being an accomplice in the bombing which killed 168 innocent people and caused millions of dollars of property damage. For his disregard for authority expressed in the bombing, Terry was sentenced to spend the rest of his life in prison.

James 1:25 has an intriguing expression: "law of liberty." We often think of law as restricting our freedom, but living in accordance to God's will and Word brings true liberty.

About God:

To Do:

March 9

Respect Improves Relationships

"Ye are my friends, if ye do whatsoever I command you."
—John 15:14

Read Psalm 119:161-176

One dark, foggy night, a lookout on a battleship saw a light. He informed the captain, who, after noting the ship's location, concluded that his ship was on a collision course with another vessel.

The captain instructed, "Signal the ship: 'We are on a collision course; advise you change course 20 degrees.' "

The return signal countered, "Advisable for you to change course 20 degrees."

The captain signaled, "I'm a captain; change course 20 degrees."

The response was, "I'm a seaman second class. You'd better change course 20 degrees."

Now angry, the captain ordered, "I'm a battleship. Change course 20 degrees!"

The reply: "I'm a lighthouse. You make the call."

God's authority is like the lighthouse. Because of who He is, He has the right to command. We can't have a good relationship with Him while we are disobeying His commands. He also delegates authority on a human level—parents, government, church leaders, and employees. A proper attitude toward delegated authority will help us avoid collisions with them.

It's hard for parents and teens to have a good relationship when the teen blatantly disregards parental instructions. If Mom says, "We don't want that kind of music in our house. We believe it stimulates carnality and worldly ideas," and the teen plays it anyway, their relationship is impaired.

A church leader faces an impossible task if the congregation does not recognize his authority. If he has been called to give leadership and maintain standards of Christian conduct, what can he do if a congregation disregards what he says? Many church divisions could have been avoided if those under authority had shown a submissive attitude. First Thessalonians 5:12, 13 says, "And we beseech you, brethren, to know them which labour among you, and are over you in the Lord, and admonish you; and to esteem them very highly in love for their work's sake."

If a foreman tells a woodworker to make a chest of drawers with three drawers, but he decides to make five drawers, there will likely be problems in their relationship. Ephesians 6:5 tells servants (which may refer to slaves or paid employees), "Be obedient to them that are your masters according to the flesh, with fear and trembling, in singleness of your heart, as unto Christ."

About God: **To Do:**

Respect Brings Blessing

"But whoso keepeth his word, in him verily is the love of God perfected: hereby know we that we are in him." —1 John 2:5

Read 1 Samuel 26:2-25

A young man was arrested in Detroit for driving without a license. Imprisoned, he felt so cooped up that he impetuously tried to escape. He climbed through an opening in the ceiling above a jailhouse sink and found himself in a tiny crawl space that led nowhere. When he tried to get back down headfirst, his pants hooked on some metalwork that left him dangling from the hole, helplessly waving his arms. Firefighters rescued him, but not without a news photographer somehow getting his picture and sending it to newspapers across the country.

Instead of creating problems for ourselves, honoring authority over us brings blessing. Take, for example, Daniel. He respected the authority of three kings with serious "I" problems—proud Nebuchadnezzar, blasphemous Belshazzar, and gullible Darius. Daniel courteously counseled Nebuchadnezzar, "Wherefore, O king, let my counsel be acceptable unto thee, and break off thy sins by righteousness, and thine iniquities by shewing mercy to the poor; if it may be a lengthening of thy tranquility" (Daniel 4:27).

Daniel's whole life expressed godliness and respect. "An excellent spirit was in him; and the king thought to set him over the whole realm. Then the presidents and princes sought to find occasion against Daniel concerning the kingdom; but they could find none occasion nor fault; forasmuch as he was faithful, neither was there any error or fault found in him" (Daniel 6:3, 4). The Lord blessed him with greatness, insight, and influence.

Every great person has learned how to obey, whom to obey, and when to obey.

David, anointed to be king after Saul, had respect for Saul because of Saul's office, as shown in today's reading. And the Lord blessed and protected David. Respect for God's authority, including delegated authority, is a good prescription for spiritual health.

Children are blessed as they respond to the authority of their parents. Ephesians 6:2, 3 says, "Honour thy father and mother; which is the first commandment with promise; that it may be well with thee, and thou mayest live long on the earth."

Whether we are eight, eighteen, or eighty, we are all under authority. Let us respond positively so that we can be blessed.

About God: **To Do:**

March 11

If You Disagree With Your Authority

"Render therefore to all their dues: tribute to whom tribute is due; custom to whom custom; fear to whom fear; honour to whom honour." —Romans 13:7

Read Daniel 1

How can you respect an authority over you if you have difficulty with his instructions or disagree with him? For example, what should you do if your dad or your foreman at work tells you to do something that is questionable or wrong?

Take a lesson from Daniel. He had a firm purpose to please God by living a holy life (v. 8). When asked to eat inappropriate food, he politely asked to be exempt. When his superior was reluctant, Daniel offered a reasonable alternative. Then his authority gave permission.

Here are some guidelines when appealing to an authority:

- Pray much and ask God for wisdom.
- Eliminate an independent spirit. Go with a humble, not a haughty, spirit.
- Think of a suitable alternative, if possible, that will be acceptable to the authority and allow him to reach his goals.
- Have the attitude of a learner rather than a superior.
- Explain politely why you have a difficulty in meeting his expectations.

What if you seriously disagree with your church leader's sermon?

"I don't agree with everything he said . . ." That is a fairly common saying, and it is understandable and sometimes to be expected. But what comes after that remark reveals whether you are respectful of authority or not.

One way to react to the sermon is to stew and fret and practically make yourself sick. A second reaction is to roast the preacher at home, feed the criticism to your family, and give indigestion to your children. A third reaction is to complain to some sympathetic person who lacks maturity or is disenchanted or out of fellowship with his church. You may have let your own steam off, but what about your listener? You have just given him another burden that he will need to handle before he can grow and rejoin the fellowship. A fourth reaction is to search the Scriptures as the Bereans did and determine whether the preacher was correct or not.

If he was wrong, go and tell him. Entreat him as a father. If you misunderstood or aren't sure, charitably ask him to clarify.

If you were wrong, humbly ask the Lord to help you see clearly so you can help maintain peace in the church.

About God: **To Do:**

The Bible: Love, Use, Remember It

"For the word of God is quick, and powerful, and sharper than any twoedged sword, piercing even to the dividing asunder of soul and spirit, and of the joints and marrow, and is a discerner of the thoughts and intents of the heart." —Hebrews 4:12

Read Psalm 119:1-24

A Massachusetts high school teacher reportedly gave a quiz to academically superior high school students on their knowledge of the Bible. According to some of the students, Eve was created from an apple; the Gospels were written by Matthew, Mark, "Luther," and John; and Jezebel was Ahab's donkey.

The teacher was also told that Jesus was baptized by Moses, Sodom and Gomorrah were lovers, and that "Golgotha was the name of the giant who slew the Apostle David."

I know the writer of Psalm 119 knew his Bible a lot better. I am not sure how old he was, but he had insight into the problems of youth and the solution to those problems. He wrote, "Wherewithal shall a young man cleanse his way? by taking heed thereto according to thy word" (Psalm 119:9). In the next four devotionals we will notice valuable things that Psalm 119 recommends that youth (and folks of all ages) do with the Bible:

1. *Love it exceedingly.* Verse 97 says, "O how love I thy law! it is my meditation all the day." We cannot overdo our love for the Scriptures, because they point to the lovely, loving Lord. "I love them exceedingly" (v. 167). When my girlfriend (now my wife) and I were separated by 4,000 kilometers, I loved her letters because I loved (and love) the author of them.

2. *Use it wisely.* The psalmist employed the Scriptures in a very helpful way in speaking to opponents of the truth. "So shall I have wherewith to answer him that reproacheth me: for I trust in thy word" (v. 42). Let's give the world in need the Word it needs.

3. *Remember it always.* "I will never forget thy precepts: for with them thou hast quickened me" (v. 93). You might forget algebra, dates (in history or courtship), your mom's birthday, or how to play a game, but don't forget God's precepts.

About God: **To Do:**

March 13

The Bible: Speak of It, Stick to It, Meditate on It

"For I am not ashamed of the gospel of Christ: for it is the power of God unto salvation to every one that believeth; to the Jew first, and also to the Greek." —Romans 1:16

Read Psalm 119:25-48

1. *Speak of it boldly.* Whether the name is Churchill, Clinton, or a common citizen, the Word is for all. "I will speak of thy testimonies also before kings, and will not be ashamed" (v. 46). This is what the Apostle Paul did before Felix, Festus, and Agrippa. Witnessing of Bible truth to our youthful peers may be just as challenging. A Christian is a nobody who is seeking to tell everybody about Somebody who can transform anybody.

2. *Stick to it tenaciously.* "I have stuck unto thy testimonies" (v. 31). This does not require "Crazy Glue" but "consecration glue."

"Will you please tell me in a word," said a Christian woman to a minister, "what your idea of consecration is?" Holding out a blank sheet of paper, the pastor replied, "It is to sign your name at the bottom of this page and let God fill it in as He wills."

Clinging to His testimonies also means sticking to accuracy in translation—not inserting "hearty handshake" for "holy kiss," or "Father-Mother" for "our Father." Suppose you would try doing the same kind of substitution to your vehicle: water instead of gasoline, molasses for oil, or Mountain Dew for antifreeze. The Bible does not need to be rewritten—just reread.

3. *Meditate on it prayerfully.* Early in the morning is often a good time. The psalmist found this to be true. "I prevented [anticipated] the dawning of the morning, and cried: I hoped in thy word. Mine eyes prevent [stay open through] the night watches, that I might meditate in thy word" (vv. 147, 148).

Andrew Bonar, a preacher who lived long ago, followed these rules: First—not to speak to any person before speaking to Jesus Christ. Second—not to do anything with his hands until he had been on his knees. Third—not to read the papers until he had read his Bible.

About God: **To Do:**

The Bible: Learn, Keep, and Respect It

"For whom the Lord loveth he chasteneth."
—Hebrews 12:6

Read Psalm 119:49-64

1. *Learn it thoroughly.* Sometimes a course in affliction rounds out our Bible education. "It is good for me that I have been afflicted; that I might learn thy statutes" (v. 71). Some of the Bible's most precious treasures are discovered only with tear-filled eyes.

A missionary in Africa learned from the natives how to walk through swift streams. The danger lay in being swept off one's feet and carried down the stream to greater depths or hurled to death against the hidden rocks. A native said, "Take a large stone, the heavier the better, and carry it across the stream. The extra weight will help keep your feet solidly on the streambed."

A load of affliction can help keep a Christian from being swept away spiritually.

2. *Keep it faithfully.* Though temptations and tempters will come, a Christian must remain determined to follow God's way. "Depart from me, ye evildoers: for I will keep the commandments of my God" (v. 115). The value of the Bible comes not from knowing it, but from obeying it. As James 1:22 says, "But be ye doers of the word, and not hearers only, deceiving your own selves."

3. *Respect it continually.* The psalmist said, "I will have respect unto thy statutes continually" (v. 117) and "my heart standeth in awe of thy word" (v. 161). We as imperfect believers need to be repeatedly renewed and revived with the water of the Word. The only way to keep a broken vessel full is by keeping the faucet turned on.

Henry Stanley, explorer of Africa in the last century, started off into the jungle with 73 books weighing 180 pounds. As he traveled farther into Africa, he lightened the load by reluctantly throwing away his books. Finally, he had just one book left—the Bible. Likewise, may we treasure the Bible above all others.

About God: **To Do:**

March 15

The Bible: Read, Appreciate, and Believe It

"Ye do err, not knowing the scriptures."
—Matthew 22:29

Read Psalm 119:65-88

1. *Read it personally.* "Thy word have *I* hid in mine heart that *I* might not sin against thee" (v. 11). The story is told of a small fishing village where a flock of seagulls fed on the scraps left by the fishermen. After some years the fishing became poor, and the fishermen moved down the coast where fishing was better. The seagulls stayed behind. Because they had become so dependent on the fishermen for food and had never learned to feed themselves, the entire flock of birds died. In the same way, believers must be able to feed themselves through personal meditation on the Word.

2. *Appreciate it frequently.* Some of us enjoy the rewards of a frequent flyer program. Greater rewards await the person who is a "frequent reader." Verse 164 says, "Seven times a day do I praise thee because of thy righteous judgments." The Bible is so deep that Bible teachers can never touch bottom, yet is shallow enough that babes in Christ cannot drown.

3. *Believe it wholeheartedly.* "Teach me good judgment and knowledge: for I have believed thy commandments" (v. 66).

God's Word has the power to make a person who is dead in sin alive (quickened). Take, for example, Etty Hillesm, a young Jewish woman living in Amsterdam in 1942. The Nazis were arresting Jews and herding them off to concentration camps. As she awaited inevitable arrest, tormented by a fear of the unknown, she began to read the Bible—and met Jesus. She simply put her hand in God's hand and found rare courage and confidence. Etty wrote in her diary: "From all sides our destruction creeps up on us and soon the ring will be closed and no one at all will be able to come to our aid. But I don't feel that I am in anybody's clutches. I feel safe in God's arms. And whether I am sitting at my beloved old desk in the Jewish district or in a labor camp under SS guards, I shall feel safe in God's arms. For once you have begun to walk with God, you need only keep on walking with Him, and all of life becomes one long stroll."

About God: **To Do:**

The Law of the Lord Is Perfect

"The law is holy, and the commandment holy, and just, and good."
—Romans 7:12

Read Psalm 119:113-136

"The law of the LORD is perfect" (Psalm 19:7). The laws of man are not. Consider, for instance, a few laws still officially on the books:

If you live in Detroit, it is illegal to fall asleep in your own bathtub.

If you live in West Virginia, it is illegal to sneeze on a train.

Did you know that in California it is technically illegal to set a mousetrap unless you have a hunting license?

What do you think happens in Kansas when this law is followed: "When two trains approach each other at a crossing, both shall come to a full stop and neither shall start up again until the other has gone."

Canada has some puzzling laws too. For example, all bicycle riders in Edmonton must signal with the arm before making a turn although said riders must keep both hands on the handlebars at all times.

In Pictou, Nova Scotia, a man may not kiss any woman, even his wife, on Sunday.

In Saanich, British Columbia, it is unlawful to let a cow walk more slowly than two miles per hour on the highway.

And, under an anti-noise bylaw, Ottawa forbids bees to buzz within the city limits!

Contrast these man-made rules with God's commands in the Bible. Some man-made rules may make us smile, but the Bible is able to make us *wise unto salvation.*

Consider the following commands:

- "And they said, Believe on the Lord Jesus Christ, and thou shalt be saved" (Acts 16:31).
- "Repent ye therefore, and be converted, that your sins may be blotted out, when the times of refreshing shall come from the presence of the Lord" (Acts 3:19).
- "Enter ye in at the strait gate: for wide is the gate, and broad is the way, that leadeth to destruction, and many there be which go in thereat: because strait is the gate, and narrow is the way, which leadeth unto life, and few there be that find it" (Matthew 7:13, 14).

A Bible scholar in his seventies was reading through the Old Testament in three weeks. His daughter asked him what he was reading. "News," was his reply. The Bible gives us relevant, sound, and up-to-date knowledge.

About God: **To Do:**

March 17

Bible Translators

"For not the hearers of the law are just before God, but the doers of the law shall be justified." —Romans 2:13

Read Joshua 1:1-9

A friend said to a young man, "I hear you are connected with a Bible society."

"I see," said the young man. "Well, in one way that report is true. I am a translator. It keeps me very busy."

"Really?" said the friend. "I didn't know you had the linguistic ability and educational background to be a Bible translator."

The young man replied, "I am busy translating the New Testament *into my daily life*."

This young man's major endeavor is very commendable. The Lord intends for His followers to demonstrate the meaning of the Bible message. The Thessalonians had the right idea. Paul wrote to them, "When ye received the word of God which ye heard of us, ye received it not as the word of men, but as it is in truth, the word of God, which effectually worketh also in you that believe" (1 Thessalonians 2:13).

We ought to immerse ourselves in the Bible and let it flavor our lives. As an analogy, let's consider tea. What makes one cup of tea stronger than another? The same ingredients, water and tea, are used for both. The difference is that in preparing the strong cup of tea, the tea leaves were immersed in the water longer, allowing the water to absorb more tea.

In the same way, the length of time we spend in God's Word determines how deeply we get into it and how deeply it gets into us. Just like the tea, the longer we are immersed in the Word, the stronger we become.

Psalm 1:2, 3 says, "But his delight is in the law of the LORD; and in his law doth he meditate day and night. And he shall be like a tree planted by the rivers of water, that bringeth forth his fruit in his season; his leaf also shall not wither; and whatsoever he doeth shall prosper." Although you may know only one language and have little inclination or potential to translate the Bible into a foreign language, by God's grace and His Spirit, you can be a strong translator of the Bible into your daily life. The Bible: know it in your head; stow it in your heart; show it in your life.

About God: **To Do:**

History Before It Happens

"Behold, the former things are come to pass, and new things do I declare: before they spring forth I tell you of them." —Isaiah 42:9

Read Isaiah 46:3-13

Do you believe it is possible for a person to travel at the speed of fifty miles per hour? This is what Sir Isaac Newton concluded several centuries ago after studying the prophecy of Daniel 12:4: "Many shall run to and fro, and knowledge shall be increased." Based on God's Word he predicted that since knowledge would be increased, a new mode of travel would be invented.

Voltaire, in his typical anti-Bible manner, wrote, "Now look at the mighty mind of Newton, who discovered gravitation. When he began to study the book called the Bible, it seems in order to credit its fabulous nonsense, he believed that the knowledge of mankind will be so increased that we shall be able to travel fifty miles an hour! The poor dotard!"

Not all man-made predictions are correct, even when they are loosely connected to the Bible. But, like Newton, we can be certain that what God says will come to pass.

The Lord says, "I am God, and there is none like me, declaring the end from the beginning, and from ancient times the things that are not yet done, saying, My counsel shall stand" (Isaiah 46:9, 10). What a wise God we serve! "Known unto God are all his works from the beginning of the world" (Acts 15:18).

He has chosen to reveal a number of things about the endtime. Consider a few Bible prophecies which have been fulfilled or are on the verge of fulfillment:

1. Jesus said, "I will come again" (John 14:3). His return is certain and imminent.
2. "As the days of Noe were, so shall also the coming of the Son of man be" (Matthew 24:37). The society Noah faced is very similar to ours.
3. Scoffers abound (2 Peter 3:3). Cults and the number of false prophets seem to be on the increase. Jesus said, "Many false prophets shall rise, and shall deceive many" (Matthew 24:11).
4. Wars and rumors of wars (Matthew 24:6) have made millions tense and anxious about widespread nuclear destruction. Terrorists may use airplanes as weapons, dirty bombs to destroy shopping malls, and beheadings to cause revulsion and fear.
5. Iniquity abounds and the love of many has waxed cold (Matthew 24:12). In my short lifetime I have witnessed tragic apostasy. The beliefs and practices of some churches could be likened to an advertisement: "For sale: a bladeless knife without a handle."

Let's be faithful.

About God: **To Do:**

The Business of Jesus

"And he said unto them, How is it that ye sought me? wist ye not that I must be about my Father's business?" —Luke 2:49

Read Luke 2:40-52

Out of the mouth of babes and youngsters have come interesting statements. For example, little Mary was visiting her grandmother in the country. Walking in the garden, Mary saw a peacock, a bird she had never seen before. After gazing in silent admiration, she ran into the house and cried out, "Oh, Granny, come and see! One of your chickens is in bloom!"

Tommy and his little brother Jack had taken their sled out to have some fun while the snow lasted. After a little while Mother looked out of the window to see how they were getting along. "I hope you are letting Jack have his share of rides, Tommy," she said.

"Oh, yes, Mother," was the reply. "I have it downhill and he has it up."

In another case a child said, "Daddy, when we sin we get smaller, don't we?"

"No," I replied, "why do you say that?"

"Well," she exclaimed, "the Bible says, 'All have sinned and come short!' "

We don't know what Jesus' earliest statements were. The first we have record of was at age 12. This experience at the temple reveals some notable things about Jesus:

- Jesus was devoted to God as He moved from childhood to youth. He was sensitive about what His Father wanted Him to be busy with (business). Many youth, despite growing up in a godly home, have their own agenda instead of God's agenda.
- Jesus showed a pattern of obedience and dependability. His parents were shocked at this apparent discrepancy to the pattern. "And when they saw him, they were amazed" (v. 48).
- Jesus' interests didn't center around basketball games, chariot racing, girls, styles, or amusements. His conversation centered around the things of His Father.
- Jesus demonstrated wisdom and understanding. Verse 47 says, "And all that heard him were astonished at his understanding and answers."
- Jesus obeyed His parents (v. 51).

You may have more knowledge than your parents. You may be more intelligent than your parents. You may be wiser than your parents. You may have greater speaking and interpersonal skills than your parents. But take a lesson from Christ in His youth. Though He was more knowledgeable, more intelligent, wiser, and more skilled, yet He was subject to His parents. You must obey your mom and dad if you are a follower of Jesus.

About God: **To Do:**

The Baptism of Jesus

"And Jesus answering said unto him, Suffer it to be so now: for thus it becometh us to fulfil all righteousness." —Matthew 3:15

It is important to be baptized. Why? First, it is a symbol of cleansing from sin. Acts 2:38 says, "Then Peter said unto them, Repent, and be baptized every one of you in the name of Jesus Christ for the remission of sins, and ye shall receive the gift of the Holy Ghost."

Second, it represents a pouring out of the Holy Spirit. First Corinthians 12:13 says, "For by one Spirit are we all baptized into one body."

Third, it is the answer of a good conscience toward God. First Peter 3:21 says, "The like figure whereunto even baptism doth also now save us (not the putting away of the filth of the flesh, but the answer of a good conscience toward God)."

Fourth, it is a formal way of being received into the church. In Acts 2:41, "Then they that gladly received his word were baptized: and the same day there were added unto them about three thousand souls."

Fifth, we should request baptism because Jesus requested baptism. He was not baptized because He had sinned. He didn't need to repent of anything. He was baptized because it is right, that is, "to fulfill all righteousness." He gave His followers an example to copy. Whatever is right, we should do. In His baptism, Jesus identified Himself with those He came to save. Still another benefit of His being baptized was the public approval it gave John's ministry.

At Jesus' baptism, the descending of the Spirit of God upon Him fulfilled the sign foretold to John that Jesus was the Messiah (see John 1:33). Jesus had the Father's smile of approval. Are your attitudes and actions such that your dad or mom can say, "This is my beloved son (or daughter) in whom I am well pleased"?

The voice from heaven came at three key points in Jesus' life: at His baptism, at His transfiguration, and just before the cross (John 12:28). Interestingly, at the transfiguration the Father said very similar words to those spoken at Jesus' baptism: "While he yet spake, behold, a bright cloud overshadowed them: and behold a voice out of the cloud, which said, This is my beloved Son, in whom I am well pleased; hear ye him" (Matthew 17:5).

Jesus was baptized. You should be too.

About God: **To Do:**

March 21

The Temptation of Jesus

"It is written, Man shall not live by bread alone, but by every word that proceedeth out of the mouth of God." —Matthew 4:4

Read Matthew 4:1-11

In my younger years, I heard a fascinating story of a bird and a snake. A traveler in South America noticed a bird fluttering over her nest in great distress. Her cries were caused by a snake starting to climb her tree.

As the traveler watched, the male bird flew away, returning shortly with a twig covered with leaves in his beak. He carefully laid the twig across the nest, covering his mate and the young. Then he flew to a higher branch and watched.

By this time the snake was twisting higher in the tree and began gliding along the branch with the nest, its forked tongue darting in and out. Just when it looked like the snake was about to attack the nest, it suddenly stopped, turned, and slithered back down the tree. The male bird began to sing.

Puzzled, the traveler climbed the tree, retrieved the leaves that the bird had laid across its nest, and took them to a native friend. From him, the traveler discovered that the leaves came from a bush that is poisonous to the snake. The bird had found a defense.

The Christian finds his defense in some other leaves—the leaves of the Bible. Each time the serpent tempted Christ, our Lord used a leaf from Deuteronomy saying, "It is written."

Jesus was led by the Spirit into the wilderness. Verse 1 says, "Then was Jesus led up of the Spirit into the wilderness to be tempted of the devil." As He faced temptation, He used the Sword of the Spirit.

What leaves of Scripture can you use?

- When worried, use the leaf of Philippians 4:6: "Be careful for nothing; but in every thing by prayer and supplication with thanksgiving let your requests be made known unto God."
- When mistreated, use Matthew 5:44:, "But I say unto you, Love your enemies, bless them that curse you, do good to them that hate you, and pray for them which despitefully use you, and persecute you."
- When lazy, consider the ant in Proverbs 6:6.
- When lonely, think of Hebrews 13:5: "I will never leave thee, nor forsake thee."
- When attracted to sexual immorality, use 1 Timothy 5:22: "Keep thyself pure."
- When discontented, check out Psalm 103.
- When tempted to boast, use Proverbs 27:2: "Let another man praise thee, and not thine own mouth; a stranger, and not thine own lips."

About God: **To Do:**

The Invitation of Jesus

"Follow me." —John 1:43

Read John 1:35-51

After John the Baptist pointed out Jesus as the Lamb of God, two of John's disciples began to follow Jesus (vv. 36, 37). Jesus noticed them following. He then invited them to the place He was staying.

The next day Jesus found Philip and invited him with the words, "Follow me" (v. 43). What does it mean to follow Jesus?

To follow means to go the same direction. When Andrew and his friend followed Jesus to His dwellingplace, they all went the same way. Since Jesus did His Father's will, His followers do the Father's will. Since Jesus went the way of the cross, His followers will take up the cross and follow Him. Since Jesus didn't lay up treasures on earth, His followers will not lay up treasures on earth. Since Jesus was pure, content, loving, thankful, and holy, His followers will also have those characteristics.

To follow means to give up your own path. You might be naturally inclined to head to the left, but if Jesus goes straight ahead or turns right, you will need to do the same. This requires trust and humility.

To follow is to keep looking at the guide, not being distracted by others and the route they are taking. After the resurrection, Jesus told Peter to follow Him even to the point of crucifixion. Peter said, "What about John?"

Jesus said to Peter, "If I will that he tarry till I come, what is that to thee? follow thou me" (John 21:22).

To follow means to keep on. You won't get to the destination if you begin to follow but then give up. It is imperative to keep following, day after day, year after year until you reach Home.

Let's follow Jesus all the way. Christ is not looking for part-time followers.

About God: **To Do:**

March 23

The First Miracle of Jesus

"Jesus saith unto her, Woman, what have I to do with thee? mine hour is not yet come." —John 2:4

Read John 2:1-11

I usually am invited to weddings months before they take place. But Jesus and His disciples seem to have been invited at the last minute to the wedding at Cana. Maybe other guests were also invited on short notice. If so, that would readily explain why there was a short supply of wine. Incidentally, the Greek word for *wine* may mean fermented or unfermented grape juice. This story of turning water into wine reveals several things about Jesus.

First, Jesus was respectful. When Jesus addressed His mother with the word *Woman,* He was not being rude. Actually, the Greek word was one used when addressing a woman of great honor such as a queen. It did, however, place some distance between them, making their relationship different from what is described in Luke 2:51. Perhaps Mary thought Jesus should reveal Himself clearly as the Messiah at this point in His life.

Second, Jesus was patient. His "hour," the time for revealing fully His purpose in coming to earth, had not yet arrived. We, too, are called to patience. James 5:7 says, "Be patient therefore, brethren, unto the coming of the Lord. Behold, the husbandman waiteth for the precious fruit of the earth, and hath long patience for it, until he receive the early and latter rain."

Third, Jesus should be obeyed. Mary wisely urged the wedding coordinators to do whatever He said. This is excellent advice for each of us: "Whatsoever he saith unto you, do it" (v. 5). Menno Simons wrote: "Christ alone is the ruler of the conscience, and besides Him there is no other. Let Him be your emperor, and His holy Word your law. You must obey God before the emperor and hold what God says above what the emperor says."

Fourth, Jesus can do miracles. His presence at the wedding made the difference between an embarrassing situation and a successful celebration.

Fifth, Jesus' ability and power should elicit faith from us. After this miracle, the disciples' trust in Him was strengthened and "his disciples believed on him" (v. 11). He pleases Christ best who trusts Him most.

About God: **To Do:**

The Night Visitor to Jesus

"Jesus answered and said unto him,
Verily, verily, I say unto thee, Except a man be born again,
he cannot see the kingdom of God." —John 3:3

Read John 3:1-17

Nicodemus, a prominent religious leader, came to Jesus at night. He had concluded that Jesus came from God—there was no other explanation in view of the miracles Jesus did (v. 2). But then Jesus threw him a curve that left him absolutely dumbfounded: "Ye must be born again" (v. 7).

This didn't make a speck of sense to this educated leader. "How can a man be born when he is old? can he enter the second time into his mother's womb, and be born?" (v. 4). Jesus then explained that He means (is describing, referring to) a spiritual birth. Being born of the Spirit is like the wind—you can't see it, but you see its power and its effects (v. 8).

A person who is born again receives a new nature, or as 2 Corinthians 5:17 says it, "He is a new creature." The new birth is a spiritual transformation brought about by the Holy Spirit in response to trust in Jesus (v. 16). It is the Spirit's work, yet it requires our commitment and cooperation.

Menno Simons wrote: "We must be born from above. We must be transformed and made new in our hearts. We must be transplanted from the unrighteous and evil nature of Adam into the true and good nature of Christ, or we can never in all eternity be saved by any means, be they of men or of God. Whoever has not truly repented and found a new life (I speak of those who are of the age of understanding) is lost. This is unmistakably clear."

Menno wrote of the difference the new birth makes: "Before, they were earthly, carnally minded, but now heavenly, spiritually; before, unrighteous, now righteous; before, evil, now good. And live no longer after the old, depraved nature of the first, earthly Adam, but after the new sincere nature of the new and heavenly Adam, Christ Jesus. . . . Their poor weak life they renew daily, more and more, and that after the image of Him who created them; their minds are after the mind of Christ, they gladly walk as He walked."

If you have not been truly born again, it's time to wake up. When Jesus spoke of the new birth, He commanded: "Ye *must* be born again." The new birth is a mystery, but it is also a necessity. There is absolutely no middle ground.

About God:

To Do:

March 25

Christ's Sermon Theme: Repent

"From that time Jesus began to preach, and to say, Repent: for the kingdom of heaven is at hand." —Matthew 4:17

Read Matthew 4:12-25

When Christ began His public ministry in Galilee, His theme was repentance. Much of today's preaching is designed to make people feel good. Jesus' preaching was intended to make them feel bad—sorry enough to change their belief system and way of life. Repentance means making a U-turn in life.

Bruce Jantzi, missionary to Ukraine, tells of how he would close Gospel services with the invitation to become a Christian. Sunday after Sunday, many would respond, but no real change was evident in their lives. One Sunday he realized that he needed to ask them to repent. They understood what that meant—a change in life. Now only a few responded, but when they did, they meant business with God.

I enjoy the story of Tommy who had difficulty saying the "R" sound. His teacher gave him a sentence to practice: "Robert gave Richard a rap in the ribs for roasting the rabbit so rare."

The next day, the teacher, wanting to hear Tommy's progress, asked him to say the sentence. Tommy said, "Bob gave Dick a poke in the side for not cooking the bunny enough." Like Tommy, theologians and popular preachers have a way of avoiding the R-word—repentance—and changing the message that Jesus taught.

Jesus said that He came to call sinners to repentance (Matthew 9:13). He rebuked the unbelieving Jews for their failure to repent, saying that "if the mighty works had been done in Tyre and Sidon, which have been done in you, they had a great while ago repented, sitting in sackcloth and ashes" (Luke 10:13). He said everyone needs to repent. Regarding those who died in the collapse of the Tower of Siloam (perhaps the first-century equivalent of 9/11), He said, "I tell you, . . . except ye repent, ye shall all likewise perish" (Luke 13:3). Jesus told stories of commendable repentance, such as that of the prodigal son. He also told of the publican who hammered his chest and said, "God, be merciful to me a sinner." Jesus said, "Joy shall be in heaven over one sinner that repenteth" (Luke 15:7).

Just before He ascended to heaven, Christ told His disciples to be witnesses, commanding them "that repentance and remission of sins should be preached in his name among all nations, beginning at Jerusalem" (Luke 24:47). Clearly, Jesus taught repentance from the beginning to the end of His ministry. Therefore, repent.

About God: **To Do:**

Jesus Loves Me

"And walk in love, as Christ also hath loved us, and hath given himself for us an offering and a sacrifice to God for a sweetsmelling savour." —Ephesians 5:2

Read 1 John 3:1-3, 16-23

"Jesus loves me, this I know." So begins the children's favorite that contains a glorious truth for everyone. The Bible tells us so, as does our Christian experience. How difficult it is to find words of praise and worship worthy of our Saviour! How impossible it is to compensate our Lord for His sacrifice! Paul prayed that the Ephesian Christians might "know the love of Christ, which passeth knowledge" (Ephesians 3:19).

The theme of the Bible and the joy of our life is the fact that Jesus loves each of us personally. We don't need to prepare a lengthy account of human evil, both past and present, to show the need of the Saviour. We only need to look at ourselves. How unworthy we are! Yet Jesus "loved me, and gave himself for me" (Galatians 2:20).

What is our response to such love? Will we be like Judas, who appeared to be a trusty treasurer for the disciples but was covertly serving the powers of darkness? Will we be like Peter, "the Rock," who rapidly backslid and denied his Lord? Will we be like the other disciples, who each boldly claimed, "Though I should die with thee, yet will I not deny thee" (Matthew 26:35), only to vanish when the Master was mistreated by the hands and mouths of men? Will we be like Peter who, in his misguided zeal, went beyond the teaching of Christ and struck off the ear of the high priest's servant? Will we be like Peter, James, and John who went to pray but fell asleep? Will we be like Pilate, who acknowledged that Christ was innocent, but would not do justice when the pressure was on?

Or will we be like the wise thief on the cross who openly received Jesus as his Lord? Will we be like the faithful women who shared Christ's sufferings, and weren't afraid to identify themselves with His shame? Will we be like the centurion who, after observing the events of Calvary, said, "Truly this was the Son of God"?

"If ye keep my commandments, ye shall abide in my love" was Jesus' promise (John 15:10). Our manner of life should be our response to Christ's unchanging love.

About God:

To Do:

March 27

The Ganges or Calvary

"If the Son therefore shall make you free, ye shall be free indeed." —John 8:36

Read Hebrews 9:11-28

Every three years, swarms of Hindus plunge into the Ganges River in northern India, believing that the frigid water from the Himalayas washes away their sins. They trust that this ritual will help them achieve *nirvana*—freedom from the cycle of death and rebirth, according to the Hindu belief in reincarnation.

Millions upon millions, stretching for miles, gather in four "holy" cities such as Haridwar to bathe in the river. Those who linger too long are pulled out of the water by police to make room for others. According to legend, during a battle between gods and demons over a pitcher containing the nectar of immortality, some of the liquid was spilled and fell to earth on the spot that is now Haridwar.

In contrast to this sad and deceptive belief, the truth of the Scripture sets one free (see John 8:32), and the Saviour makes a person thoroughly free (see John 8:36).

1. There is a need for cleansing, but the removal of sins comes not from the water of the Ganges but by faith in Jesus who shed His blood. "In whom we have redemption through his blood, the forgiveness of sins" (Ephesians 1:7).
2. There is a future bliss, but it is not nirvana; it is heaven. Furthermore, a sinful person does not face reincarnation (being born as a donkey, baboon, salamander, etc.), but eternal damnation. Rather, admission to heaven through the Way, Jesus Christ, frees one from judgment and eternal damnation.
3. The door to salvation does have a time limit, but it is not at the end of a festival; it is at the end of one's life (or at Christ's return). There is no second chance as a giraffe, weasel, or trout. Hebrews 9:27 says, "It is appointed unto men *once* to die, but after this the judgment."
4. Eternal life can be obtained—not at Haridwar—but at Calvary. It was not the nectar of immortality that was spilled, but the blood of Jesus.
5. There is room for all at the cross. As Romans 10:13 says, "For *whosoever* shall call upon the name of the Lord shall be saved."

About God: **To Do:**

Jesus, Saviour

"In whom we have redemption through his blood, the forgiveness of sins, according to the riches of his grace." —Ephesians 1:7

Read Hebrews 5:1-9

"Consider the Apostle and High Priest of our profession, Christ Jesus" (Hebrews 3:1). Ponder these profound paradoxes:

1. He, the Life, suffered death to give men life.
2. He, the Man of Sorrows, experienced anguish so that all mankind could experience everlasting joy.
3. He, our Redeemer, was sold for thirty pieces of silver.
4. He, the Light, hung in the darkness on the cross.
5. He, the Sinless One, was crucified by sinful men for sinful men.
6. He, being wounded by men, brought about man's spiritual healing.
7. He who gives rest was so weary that He could not carry His cross to Calvary.
8. He, the Son of God, died a criminal's death.
9. He, the Water of Life, gave His life, crying, "I thirst."
10. He, the Mighty God, was put to death by puny men.
11. He, our Saviour, laid down His life, and by death destroyed death.

Truly, we can never praise Jesus too much. Every Christian should wear a sign on his heart: "Not for sale."

About God: **To Do:**

March 29

Jesus Gave Himself for Me

"The good shepherd giveth his life for the sheep." —John 10:11

Read Titus 2:11-14

Nikolai Berdyaev was at a concentration camp when the Nazis were killing Jews in the gas chambers. One distraught mother refused to part with her baby. Nikolai noticed another woman prisoner, Maria, observing the tragic scene. When Maria saw that the officer was interested only in numbers, she wordlessly pushed the mother aside and quickly took her place. Nikolai, who had been a Marxist, saw a vivid portrayal of the essence of Christianity—Christ giving His life for others. This selfless act of love moved him to accept Christianity.

"The Son of God . . . *gave himself* for me" (Galatians 2:20). Why?

1. He died *as a ransom for you.* Each accountable person has been taken captive by Satan through sin. Through Christ, our kidnapped experience can come to an end. "For there is one God, and one mediator between God and men, the man Christ Jesus; who *gave himself* a ransom for all" (1 Timothy 2:5, 6). In regards to redemption, it's who you know that counts. We are saved by Christ's mediation, not our merits.
2. He died *to be a satisfactory and pleasing offering to God.* That's the idea of a sweet-smelling savor that Christ's death brought to His Father. Christ has "loved us, and hath *given himself* for us an offering and a sacrifice to God for a sweet-smelling savour" (Ephesians 5:2). Salvation is by atonement—not by attainment.
3. He died *to deliver us.* How wonderful to receive grace and peace from Jesus "who *gave himself* for our sins, that he might deliver us from this present evil world" (Galatians 1:4).
4. He died *to redeem and purify us.* Titus 2:14 says that Jesus *"gave himself* for us, that he might redeem us from all iniquity, and purify unto himself a peculiar people, zealous of good works." The sinner has only two options: be pardoned or be punished.
5. He died *to have a holy, glorious church.* This church is like a bride who will be gloriously presented at the marriage supper of the Lamb. "Christ also loved the church, and *gave himself* for it; that he might present it to himself a glorious church, not having spot, or wrinkle, or any such thing; but that it should be holy and without blemish" (Ephesians 5:25, 27).

About God: **To Do:**

A Man of Sorrows

"Surely he hath borne our griefs, and carried our sorrows: yet we did esteem him stricken, smitten of God, and afflicted." —Isaiah 53:4

Read Isaiah 53

"Behold the man!" This is what Isaiah said prophetically. Under divine inspiration he declared that the King would be a "man of sorrows and acquainted with grief." Perhaps our appreciation of Christ's love for us can be deepened by meditating on the nature of His grief.

Jesus endured the same sorrows which many others have passed through. He wept when His dear friend Lazarus died and his sisters were mourning. His earthly "father," Joseph, evidently passed away before Christ's crucifixion. During His ministry, Jesus became very hungry and thirsty. He did not even have a regular place to lay His head. But other extraordinary factors caused Him the greatest anguish.

His friends forsook Him. During the great agony of the Garden, His closest friends fell asleep repeatedly instead of watching and praying, even though He told them, "My soul is exceeding sorrowful, even unto death." The disciples had insisted they would never leave their beloved Master, yet what do we read in Matthew 26:56? "Then all the disciples forsook him, and fled." Bold Peter shamefully denied his Lord. And Judas, "mine own familiar friend, in whom I trusted" (Psalm 41:9), betrayed Jesus with a symbol of affection.

Men misunderstood His mission, time after time. When asked for a sign, "he sighed deeply in his spirit" (Mark 8:12). He was truly "despised and rejected of men" even though He loved them sincerely. His compassion for those that hated Him is revealed by His lament over Jerusalem, "How often would I have gathered thy children together . . . and ye would not" (Matthew 23:37).

Sorrows came to Him in anticipation. He knew the cross was ever before Him. "The Son of man must suffer many things, and be rejected of the elders and chief priests and scribes, and be slain" (Luke 9:22).

Physically, Christ's suffering surrounding His crucifixion was excruciating. His face was marred (Isaiah 52:14); His brow was scarred (Matthew 27:29); His back was lacerated (Isaiah 50:6); His side was pierced (John 19:34); His feet were torn (Psalm 22:16); His hands were nailed to the cross (John 20:27).

The man of sorrows experienced grief and suffering, so that we could have joy and bliss. We will be forever grateful.

About God: **To Do:**

March 31

In the Cross of Christ I Glory

"But God forbid that I should glory, save in the cross of our Lord Jesus Christ." —Galatians 6:14

Read 1 Corinthians 1:17-24

In China, on a hill overlooking the harbor of Macao, Portuguese settlers built a huge cathedral. During a typhoon the building collapsed—all except the front wall. On the top of that wall, stood a great bronze cross that withstood the elements through the years.

In 1825 Sir John Bowring was shipwrecked nearby. Clinging to the wreckage of his ship, he caught sight of that great cross, which showed him where he could reach the shore and safety.

The importance of that cross in his survival moved him to write this hymn:

In the cross of Christ I glory
Towering o'er the wrecks of time,
All the light of sacred story
Gathers round its head sublime.

The cross represents Christ's desire to save. Like a shepherd, He seeks for the lost sheep. He took the initiative with many people in His earthly ministry: Peter and Andrew (Matthew 4:18); the Samaritan woman (John 4:7); the crippled man (John 5:14); and the blind man (John 9:35).

The story is told of a woman who was driving home one evening when she noticed a big truck behind her, following uncomfortably close. She accelerated to gain some distance from the truck, but when she sped up, so did the truck. The more rapidly she drove, the faster the truck followed. Frightened, she exited the freeway. The truck stuck with her. Growing frantic, the woman turned up a main street, hoping to lose her persistent pursuer in traffic. But the truck ran a red light and continued the chase.

The woman, reaching the point of panic, whipped her automobile into a service station, and darted out of her vehicle, screaming for help. The truck driver sprang from his truck and ran toward her car. Yanking the back door open, the driver pulled out a man that had been hiding in the backseat.

The woman had been trying to escape from someone intent on delivering her from danger and possible death. From his high vantage point, the truck driver had spotted the would-be attacker in the woman's car.

Many people are trying to evade the Lord Jesus, who is pursuing them in love to save them from spiritual danger and death. He died on the cross to "save that which was lost" (Luke 19:10).

About God:

To Do:

Christ Invites You

"And the Spirit and the bride say, Come.
And let him that heareth say, Come.
And let him that is athirst come." —Revelation 22:17

Read Luke 14:15-27

According to Henry Taylor, the ten most persuasive words in the English language are: *you, easy, money, save, love, new, discovery, results, proven,* and *guarantee.* I think one of the most wonderful words I've ever heard is the word *come.*

That glorious word is used in Christ's invitation to burdened, sinful individuals: "Come unto me, all ye that labour and are heavy laden, and I will give you rest. Take my yoke upon you, and learn of me; for I am meek and lowly in heart: and ye shall find rest unto your souls. For my yoke is easy, and my burden is light" (Matthew 11:28-30). In this invitation, Christ tells us to do three things:

First, "Come." If you have been working outdoors, you are glad when Mom says, "Come for dinner." If you are pulling weeds in the hot sun, you don't delay when Dad says, "Come to the shade to rest." When a friend says, "Come over for a wiener roast tonight," you are probably overjoyed. But far greater is Jesus' invitation: "Come unto Me." He can satisfy better than your mom's cooking. His rest is far superior to the rest granted by your father. And He can fulfill your need for fellowship more deeply than any other friend.

Second, "Take My yoke upon you." This is a comparison to a wooden yoke worn by working animals. What does it mean for us? Be linked to Christ in loving obedience. Work with Him to discover that He makes the way easy for you. Walk beside Him to learn of Him. Learn of the meek and lowly way. Learn of His strength and power. Yoked with Him, we find deliverance from the unrest of self-will. Yoked with Him, we find rest, peace, and purpose.

How does being yoked to Jesus make life *easy*? It is easy in contrast to the way of sin. "The way of transgressors is hard" (Proverbs 13:15). It is easy because Jesus, to whom all power has been given (Matthew 28:18), bears the burden for us and with us, making it light.

Third, "Learn of me." Why? Not because He could do miracles. Not because He was a great teacher. Not because large crowds surrounded Him. No, the reason is simply that Jesus lived the way we should live—in meekness and lowliness.

About God: **To Do:**

Word of Forgiveness

"Father, forgive them; for they know not what they do." —Luke 23:34

Read Luke 23:13-34

I'm impressed with the story of Joe Roberts, and wonder whether I would have had the same sacrificial courage had I been in his shoes.

Joe, a youthful pastor, arrived in Wyoming by stagecoach in 1883, intending to minister to the natives. Soon after arriving, a major crisis occurred. The son of Chief Washakie was shot by a soldier in a brawl, and the chief vowed to kill the first white man he met. Since this could mean the start of a long, bloody feud, young Roberts decided to take action. Seeking out the chief's tepee fifteen miles away in the mountains, he stood outside and called the chief's name. When Washakie appeared, Roberts opened his shirt.

"I have heard of your vow," he said. "I know that the other white men have families, but I am alone. Kill me instead."

Astonished, the chief motioned him to enter his tent. "How do you have so much courage?" he asked.

Joe Roberts told him about Christ, His death, and His teachings. They talked for hours. When Joe left, the chief of the Shoshones had renounced his vow to kill and had resolved to become a Christian. Chief Washakie had seen the love of the cross in action.

The penitent thief also saw the love of the cross. He heard the first of seven "words" from the cross: "Father, forgive them; for they know not what they do" (Luke 23:34). Due to his response of repentance and faith, the second word from the cross was directed to him, "To day shalt thou be with me in paradise." In His first statement, Christ interceded for pardon; in the second, He granted pardon.

Christ's prayer, "Father, forgive them," expresses perfect love—no revengeful attitude, no harsh words, no bitterness, no anger at the injustice of it all.

Whom did Jesus have in mind? Was He thinking of Peter and the cowardly disciples? Was it Pilate He had in mind? Caiaphas? Herod? the soldiers? Was He thinking of you and me? Really, His plea applies to everyone because He "gave himself a ransom for all" (1 Timothy 2:6). Whosoever will, may come and find salvation.

His prayer of forgiveness teaches us two things: We must be forgiving and we must be forgiven.

About God: **To Do:**

Word of Companionship

"To day shalt thou be with me in paradise." —Luke 23:43

Read Luke 23:25-49

Two thieves, one on either side of Jesus, hung from the crosses on Golgotha. Multiple crucifixions saved the Romans time and money.

The Roman soldiers often gagged criminals whom they crucified so the executioners wouldn't need to hear abusive, vile words. I'm so glad the three on Golgotha were permitted to speak: their words are instructive.

Why did the penitent thief hear the words, "To day shalt thou be with me in paradise"? Consider six of his actions and attitudes:

1. *He looked to Christ and called Him Lord* (v. 42). He saw the title above Christ calling Him "King." He heard the mocking words of the chief priests referring to Jesus' claim to be Christ, the chosen of God. He heard Jesus' authoritative words to the weeping women. He saw the calmness and self-control of Jesus. He may have heard Pilate's words, "I find no fault in Him." He heard Christ's gracious words of forgiveness to those crucifying Him.
2. *He feared God and rebuked sin.* That he feared God is implied by his question to his fellow thief, "Dost not thou fear God, seeing thou art in the same condemnation?" (Luke 23:40). He forthrightly rebuked the other for his railing words.
3. *He faced up to his sin.* Concerning the punishment that he and the other thief were receiving, he said, "And we indeed justly; for we receive the due reward of our deeds" (v. 41). His confession was audible. He did not blame others.
4. *He recognized Jesus as sinless.* He said, "This man hath done nothing amiss." Did he know Christ before? Did he hear other reports about Jesus' innocence? Or did he come to his conclusion solely by careful observation?
5. *He believed.* He said, "Lord, remember me." In contrast, the other thief said, *"If . . ."*
6. *He prayed humbly.* To the King, he asked to be remembered. Jesus assured him, "Verily I say unto thee, To day shalt thou be with me in paradise." The word *verily* means "Amen—so be it, so it is." It was a confirmation. The penitent thief could count on it.

This account serves to remind us that the Lord remembers us too—in sickness, in bereavement, in perplexity, in temptation, and in death. Be assured: God remembers you as you remember Him.

About God: **To Do:**

April 4

Word of Comfort

"When Jesus therefore saw his mother, and the disciple standing by, whom he loved, he saith unto his mother, Woman, behold thy son! Then saith he to the disciple, Behold thy mother!" —John 19:26, 27

Read John 19:25-42

Jesus, as Mary's oldest son, spoke words of concern and comfort to His mother. He asked John to care and provide for her. In His agony, as He bore the sins of the world, Christ still remembered His mother.

There's a lesson here for youth. Even when you are very busy with your schooling or your job, don't forget your mother. Even if you are facing trials and troubles, anxiety and anguish, decisions and debts, think of your mother's emotional and physical needs.

Jesus saw His bosom friend nearby and spoke to ensure that His mother would be cared for. We do well to behold John and learn lessons from him. For one thing, he returned to Christ. Previously, he was among the other disciples of whom Matthew 26:56 says, "Then all the disciples forsook him, and fled." We, like John, need to be sorry for turning from Christ and, in repentance, come to the cross. If you have stopped following Jesus, go to the cross, look at Jesus, and hear His words.

John also listened to Jesus. This means he needed to be close to Jesus. Are you close enough to Christ to be directed by Him in paths of service?

In addition, John accepted the responsibility that Jesus gave him. When Jesus said, "Behold . . . behold," He was using a variation of marriage vows that was common among the Jews. It is my understanding that He substituted the words *woman* and *son* for *husband* and *wife*. It seems that John saw and accepted the seriousness of his responsibility as he took Mary to his own home.

Interestingly, Jesus was on the cross on John's behalf. So He asked John to take His place in the home. Likewise, Jesus went to the cross for us and wants us to help others.

Some people spell service, "serve us," but not so the apostle of love. Like Mary and John, you can do great things for Christ by doing small things for others.

About God:

To Do:

Word of Suffering

"My God, my God, why hast thou forsaken me?" —Matthew 27:46

Read Psalm 22

It is reported of Martin Luther that he sat for long hours without food or rest in silent meditation on this fourth saying. When he broke the long silence he said, "God forsaken of God! Who can understand that?"

Although I don't understand everything about this cry of Christ, it tells me three things:

1. *It was a cry of loneliness.* He was forsaken by His friends. His brothers didn't believe Him. His neighbors in Nazareth rejected Him. His nation didn't receive Him. Judas betrayed Him and Peter denied Him. In fact, "all the disciples forsook him, and fled" (Matthew 26:56). Now He felt very much alone.

We all have the need for companionship and sympathy, especially in difficult hours. And it was dark. Those who suffer bodily tend to dread the night.

A little boy was responsible to put the milk bottles out on the porch. One night he took only a step or two outside the door and came back. His father asked, "Son, why didn't you put the bottles on the porch?"

He replied, "It's too dark to go out there without a father."

The street light was out; it was darker than usual. When the father went with him, the boy placed the bottles where they belonged.

How wonderful that we as children of God need never go into the dark and into the unknown without our Father. Jesus willingly suffered on the cross to provide forgiveness and bring us into fellowship with the Father who says, "I will never leave thee, nor forsake thee" (Hebrews 13:5).

2. *It was a cry of suffering.* He felt pain from the nails, the thorns, the scourging, the beatings. But there was also the emotional pain of the taunts, the ridicule, and the curses. Yet He willingly suffered it all to redeem us from the bondage of sin.

3. *It was a cry of trust.* He refers to "*my* God." This prayer comes from Psalm 22, a messianic psalm which concludes with faith, even praise.

True, Psalm 22 refers to many of the painful experiences of Calvary: the reproach (vv. 6-8), the desertion of friends (v. 11), the suffering (v. 14), the thirst (v. 15), the pierced hands and feet (v. 16), the nakedness (v. 17), the casting of lots (v. 18). Yet note the trustful tone of verses 26-28 and 31.

About God: **To Do:**

April 6

Word of Humanness

"I thirst." —John 19:28

Read Psalm 69:1-21

Christ had created the rivers and streams, the springs and the waterfalls, the rain and the snow—yet He cried, "I thirst."

He had given living water to the Samaritan woman and to those who heard her testimony and believed on Him as the Messiah—yet He cried, "I thirst."

He had promised believers rivers of living water flowing from one's innermost being, saying, "If any man thirst, let him come unto me, and drink" (John 7:37)—yet He cried, "I thirst."

How ironic that He, the Water of Life, should thirst.

The fact that He thirsted declares His humanity. Although God, He was fully human. He identifies with our thirst, our hunger, our pain, our weariness, and our human limitations. "For we have not an high priest which cannot be touched with the feeling of our infirmities; but was in all points tempted like as we are, yet without sin" (Hebrews 4:15).

It was probably sixteen to eighteen hours since Jesus had taken any liquid, likely not since the Passion meal. He had sweated greatly in Gethsemane. Because of the scourging, the thorn punctures, and the nails, He was suffering from loss of blood and dehydration. No wonder His mouth was parched.

The verses from the daily reading vividly portray His extreme suffering—emotionally and physically. "Reproach hath broken my heart; and I am full of heaviness: and I looked for some to take pity, but there was none; and for comforters, but I found none. They gave me also gall for my meat; and in my thirst they gave me vinegar to drink" (Psalm 69:20, 21).

In the 1700s a Moravian missionary went to the slaves of the West Indies. But they mistrusted this white man because they had been so terribly mistreated by whites. The missionary pondered and prayed about how to get through to these slaves.

He decided he needed to identify with them and share their lot, even as Jesus became like those He came to save. So the missionary sold himself into slavery. Now the slaves listened and responded.

Because Jesus said, "I thirst," we can have living water eternally. "Whosoever will, let him take the water of life freely" (Revelation 22:17). The birth of Christ brought God to man, but it took the death of Christ to bring man to God.

About God: **To Do:**

Word of Completion

"It is finished." —John 19:30

Read Hebrews 2:9-18

A carpenter smoothed the last coat of lacquer over the gleaming, stained chest of drawers. Stepping back, he surveyed the carefully crafted piece of furniture. With a deep sense of satisfaction, he exulted, "Finished."

Jesus' last exclamation from the cross, "It is finished" (John 19:30), carried similar meaning. In dying, Jesus was victorious over Satan and sin. His work was finished. He had completed His part in the plan of salvation. His was a conqueror's cry. Jesus "cried with a loud voice, and gave up the ghost" (Mark 15:37). It was a shout of jubilation, not lamentation.

What was finished? The Old Testament prophecies concerning Christ's work prior to His death had been fulfilled. Consider, for example, the prophecies concerning His birth in Bethlehem, the virgin birth, being of the seed of Abraham and the lineage of David, the rejection of the Jews, His triumphal entry, the betrayal by a friend, the treachery involving thirty pieces of silver, the smiting, the spitting, the scorning, and His silence.

Also, His personal sufferings were finished. Repeatedly He had referred to the sufferings that awaited Him.

Furthermore, the plan of salvation was completed. He could honestly say to the Father, "I have finished the work which thou gavest me to do" (John 17:4). He gave His life as the Lamb of God, shedding His blood to bring redemption. To signify His finished work, the veil of the temple was torn from the top to the bottom immediately after His death (Mark 15:38).

In addition, the harassment and temptations by Satan upon Christ were finished. As the daily reading says, "That through death he might destroy him that had the power of death, that is, the devil" (v. 14).

Thank God that Christ could exclaim "Finished!" at His death. Now new life could begin in the believer who claimed salvation through Him.

Yes, "It is finished!" That cry went up to the Father who so loved the world that He gave His only Son. That cry, no doubt, went down to the imprisoned spirits of men, alerting them to the impending ascension of Christ. That cry went back to the beginning of mankind, completing salvation for every Old Testament believer. That cry went forward to the twenty-first century and to the end of the age, offering salvation to every person who would believe in the Lord Jesus Christ.

About God: **To Do:**

April 8

Word of Commitment

"Father, into thy hands I commend my spirit." —Luke 23:46

Read Psalm 31

The first prayer I learned was the bedtime prayer, "Now I lay me down to sleep." Probably the first prayer Jesus learned was verse 5 of the daily reading: "Into thine hand I commit my spirit: thou hast redeemed me, O LORD God of truth." Every Jewish child was taught this bedtime prayer.

Christ, upon the cross, prayed this prayer in the evening of His life. Christ was expressing *confidence*. He was acutely conscious of God as His Father. At age twelve He referred to His Father's business. In the Sermon on the Mount, He refers to God as Father seventeen times. In His observance with the disciples the previous night, as recorded in John 14–16, He called God His Father forty-five times. Christ knew His Father and knew His Father's hands were a place of security.

The last word from the cross not only denotes confidence, but also *conquest.* It was a loud cry. In Roman times a victorious general, when leaving the battle site, uttered a loud cry as a token that he had triumphed. Clearly, Christ laid down His life. It was voluntary. The previous prayer about God forsaking Him tells of the serpent bruising the heel of the woman's seed. But the last prayer tells of the seed crushing the serpent's head. "For this purpose the Son of God was manifested, that he might destroy the works of the devil" (1 John 3:8).

This last prayer of commitment also denotes *completeness.* Christ was, as it were, handing His spirit over to the Father. It reminds me of my young children cuddling up against me at bedtime and asking me to put them to bed.

We, too, can face death with confident commitment. Stephen prayed a similar prayer, saying, "Lord Jesus, receive my spirit" (Acts 7:59). Other martyrs, such as Polycarp and John Huss, echoed Christ's prayer.

Felix Manz, the first Anabaptist martyr at the hands of Protestants, was thinking about this prayer as they put him aboard a boat on the Limmat River in Zurich, Switzerland. Felix was helpless because his bound hands had been pushed over his knees and a stick thrust between them. A Reformed priest accompanied Felix in case he should wish to recant, but his mother on the bank cheered him on to be faithful. Before they threw him into the water, Felix cried out, "Father, into thy hands I commit my spirit."

About God:

To Do:

Peace Be Unto You

"Peace be unto you." —John 20:21

Read John 20:11-23

In 1815 the population of England eagerly awaited news of the outcome of a battle between English soldiers under Wellington and French troops commanded by Napoleon. Finally the message was slowly signaled from the top of Winchester Cathedral letter by letter. WELLINGTON DEFEATED was spelled, and then a dense fog settled over the area. The signals could no longer be seen and thus the tragic news spread that Wellington had been defeated.

After awhile the fog lifted and the message became clear: WELLINGTON DEFEATED THE ENEMY.

The death of Jesus seemed like a tragic defeat. Then the glorious resurrection on Easter morning made the message clear and complete: JESUS DEFEATED THE ENEMY, DEATH.

On the evening of Easter Sunday, the complete message wasn't seen by the disciples. The daily reading tells of fearful ones behind closed doors. Suddenly Jesus was in the midst of them, saying, "Peace be unto you."

Peace has been translated into an Indian tongue in Mexico as "a quiet heart." The disciples had peace and gladness when they saw the nail prints in Christ's hands and realized it was truly Jesus. Now they understood that He had conquered death.

Christ's legacy to His followers is peace. It is in His will that we receive peace. "Peace I leave with you, my peace I give unto you" (John 14:27). Through His atoning death and justifying resurrection, we have peace with God. Romans 4:25 and Romans 5:1 say, "Who was delivered for our offences, and was raised again for our justification. Therefore being justified by faith, we have peace with God through our Lord Jesus Christ." As we come to God through Christ, we will receive the peace of God. Philippians 4:6, 7 says, "Be careful for nothing; but in every thing by prayer and supplication with thanksgiving let your requests be made known unto God. And the peace of God, which passeth all understanding, shall keep your hearts and minds through Christ Jesus."

God does not remove all trouble for the believer. In fact, the disciples were facing an increase in trouble. But God gives peace because of His presence through the problems and perplexities of life. These messengers of peace went into the entire world with the word of peace upon their lips, the gift of peace in their hearts, and the light of peace upon their faces.

About God: **To Do:**

April 10

Slow of Heart to Believe

"And he said unto them, What manner of communications are these that ye have one to another, as ye walk, and are sad?" —Luke 24:17

Read Luke 24:13-35

I love Jesus' sense of humor as shown in the daily reading. When asked by Cleopas and his companion, "Haven't you heard about the things that have happened here in Jerusalem?" I can imagine the twinkle in Jesus' eyes as He said, "What things?"

The two were "slow of heart" to believe how Christ had fulfilled the Old Testament prophecies about the Messiah (v. 25). Then a tremendous Easter Bible Conference took place. It featured the greatest Teacher explaining the greatest themes from the greatest Book, revealing the greatest fulfillment of prophecy, and bringing the greatest blessings. It ended with a fellowship meal (v. 30) and a real eye-opening experience (v. 31).

These two disciples started off walking with Jesus with slow hearts; they ended up with burning hearts, hot with understanding and joy. First, Jesus opened the tomb; then He opened the Scriptures; and then He opened their eyes.

Easter brings to me joy and understanding. I'm glad Jesus' life didn't end with His death. I remember looking at the Thomas Jefferson Bible that a friend of mine had in his collection of Bibles. Jefferson had removed anything that was supernatural.

His "Bible" ends with the words, "And they laid Jesus in the tomb and departed." Like Jefferson, there are millions of Americans who quickly close their minds and hearts to the reality of Jesus' Resurrection.

You would have had a hard time convincing Cleopas and companion that Christ was still in the tomb. They walked with Him. They talked with Him. They were fed by Him. They knew Him (v. 31).

Are you slow of heart to believe? Believe of a certainty that Jesus is alive. Faith honors God; God honors faith.

About God: **To Do:**

All Things Must Be Fulfilled

"Then he said unto them, O fools, and slow of heart to believe all that the prophets have spoken." —Luke 24:25

Read Luke 24:36-53

I love to explain an idea or concept and see the other person's face light up as he says, "I see it now!" After the resurrection, Jesus opened up minds to see how His death and resurrection fulfilled the Old Testament teachings and prophecies. Mr. Cleopas (and Mrs. Cleopas, if that's who was traveling with him) said, "He opened to us the scriptures" (Luke 24:32). In today's reading, verse 45 says, "Then opened he their understanding, that they might understand the scriptures."

The Jews divided the Old Testament into three parts. Jesus showed them that in all sections of the Old Testament, He fulfilled the teachings and symbolisms of the future Messiah.

Perhaps Christ began with the first Messianic prophecy of Genesis 3:15 that the seed of a woman would bruise Satan's head. He may have expanded on the sacrifice of Abel, Noah's ark of safety, and the sacrifice of Isaac on Mount Moriah (called Mount Calvary at the time of Christ). He may have shown how the Old Testament sacrifice of blood pointed forward to His blood that was shed. Maybe He explained the meaning of the activities on the Day of Atonement, and the significance of the scapegoat. Perhaps He referred to the symbolism of the tabernacle articles that He fulfilled—the shewbread, the candlestick, the mercy seat, and the veil shielding the holy of holies.

No doubt, He referred to messianic Psalms such as Psalm 22, and messianic prophecies such as Isaiah 53, and Zechariah's prophecy that a fountain would be opened for sin and uncleanness (13:1). As one Bible teacher said, "If the Bible were cut, every page would bleed." There is a crimson thread running from Genesis to Revelation—the thread of redemption through the blood of the Lamb.

The fact that Christ died during the Passover is significant. In the first place, it was on the tenth day of the month, the day that the Passover lamb was chosen, that Christ arrived in Jerusalem. Furthermore, on the day of Passover, the Passover lamb was killed at 3:00 p.m. At that time the priest stood in the pinnacle of the temple and blew the shofar (ram's horn). Jesus died at 3:00 p.m. There, while nailed to the cross as the Lamb of God, Jesus would have heard the shofar announcing that the lamb's throat had been cut and the sacrifice was complete. It was at that point that the Lamb of God loudly and victoriously proclaimed, "It is finished." All things had been fulfilled.

About God: **To Do:**

April 12

Be Not Faithless But Believing

"Then saith he to Thomas, Reach hither thy finger, and behold my hands; and reach hither thy hand, and thrust it into my side: and be not faithless, but believing." —John 20:27

Read John 20:24-31

Doubting Didymus became Trusting Thomas. As Doubting Didymus, he declared concerning the report of Jesus' rising from the dead, "Except I shall see in his hands the print of the nails, and put my finger into the print of the nails, and thrust my hand into his side, I will not believe." As Trusting Thomas, having met the risen Lord in person, he exclaimed, "My Lord and my God."

What lessons can we learn from Thomas?

1. *Doubt is a real possibility.* The Christian life is one of faith. We, therefore, need to meet together to encourage one another, "not forsaking the assembling of ourselves together" (Hebrews 10:25). Thomas missed out on one meeting (Easter evening) and so acquired the name of "Doubting Thomas." If we skip services, we, too, miss out on encouragement that inspires faith.
2. *Jesus calls all types of personalities.* Thomas's nature seems to have been set in a minor key. But Jesus saw the hidden potential and led him to give a clear confession of faith, "My Lord and my God."
3. *Jesus gives special help to those who are weak.* After the resurrection, He gave special attention to Peter, who denied Him, and to Thomas, who doubted Him. Christ specializes in mending broken reeds and fanning smoking wicks.
4. *There is a beatitude for believing.* "Blessed are they that have not seen, and yet have believed" (v. 29). While it's good to avoid being gullible, when the Lord speaks, we should believe.
5. *Even if we have doubts, we can be strong in faith.* According to tradition, Thomas became a missionary to Persia, China, and also to India, where a group of Christians were named after him. So committed was Didymus that he became a martyr. *Martyrs Mirror* (pages 89-91) records that Thomas put a stop to the abominable idolatry of the heathen in the East Indies who worshiped the sun. He was tormented with red-hot plates, then cast into a glowing furnace. But the fire did not hurt hurt him, so the idolatrous priests killed him with spears and javelins. Throughout the ordeal, Thomas was steadfast.

No longer was he "Doubting Didymus," but "Devoted Didymus."

About God: **To Do:**

Lovest Thou Me

"Simon son of Jonas, lovest thou me?" — John 21:16

Read John 21:1-17

Peter denied Jesus three times (Luke 22:54-62). I think it is significant that three times Jesus asked Peter, "Do you love Me?" (see vv. 15-17). Jesus longs to restore the fallen to full fellowship and usefulness. Thrice Peter denied his love for Jesus. Thrice Christ led him to renew his declaration of love.

Is your love for Christ up-to-date? Love for the Lord is foundational to Christian life and growth. Love to God is the first and greatest commitment. Do you need to renew your love to Jesus? Why not whisper it to Him now in private, and show it openly henceforth?

Peter was told to show his love for Jesus by service—feeding the lambs and sheep the truth. Are you serving the Lord by sharing the truth? Dying for us was the most Jesus could do; living for Him is the least we can do.

Love for Christ must have priority. "Simon, son of Jonas, lovest thou me *more* than these?" (v. 15). Earlier that morning Peter had said, "I go a fishing." Fishing was his source of income. Making money and adding possessions dare not supersede love for Jesus. We need to consider what is truly (eternally) valuable. In an age of affluence, does Jesus or things have our affection? Money is useful to meet our personal and family needs but dare not be a rival or replacement for the Lord.

Two snowmobilers were caught in a blizzard in the Rocky Mountains. They abandoned their machines to find shelter from the storm. Unless they could find some way to keep warm, they would die from exposure. In their frantic search for wood they found some larger pieces, but without kindling, they couldn't get a fire going. They despaired of staying alive. Then one of them thought of their money. They dug out their wallets and made a loose pile of twenties, tens, fives, ones, and fifties. Soon a heartwarming—and bodywarming—blaze was started.

Money makes a good servant but a bad master. Jesus is our Master and must have priority. The more of heaven that is in our lives, the less of earth we will covet.

About God: **To Do:**

April 14

Go and Teach All Nations

"And he said unto them, Go ye into all the world, and preach the gospel to every creature." —Mark 16:15

Read Matthew 28:1-20

In fifth grade I studied about the travels of Marco Polo, an explorer from Italy who went to China in the 1200s. What I didn't know was that the emperor of China, Kublai Khan, had asked Marco Polo's father and uncle, who had visited China a few years before Marco did, to send 100 missionaries from Europe to China to teach the Chinese about Christ. Kublai Khan was very interested in Christianity and said, "When we learn about Christianity, there will be more Christians in my empire than in all Europe." (He ruled over more territory than any man has ever ruled—from India to Siberia and from China to Eastern Europe.)

The Polo brothers conveyed the request, but few people were interested in going. Two friars agreed to go to China with the Polos (including Marco). However, along the way, these religious teachers lost heart and returned to Europe.

When the Polos arrived in China, Kublai Khan asked, "Where are the missionaries?" Although some missionaries eventually came, things had changed in China and a great opportunity was lost.

How much enthusiasm do you have for missions? Are you willing to go to China? to Bolivia? to India? to Central America? to Ukraine? to Belgium? to Liberia? to Chile? to Turkey? to Sudan? to wherever the Lord might call? to the uttermost part of the world?

Does having a well-paying job or pursuing a business career have priority in your life? Someone predicted that if the evangelization of this world were a commercial proposition with a reward of even a ten-percent dividend, there would not be a village on earth without a church.

"Go ye therefore, and teach all nations, baptizing them in the name of the Father, and of the Son, and of the Holy Ghost" (v. 19) is the last mandate of the Risen Christ. You have heard the Gospel because of past missionary efforts. By what right do you choose the King's final command, "Go ye," as the thing to be squeezed out of your life?

It is imperative not only to go and to baptize, but also to teach all things that make up Christ's commands. Thankfully, Christ promises His power (v. 18) and His presence (v. 20).

Go ye, therefore. Has your Master given you permission to stay at home?

About God: **To Do:**

Ye Shall Receive Power

"But ye shall receive power, after that the Holy Ghost is come upon you: and ye shall be witnesses unto me both in Jerusalem, and in all Judaea, and in Samaria, and unto the uttermost part of the earth." —Acts 1:8

Read Acts 1:1-14

A missionary once said, "The light that shines the farthest will shine the brightest at home." Jesus first wanted His followers to let their light shine through the power of the Holy Ghost in their country's capital, Jerusalem.

Just before Jesus ascended into heaven, He gave His final words: "Ye shall receive power" and "ye shall be witnesses" (Acts 1:8). Ordinary people were able to do extraordinary things because of the power of the Spirit. *Witness* is a key word in Acts, appearing twenty-nine times. It means someone who tells what he has seen and heard (Acts 4:19, 20). Actually, our English word *martyr* comes from the Greek word *witness*. Eleven out of the twelve apostles did conclude their witness by being a martyr for Christ.

Interestingly, Acts 1:8 gives an outline of the Book of Acts. Chapters 1 to 7 tell about witnessing at Jerusalem; Chapters 8 and 9 tell about the extension of the witness to all Judaea and Samaria, and Chapters 10 to 28 tell about the Gospel witness to Europe and to the uttermost part of the earth. *Martyrs Mirror* tells us some of the faraway places to which the Twelve took the Gospel, according to historical tradition. For example, Bartholomew went to the Middle East and to India. Matthew went to Ethiopia. Simon Zelotes went to Northern Africa and then to England. Thomas traveled widely to Ethiopia, India, and the East Indies. Philip ventured into Asia. Peter journeyed to Rome. Andrew went to Greece.

The apostles went all directions to many countries and cultures. Then, in the next century or two after the apostles, their converts led many more people to Christ. The historian Schaff wrote in *History of the Christian Church*, "Christianity once established was its own best missionary. It grew naturally from within. It attracted people by its very presence. It was a light shining in darkness and illuminating the darkness. And while there were no professional missionaries devoting their whole life to this specific work, every congregation was a missionary society, and every Christian believer a missionary, inflamed by the love of Christ to convert his fellow men. . . . Every Christian told his neighbour, the labourer to his fellow labourer, the slave to his fellow slave, the servant to his master and mistress, the story of his conversion as a mariner tells the story of the rescue from shipwreck."

About God: **To Do:**

Dealing With Feelings of Inferiority

"For I say through the grace given unto me, to every man that is among you, not to think of himself more highly than he ought to think; but to think soberly." —Romans 12:3

Read Romans 12:1-8

Many people struggle with feelings of inferiority. I am one of them. I was born fifth in a family of six. As a youngster, I couldn't do what my older siblings could do. In school I detested art class. My rabbits looked like dogs; my pigs were taken for horses—so usually I drew cows because their udders identified them.

In my pre-adolescent years, I was bothered by some big boys of whom I was afraid. As an adolescent I was terrified of public-speaking because I felt so inferior. I was so shy, I didn't use a telephone at all until I was a teen.

Many youth have feelings of personal inadequacy and insecurity. In comparing ourselves with others, we see others who are more attractive, more intelligent, more athletic, more skilled in music or public speaking or sewing or tiddlywinks or—the list goes on. These comparisons usually lead to questioning one's worth. If we have intense or repeated feelings of inferiority that cause us to be withdrawn, or, on the other extreme, very aggressive, we have an inferiority complex. Many people have a temporary or moderate form of this problem.

How should a Christian feel about himself or herself? Romans 12:3 has the answer. A person is "not to think of himself more highly than he ought to think; but to think soberly, according as God hath dealt to every man the measure of faith." We should not think of ourselves more highly nor (by implication) too lowly of ourselves. We should think soberly and rightly, viewing ourselves as God sees us. This means rejecting thought patterns such as: "I'm worthless, no good," and "poor me." On the other hand, we should eliminate ideas such as: "I'm really great. I deserve praise and honor. I'm better than others."

Moses needed to learn to think soberly. At first he seemed overconfident as he went about to establish justice for the Israelites in Egypt, killing an Egyptian who was flogging an Israelite. Then Moses fled to the desert.

After Moses' forty years of wilderness education, God called him to go to Egypt to speak to Pharaoh. Moses said, "Who am I, that I should go unto Pharaoh?" (Exodus 3:11) and "O my Lord, I am not eloquent, neither heretofore, nor since thou hast spoken unto thy servant: but I am slow of speech, and of a slow tongue" (Exodus 4:10).

Isaiah had a better attitude. He said, "Here am I, send me." You don't need to know where you are going provided you know who you arc following.

About God: **To Do:**

You Are Special: God Made You

"For thou hast made him a little lower than the angels, and hast crowned him with glory and honour." —Psalm 8:5

Read Psalm 139

You may not feel special. Why? First, maybe you've compared yourself with others and concluded that because you're less capable and skilled, you are worth less. Many youth buy into the erroneous idea that our worth is rated by achievement or appearance. Those who are "comparing themselves among themselves, are not wise" (2 Corinthians 10:12). True, we possess varying gifts and abilities, but nonetheless, we are of equal worth.

Second, you may have absorbed negative messages about yourself from others. For example, "You'll never amount to much." Your father may have frequently pointed out your faults and rarely praised you. You may have sensed from your mom that you were an unwanted child or were considered a bother.

A downward progression of thinking goes like this: Let's say that you have difficulty with math (or cooking or basketball) and hear, "You're not much good at math." Then you begin to think, *I'm not good at anything. I can't do anything right.* Finally you conclude, *I'm not worth anything.*

Third, you may have heard a lot of overly positive comments about yourself. If you have continually been told how wonderful and exceptionally talented you are by well-meaning parents and teachers, you may feel guilt and shame because you know that you have weaknesses and faults. It is important that parents give positive input to children, but their evaluation should be realistic and honest.

There are other factors, too, which contribute to inferiority feelings such as poor social skills, parental dominance, sexual abuse and other hurts, perfectionism, and physical blemishes.

However, there are six major reasons for knowing you are special: First, God created you. "I am fearfully and wonderfully made" (v. 14). God superintended the development of your body and mind (vv. 15, 16). You and I are not assembly line products—we're unique. "God don't make no junk," said a person with poor grammar but excellent theology.

You have been made in the image of God. Genesis 1:26 says, "And God said, Let us make man in our image, after our likeness." Thus we are immortal, conscious of self, and can know right from wrong.

True, man has been marred by the Fall. But a Christian becomes a new person in Christ, and will be fully restored in the Resurrection.

About God:

To Do:

April 18

God Knows You and Cares for You

"Casting all your care upon him; for he careth for you." —1 Peter 5:7

Read Isaiah 43:1-7

Here's a second major reason for knowing you are special in God's eyes. God knows you. I like to personalize Isaiah 43:1, "Fear not: for I have redeemed thee, I have called thee by thy name; thou art mine." Wouldn't you feel special and significant if a world leader like the U. S. president called you by name? But that is minor compared with the Sovereign of the universe knowing not just your name, but everything about you.

This great God wants to take you by the hand. Isaiah 42:6 says, "I the LORD have called thee in righteousness, and will hold thine hand, and will keep thee, and give thee for a covenant of the people, for a light of the Gentiles." I only walk hand-in-hand with special people like my wife or children.

This great God wants to help you. Isaiah 41:10 says, "Fear thou not; for I am with thee: be not dismayed; for I am thy God: I will strengthen thee; yea, I will help thee; yea, I will uphold thee with the right hand of my righteousness."

This great God knows all about your problems and griefs. As He said to Moses in reference to the children of Israel, "I know their sorrows; and I am come down to deliver them" (Exodus 3:7, 8).

So intimate and personal is His knowledge of us that He knows the number of our hairs. "But the very hairs of your head are all numbered" (Matthew 10:30).

Even if you aren't known for your beauty, skills, strength, and talents, you are of value (Matthew 10:31). God made you with certain features, and He knows you and loves you just the way you are.

The third big reason for knowing you are special relates to God's care for you. "He careth for you" (1 Peter 5:7). Literally, this means "concerning you, it matters to Him." Got a big exam coming up? It matters to Him. Friends prove false? It matters to Him. Hurt your back? It matters to Him. Feeling lonely and frustrated? It matters to Him. Got an irritating co-worker? It matters to Him. Had a disappointment? It matters to Him. Need a job? It matters to Him. Feeling misunderstood? It matters to Him.

Therefore, cast all your concerns and anxieties upon Him. If you do the casting, He'll do the caring.

About God: **To Do:**

God Has a Plan for You

"For I know the thoughts that I think toward you, saith the LORD, thoughts of peace, and not of evil, to give you an expected end."
—Jeremiah 29:11

Read 1 Peter 1:13-25

You can usually tell how much something is worth by what it cost. Think of the relative cost of a house, a pack of gum, a Corvette, and a volleyball, for instance.

Now think of Christ purchasing your salvation—at a price more than the combined worth of Microsoft, Wal-Mart, General Motors, and a thousand other big companies. As 1 Peter 1:18, 19 says, "Ye were not redeemed with corruptible things, as silver and gold . . . but with the precious blood of Christ." It is part of God's plan that you be saved.

You and I are unworthy, yet in God's eyes we are of great worth as we abide in Christ. The fact that Christ died for you is the fourth big reason for knowing you are special.

The fifth big reason relates to God's guidance. He wants to direct and bless your life. As Jeremiah 29:11 says, "For I know the thoughts that I think toward you, saith the LORD, thoughts of peace, and not of evil, to give you an expected end." Or as the NIV puts it, "For I know the plans I have for you," declares the Lord, "plans to prosper you and not to harm you, plans to give you hope and a future."

To know God's will is life's greatest treasure—to do God's will is life's greatest pleasure. "In all thy ways acknowledge him, and he shall direct thy paths" (Proverbs 3:6). Outside of God's will there is no such thing as success; in His will there can be no failure. You are important and special to God. Believe and follow Him. Never be afraid to trust an unknown future to a known God.

A sixth big reason for understanding that you are special relates to God's desire to fellowship with you. If Christ is outside of your heart because you have backslidden in sin, hear His voice, "Behold, I stand at the door, and knock: if any man hear my voice, and open the door, I will come in to him, and will sup with him, and he with me" (Revelation 3:20).

We can all be special to God eternally. Jesus said, "I go to prepare a place for you. And if I go and prepare a place for you, I will come again, and receive you unto myself; that where I am, there ye may be also" (John 14:2, 3).

About God: **To Do:**

April 20

Coping With an Inferiority Complex

"I come to thee in the name of the LORD of hosts, the God of the armies of Israel, whom thou hast defied." —1 Samuel 17:45

Read 1 Samuel 17:1-37

In counseling hundreds of people, both young and old, I have discovered feelings of inferiority are very common. How can we get past such an ingrained attitude and instead serve the Lord with gladness, hope, and courage?

The attitude of the Israelites facing Goliath, as recorded in 1 Samuel 17, is a striking example of an inferiority complex. Verse 11 says, "When Saul and all Israel heard those words of the Philistine, they were *dismayed, and greatly afraid.*" Life itself may confront us like a giant, causing fear and dismay. We may flee from such situations as did the Israelites. "All the men of Israel, when they saw the man, *fled from him,* and were *sore afraid*" (v. 24). As a result they were immobilized in their service for God, and the living God was defied and defamed (v. 26). Those of us who have struggled with feelings of inferiority know the fear, the failure, the desire to flee, and the paralysis that can come from comparing oneself to others.

David's example in facing intimidating circumstances can teach us how to deal with an inferiority complex.

1. *Face the giant.* It's easier to surrender and run away than to meet the giants of life. But David "drew near to the Philistine" (v. 40).
2. *Face the giant with faith.* "I come to thee in the name of the Lord of hosts," said David. We should solicit the help of God, beg for His presence, and depend upon His unfailing grace and unending strength. We must recognize that He has a personal interest in each of us.
3. *Face the giant realistically.* David recognized that Goliath had a sword, spear, and shield (v. 45). But he also saw the far greater resources of God.
4. *Face the giant with gratitude.* Remember how God helped you overcome in the past. David recalled overcoming a lion and a bear (vv. 34-36). Recall the times when circumstances threatened to overwhelm you, but God helped you succeed.

About God: **To Do:**

Four Attitudes to Avoid

"For the battle is the LORD'S and he will give you into our hands."
—1 Samuel 17:47

Read 1 Samuel 17:38-51

David's response to the intimidation and threats of Goliath teach us valuable lessons about how to deal with an inferiority complex.

First, don't try to be somebody else. David tried on Saul's armor. He soon took it off. He was wise. He didn't put on a false front and try to be someone else. He realized he just needed to be himself. If God wanted you to be someone else, He would have made you like that person.

Second, don't let negative comments disturb or discourage you. Upon meeting David, Saul exclaimed, "Thou art but a youth!" And when Goliath spotted David, "he disdained him." But David was undeterred. He accepted himself and his limitations, and did the best with what he had.

Third, don't minimize the resources and abilities you have been given. David took his staff, scrip, sling, and five stones. He wasn't equipped like Saul or Eliab or the armor-bearer, but he effectively used what he did have.

Fourth, don't make excuses and withdraw. David could have run away from the situation, saying, "All I have is a sling." But he went forward in the name of the Lord and defeated the giant.

We need to discard our pet excuses!

"I can't."

"Someone else can do it better."

"I think I'll just stay at home."

"I'm no good at anything."

"What would others say?"

"I don't feel the best so get someone else."

"What if . . . ?"

"God didn't really give me any talents."

"I'd rather not."

Verse 50 says, "So David prevailed over the Philistine." We can prevail too, being effective in God's service. Realize what you can do for God by trusting, trying, and triumphing.

About God: **To Do:**

Thinking Soberly About Self

"For as we have many members in one body, and all members have not the same office." —Romans 12:4

Read 2 Corinthians 3:12–4:5

First, accept what you cannot change about yourself.

In one survey of evangelical Christian youth, over ninety-five percent said that they were dissatisfied with their appearance, height, complexion, shape of nose and ears, etc. We need to remember that Jesus was not attractive by outward, human standards. Isaiah 53:2 says, "He hath no form nor comeliness; and when we shall see him, there is no beauty that we should desire him."

We need to accept not only our appearance, but things such as who our parents are and what our economic and social status is. Our appearance, physique, and background do not determine our worth. David's brothers looked kingly in Samuel's eyes, but God saw David's heart and chose him to be king. "For the LORD seeth not as man seeth; for man looketh on the outward appearance, but the LORD looketh on the heart" (1 Samuel 16:7).

Rather than being discontented with what God has given you, be thankful for your abilities, blessings, gifts, and opportunities.

Of course, change what you can change. If you smell like a locker room, take a shower and use deodorant. If you talk with your mouth full, interrupt, belch, etc., get some help in developing social graces. If your teeth are grimy, brush them. If your clothes are dirty, wash them. If you don't like your weight, eat differently and exercise. If you barely pass tests, study and get help. If you don't have friends, be friendly. Do what you are asked to do to the best of your ability, even if someone else could do it better.

Second, realize you are special. This does not mean you are more special than anyone else. But it does mean that God values and loves you.

Third, focus on God, not self. Adopt the mentality of being God-centered and others-focused. How can I please God? How can I serve others?

Some youth who don't feel good about themselves may try to compensate. They become loud in voice and dress. They flirt. They try to be the life of the party. They play practical jokes. They may spend extravagantly to gain attention. Rather than seeking the admiration of people, make it your aim to be "approved unto God" (2 Timothy 2:15).

Fourth, let God change you. As the daily reading says, be changed into the image of the Lord.

About God: **To Do:**

The Blessings of Work

"Work with your own hands, as we commanded you."
—1 Thessalonians 4:11

Read Genesis 2:1-20

The Lord didn't burden us with work, He blessed us with it. We tend to be happier when we fill our days with real work and our nights with real rest. It's better to get bent from hard labor than to grow crooked from trying to avoid it.

The daily reading tells us that God worked and then rested on the seventh day (v. 2). In the paradise known as the Garden of Eden, God blessed Adam with physical work, telling him to cultivate and keep it (v. 15). God also gave Adam mental work by having him name all the animals and birds (v. 19). I believe hard work is a thrill and joy when you are in the will of God.

It's no credit to you to try to avoid work. One old wag said, "Two good openings for a young man are the legs of a pair of coveralls." And when at work, work. "Whatsoever thy hand findeth to do, do it with thy might" (Ecclesiastes 9:10).

A fellow applied for a job at a grocery store, "I'm interested in filling the vacancy left by the one who left."

"I'm sorry, but when he left, he didn't leave a vacancy."

Work is honorable. Jesus was a carpenter. He worked with His hands, handling wood and probably cutting stones as a mason. He was a teacher. He worked with His mind.

"Six days shalt thou labour," says the fourth of the Ten Commandments. Ephesians 4:28 says, "Let him that stole steal no more: but rather let him labour, working with his hands the thing which is good, that he may have to give to him that needeth."

About God: **To Do:**

April 24

Choosing a Vocation

"Whether therefore ye eat, or drink, or whatsoever ye do, do all to the glory of God." —1 Corinthians 10:31

Read 1 Corinthians 16:5-24

If you are deciding on a vocation or thinking of changing jobs, here are six questions for you to consider:

1. *Does it glorify God?* Whether we eat or drink or work, we should do it all for the glory of God. This immediately closes the door to being a brewery worker, a movie star, a hair stylist, a professional athlete, or a jeweler like Demetrius. It opens the door to the possibility of being a carpenter like Jesus, a farmer like Boaz, a fisherman like Peter, a seamstress like Dorcas, a teacher like Moses, a shepherd like David, a fruit gatherer like Amos, or a mobile home worker like Paul, who made tents.
2. *Is it for the good of your fellowmen?* Philippians 2:4 says, "Look not every man on his own things, but every man also on the things of others." How can a farmer grow tobacco if he is interested in the good of others? Or how can a sales clerk sell it?

   A friend of mine worked herself into a responsible position in a store. Upon her promotion, she was expected to sell lottery tickets. She couldn't do this in good conscience, so she resigned.
3. *Does the work environment include overwhelming temptations?* Although all jobs present temptations and we ought to be a witness to unbelievers at work, some jobs do not provide a fit environment. It may be continual cursing, foul language, and pornography on the walls. A Christian who has been saved from an addiction to drink shouldn't be working where coworkers do social drinking.
4. *Does it involve unnecessary Sunday work?* There is a difference between caring for the needy in a nursing home and working in a restaurant on the Lord's Day. There is a difference between milking cows versus pumping gas or operating a lathe on the day of rest.
5. *Does it prevent active participation in the local congregation?* Jobs such as long-distance truck driving may limit your involvement in church activities and home life. It's better to be like the household of Stephanas, who addicted themselves to the ministry of the saints (v. 15).
6. *Does it involve compromising any Bible principles?* In my first job, it was compulsory to be part of a group life insurance plan. I appealed for exemption due to my religious beliefs and, fortunately, it was granted.

About God: **To Do:**

Employee Attitudes

"And whatsoever ye do, do it heartily, as to the Lord, and not unto men." —Colossians 3:23

Read
2 Thessalonians
3:6-18

If you are an employee, what attitudes should you portray at work?

1. *Be diligent at work.* An employer said to a job applicant, "Sorry, I have no job for you. I wouldn't find enough work to keep you busy."

The applicant replied, "But you have no idea how little work it takes to keep me busy."

In contrast to that applicant's attitude, a Christian should do his work heartily—energetically and thoroughly—as though the Lord were his immediate boss.

Don't be stubborn. Two ships collided in the Black Sea in 1986, hurling hundreds of passengers into the icy waters and causing a tragic loss of life. An investigation showed that the accident was caused by human stubbornness. Each captain was aware of the other ship's presence, and both could have averted the collision. But neither would yield. By the time they saw the error of their ways, it was too late.

2. *Value work.* Work is God-ordained. Work was one of the pleasures of paradise, and we cannot be happy without it. Unless retirees find some way to stay occupied, they are likely to become despondent. Actually, the death rate for idle retirees is significantly higher than that of the active retired.

The Apostolic Constitution of the Early Church said, "Attend to your employment with all appropriate seriousness, so that you will always have sufficient funds to support both yourselves and those who are needy. In that way, you will not burden the church of God. . . . Some of us are fishermen, tentmakers, and farmers, so that we may never be idle. Solomon says, 'Go to the ant, you sluggard; consider her ways diligently and become wiser than she.'"

3. *Seize opportunities at work.* Remember, your work reflects your commitment to Christ. A person's work is a portrait of himself. It is, in effect, your silent testimony that speaks loudly. If your life is hid with Christ, then Christ should be seen in your work.

4. *Respect the boss.* Don't give eyeservice—that is, working diligently when the boss is around and slacking off when he leaves. I think this sign is interesting: "Wanted, clerk to work eight hours a day to replace one that didn't."

About God: **To Do:**

April 26

Instructions for Employees

"Servants, obey in all things your masters according to the flesh; not with eyeservice, as menpleasers; but in singleness of heart, fearing God." —Colossians 3:22

Read Luke 19:11-28

If you want to know what makes a good employee, consider Ephesians 6:5, 6: "Servants, be obedient to them that are your masters according to the flesh, with fear and trembling, in singleness of your heart, as unto Christ; not with eyeservice, as menpleasers; but as the servants of Christ, doing the will of God from the heart."

1. *Be yielding.* Sometimes employees think they know better than their boss. But the Bible is clear that we should obey those who are over us in the workplace. Carry out your work assignments well. Nobody ever became the man of the hour by watching the clock.
2. *Be respectful.* Watch out lest you be affected by complaining, disrespectful talk among your coworkers. At one job I needed to repent of some attitudes about my boss.
3. *Be sincere.* Have singleness of heart. Be like Daniel whose jealous co-workers tried to find fault with his work. "But they could find none occasion nor fault; forasmuch as he was faithful, neither was there any error or fault found in him" (Daniel 6:4). It's not the number of hours you put in, but what you put into those hours that counts.
4. *Be diligent.* Do quality work. I believe Jesus was a good carpenter, David a good shepherd, and Paul a good tentmaker.
5. *Be servants of God.* Ephesians 6:7 and 8 says, "With good will doing service, as to the Lord, and not to men: knowing that whatsoever good thing any man doeth, the same shall he receive of the Lord, whether he be bond or free." Look beyond the shingles, the dishes, the workbooks, the shovels, or the computer to the grander purposes of glorifying God and serving mankind.

There is a story that when the famed English architect, Sir Christopher Wren, was directing the building of St. Paul's Cathedral in London, some of the workers were interviewed by a journalist who asked them, "What are you doing here?"

The first one said, "I'm cutting stone for three shillings a day."

The second replied, "I'm putting ten hours a day in on this job."

The third replied, "I'm helping Sir Christopher Wren build the greatest cathedral in Great Britain for the glory of God."

About God: **To Do:**

Do Not Purloin

"Thou shalt not steal." —Exodus 20:15

Read Titus 2:6-15

A father learned that his son had stolen several pencils from a store. He scolded him severely, saying, "You ought to know better than to steal. I can pick up all the pencils you need at the office."

This father should have read the instructions to employees in verse 10, "Not purloining, but showing all good fidelity." To *purloin* is "to take dishonestly, to pilfer, and to steal." I connect the word *purloin* with *sirloin*—a person may be tempted to purloin sirloin.

This command to employees is pertinent as well as practical. Studies have indicated that fifty to ninety percent of business thefts are the result of workers who go home with more than their paychecks. Many stores lose fifty percent of their profits through "inventory shrinkage" due to damage, shoplifting, and unfortunately, purloining.

Security officials have estimated that nine percent of all employees steal on a regular basis, and that seventy-five percent of all employees in retail establishments pirate things home to some degree.

The Bible is clear that any form of theft is not acceptable. "Ye shall not steal, neither deal falsely. Thou shalt not defraud thy neighbour [employer], neither rob him" (Leviticus 19:11, 13).

Employees can steal in other ways besides taking items home without permission or payment. Some workers are careless with the employer's equipment, vehicles, tools, and supplies. Although the worker hasn't actually taken anything, the owner has experienced loss, and so the worker has, in effect, stolen. The employee may also steal by taking more time than is permitted for coffee breaks, lunch, etc. Thus a person earning ten dollars an hour who takes ten minutes longer than the allotted time for each of three breaks is taking from his employer five dollars which is not rightfully his. (I heard of an employee who stretched his coffee break all the way to the unemployment office!) It seems that some employees take so long to get back to work after the afternoon break that they are in danger of being late for quitting time. Likewise, shoddy workmanship and wasting materials because of careless mistakes are costly to the owner and violate the standards of integrity for Christian employees.

Don't purloin. Ill-gotten *gain* is always great *loss.*

About God: **To Do:**

April 28

Tough Days at Work

"Rejoicing in hope; patient in tribulation; continuing instant in prayer." —Romans 12:12

Read Philippians 4:1-13

After coming home from a day of work, you may be asked, "How was your day?"

You reply, "It was a tough day."

Take some advice found in the daily reading from that veteran of tough days, the Apostle Paul:

1. *Rejoice in the Lord* (v. 4). We may find it difficult to always rejoice in our circumstances, but there is always abundant reason to rejoice in the Lord. When appliances and machinery break, rejoice that He knows your load limit (1 Corinthians 10:13) and will not permit too much strain or stress. When you make "stupid mistakes," rejoice that He forgives his children's sins and knows that we are dust (Psalm 103:12-14). When others seem unloving and brusque, rejoice that He personally loves and cares, wanting you to cast your cares upon Him (1 Peter 5:7).
2. *Be sweetly reasonable.* "Let your moderation [yieldedness, self-control] be known unto all men" (v. 5), including your co-workers. True, we meet many unreasonable people on the job; we shouldn't make the situation worse by being as unreasonable as they.
3. *Look for Jesus' return.* "The Lord is at hand" (v. 5). A better day is coming when there will not be boring, routine, or unpleasant tasks. When you start feeling down, look up!
4. *Refuse anxiety.* Rather, "in every thing by prayer and supplication with thanksgiving let your requests be made known unto God" (v. 6). Don't worry about being laid off. Don't worry about the rising cost of living. Don't worry about an empty retirement fund—on earth, that is!
5. *Think good things* (v. 8). If a co-worker treats you unfairly, don't concentrate on the injustice and pity yourself. We may not be able to control what crosses our minds, but we can determine what stays there.
6. *Learn contentment.* Paul said, "I have learned, in whatsoever state I am, therewith to be content" (v. 11). Another person wrote, "The secret of contentment lies in knowing how to enjoy what you have, and to be able to lose all interest in things beyond your reach." John the Baptist told workers of his day, "Be content with your wages."
7. *Let Christ strengthen you.* In many jobs, great power is available at the flick of a switch. In Christ we have unlimited power. Therefore, be strong in the Lord as you erect buildings, care for children, work in a hospital, or operate a dairy farm.

About God: **To Do:**

Good Job

"Servants, be subject to your masters with all fear; not only to the good and gentle, but also to the froward." —1 Peter 2:18

Read 1 Timothy 6:1-12

What is the best job to have in North America? According to Les Krantz's *Jobs Rated Almanac,* which rates 250 jobs, a web site manager has the best job, followed by an actuary, computer systems analyst, software engineer, and fifthly, a mathematician. At the very bottom is the oil field laborer. Six categories were considered in the evaluation: environment, income, outlook, physical demands, security, and stress.

The four best incomes were all in professional sports, followed by surgeons. The five lowest incomes were maid, waiter, cashier, childcare worker, and lowest of all, dishwasher.

The best working environment ratings were for statistician, followed by mathematician, computer systems analyst, hospital administrator, and historian. The worst were taxi driver, NFL football player, racecar driver, firefighter, and at the very bottom, President of the United States.

Are the best jobs easy ones? The word *easy* appears only once in the New Testament, and this in connection with *yoke.* So the instructions to Christians who are employed are not directed to doing easy work but to doing work commendably.

Note four specific points made in Titus 2:9, 10: "Exhort servants to be obedient unto their own masters, and to please them well in all things; not answering again; not purloining, but shewing all good fidelity; that they may adorn the doctrine of God our Saviour in all things."

1. *Obey.* The word *servant* can refer to a slave or to a paid employee. In either case, instructions from the boss are to be followed. (Who, by the way, are always early when you are late and late when you are early?) As the daily reading shows, don't take advantage of a Christian boss.
2. *Work well.* Try to please the boss by doing the job satisfactorily, even superiorly. People may not remember how fast you did your work, but they will remember how well you did it. Work well whether the boss is observing you or not. Make your employer think he's getting good value for the wages he's paying you. Don't tempt your foreman to resort to his best incentive plan—"Get busy, or you're fired."
3. *Honor.* It is very easy to evaluate a boss in a disrespectful, griping way. Don't give backtalk and don't talk behind his back.
4. *Be a model employee.* Adorn the doctrine of Christ by being an exemplary employee. Your work is the most accurate commentary on your character.

About God: **To Do:**

Fear God

"O that there were such an heart in them, that they would fear me, and keep all my commandments always, that it might be well with them, and with their children for ever." —Deuteronomy 5:29

Read Exodus 20:18-26

One time my audience braced itself for confusion when I assigned four people to read simultaneously the following parts of the Bible: the third sentence of 1 Peter 2:17; the sixth and seventh words of Revelation 14:7; the tenth and eleventh words of Ecclesiastes 12:13; the third from the last word and the last word of Ecclesiastes 5:7. What the audience heard, however, was not confusing but clear. Look up the verses and you will see.

One beautiful, sunny August afternoon, my wife and I traveled to Tobermory, a port on Georgian Bay, which is a watery graveyard for many a ship traversing the Great Lakes. We were hoping to enjoy God's handiwork on a sunset cruise, but to our surprise it was cancelled because of a stiff breeze that had sprung up. The captain was afraid that the ship might be forced aground. Although disappointed, we understood the need to avoid having our marriage end up on the rocks (literally).

In contrast, a group of university students from Toronto went to Georgian Bay for a fishing trip. They hired a boat and a captain to take them out on the bay. Without much warning a storm broke. The captain sat at the helm, looking worried. The students laughed at his fear and declared, " We're not afraid!"

The old sailor looked at them and said, "Yes, you are too ignorant to be afraid."

A slogan I often see on trucks and T-shirts says, "No fear." It corresponds to Romans 3:18, "There is no fear of God before their eyes." This lack of fear and respect for holy God is indicated by blasphemous speech, disregard for the Lord's Day, disrespect for human life, and pride in an ungodly lifestyle.

Presently, there is no fear. But in the future there will be great fear. Here is a description of the great day of God's wrath: "And the kings of the earth, and the great men, and the rich men, and the chief captains, and the mighty men, and every bondman, and every free man, hid themselves in the dens and in the rocks of the mountains; and said to the mountains and rocks, Fall on us, and hide us from the face of him that sitteth on the throne, and from the wrath of of the Lamb" (Revelation 6:15, 16).

About God: **To Do:**

Don't Fear God

"There is no fear in love; but perfect love casteth out fear." —1 John 4:18

Read Hebrews 4:1-16

I love the beautiful invitation of Hebrews 4:16, "Let us therefore come boldly unto the throne of grace, that we may obtain mercy, and find grace to help in time of need." Although we are to have a godly fear of Almighty God, yet He wants us to come to Him through Jesus, our great High Priest who understands our weaknesses.

Heathen religions for centuries have operated on fear of the gods, fear of evil spirits, fear of spells. Witch doctors and shamans have capitalized on this fear to control people and siphon goods from them. In contrast, God wants us to trust Him and draw close to Him. His truth will set us free from unnecessary fears.

One January day in 1960, a very smelly, gaunt peasant appeared before his shocked neighbors in a village in Ukraine. Grisha Sikalenko's neighbors hadn't seen him for eighteen years and no longer expected to see him. Everyone thought he had died a hero's death fighting the Germans in World War II.

The night that Grisha was thought to have marched away to war, he had actually deserted and sneaked back home. His mother had made a hiding place for him under the manure pile at the back of the goat shed. Day after day, year after year, his mother slipped food to him. Grisha shivered through the winters and nearly suffocated through the summers from the stench and heat.

After overcoming his fear of punishment for desertion, Grisha finally emerged from the reeking pit. His fears were groundless. The statute of limitations had long since made him immune from being prosecuted.

David said, "I sought the LORD, and he heard me, and delivered me from all my fears" (Psalm 34:4). Fear God and don't have fear. Respect Him, but don't be afraid to come to Him with your burdens, fears, and frustrations.

It's something like working with fire. If you have a proper relationship with fire, it is of great benefit; but if you are careless, it will destroy you. Likewise, electricity. Respect it, and its power is helpful. Play with it, and it will kill you.

The Hebrew writer says that we can come boldly to God. "Let us draw near with a true heart in full assurance of faith" (Hebrews 10:22). But he also says, "It is a fearful thing to fall into the hands of the living God" (Hebrews 10:31).

About God: **To Do:**

May 2

Cultivating a Fear of God

"Fear before him, all the earth: the world also shall be stable, that it be not moved." —1 Chronicles 16:30

Read Revelation 15:1-8

People have all types of phobias. They might fear spiders, heights, black cats, elevators, the dark, germs, and snakes. And they sometimes cultivate their fear.

For example, an outdoorsman from Detroit who had been bitten by his share of ticks, heard about Lyme disease, which is carried by deer ticks. Since he had often been bitten by ticks, he was convinced that he had been bitten by a tick carrying Lyme disease and that he had passed the disease on to his wife.

He took medical tests. They were negative. Doctors assured him that he didn't have Lyme disease. They said, "Even if you have Lyme disease, it is virtually impossible to transmit it to your wife."

The man thought he knew more than the doctors. Finally, obsessed with the thought of Lyme disease, the man killed his wife and then himself. The police found his mailbox jammed with material about Lyme disease. They also found a slip confirming a medical appointment for still another Lyme disease test.

How can we cultivate a proper fear of God?

1. Recognize the *power of God.* He hung the stars in the sky. He positioned the sun and moon. He created life. He has power of life and death. He created and controls natural phenomena. God did tremendous things for Israel on the way to Canaan. Joshua said, "That all the people of the earth might know the hand of the LORD, that it is mighty: that ye might fear the LORD your God for ever" (Joshua 4:24).
2. Recognize His *goodness*. Samuel told the fickle people of his day, "Only fear the LORD, and serve him in truth with all your heart: for consider how great things he hath done for you" (1 Samuel 12:24).
3. Recognize His *readiness to forgive.* The psalmist gave us the mental picture of the Lord writing down the sins of last year and last week and yesterday and today, but then says, "No, that's not the way it is." Psalm 130:3, 4 says, "If thou, LORD, shouldest mark iniquities, O Lord, who shall stand? But there is forgiveness with thee, that thou mayest be feared."
4. Recognize the *judgment of God.* The angel having the everlasting Gospel said with a loud voice, "Fear God, and give glory to him; for the hour of his judgment is come" (Revelation 14:7).

About God: **To Do:**

Commands to Fear God

"Fear before him, all the earth." —Psalm 96:9

Read Psalm 96

Jesus put it plainly, "But I will forewarn you whom ye shall fear: Fear him, which after he hath killed hath power to cast into hell; yea, I say unto you, Fear him" (Luke 12:5). Sober thoughts of death and hell have a way of putting life into perspective. Yet some theologians and clergymen downplay these realities.

Years ago a preacher was robbed on the road by a former employee. The man was arrested and sentenced to a long punishment. Thinking he would try to touch the condemned man's conscience, the preacher queried, "How could you be so base as to rob your kind old employer?"

The man's reply utterly silenced him: "You yourself tempted me to commit this offence against the law. I often heard you say both in public and in private that all men will enjoy everlasting bliss after death and that there is no such thing as eternal punishment or hell in the next world. Since you have removed my greatest fear, why should I dread the lesser one?"

The writer of Ecclesiastes gave this concise conclusion, "Fear God, and keep his commandments: for this is the whole duty of man. For God shall bring every work into judgment, with every secret thing, whether it be good, or whether it be evil" (Ecclesiastes 12:13, 14).

Both the Old Testament and New Testament of the Bible repeatedly urge us to fear God. For example, Deuteronomy 10:12 says, "And now, Israel, what doth the LORD thy God require of thee, but to fear the LORD thy God, to walk in all his ways, and to love him, and to serve the LORD thy God with all thy heart and with all thy soul."

Psalm 2:11 says, "Serve the LORD with fear, and rejoice with trembling."

In view of the fact that we are sons and daughters of God, 2 Corinthians 7:1 says, "Having therefore these promises, dearly beloved, let us cleanse ourselves from all filthiness of the flesh and spirit, perfecting holiness in the fear of God."

And Hebrews 12:28 sums it up this way: "Wherefore we receiving a kingdom which cannot be moved, let us have grace, whereby we may serve God acceptably with reverence and godly fear." The early church leader, Tertullian, rightly said, "Where the fear of God is, there is seriousness and an honorable and yet thoughtful diligence."

About God:

To Do:

Consequences of a Lack of Fear of God

*"Blessed is every one that feareth the LORD;
that walketh in his ways."* —Psalm 128:1

Read Romans 3:10-18

Over and over in the Bible appears the phrase "the fear of the Lord." In fact, there are over three hundred references in the Old Testament that speak of the fear of the Lord.

The fear of the Lord includes a mixture of awe, reverential trust, hatred of evil, and recognition that the divine Judge sees my deeds, hears my words, and knows my thoughts.

What happens when a fear of God diminishes or disappears? Romans 3:10-18 gives six results:

1. *Little interest in spiritual things.* "There is none that understandeth, there is none that seeketh after God" (v. 11). In America, fewer and fewer people go to church or read their Bible regularly.
2. *Unrestrained living.* "They are all gone out of the way, they are together become unprofitable; there is none that doeth good, no, not one" (v. 12). This is reflected in drunken parties, big problems with sexually transmitted diseases, pursuit of expensive and sinful pleasures, drugs, etc.
3. *Evil speech.* Verse 13 is very descriptive. "Their throat is an open sepulchre; with their tongues they have used deceit; the poison of asps is under their lips." Doesn't this describe modern Western culture—deceptive words, poisonous speech plus lots of "cursing and bitterness" (v. 14). Some people can't seem to talk a minute without using God's name in vain.
4. *Rejection of the sanctity of life.* "Their feet are swift to shed blood" (v. 15). No fear of God has resulted in tens of millions of abortions yearly. Suicide and assisted suicide correspond to a low view of human life.
5. *Involvement in harmful activities.* "Destruction and misery are in their ways" (v. 16). Lord Byron, a skilled poet, pursued sinful pleasures in his youth. He really "lived it up." But within a few years, he experienced the results of sin. In despair he wrote:

   The thorns I have reaped are of the tree I planted.
   They have torn me and I bleed.
   I should have known what fruit would spring
   From such a tree.
6. *Conflict.* "And the way of peace have they not known" (v. 17). There can be no peace where pride reigns.

Verse 18 summarizes the sorry situation, "There is no fear of God before their eyes."

About God: **To Do:**

Consequences of Fearing God

"Though a sinner do evil an hundred times, and his days be prolonged, yet surely I know that it shall be well with them that fear God, which fear before him." —Ecclesiastes 8:12

Read Acts 10:1-8, 34-45

Some people have irrational fears, for instance, driving over large bridges. Some motorists will drive hours out of their way to avoid them. Others start across the bridge but have a panic attack halfway across. They block traffic because they can't force themselves to go farther.

Some bridge operators have begun to offer a driving service. For those who request help, bridge attendants will drive their car over the bridge. In 1996 Michigan's Timid Motorist Program helped over 1000 motorists across the five-mile-long Mackinac Bridge which rises 62 meters (200 feet) into the air.

There are many other irrational fears—fear of open spaces, fear of frogs, and fear of blushing. But the fear of the Lord makes total sense. Look at the good results:

1. *It gives wisdom.* As Job 28:28 says, "Behold, the fear of the LORD, that is wisdom; and to depart from evil is understanding."
2. *It brings blessing.* Psalm 115:13 says, "He will bless them that fear the LORD, both small and great."
3. *It helps prevent sin.* As Israel was told, "Fear not: for God is come to prove you, and that his fear may be before your faces, that ye sin not" (Exodus 20:20).
4. *It pleases the Lord.* As Psalm 147:11 says, "The LORD taketh pleasure in them that fear him, in those that hope in his mercy."
5. *It encourages salvation and evangelism.* Noah who was "moved with fear, prepared an ark to the saving of his house; by the which he condemned the world, and became heir of the righteousness which is by faith" (Hebrews 11:7).

The wonderful thing about fearing God is that when you fear the Lord, you fear nothing else, whereas if you do not fear the Lord, you are open to fearing everything.

About God: **To Do:**

May 6

More Advantages of Fearing the Lord

"By humility and the fear of the LORD are riches, and honour, and life." —Proverbs 22:4

Read Proverbs 14:2-27

American natives gave a final test when training young braves. When each boy turned thirteen, having been taught how to scout, hunt and fish, he was blindfolded and taken several miles away. For the first time away from the security of his family, he would spend the night alone in the wild.

When he took off the blindfold, he was in a dense forest. Imagine what a terrifying experience it must have been—in the pitch dark, hearing twigs snap, not knowing when a wild animal might pounce. Surviving the long, lonely night hours, he finally saw dawn break. Looking around he saw trees, flowers, and a path. Then to his amazement, he made out the figure of a man standing only a few paces away, armed with bow and arrow. It was the boy's father. He had been there all through the night.

Our heavenly Father is near through the dark, lonely times in life. We don't see Him, but He promises to be there to remove our dread if we fear Him. "Behold, the eye of the LORD is upon them that fear him, upon them that hope in his mercy" (Psalm 33:18). God's presence and protection is a wonderful result of godly fear.

Another result is hearing our prayers. "He will fulfil the desire of them that fear him: he also will hear their cry, and will save them" (Psalm 145:19).

Furthermore, God's mercy and compassion flow to those who fear Him. As Psalm 103:11 says, "For as the heaven is high above the earth, so great is his mercy toward them that fear him." Still another blessing of godly fear is acceptance by God. Peter declared this to Cornelius and company who gathered to hear God's message: "God is no respecter of persons: but in every nation he that feareth him, and worketh righteousness, is accepted with him" (Acts 10:34, 35).

God is interested in our good. The fear of the Lord is interwoven with our being blessed. Jeremiah 32:39, 40 says, "And I will give them one heart, and one way, that they may fear me for ever, for the good of them, and of their children after them: and I will make an everlasting covenant with them, that I will not turn away from them, to do them good; but I will put my fear in their hearts, that they shall not depart from me."

About God: **To Do:**

Appreciating a Mother's Loyalty: Mary

"Now there stood by the cross of Jesus his mother, and his mother's sister, Mary the wife of Cleophas, and Mary Magdalene." —John 19:25

Read Luke 2:25-38

When Jesus looked down from the cross toward His mother, what do you think He saw? He saw first of all that His mother was *there* near the cross. "Now there stood by the cross of Jesus his mother, and his mother's sister, Mary the wife of Cleopas, and Mary Magdalene" (John 19:25). How wonderful to have a mother, a family member, or a friend "stand by" in painful experiences of life such as illness, rejection, bereavement, and disappointment.

Second, He saw the loyalty of His mother along with that of the other two Marys. Although Judas had betrayed Him, Peter had denied Him, and the disciples had largely deserted Him and fled, yet His mother was faithful to Him.

Third, He saw her pain—the pain prophesied by Simeon soon after Jesus' birth. She had been told, "A sword shall pierce through thy own soul also" (Luke 2:35). I think that, in a sense, she felt the blows of the hammer, the piercing of the thorns, the sting of the scourging, and the taunts of the priests. No doubt part of her pain was her inability as a mother to help. Her Son's back was bleeding, but she couldn't bandage His wounds. His mouth was parched, but she couldn't moisten His lips. His hands were held by spikes, but she couldn't remove them.

It seems to me that Mary experienced to the full the prophecy of Simeon. She saw the forehead she had kissed, now adorned by thorns. She saw the head she had patted, now wounded and bleeding. She saw the hands she had held, now held by spikes. She saw the feet that had padded beside her, now held immobile. She saw the back that she had bathed, now bruised and torn and broken.

Finally, Jesus saw her courage. It takes bravery to stand with a person whom all others seem to stand against.

Jesus said to John, "Behold thy mother." *We* do well to behold her also—appreciating her love, her sympathy, her courage, and her loyalty to Christ. May we follow her example.

About God: **To Do:**

Appreciating a Mother's Care: Jochebed

"By faith Moses, when he was born, was hid three months of his parents, because they saw he was a proper child; and they were not afraid of the king's commandment." —Hebrews 11:23

Read Exodus 2:1-10

A little three-year-old girl said:

Doggie says Bow-wow,
Sheep says Baa-baa,
Cow says Moo-moo,
Mommy says No-no.

However, mothers do much more than say "No-no." A child depends on his mother for his or her very life.

Jochebed, as told in the daily reading, defied Pharaoh's command to toss all the baby boys into the Nile. She obeyed the higher law of God. Many governments of the world presently permit mothers to dispose of their unborn babies. But the godly Jochebeds of today see the value and potential of babies.

Jochebed cared for her baby. Instead of taking his life, she risked her own life to hide him. When he became too old to hide, she placed him in a basket in the river, positioning big sister Miriam nearby to watch. What was Jochebed thinking? Did she expect the princess to find Moses and perhaps feel sorry for him? Or did she just hope for the best? We do know she trusted God.

Do you appreciate your mother's hard work on your behalf—washing, folding laundry, making meals and cleaning up, her care of you as a baby and toddler? Do you appreciate her spiritual labors for your good—her prayers, her training, her discipline, and the Bible stories and songs she taught you? Are you thankful for the sacrifices she has made on your behalf?

A girl was looking at her mother. "You have pretty hair and such nice eyes and a kind face, Mommy. But, Mommy, why are your arms so ugly?"

"Let me tell you what happened. When you were a baby, a fire started in our house. I ran through the smoke to get you in your crib. I brought you out safely, but my arms got burned as I shielded you. I recovered from the burns, but my arms are scarred. You are right, they are ugly."

The little girl thought about what she had heard. "Mommy," she said, "you have pretty hair, nice eyes, and a beautiful face. But I think your arms and hands are the most beautiful of all."

About God: **To Do:**

Appreciating a Mother's Prayers: Hannah

"And Hannah prayed, and said, My heart rejoiceth in the LORD, mine horn is exalted in the LORD: my mouth is enlarged over mine enemies; because I rejoice in thy salvation." —1 Samuel 2:1

Read 1 Samuel 1:9-28

An unknown poet wrote about his mother's prayers:

Among the treasured pictures
  That I'll hang on memory's wall,
There's one that's clearer than the rest
  And sweeter far than all.

'Tis a picture of my mother
  When I, a little chap,
Was folded in her loving arms,
  To slumber on her lap.

I felt her hands caress my head,
  I heard her softly say,
"Dear Jesus, take this little life
  And use it every day."

There must have been a mighty weight
  Behind that simple prayer,
For through the seasons, year on year,
  That picture lingers there.

And whether I'm on hill or plain
  Or on the deep blue sea,
The memory of that sacred scene
  Forever comforts me.

Among the treasured pictures
  That I've hung on memory's wall,
My mother's supplication
  Is the sweetest one of all.

I think Samuel treasured the memory of Hannah's prayers. She no doubt told him how she prayed for a son, how she promised to commit him to the Lord's work, how she was misunderstood by her spiritual leader, how God answered her prayers, and how she praised God (1 Samuel 2:1-10).

Like Samuel, I have a godly mother. She prays for me each day. As I write this, she is ninety-three years old. If she has prayed for me each day, I have been remembered at God's throne approximately 20,000 times.

Have you ever thanked your mother for praying for you? The chain of a mother's prayers can link her child to God.

About God: **To Do:**

Appreciating Fathers

"And he arose, and came to his father. But when he was yet a great way off, his father saw him, and had compassion, and ran, and fell on his neck, and kissed him." —Luke 15:20

Read Genesis 22:1-19

One Saturday in April, when I was thirteen, the large dairy barn on our farm burned to the ground. Although my brother and I were able to free the cows from the barn, it was a major financial loss. My dad and mom were just emerging from being in debt, and the fire was a real setback. What I remember best about my dad from that experience was his testimony in church the next day. He said, "The Lord hath given and the Lord hath taken away. Blessed be the name of the Lord." His trust and submission to God made a real impact on me.

I'm sure Abraham's trust in God deeply impacted his son. Abraham was not only a great father of the Jews, he was also a good father to Isaac. How?

- He loved his son (v. 2).
- He set an example of obedience. He "rose up early in the morning" to follow God's instructions (v. 3).
- He led out in worship (vv. 5, 6).
- He kept lines of communication open with his son on a very difficult topic (vv. 7, 8).
- He arranged to provide for his son's social needs. He sent his servant to find a wife for his son (see Genesis 24).
- He commanded his children after him. Genesis 18:19 says, "For I know him, that he will command his children and his household after him, and they shall keep the way of the LORD, to do justice and judgment; that the LORD may bring upon Abraham that which he hath spoken of him."

Parents can never teach unless they practice what they preach. A father is generally happier to have his child look like him than act like him. It ought to be the other way around. It's hard to train a child in a way that parents don't go themselves.

About God: **To Do:**

Appreciating Parental Discipline

"My son, forget not my law; but let thine heart keep my commandments." —Proverbs 3:1

Read Hebrews 12:1-14

I remember the last time my dad spanked me. I had been quarreling with my younger sister, and I used some words I would not have chosen had I realized my father was listening. I didn't appreciate my father's discipline then, but as I became an adult I did. I realize he took time to correct me because he loved me. Proverbs 3:11, 12 makes this connection, "My son, despise not the chastening of the LORD; neither be weary of his correction: for whom the LORD loveth he correcteth; even as a father the son in whom he delighteth."

The priest, Eli, failed to discipline his sons as he should have. He scolded them for their sins (see 1 Samuel 2:23-25). However, he failed to stop them or correct them. The Lord was displeased with his permissiveness. God told Eli that he honored his sons above God. Through Samuel, God described the problems to Eli. "For I have told him that I will judge his house for ever for the iniquity which he knoweth; because his sons made themselves vile, and he restrained them not" (1 Samuel 3:13).

David was another godly leader who was a poor father. Maybe he was too busy. (If fathers took their sons fishing when they were young, they wouldn't have to go hunting for them when they are older.) Maybe David was too affluent. (Very frequently rich parents are poor parents.) Maybe he was too indulgent. (Parents who are afraid to put their foot down often have children who step on their toes.)

When Adonijah wanted to replace David as king, 1 Kings 1:6 says, "And his father had not displeased him at any time in saying, Why hast thou done so?"

Have you ever thanked your parents for the corrective discipline that they have given you? I'm sure an appreciative letter to them would be welcomed.

About God: **To Do:**

May 12

Appreciating Siblings

"A friend loveth at all times,
and a brother is born for adversity." —Proverbs 17:17

Read Genesis 37:2-13, 18-34

My older sister remembers my singing in the house loudly, not exactly on key, repeating the same folk song ad nauseam. Why? She says it was to irritate her. I admit she is right.

Siblings often have trouble appreciating each other. And this trouble goes back to the first siblings. Cain became jealous of Abel and, after exchanging words with him in the field, rose up and killed him.

Jacob and Esau, twins, but certainly not identical twins nor loving twins, had serious trouble relating to each other. Jacob took advantage of Esau. Jacob schemed with their mother and cheated Esau. Esau then hated Jacob and held a grudge, intending to kill him when he had the opportunity. Jacob fled and didn't see his brother again for twenty years.

Joseph and his eleven brothers had major problems. Joseph told them some of his dreams, which implied his future greatness in comparison to them. They envied him. They hated him. They conspired to kill him, but when the opportunity arose, they sold him as a slave into Egypt as told in the daily reading. Siblings can be very mean to each other. Think also of Absalom and his brothers, of the older brother and the prodigal son, of David and his elder brother Eliab, of Jesus and His skeptical brothers.

But the Bible also shows examples of sibling appreciation. For example, Andrew and Peter seem to have gotten along well together. They worked together as fishermen, and, upon meeting Jesus, Andrew immediately wanted to introduce his brother to Him (John 1:40-42).

Although Mary and Martha had some differences, their relation with each other and with their brother Lazarus was quite close. Miriam watched over her baby brother, Moses, and Aaron helped him as a spokesman (although they later became jealous of his prominence).

The Proverb writer assumed that normally there is a good relationship among siblings. He wrote, "A brother is born for adversity" (Proverbs 17:17). He implied that brothers tend to be close, although "there is a friend that sticketh closer than a brother" (Proverbs 18:24).

Do your part to have a happy family. Nowadays there are a lot of model homes advertised, but few model families are evident. It's a happy home when the only scraps are those brushed off the kitchen table.

About God: **To Do:**

Appreciating Grandparents

"When I call to remembrance the unfeigned faith that is in thee, which dwelt first in thy grandmother Lois, and thy mother Eunice; and I am persuaded that in thee also." —2 Timothy 1:5

Read Psalm 71

Grandparents can be a grand blessing to youth. Thirty-five years before I was born, my grandfather and grandmother on one side died from malaria contracted while he was serving in the British army in India. My other grandpa died of a heart attack five years before I was born. But I had a grandma whom I would stay with for several days at a time during holidays and whom I would see at church. She blessed me.

What should youth appreciate about grandparents?

- Their faith. The daily reading tells of an older person's trust (v. 1). Paul encouraged young Timothy to appreciate the genuine faith of Grandma Lois.
- Their prayer life (vv. 2-4). The gray-headed person asked God for deliverance, salvation, and refuge.
- Their gratitude to God (vv. 5-8). The psalmist looked back over the decades. He saw that God had blessed him from his youth as he trusted in God. In fact, from the time of his birth, God had been good. He had much to praise God for all through the day.
- Their steadfastness (vv. 9-16). What an encouragement to youth when their grandparents remain firmly standing on the truth of God's Word, going "in the strength of the Lord GOD."
- Their testimony. The psalmist declared God's "wondrous works" (v. 17). He showed God's strength (v. 18). He said God had done "great things" (v. 19). He praised God's truth (v. 22). He intended to talk about God all day long (v. 24).

How can we show appreciation to godly grandparents?

1. *Show respect.* Proverbs 16:31 says, "The hoary head is a crown of glory, if it be found in the way of righteousness."
2. *Visit and communicate with them.* This is an application of the Golden Rule.
3. *Be helpful.* For example, get up from your chair and offer it to Grandpa. Leviticus 19:32 says, "Thou shalt rise up before the hoary head, and honour the face of the old man, and fear thy God: I am the LORD."
4. *Pray.* Old age brings with it many trials. Grandparents need "foreign aid"—the kind God in heaven sends.

About God: **To Do:**

Food

"Thy words were found, and I did eat them; and thy word was unto me the joy and rejoicing of mine heart: for I am called by thy name, O LORD God of hosts." —Jeremiah 15:16

Read Psalm 119:89-112

A baby without an appetite spells trouble. My wife worked with premature babies in a hospital. She needed to wake them up for feeding, otherwise some would have slept themselves to death.

Friends of ours said they had such a good baby who spent a great deal of time sleeping. Problem was, the child wasn't gaining any weight. The reason: too much sleep and not enough appetite.

Spiritually, a baby Christian needs food. First Peter 2:2 says, "As newborn babes, desire the sincere milk of the word, that ye may grow thereby." The Bible also tells us that maturing Christians should have "meat." Hebrews 5:13-14 refers to the desirability of strong meat rather than only milk. "For every one that useth milk is unskilful in the word of righteousness: for he is a babe. But strong meat belongeth to them that are of full age, even those who by reason of use have their senses exercised to discern both good and evil."

The milk and meat of the Bible can be consumed privately in personal devotions and publicly in worship services. Whether in private or in public, don't neglect "eating" the Scriptures.

Christ is our example. He knew the Scriptures. He memorized many verses. He quoted them. He lived the truth of them.

Children need to eat, but they shouldn't eat just anything—not cleaning solutions, nor lead in paint, nor detergent, nor bottles of aspirin. Children of God need a restricted diet too. Philippians 4:8 tells us what our food for thought should be: "Finally, brethren, whatsoever things are true, whatsoever things are honest, whatsoever things are just, whatsoever things are pure, whatsoever things are lovely, whatsoever things are of good report; if there be any virtue, and if there be any praise, think on these things."

Avoid, therefore, feeding on any words or pictures that present evil as acceptable and good, that imply that a life without God is fulfilling, or that portray sin as having no bad effects.

Nor dare we feed on wrong and injustices done to us. Rather forgive. Don't regurgitate and chew on grievances and hurts.

The Bible is good food for our minds and hearts. It is essential for spiritual growth. Be like Job who said, "I have esteemed the words of his mouth more than my necessary food" (Job 23:12).

About God: **To Do:**

Air

"And he withdrew himself into the wilderness, and prayed." —Luke 5:16

Read Daniel 6:4-24

What word rhymes with *air* and, as a poet said, is "the Christian's vital breath"? Even as oxygen is needed for the body, so prayer is essential for the soul's survival.

Daniel's life teaches us to pray regularly. He chose to spend a night with the lions rather than miss a day of prayer.

Elijah's life teaches us to pray fervently. James 5:17, 18 says, "Elias was a man subject to like passions as we are, and he prayed earnestly that it might not rain: and it rained not on the earth by the space of three years and six months. And he prayed again, and the heaven gave rain, and the earth brought forth her fruit."

The publican teaches us to pray humbly. Unlike the proud Pharisee, "the publican, standing afar off, would not lift up so much as his eyes unto heaven, but smote upon his breast, saying, God be merciful to me a sinner" (Luke 18:13).

Paul's blessing the food on board a ship teaches us to pray openly. "He took bread, and gave thanks to God in presence of them all: and when he had broken it, he began to eat" (Acts 27:35).

David's life teaches us to pray penitently. He said, "Wash me throughly from mine iniquity, and cleanse me from my sin. For I acknowledge my transgressions: and my sin is ever before me" (Psalm 51:2, 3).

To stay alive and grow, we must breathe constantly. We should "pray without ceasing" (1 Thessalonians 5:17). A student said to a godly Bible teacher, "I understand you get up very early in the morning, read your Bible, and pray."

"Oh, yes," said the teacher. "I've been doing that for many years."

"How do you manage to do it? Do you pray about it?" asked the student.

"No," he replied. "*I get up!*"

A person generally doesn't pray about breathing—he just breathes.

Martin Luther wrote, "To be a Christian without prayer is no more possible than to be alive without breathing."

Keep breathing and keep praying.

About God: **To Do:**

May 16

Cleanliness

"Now ye are clean through the word which I have spoken unto you." —John 15:3

Read Leviticus 14:1-20

Hundreds die daily because of unsanitary conditions. Inadequate waste disposal, polluted water, poor hand-washing habits, and the spread of germs make people sick and inhibit growth.

One little boy who was asked to complete the statement, *Cleanliness is next to godliness,* said, "Cleanliness is next to impossible." Perhaps absolute freedom from germs is next to impossible for most of us, but I appreciate our emphasis on cleanliness to promote health.

God's people from the time of the Israelites in the wilderness have emphasized cleanliness. The children of Israel were to wash numerous times, especially when they were suffering from poor health. See Leviticus 14:8, 9, for example. They were commanded to bury their wastes (Deuteronomy 23:12-14). The Israelites were to burn the germ-filled waste of sacrificial animals outside the camp (Leviticus 4:11, 12). This incineration destroyed many infectious agents. There were rules to follow when a person was exposed to dead bodies of people or animals.

The emphasis on sanitation was in stark contrast to the conventional medical "wisdom" of the day. That Moses did not get the excellent guidelines for health from Egyptian education but rather from the Lord is very evident. Take, for instance, a prevailing treatment from Egyptian medical authorities. For embedded splinters, the application of donkey's dung was recommended. Many people with splinters died from lockjaw since dung is loaded with tetanus spores. Other remedies from *Papyrus Ebers,* an Egyptian medical book, include lizards' blood, putrid meat, swine's feet, stinking fat, moisture from pigs' ears, and dung from dogs, cats, and humans.

Although being clean is vitally important for physical health, becoming clean spiritually is even more important. We need to be cleansed from the contamination of sin by the blood of Jesus. Walk in the light; that is, be serious in your walk with God. Then you can stay clean and have the germs of sin removed. As 1 John 1:7 says, "But if we walk in the light, as he is in the light, we have fellowship one with another, and the blood of Jesus Christ his Son cleanseth us from all sin."

Jesus said, "If I wash thee not, thou hast no part with me" (John 13:8). You can be clean by letting Jesus cleanse your heart.

Be clean. It is essential for both physical and spiritual health and growth.

About God:

To Do:

Exercise

"I press toward the mark for the prize of the high calling of God in Christ Jesus." —Philippians 3:14

Read 1 Corinthians 9:24-27

Some people get a lot of exercise in a day. Take, for instance, a man who did an incredible 46,000 push-ups within twenty-four hours. I admire an eighty-two-year-old woman from New Zealand who ran a twenty-six-mile marathon (forty-two kilometers), and did it in eight hours. I'm also impressed by a ninety-eight-year-old man from Greece who ran the marathon in seven and one-half hours.

But what really impresses me is the amount of exercise done by a toddler.

Ever watch a normal little child? Talk about being active—running, climbing, crawling—he is a super-charged bundle of energy. Even a baby with wiggling body, waving arms, and flailing legs gets a tremendous amount of exercise. And exercise is essential for growth of muscles and bones.

The Bible recognizes the benefit of physical exercise. First Timothy 4:8 says, "For bodily exercise profiteth little: but godliness is profitable unto all things, having promise of the life that now is, and of that which is to come." Exercising the body is profitable, although little in comparison with spiritual exercise. Also, it is profitable for only a little (short) while, that is, as long as physical life lasts. But the exercise of godliness is totally (highly) profitable and continues eternally.

What are some spiritual exercises to help a Christian grow? First, run the Christian race. Hebrews 12:1, 2 says, "Let us run with patience [since it is a marathon] the race that is set before us, looking unto Jesus." And nearing the end of the race, Paul writes, "I have finished my course" (2 Timothy 4:7).

Second, exercise yourself in witnessing. Immediately following his conversion, Saul "preached Christ in the synagogues, that he is the Son of God. But Saul increased the more in strength . . . proving that this is very Christ" (Acts 9:20, 22). His witnessing helped to make him a strong and growing Christian.

Third, exercise yourself in resisting the devil. "For we wrestle not against flesh and blood, but against principalities, against powers, against the rulers of the darkness of this world, against spiritual wickedness in high places" (Ephesians 6:12). The young Christian, Timothy, was told to "flee youthful lusts: but follow righteousness, faith, charity, peace, with them that call on the Lord out of a pure heart" (2 Timothy 2:22).

Get physical exercise. But more importantly, get active spiritually.

About God: **To Do:**

Love

"And this I pray, that your love may abound yet more and more in knowledge and in all judgment." —Philippians 1:9

Read 1 John 4:7-21

Is it important for a young child to be held, cuddled, talked to, played with, and shown love?

Babies at an orphanage were divided into two groups. The nurses and caregivers gave each group routine care—food on schedule, diapers changed regularly, and necessary medical care.

But the first group were also given personal loving attention. They were rocked, gently bounced, cuddled—the sorts of things loving parents do.

Before long the second group was having problems. Not only were they experiencing serious emotional maladjustments, but they were also not as healthy physically. In contrast, the first group had bright, sunny personalities and good health.

In one understaffed orphanage where the children got only about ten percent of the affection a mother would normally give, thirty percent of the babies died before they had their first birthday.

Young Christians also need the fellowship and warmth of Christian love. Love in a Christian brotherhood is mutual and reciprocal. We are to "be kindly affectioned one to another with brotherly love" (Romans 12:10). Jesus desires "that ye love one another, as I have loved you" (John 15:12). Paul prayed that the Thessalonians would "increase and abound in love one toward another" (1 Thessalonians 3:12). Peter tells us to "have fervent charity among yourselves" (1 Peter 4:8). John says, "If we love one another, God dwelleth in us, and his love is perfected in us" (1 John 4:12).

If you want to grow, let love show. When God measures your growth, He puts a tape around your heart—not your head. Augustine wrote: "What does love look like? It has the hands to help others. It has the feet to hasten to the poor and needy. It has the eyes to see misery and want. It has the ears to hear the sighs and sorrows of men. That is what love looks like."

About God: **To Do:**

Rest

"And he said, My presence shall go with thee, and I will give thee rest." —Exodus 33:14

Read Hebrews 4:1-11

If a person goes an entire day without sleep, he becomes less energetic and more quick-tempered. After two days without sleep, a person finds it very hard to concentrate, makes many mistakes even at routine tasks, and dozes off. According to researchers, after three days a person has trouble thinking and seeing clearly. He may lose his train of thought in mid-sentence and have hallucinations. A few people have gone for a week and one-half without sleeping, but they acted very strangely and lost touch with reality.

Not only do our bodies need rest, but our souls do also. "Blessed be the LORD, that hath given rest unto his people" (1 Kings 8:56). We are encouraged to "rest in the LORD, and wait patiently for him" (Psalm 37:7). Do you truthfully rest in God, or do you fret and worry? There is no greater security than resting in the Father's arms. Victor Hugo said, "Have courage for the great sorrows of life and patience for the small ones. And when you have finished your daily task, go to sleep in peace. God is awake!"

Christ sets the example. He slept during a storm at sea. He went into dangerous situations among His enemies because He knew the hour hadn't come for them to put Him to death.

Anxiety is like the rust of life, destroying its brightness and weakening its power. A childlike, abiding trust in God is its best prevention and remedy.

Christ offers rest to the sinner who is tired of carrying the load of guilt. "Come unto me, all ye that labour and are heavy laden, and I will give you rest. Take my yoke upon you, and learn of me; for I am meek and lowly in heart: and ye shall find rest unto your souls" (Matthew 11:28, 29).

In contrast, Isaiah 57:20, 21 points out the unrest of the ungodly. "But the wicked are like the troubled sea, when it cannot rest, whose waters cast up mire and dirt. There is no peace, saith my God, to the wicked."

Peace rules the day when Christ rules the heart.

About God: **To Do:**

May 20

Growing in Sunlight

"For God, who commanded the light to shine out of darkness, hath shined in our hearts, to give the light of the knowledge of the glory of God in the face of Jesus Christ." —2 Corinthians 4:6

Read John 9:1-25

Would you like to grow taller? Not only genetics, diet, and health, but also the amount of sunshine apparently causes variations in height.

Scientists in Austria announced in 1998 a connection between the time of year when a person is born and the height that they reach. Scientists looked at the heights attained by over one-half-million Austrian army conscripts over a period of ten years. It appears that babies born in the spring grow taller because of the amount of light and sunshine they experience. A clear link between height and the month of birth followed a pattern that peaked at the beginning of April and fell to its lowest point in October. After eliminating other factors, the Austrian scientists concluded that the time of year had a 4.6 percent influence on their height (a three-inch difference for a six-footer).

Why might sunlight make such a difference? One explanation is that sunlight causes a reaction between a human growth hormone in the pineal gland (located at the back of the skull) and melatonin, which controls the body's day and night rhythms. Sunlight is believed to stimulate the body's production of melatonin.

Light is also vital for spiritual growth. Christ is the Source of light. Therefore come to Jesus, abide in Jesus, and follow Jesus. "Christ shall give thee light" is the promise of Ephesians 5:14. Jesus says, "I am the light of the world" (John 8:12). A relationship with Jesus is the foundation for spiritual growth.

The Bible is another source of light for stimulating growth. If a Christian fails to give himself exposure to the life-giving beams of the Word, he will become sickly and stunted. "For the commandment is a lamp; and the law is light" (Proverbs 6:23). Are you in need of insight and illumination? Expose yourself to the light of God's Word. As Psalm 119:130 says, "The entrance of thy words giveth light; it giveth understanding unto the simple." Are you in need of direction and guidance? Let God's Word beam its life-giving teachings into your experience. As Psalm 119:105 says, "Thy word is a lamp unto my feet, and a light unto my path."

Walk in spiritual sunlight so that you can grow tall, "unto a perfect man, unto the measure of the stature of the fulness of Christ" (Ephesians 4:13).

About God: **To Do:**

God's Call to Go

"Go ye therefore, and teach all nations, baptizing them in the name of the Father, and of the Son, and of the Holy Ghost." —Matthew 28:19

Read Isaiah 6:1-11

Thomas Lambie had been a doctor in Africa. When he returned to America, he was urged by his brother-in-law to stay in America and share in the brother-in-law's prospering medical practice.

One night when Dr. Lambie was very tired, he either dozed off and had a dream, or he had a vision while he was awake. He never knew which. But at that midnight hour, he saw a map of Africa. From the center of the map came a hand and an arm. It was stretched toward him, pleading and beckoning. It was the hideous hand of a leper. Dr. Lambie hesitated. He did not want to grasp that hand, but he could not evade it. And at last he took the hand in his. To his surprise, he found that it was not the hand of a leper, but the hand of Christ, with the print of the nails!

After that dream or vision, Dr. Lambie knew he could not remain in America. He had to return to Africa and continue to give the Gospel to the lost. He had to do the work to which Christ had called him.

If we catch a vision of the need and a vision of the awesomeness of God, we will feel compelled to respond to God. In the daily reading, Isaiah is overwhelmed by the majesty and holiness of God. The King was on the throne. He was high and exalted. The train of His robe filled the temple.

Isaiah's response was one of willingness when God said, "Whom shall I send, and who will go for us?"

Mike enjoyed the farm—especially working with farm machinery. But at age nineteen, he was seriously pondering what the Lord's will for him really was. Should he stay on the farm? He felt burdened about the souls of men and women passing into eternity without Christ as their Saviour. He was really stirred by the message of a missionary from Central America who described the joys and difficulties of being a missionary. One major need was a mechanic to keep trucks and equipment working. Mike knew he had some talent, as well as experience, in working with motors and machinery. The missionary had said that if anyone might be able to fill the need for a mechanic, he should contact the mission board chairman.

What would you do if you were Mike?

About God: **To Do:**

May 22

Christ, the Missionary

"As my Father hath sent me, even so send I you." —John 20:21

Read John 4:27-42

"God had only one Son and He was a missionary," said David Livingstone.

Jesus was a foreign missionary sent from His homeland of heaven to the sin-cursed sphere called earth. "When the fulness of the time was come, God sent forth his Son" (Galatians 4:4).

Jesus was a city missionary. He went to the capital city, Jerusalem, and said, "If any man thirst, let him come unto me, and drink" (John 7:37).

Jesus was a home missionary. In His hometown of Nazareth He identified Himself as their Messiah who had fulfilled Isaiah's messianic prophecy.

Jesus was an itinerant missionary. He went from town to town preaching the Gospel. He even went to Samaria and gave living water to the many who believed on Him in Sychar.

Jesus was a missionary to the poor. He offered them salvation, healed the sick, and opened the eyes of the blind and offered them salvation

Christ was a missionary to the rich; recall His interest and involvement with Zacchaeus.

Even at the cross Christ was a missionary as He provided salvation for the penitent thief.

His last command was the missionary commission, "Go ye therefore, and teach all nations, baptizing them in the name of the Father, and of the Son, and of the Holy Ghost: teaching them to observe all things whatsoever I have commanded you: and, lo, I am with you alway, even unto the end of the world. Amen" (Matthew 28:19, 20).

The first message at the birth of Christ was a missionary message. Luke 2:10 says, "And the angel said unto them, Fear not: for, behold, I bring you good tidings of great joy, which shall be to all people."

The first prayer Christ taught was a missionary prayer. Matthew 6:10 says, "Thy kingdom come."

The first message of the risen Lord was a missionary message. John 20:17 says, "Jesus saith unto her, Touch me not; for I am not yet ascended to my Father: but go to my brethren, and say unto them, I ascend unto my Father, and your Father; and to my God, and your God."

The first command of the risen Lord to His disciples was a missionary message. John 20:21 says, "As my Father hath sent me, even so send I you."

Christ alone can save the world—but He cannot save the world alone; He needs your help.

About God: **To Do:**

Brother Andrew, a Missionary in Palestine and Greece

"Now then we are ambassadors for Christ,
as though God did beseech you by us: we pray you in Christ's stead,
be ye reconciled to God." —2 Corinthians 5:20

Read John 1:29-42

A one-legged schoolteacher from Scotland came to Hudson Taylor to offer himself for service in China.

"Why do you, with only one leg, think of going as a missionary?" asked Taylor.

"I do not see those with two legs going, so I must," replied George Stott.

He was accepted.

Andrew, a disciple of John the Baptist, felt a compulsion to evangelize. When he heard John say about Jesus, "Behold the Lamb of God," Andrew began to follow Jesus. Jesus invited him to the place He was living and he stayed with Jesus for awhile. But soon he went to find his brother, Simon Peter. Excitedly he brought his brother to Jesus. So right away, Brother Andrew was a missionary.

Next we see Andrew introducing a boy with five loaves and two fishes to Jesus. John 6:8, 9 says, "One of his disciples, Andrew, Simon Peter's brother, saith unto him, There is a lad here, which hath five barley loaves, and two small fishes: but what are they among so many?" Jesus then multiplied the food. Andrew and the other disciples distributed it to over 5,000 people. There's enough Bread of Life to supply the whole world, but are there enough volunteers to distribute it?

Next we observe Andrew introducing some Greeks to Christ, who said, "Sir, we would see Jesus" (John 12:21). According to tradition, one of those Greeks was Luke.

Whenever we read of Andrew's life, we see him bringing people to Jesus. What an example for us! There are some who will never know Christ unless you introduce Him to them.

After Christ's Resurrection, Andrew heard Jesus say, "Go ye into all the world, and preach the gospel to every creature" (Mark 16:15). *Martyrs Mirror* informs us that Andrew went "everywhere preaching Christ whereby he converted many to the Christian faith." One of his converts was the wife of the governor of Achaia. So the governor had him crucified. From the cross Andrew still spoke for Jesus. He said, "I thank my Lord Jesus Christ, that He, having used me for a time as an ambassador, now permits me to . . . obtain everlasting grace and mercy."

Be like Andrew. Introduce your brother and sister to Jesus. Introduce friends that you make to Jesus. Let's reach out to a world in need with the Word it needs.

About God: **To Do:**

May 24

Jesus' Example and Exhortation

"Pray ye therefore the Lord of the harvest,
that he will send forth labourers into his harvest." —Matthew 9:38

Read Matthew 10:1-15

How does Jesus' example illustrate missionary effort? Observe Him in this glimpse that Matthew gives. "And Jesus went about all the cities and villages, teaching in their synagogues, and preaching the gospel of the kingdom, and healing every sickness and every disease among the people. But when he saw the multitudes, he was moved with compassion on them, because they fainted, and were scattered abroad, as sheep having no shepherd" (Matthew 9:35, 36).

First, Jesus went. He didn't just wait for people to come to Him. Second, He went to both urban centers (cities) and more rural areas (villages). Third, He saw the need: the multitudes fainting, scattered, and leaderless. Fourth, He didn't ignore their physical or spiritual need. As the Great Teacher, He taught in the usual places, synagogues. As the Great Preacher, He, the King, proclaimed the Good News. As the Great Physician, He found no disease incurable. Fifth, He was motivated by love and compassion.

As recorded in the daily reading, He also gave instructions to those He sent out:

1. Follow the direction of God. God may lead you to a certain individual or group. The disciples were to limit their work to the Jews at this time. Later they were told to witness to the Samaritans and all the world (Acts 1:8). This was God's plan for the spread of the Gospel.
2. They went to the lost (v. 6). Christ, the Good Shepherd, is always interested in the lost sheep.
3. They told the good news of salvation (v. 7). Mark 6:12 adds that they "preached that men should repent."
4. They remembered the physical needs of people (v. 8). The miracles done would confirm what the disciples said.
5. Salvation is free to you (v. 8). Freely and generously give of yourself to help others.
6. They stayed with those who tended to be receptive to the Gospel (v. 11). They were to be satisfied with their accommodation.
7. They were to be courteous and peaceable (vv. 12, 13). Rudeness and the story of redemption do not go together.
8. They were to be realistic (v. 14). Some would accept the message; others would reject. Keep working without discouragement. Jesus' servants can expect to be rejected even as the Servant was "despised and rejected of men."

Christ never told His disciples to stay at home and wait for sinners to come to them.

About God: **To Do:**

When Good Comes From Bad

"And we know that all things work together for good to them that love God, to them who are the called according to his purpose." —Romans 8:28

Read Philippians 1:9-21

William Carey and two of his missionary associates are examples of Christians who trusted the Lord in spite of what appeared to be a terrible setback to their labors. In March of 1812, a devastating fire swept through one of their buildings. They lost a large amount of newly cast type, nearly all of their Indian versions of the Bible, the Bengali dictionary, and much vital equipment. Undismayed, they declared, "God will certainly bring good out of this evil and promote our interest. He will never forsake the work of His own hands." Within months they began to understand why the "disaster" had occurred. When the news of the fire reached England, many people were awakened from their spiritual apathy. Thousands became burdened for the lost and were moved to give sacrificially for the spread of the Gospel. Out of a seeming tragedy was born a new missionary zeal among God's children, and the work in India advanced as never before.

The Apostle Paul also saw good results from adversity. He had desired to be traveling from place to place as a missionary. However, he was imprisoned. But that didn't stop his missionary efforts, and, as shown by the daily reading, the result was a greater boldness to witness.

Paul's prison became a pulpit. Many workers employed by Caesar heard the Gospel. Another thing Paul was happy about was the boldness that other Christians were showing in sharing their faith.

Perhaps you have desired to go to a foreign mission but the door has not opened for you to leave home. Let God use you where you are.

Upon his acceptance for mission work in Africa, a young man and his wife sailed from New York to the dark continent. Before long it was clear that his wife could not tolerate the climate. He was heartbroken, but he prayerfully returned home with the determination to make as much money as possible and use it to spread the kingdom of God. His father, a dentist, had started to make on the side an unfermented wine for the Communion service. The young man took the business over and developed it until it was a prosperous enterprise. His name was "Welch," and his family still manufactures grape juice. He gave literally hundreds of thousands of dollars to the work of missions.

About God: **To Do:**

May 26

Missionaries: Misunderstood and Misused

"Yea, and all that will live godly in Christ Jesus shall suffer persecution." —2 Timothy 3:12

Read Acts 14:7-22

Like the missionary Paul, John Wesley preached the Gospel fearlessly. One cold night in northern England, a mob of miners came pounding on his door, breaking it down. They stripped his clothing from him; they smeared hot tar on him; they pasted feathers to the tar, they dragged him to the edge of town and left him for dead. But, like Paul in the daily reading, he revived. After finding a friend, he cleaned himself up.

Like Paul, he did not give up his missionary message and endeavors. The next morning found John Wesley standing, stiff and sore, on a rock by the side of the road in the chilly dawn as the miners trudged to their dreary jobs. He shouted to them as they passed by. Threats? Angry words? Revengeful denunciations? No! He cried, "To you I come with glad tidings."

At Lystra, Paul and Barnabas brought glad tidings but were severely misunderstood. The miraculous healing of the lame man should have confirmed the Gospel message in the people's minds. Instead, they concluded that God's representatives were gods.

Paul and Barnabas attempted to correct the people's misunderstanding in different ways:

- They showed their disagreement and horror at the idea that they were gods.
- They respectfully addressed them with the term, "Sirs."
- They reproved their idolatrous intentions with the question, "Why do ye these things?"
- They explained they were just ordinary people with like passions, that is, feelings, needs, and nature of men.
- They encouraged the people to turn from idols to serve the living God.
- They declared the goodness of God as shown in nature.

Unfortunately, antagonistic Jews from neighboring cities persuaded the people to stone Paul. Miraculously, he recovered or was resurrected. The mistreatment he received made his message compelling. He said, "Let no man trouble me: for I bear in my body the marks of the Lord Jesus."

Missionary Adoniram Judson, on one occasion, after unspeakable sufferings in a filthy prison, appeared before the king of Burma and asked permission to go to a certain city to preach.

"I am willing for a dozen preachers to go, but not you," was the king's answer. "Not with those hands! My people are not such fools as to take notice of your preaching, but they will take notice of those scarred hands."

About God: **To Do:**

Problems and God's Presence

"Fear not: for I am with thee." —Isaiah 43:5

Read Acts 18:1-17

Cruel tomahawks in hand, the Indians crept toward the tent. As they cautiously peered under the flap, their murderous intentions were forgotten. There, in the center of the tent, they saw a young man on his knees. As he was praying, a rattlesnake crossed his feet and paused in position to strike. But the snake did not strike. Instead, it lowered its deadly fangs and, amazingly, glided out of the tent. The missionary to North American natives, David Brainerd, prayed on.

Sometime later he discovered why the Indians treated him with such respect instead of trying to kill him. Since God had protected him in such a marvelous way from the rattler's attack, they regarded him as a messenger from God.

When God gives His child a work to do, He protects His worker. This truth gave boldness in unfavorable circumstances to missionaries in the past and can encourage us too.

As seen in the daily reading, Paul faced problems. For one thing, in a heathen city, he was isolated from his Christian friends, Silas and Timothy, coming from Macedonia. In addition, he may have been short of funds—at least Paul spent time making tents. And besides these unfavorable circumstances, the Jews were violently opposed to Paul preaching that Jesus was Christ.

But these problems did not stop Paul. He was encouraged by the appearance of Silas and Timothy who may have brought him a gift of money from the Thessalonians. He was encouraged by the chief ruler of the synagogue himself, Crispus, who became a Christian along with his family.

He was also encouraged by the Lord's voice in a vision. What blessed words of cheer to Paul!

1. Do not be afraid. It is less important to die the martyr's death than to live the courageous life.
2. Speak and continue to speak for Jesus. Silence is not always golden: sometimes it is yellow if we fearfully refuse to witness.
3. The Lord restated what He said in Matthew 28:20, "Lo, I am with you alway." This same message which so inspired David Livingstone applies to all believers.
4. No one would be able to hurt Paul, for he was in the haven of God's hands.
5. Paul had or would soon have many brothers and sisters in the Lord right in the wicked city of Corinth.

About God: **To Do:**

Who Is the Holy Spirit?

"And I will pray the Father, and he shall give you another Comforter, that he may abide with you for ever." —John 14:16

Read 1 Corinthians 2:2-16

Roald Amundsen, an explorer from Norway, was the first person to travel to both the South and the North Poles. On one of his trips he took a homing pigeon along. When he arrived at the Pole, he opened the bird's cage and set it free. When the bird arrived back home, Mrs. Amundsen knew her husband was alive and had arrived at his destination. No doubt she was thrilled and joyous.

Before Jesus left, He said He would send the Heavenly Dove to the disciples. When the Holy Spirit descended at Pentecost and remained with the disciples, they were reminded that Jesus had arrived in heaven, and this thought gave them great joy and power.

The dove is a symbol of the Holy Spirit. The Holy Spirit is a person or, perhaps more accurately, a personality. He has emotions. For example, He can feel grief. Ephesians 4:30 says, "And grieve not the holy spirit of God, whereby ye are sealed unto the day of redemption." He feels love. Romans 15:30 says, "Now I beseech you, brethren, for the Lord Jesus Christ's sake, and for the love of the Spirit, that ye strive together with me in your prayers to God for me."

He makes decisions. Concerning gifts, 1 Corinthians 12:11 says, "But all these worketh that one and the selfsame Spirit, dividing to every man severally as he will."

He does what a person does. He leads, He intercedes, He teaches, and He empowers.

The Holy Spirit is God. In Peter's discussion with deceitful Ananias, he says, "Why hath Satan filled thine heart to lie to the Holy Ghost?" (Acts 5:3). In the next verse, Peter says, "Thou hast not lied unto men, but unto God." Clearly, the Holy Spirit is God.

Second Corinthians 3:17 calls Him Lord. "Now the Lord is that Spirit: and where the Spirit of the Lord is, there is liberty."

The Holy Spirit has the attributes of God. He is "the eternal Spirit" (Hebrews 9:14). He is omnipresent (Psalm 139:7-10), and our daily reading shows He has knowledge of the things of God.

Let me conclude this devotional about the Third Person of the Trinity with the beautiful words of 2 Corinthians 13:14: "The grace of the Lord Jesus Christ, and the love of God, and the communion of the Holy Ghost, be with you all. Amen."

About God: **To Do:**

How the Holy Spirit Helps Us

"Likewise the Spirit also helpeth our infirmities: for we know not what we should pray for as we ought: but the Spirit itself maketh intercession for us with groanings which cannot be uttered." —Romans 8:26

Read Acts 2:33-47

Have you heard of the "dove man" who led travelers through the deserts of Saudi Arabia? He never lost his way. How? He carried with him a homing pigeon with a very fine cord attached to one of its legs. When in doubt as to which path to take, he threw the bird into the air. The pigeon quickly strained at the cord to fly in the direction of home, and thus led the guide accurately to his goal.

The Holy Spirit, the Heavenly Dove, will direct us to our destination.

On the day of Pentecost, as the daily reading shows, the Holy Spirit helped in three ways. So it is today.

1. *He convicts.* Verse 37 says, "Now when they heard this, they were pricked in their heart, and said unto Peter and to the rest of the apostles, Men and brethren, what shall we do?" Peter's audience was convinced and convicted of their sin. They saw that they needed help.

   The Holy Spirit works in the sinner prior to conversion to produce a discomfort and a desire. Jesus had explained to His disciples the work of the Holy Spirit. John 16:8, "He will reprove the world of sin, and of righteousness, and of judgment."

   First, the Holy Spirit produces guilt and an awareness of sin. He uses the Spirit-breathed Bible. He uses preaching. He uses the conscience. Second, the Holy Spirit produces knowledge of right and wrong. He points to the only One who was righteous and thus able to provide atonement for sin. The Father's readiness to receive Jesus back to glory is proof that He found in Jesus no defect.

   Third, the Holy Spirit produces fear. For Felix, the thought of judgment to come because of sinful living caused him to tremble. "And as he reasoned of righteousness, temperance, and judgment to come, Felix trembled, and answered, Go thy way for this time" (Acts 24:25).

2. *He converts.* As Peter's audience repented and believed in the name of Jesus, they received the gift of the Holy Spirit (v. 38). What a change—they were converted from rejecting and crucifying to believing and receiving.

3. *He comforts.* The new believers after Pentecost were strengthened and comforted. They had teaching, fellowship, Communion, and prayers (v. 42). They also had joy as they praised God (vv. 46, 47).

About God: **To Do:**

The Spirit of Truth

"But when the Comforter is come, whom I will send unto you from the Father, even the Spirit of truth, which proceedeth from the Father, he shall testify of me." —John 15:26

Read John 14:15-31

Numerous times I have gone to see the Queen of England (and Canada) when she came to visit my area. (Once she looked at me and waved!) Suppose she comes to speak at a local auditorium. The band plays "God Save the Queen." The spotlight follows her steps to the podium. Then the crowd rises, looks up at the spotlight operator and bursts into applause. Instead of praising the Queen, they shower their attention on the person shining the spotlight on the Queen.

This is a bit like those who focus their attention on the Holy Spirit instead of the King of kings, Jesus. Jesus said that "when he, the Spirit of truth, is come, he will guide you into all truth: for he shall not speak of himself; but whatsoever he shall hear, that shall he speak: and he will shew you things to come. He shall glorify me: for he shall receive of mine, and shall shew it unto you" (John 16:13, 14). F. B. Meyer put it this way: "The Holy Spirit glorifies Christ, and when the Holy Ghost works most, you do not think about the Holy Ghost, but you think about our dear Lord."

The Spirit of truth directs attention and glory to the One who said, "I am the Truth." The Holy Spirit also testifies of the truth. John 15:26 says, "But when the Comforter is come, whom I will send unto you from the Father, even the Spirit of truth, which proceedeth from the Father, he shall testify of me."

The Holy Spirit is a teacher of truth. "He shall teach you all things" (John 14:26). In times of stress and persecution, count on the Holy Spirit to teach you what to say. "But when they shall lead you, and deliver you up, take no thought beforehand what ye shall speak, neither do ye premeditate: but whatsoever shall be given you in that hour, that speak ye: for it is not ye that speak, but the Holy Ghost" (Mark 13:11). The normal method of teaching by the Holy Spirit is indicated by 1 Corinthians 2:13: "Which things also we speak, not in the words which man's wisdom teacheth, but which the Holy Ghost teacheth; comparing spiritual things with spiritual."

The Spirit of Truth will also "guide you into all truth" (John 16:13).

About God: **To Do:**

How to Be Filled

"And be not drunk with wine, wherein is excess; but be filled with the Spirit." —Ephesians 5:18

Read Luke 11:1-13

"Be filled with the Spirit" says Ephesians 5:18. How is this done?

1. *Be Christ-centered.* Become a Christian by being born again through repentance and faith. At conversion, the Holy Spirit baptizes us into the body of Christ. First Corinthians 12:13 says, "For by one Spirit are we all baptized into one body, whether we be Jews or Gentiles, whether we be bond or free; and have been all made to drink into one Spirit." As Christians, we want to show our commitment to Jesus in love and discipleship. This takes the work of the Holy Spirit. The baptism of the Spirit means I belong to Christ's body. The filling of the Spirit means my body belongs to Christ.

To be filled with the Spirit means to be controlled by the Spirit.

2. *Be desirous.* Jesus said with reference to conversion and the filling of the Spirit, "If any man thirst, let him come unto me, and drink. He that believeth on me, as the scripture hath said, out of his belly shall flow rivers of living water. (But this spake he of the Spirit, which they that believe on him should receive: for the Holy Ghost was not yet given; because that Jesus was not yet glorified.)" (John 7:37-39). He said, "Blessed are they which do hunger and thirst after righteousness: for they shall be filled" (Matthew 5:6). The Lord says, "For I will pour water upon him that is thirsty, and floods upon the dry ground: I will pour my spirit upon thy seed, and my blessing upon thine offspring" (Isaiah 44:3).

3. *Be emptied of self.* If I want to fill a glass with milk which presently is filled with tomato juice, I will need to empty the glass of the tomato juice. Or, consider a house already occupied. How can another person come in and be in control? When the sin principle controls, how can the Spirit control? We need to invite the Holy Spirit to take control of our "house." This means cleaning out the house of one's life—pride must go, selfish ambition must go, as must bitterness, impurity, envy, and the love of money. The *Holy* Spirit does not dwell amidst *unholiness*.

About God **To Do**

June 1

Results of Being Spirit-Filled

"The Spirit itself beareth witness with our spirit, that we are the children of God." —Romans 8:16

Read Ephesians 5:18-25

A theologian of years gone by, A. J. Gordon, told of going for a walk and looking across a field at a house. He was intrigued by a man pumping furiously with a hand pump. As he watched, the man continued to pump at a tremendous rate; he seemed absolutely tireless, pumping on and on, up and down, without ever slowing in the slightest, much less stopping.

It was an impressive sight, so Gordon decided to have a closer look. As he got closer, he could see it was not a man at the pump, but a wooden figure painted to look like a man. The arm that was pumping so rapidly was hinged at the elbow and the hand was wired to the pump handle. The water was pouring forth, but not because the figure was pumping it. It was an artesian well, and the water was pumping the man!

The Holy Spirit is like that artesian well. He empowers the believer. But the believer needs to keep his hand on the handle. Acts 1:8 says, "But ye shall receive power, after that the Holy Ghost is come upon you: and ye shall be witnesses unto me."

Not only does the Holy Spirit empower, but there are other results of being Spirit-filled. Notice these from the daily reading:

- Self-control. Be not drunk with wine, wherein is excess (v. 18). In contrast to drunkenness, the Spirit's fruit is self-control and a temperate life.
- Joy and singing to the Lord (v. 19). A Hindu once asked a native Christian of India, "What medicine do you put on your face to make it shine so?"

  "I don't put anything on it," said the Christian.

  "Yes, you do. All you Christians do. I've seen shining faces wherever I have met Christians!"

  Then the Christian said, "I will tell you what 'medicine' makes our faces shine—it is the joy in our hearts because Jesus dwells there."
- Gratitude (v. 20). Giving thanks *always* for *all* things is very comprehensive. Instead of grumbling, whining, and being discontented, a Spirit-filled person is filled with thanks.
- Mutual submission (v. 21). This yield sign applies not only while operating a vehicle—it also applies to the house and church.
- Godly home life (vv. 22-25). The quality and depth of a Christian's life will be shown at home.

About God: **To Do:**

Fruit of the Spirit

"For the fruit of the Spirit is in all goodness and righteousness and truth." —Ephesians 5:9

Read Galatians 5:13-26

I love fruit. If I have a choice between cake or fruit, I take fruit. Do you agree with me that the nine best kinds of fruit are apples, grapes, peaches, bananas, pears, nectarines, watermelon, pineapple, and cherries?

There are nine other fruits that are more important. Our daily reading (vv. 22, 23) lists nine spiritual fruit.

- *Love.* This lovely fruit reveals whether you are a genuine Christian. "By this shall all men know that ye are my disciples, if ye have love one to another" (John 13:35). It grows at home, at school, at church, among your neighbors, among the youth group. It is shown to all ages, to all ethnic groups, to both genders, and to friends and enemies. It is impossible for people to hate each other and still love.
- *Joy.* Happiness is based on happenings, but joy is based on Jesus. Jesus said, "These things have I spoken unto you, that my joy might remain in you, and that your joy might be full" (John 15:11). Joy isn't found in SUVs, money, amusements, or the latest electronic inventions on the market. The Christian has received the Lord "with joy of the Holy Ghost" (1 Thessalonians 1:6).
- *Peace.* At conversion, the Christian has peace *with* God. Romans 5:1 says, "Therefore being justified by faith, we have peace with God through our Lord Jesus Christ." The peace *of* God can be ours in daily living as we trust, pray, and obey.
- *Longsuffering.* This will be demonstrated toward a sibling still getting ready while you wait in the car, toward an annoying coworker who whistles too loudly, and toward slow motorists in the left lane. If you have a short fuse, work with God to lengthen it.
- *Gentleness.* This means being kind, reasonable, and gracious. It is a word used by Greek writers to describe an exemplary nurse with a trying patient, or a teacher with a difficult pupil.
- *Goodness.* The words *good* and *God* have the same root. To be good is to be like God.
- *Faithfulness.* There are no shortcuts in the maturing of this fruit. God expects us to be faithful, not famous.
- *Meekness.* This is controlled strength no matter what the circumstances. It is closely linked with humility.
- *Temperance.* This means self-control, moderation, and mastery of one's appetites. We can only have godly self-control if the Spirit has control of us.

About God: **To Do:**

June 3

Grieve Not the Spirit

"And grieve not the holy Spirit of God, whereby ye are sealed unto the day of redemption." —Ephesians 4:30

Read Ephesians 4:1-3, 17-31

Think of how you could cause sorrow to a friend: hitting her with your fists, ignoring her, questioning her motives, giving her verbal blasts, deliberately going against her wishes, or totally ignoring her appeals.

Just as we may grieve an earthly friend, so we may grieve our heavenly Guest, the Holy Spirit. *Grieve* is not a word used when referring to an enemy or a stranger. It is a love word.

In general, a Christian grieves the Spirit by sin. The Third Person of the Trinity is a guest in the body of the believer. He will remain only where He is made to feel welcome.

If we ignore Him, He can hardly feel welcome. Some church members live as though the Holy Spirit doesn't exist. Apart from the doxology at the end of the Sunday morning service, they may give Him no thought from Monday morning to Sunday night. What person appreciates being ignored?

If we go against His leading and impulses, we do not make Him feel welcome. Philip, who was leading a very successful evangelistic campaign in the present day West Bank, was nudged by an angel to go to the desert near the Gaza Strip where he met a traveler from Ethiopia. "Then the Spirit said unto Philip, go near, and join thyself to this chariot" (Acts 8:29). And Philip obeyed.

If we act or speak contrary to the Spirit's written instruction, the Bible, we do not make Him feel welcome. Our daily reading mentions several specific sins that grieve the Holy Spirit:

- Lying (v. 25). The Holy Spirit is the Spirit of Truth, and He is repelled by that which is dishonest and deceitful.
- Anger (v. 26). Don't prolong the angry feelings. Forgive. No matter how long you nurse a grudge, it won't get better.
- Stealing (v. 28). A person on the straight and narrow has no room for crooked dealings.
- Clamor (v. 31). The fruit of the Spirit is peace. Many an argument is sound—and only sound. It will do no good to argue if you are wrong, and if you are right—you don't need to.

About God: **To Do:**

From a Frog to a Prince

"And be not conformed to this world: but be ye transformed by the renewing of your mind, that ye may prove what is that good, and acceptable, and perfect, will of God." —Romans 12:2

Read Mark 9:2-12

"And he was *transfigured* before them." "But we all . . . are *changed* into the same image." "But be ye *transformed.*" Metamorphosis: to change into another form, to transform, to transfigure. Not only does this occur spiritually every day in lives all over the world, but there are also remarkable examples in nature of new creatures coming from old. What creature changes from a "fish" to an amphibian? Of course, the frog. In the spring this miracle occurs thousands of times.

When tadpoles hatch from the egg, they are very hungry. One has described them as an eating-machine. Tadpoles have a set of organs designed for the environment they exist in. With gills for breathing, a long digestive tract curled up inside of them, a two-chambered heart (like a fish's), and mouthparts designed for feeding on vegetative material, they are truly a unique creature.

The change from "fish" to frog is controlled by the release of a single hormone. The window of time needed for this process is very narrow. Considering that this occurs while the creature is still "running around," this process is truly amazing. Remember that a frog breathes with lungs, not gills; has a three-chambered heart; is strictly carnivorous; and has four appendages . . . truly a miracle of design occurs.

As a frog changes its diet, and as its mouth adapts for its new menu, there is a period during which it is unable to eat. How does it survive? If you recall, tadpoles have a large tail and frogs don't—here lies the answer. As the "frog" needs energy, its tail is reabsorbed into its body, and the nutrients from the tail feed the frog until the rest of the needed changes occur.

As we consider God in His infinite creative power, designing a creature with a life-cycle such as the frog's, how can we doubt His ability to metamorphose us into new creatures! By His grace we become princes and princesses as children of the King. Second Corinthians 3:18 says, "But we all, with open face beholding as in a glass the glory of the Lord, are changed into the same image from glory to glory, even as by the Spirit of the Lord."

About God: **To Do:**

Shocking Information

"God hath power to help, and to cast down." —2 Chronicles 25:8

Read Romans 1:1-16

Your parents told you not to play with electricity—especially not when standing in water. The stories of intense agony from the resulting shock has been enough to keep most of us obedient. But what if the electricity is in the water—swimming around? In two South American rivers, the Amazon and Orinoco, there lives a creature called the electric eel. The electric eel is a self-contained battery pack, "cattle prod," electrical guidance system, and stun gun.

Adult electric eels have the capability of generating approximately 500 volts of power in a single discharge—enough to stun or kill most prey. This is equivalent to five times the shock received when you stick your finger into an electrical socket. This would also be enough to cause serious respiratory problems or even cardiac failure in humans.

The electric eel, which has an average length of 1 to 2.5 meters, is a strange, ugly-looking creature that is mostly tail. Contained in this tail is the electricity-generating device that the electric eel depends on: an array of 100,000 discs arranged in horizontal and vertical rows that generate the electric current. This arrangement is similar to a battery. In a battery the current is produced by chemical change, while in the eel the current is produced by the eel's metabolism. The head of the eel has a positive charge, and the tail has a negative charge. When the eel is able to touch its prey, it can complete the circuit, causing a shock. It has also been shown that an eel can send a current without touching its prey, with stories of an eel dropping a horse from 20 feet away!

In the Vancouver Aquarium they have a special display at Christmas with lights that are powered by an electric eel. When the eel discharges current, the lights come on! It is easily understood that the electric eel would not make a good pet, due to its shocking personality. I find it interesting that once again, man, with all his attempts at ingenuity, only copied something that God, the Master Designer, had already made: a self-contained battery.

Much more amazing and significant is the power that comes from God to change a sinner into a saint victorious over sin. As the daily Scripture says, the Gospel is the power of God unto salvation.

About God:

To Do:

A Fruitful Discussion

"Even so every good tree bringeth forth good fruit; but a corrupt tree bringeth forth evil fruit." —Matthew 7:17

Read John 15:1-17

I love the taste of a nice ripe apple—but did God create fruit just to be a flavorful food? My wife and I cannot agree at which stage pears should be eaten: I like them hard and she likes them soft. How does fruit know how to ripen? It's intriguing to see the little miracles that are constantly occurring for our benefit.

For the first question we need to go to Genesis 1:11 to find the answer. It reads as follows: "And God said, Let the earth bring forth grass, the herb yielding seed, and the fruit tree yielding fruit after his kind, whose seed is in itself, upon the earth: and it was so." One reason we have fruit is for the production and distribution of seeds. The Creator, in His ultimate wisdom and design, also saw fit to use this as a method to feed His creation.

If you've ever watched the process of an apple or banana ripening, you've probably wished at some point that there would be a method to speed up or slow down the ripening process.

The process of ripening is actually a deterioration of the cell walls within the fleshy part of the fruit. As enzymes break down the cell walls, juice is produced, causing the fruit to be softer than the "green" original. Take this to the extreme, and you have rotten fruit, devoid of organized cellular structure.

Triggering the ripening of fruit is the natural release of the chemical ethylene. As ethylene produced by the fruit itself accumulates in the air around the fruit, the ripening process begins. As plants continue to ripen, they produce more and more ethylene, causing the ripening process to accelerate. If you confine the fruit within a paper bag, you can significantly speed up this process because the ethylene is contained around the fruit, but oxygen can still enter the bag through the walls of the bag, allowing the rest of the ripening process to continue. Commercial fruit growers are naturally concerned about the amount of ethylene in their warehouses, as this speeds up fruit ripening. Banana growers ship bananas green, and upon arrival "gas" them with ethylene to hasten the ripening.

No one but God could have developed such a complex method for plants to reproduce themselves, yet benefit mankind in the process.

About God: **To Do:**

June 7

The Little Beasties

"God hath spoken once; twice have I heard this; that power belongeth unto God." —Psalm 62:11

Read Romans 1:13-25

In 1676 Antonie van Leeuwenhoek viewed a sample of stagnant pond water and was shocked to find it swarming with what he termed "tiny little beasties." Using a microscope made of small hand-ground lenses, this linen-draper was able to view the creatures we now call protozoa—tiny one-celled animals. Leeuwenhoek went on to discover many new things with his world-famous lenses, but I find these protozoa to be unique!

There are thousands of different one-celled animals, but the little amoeba is the most fascinating. Amoeba can be collected from the bottom soil of many ponds and observed under a microscope. Most famous for their pseudopods (false feet) that seem to grow wherever they wish, these "blobs" are testimony to God's creative nature even in the minute details of unseen nature.

Most amoeba are only microscopic in size, though one species can grow to a whopping 3-5 mm in length. Amoeba move by extending their pseudopods and reorienting their body. The fluid in the pseudopod changes from a liquid to a semi-solid if the pod will be used for anchoring. The quickest way for an amoeba to move is to shape itself like a star with many extensions, and catch the water current and float with it. Amoeba will assume this position if they feel threatened. One scientist estimated that amoeba can move on their own at the astounding pace of 1 mm in five minutes, depending on the species.

Amoebas survive by eating other microorganisms. Their unique chemical sensors detect whether they must act quickly to capture a mobile prey (usually another mobile microorganism), or if they can enjoy a relaxed meal on an immobile alga. As an amoeba prepares to eat its catch, it sends its pseudopods out to engulf and enclose the prey, and then begins to digest it all within this makeshift stomach. When it is finished eating, it will open its pseudopods and expel any of the wastes back into the water.

Truly the Apostle Paul was right when he said, "For the invisible things of him from the creation of the world are clearly seen, being understood by the things that are made, even his eternal power and Godhead; so that they are without excuse" (Romans 1:20). Even the tiny amoeba is testimony to the creative power of God, even though it went unnoticed for several thousand years!

About God: **To Do:**

A Spongy Topic

"And straightway one of them ran, and took a spunge, and filled it with vinegar, and put it on a reed, and gave him to drink." —Matthew 27:48

Read Acts 18:18-28

A preschooler learns so rapidly that he seems to soak everything up like a sponge. This is an interesting cliché, considering where "sponges" originate. When we talk of sponges, we typically think of those multicolored items we buy at the local store, not a living animal found in the depths of the sea.

The only reference recorded in the Bible to a sponge is during the crucifixion, when Jesus called for liquid, and vinegar was provided . . . via a sponge! Sponge fishing was common in Jesus' day, and still is. It involves diving to the floor of the sea and ripping the sponge off the bottom. It is then left to die and decay on shore. When all the living tissue is gone, you are left with the "skeleton" of the sponge. This is washed, dried, and ready for use.

Sponges are spineless, "brainless," organless sessile animals that live on the sea floor. Though they seem to be lacking in many animal-like qualities, they are efficiently designed for their specific application. They have been called poor animals because of their apparent deficiencies, but have thousands of pores that they use for feeding. If you visualize an inverted thimble with porous sides, you can imagine what some sponges look like. Water constantly flows through the tiny pores. Special cells filter out any particles in the water which the sponge uses for food. Sponges can filter out particles as small as bacteria, making a significant contribution to the cleanliness of a reef. Excess water is exhaled through the large opening. Sponges are sensitive to touch and can be seen to close their pores when threatened.

There is one type of sponge in the Mediterranean Sea that is actually carnivorous. Using velcro-like hooks it is capable of snagging shrimp-like crustaceans as they pass by. The sponge then grows over the captured animal within one day, completely enveloping it, and then digesting it for nutrients.

When it comes to spiritual insights, absorb them like a sponge. But don't be stingy; let those good things be wrung out of you so they can bless others!

Be like Apollos who soaked up spiritual knowledge from Aquila and Priscilla. Then he mightily shared the truth with others. For a Christian, two events must always be taking place: something should be happening in us and something should be happening through us.

About God: **To Do:**

June 9

The Head as a Hammer

"God created . . . every winged fowl after his kind: and God saw that it was good." —Genesis 1:21

Read Luke 12:6-24

The rapid-fire sound of a woodpecker resembles a machine gun. No other creature created by God endures quite the cranial abuse as this bird. This lowly head-banger is one of God's powerful instruments in controlling the infestation of insects, and comes specially designed for this role, like no other bird in God's creation.

A woodpecker hammers wood at the incredible rate of 15 to 16 times per second, creating g-forces 250 times greater than that experienced by astronauts during shuttle launches. What protects the bird from irreparable brain damage? God has given woodpeckers several unique design enhancements. The first one is a specially designed beak—specially hardened and chisel-tipped. To handle the sawdust, God gave them a special set of slit-nostrils which are covered by tiny hairs, not unlike the filters we might use to cover our nostrils! A second feature is that, unlike most birds with a beak connected directly to the cranium, the woodpecker has a special sponge-type tissue between the two that acts like a shock absorber, cushioning the blows to the cranium. As of yet, man has never invented a shock absorber close to this quality or reliability. The woodpecker needs his quality shock absorber in order to handle 30,000 blows to the head per day.

God has given the woodpecker a keen sense of hearing. It can actually hear the munching of a larvae beetle inside a tree. Then all it has to do is drill a hole and find the tunnel. But how does it get the larvae out of the tree?

God has designed the woodpecker so that its tongue extends from the beak, back to the rear of its mouth, up and around inside its skull, and anchored in its nostril! Coupled with much longer tongue muscles than other birds, the woodpecker tongue can be sent out of its beak much like a javelin, extending two to three times farther than a normal bird tongue. If that weren't enough, the end of the tongue is a double-barbed spear that has sticky saliva on it. All in all, I'm glad I'm not a beetle larva!

Interestingly, woodpeckers can communicate with each other in their hammering, much like a rapid-fire Morse code.

Jesus said God cares about sparrows (v. 6) and ravens (v. 24). How much more He values you (v. 7)!

About God: **To Do:**

Cool Crystals

"Wash me, and I shall be whiter than snow." —Psalm 51:7

Read Psalm 147

What is small yet powerful, unique yet common, simple yet complex? Arriving in high volumes, these units have the power to grind society to a halt, yet children look forward to its appearance. Sometimes we are held hostage by several million of these tiny little objects. As our daily reading says, "He giveth snow like wool." In His dialogue with Job, God asks the question: "Hast thou entered into the treasures of the snow? or hast thou seen the treasures of the hail?"(Job 38:22)

Whether you watch a graceful snowfall with large, lustrous flakes, or brace against the furor of a blizzard, you can find beauty and design in every snowflake. In 1611 Johann Kepler was the first to publish a scientific paper on the "six-sided" snowflake. In 1665 Robert Hooke viewed and sketched these tiny wonders with the newly developed microscope. But the most prestigious work must go to Michael Bently, an American farmer who photographed over 5,000 snowflakes and eventually published his work in his book, *Snow Crystals.*

The life of a snow crystal begins with a tiny particle of dust on which water vapor condenses to a solid. When water vapor condenses, it creates a hexagonally-shaped crystal structure. As more water vapor condenses on this crystal, it continues to grow. Because the corners of the crystal project into the supersaturated air, they tend to grow faster than the flat sides of the crystal. This begins the six arm-like projections that we typically associate with snowflakes. As the snow crystal continues to move through the cloud, it will enter several temperature and humidity zones which will affect its overall growth and shape. When the snowflake begins to fall, it may combine with other crystals, producing the puff-ball snowflakes you can catch on your tongue. The colder it is, the more likely it is that the crystals will not combine but will fall as smaller units. Though snowflakes can be categorized by common shapes, they are truly unique because one cannot completely predict the conditions under which they will form.

The next time you find yourself wishing for warmer weather and for the snow to stop falling, take a minute to catch a few flakes in your hand to see the treasures they hold. Just as God made each of us unique with our own characteristics, we also can see His fingerprints in the snow.

About God:

To Do:

Ten Commandments for Honoring Parents

"And he that curseth his father, or his mother, shall surely be put to death." —Exodus 21:17

Read Deuteronomy 5:7-21

1. Thou shalt make no mocking, nor disparaging words about thy parents.
2. Thou shalt obey thy parents cheerfully when they say:
   "It's time to get up."
   "Clean your room."
   "Those clothes aren't acceptable—return them to the store."
   "Once per week with one's special friend is often enough."
   "Take out the garbage, please."
3. Thou shalt not take the name of thy parents in vain and spoil their reputation by evil speaking, nor by forging checks, nor by sinful living in a far country, wasting the inheritance of godly example.
4. Remember the kindness they showed in many ways—hugs to make a child feel secure, discipline to make a child well-adjusted, kisses to remove the sting of "ouchies," food to nourish the body, Bible reading to feed the soul, and advice to direct the mind.
5. Honor thy father and thy mother in thy adult years, that when their days may be long upon the rocking chair or the nursing home bed, they may experience thy frequent visits, caring words, and comforting touch.
6. Thou shalt not steal from thy parents. Do not steal their sleep by arriving home late from youth activities, nor health from failing to help with work, nor self-respect by being ashamed of thy father or thy mother.
7. Thou shalt not kill communication by using evasion instead of conversation, shrugs instead of hugs, curtness instead of openness. Rather, foster communication by speaking courteously, listening attentively, writing notes of appreciation, taking them out occasionally to eat, and forgiving rather than reliving offences.
8. Thou shalt not neglect to pray for thy parents. They surely need it! Pray that they would be a godly example. Pray that they would have wisdom to instruct thee. Pray that they will have patience to put up with thy immaturity and shortsightedness.
9. Thou shalt not covet thy neighbor's parents but shalt appreciate thy parents for providing a pleasant home atmosphere, decent clothes, affirming words, needful corrections, and unselfish care.
10. Thou shalt encourage thy parents by words but especially by a godly example of the believer so that their testimony can be, "I have no greater joy than to hear that my children walk in truth" (3 John 4).

About God: **To Do:**

Beatitudes for a Happy Home

"Behold, how good and how pleasant it is for brethren to dwell together in unity!" —Psalm 133:1

Read 1 Kings 1:5-31

Blessed are the family members who humble themselves and help with daily household chores, for their home shall be a foretaste of heaven.

Blessed are the family members who mourn and apologize when they have wronged each other, for they shall find home to be a comfort and a refuge.

Blessed are the family members who do not retaliate with angry words, pouting, unkind actions, or the silent treatment, for they shall live happily on earth.

Blessed are the family members who help each other live righteously, for their home shall be filled with happiness.

Blessed are the family members who show mercy in dealing with the mistakes of others in the home, for they shall be shown consideration and mercy when they err.

Blessed are the family members who enjoy pure thoughts, pure actions, clean speech, and sincere motives, for they shall sense God's presence with them.

Blessed are the family members who control themselves when provoked, help to settle disagreements, and remember that it takes two to quarrel, for they shall be called God's children of peace.

Blessed are the family members who are loyal to each other and to Bible ideals in the face of scorn, a changing moral climate, and the untruths of worldly family psychologists, for such family members have heaven's smile of approval.

About God: **To Do:**

June 13

Do You Rob Your Parents?

"Honour thy father and thy mother, as the LORD thy God hath commanded thee; that thy days may be prolonged, and that it may go well with thee, in the land which the LORD thy God giveth thee." —Deuteronomy 5:16

Read Proverbs 23:9-26

"Why, of course not!" you say. "I don't pilfer cash from my dad's wallet. I don't write checks on his account. I don't even snitch cookies from the jar as I used to. I don't rob my parents."

That's commendable, for the Bible says, "Whoso robbeth his father or his mother, and saith, It is no transgression; the same is the companion of a destroyer" (Proverbs 28:24). There have been cases of teenagers who actually have robbed their parents of money.

But perhaps there are other ways of robbing parents, or removing or depriving them of that which is rightfully theirs. Consider a few possible thefts:

Don't rob your parents of *sleep*. Get home at a reasonable time and stay within your curfew. Many parents have difficulty going to sleep if a son or daughter hasn't come home, because they're so concerned for their child. Others wake up upon the young person's arrival.

Don't rob your parents of *respect*. Being ashamed of your father or mother is disrespectful. "Despise not thy mother when she is old" (Proverbs 23:22). Don't make them feel cheap or uncomfortable by your attitudes or comments when you invite your friends to your home.

Don't rob your parents of *health*. Be sure you don't contribute to poor wellbeing of parents due to overwork. Do your share.

Don't rob your parents of *appreciation*. They deserve your thanks. Express gratitude to them for making meals, providing shelter, giving advice, and granting special privileges. Complaining to parents may steal from them mental calmness and peace of spirit. Have you steered clear of griping? "Why do I have to have parents who are so strict? You never let me do what I want. You're always treating me like a baby."

Don't rob your parents of *self-respect*. Parents of wayward, rebellious, mouthy teenagers may feel crushed and disappointed. Your respect for your parents lets them retain their self-respect.

Don't rob your parents of *fellowship*. Spend time at home. Discuss your struggles. Ask them questions. Share joys and disappointments. Confide in them. Talk with parents a lot. At the family supper table don't serve cold shoulder or pickled tongue or "beefs."

Have you robbed your parents? Seek their forgiveness. Make restitution where possible. And in the future, avoid robbing your parents in any way.

About God: **To Do:**

How to Treat Your Mother

"And he went down with them, and came to Nazareth, and was subject unto them: but his mother kept all these sayings in her heart." —Luke 2:51

Read John 19:13-27

Mary had the perfect son, Jesus. Observe how He treated His mother when He was under tremendous emotional and physical stress. Sometimes teens and older youth excuse their lack of respect and attention to parents by saying they were stressed out. But notice how Jesus related to His mother as He hung on the cross.

First of all, He *saw* His mother. As John 19:25, 26 says, "Now there stood by the cross of Jesus his mother. . . . Jesus therefore saw his mother."

Although Jesus was suffering excruciating pain, although He was hearing insults and taunts from those He was dying to save, although He was bearing the sins of the world, yet He saw His mother and her needs. Perhaps He saw her in the past—being held in her arms, hearing her lullaby, sensing her love and comfort when He was a boy. Perhaps He saw her in the future, bereft of her oldest Son and needing someone to care for her.

Youth, do you see your mom, or are you practically always gone from home? Do you see your mother's needs or are you so preoccupied with work, sports, social activities, or school that you scarcely pay any attention to her? Take a specific lesson from Jesus' example.

Jesus communicated with His mother. "When Jesus therefore saw his mother, and the disciple standing by, whom he loved, he saith unto his mother, Woman, behold thy son!" (John 19:26). Notice that He talked to His mom. Talking to Mom and Dad doesn't seem to be a favorite pastime of many youth. Young person, remember that although you have many exciting things on the go and more exciting people to talk to, don't forget to talk things over with your parents. Tell them what is happening in your life.

Jesus respected His mother. The term "Woman" that He used to address Mary was a term of honor, a term one would use in addressing a person of great distinction. Are your words to your mother clearly respectful?

Not only should our words *to* our mothers be respectful but also *about* our mothers. Terms beginning with the words "the old _____," which are common in the world, wouldn't have come from Christ's mouth and shouldn't come from the mouths of Christian youth.

Jesus—what a Saviour! Jesus—what a son!

About God: **To Do:**

June 15

Honor Her Parents

"Ever follow that which is good." —1 Thessalonians 5:15

Read Philippians 2:1-5

Young man, how you view the father of a girl may hinder the start or progress of a courtship with her.

To illustrate: A man from North Carolina remembers a disconcerting blunder. He had a crush on a high school classmate. While on the bus one afternoon, he noticed a scarecrow with a torn straw hat, ragged overalls, and a faded shirt in the garden near the girl's home. To complete its effectiveness, a hoe rested under its right arm.

"Laura Mae," he said, currying her favor by displaying his wit, "your daddy doesn't have to worry about crows." He pointed. "That's so ugly that it will keep everything away."

Just then the "scarecrow" moved, as Laura Mae's father began to hoe.

Young man, what you think of your girlfriend's father is important. Your attitude toward, words to, and conversation about him may cause you happiness or heartache.

How can a young suitor relate well to a potential father-in-law?

1. *Recognize his position.* Before having a date with a girl, have the approval of her father. After all, he is her father and, as such, carries responsibility for her protection, welfare, and happiness.

Consider some benefits of asking the father's approval. It builds trust. It provides a basis for further communication. It may help a young man to sense accountability to the father. It brings a sense of satisfaction, knowing that parents approve of the courtship.

2. *Respect his person.* Talk to him—respectfully, openly, cordially. Don't ignore him. Get to know him, his views, his personality. Don't have a chip on your shoulder toward him. Don't flatter him either. If he states a curfew, honor it. Listen to his advice and viewpoints. You can learn a lot. Remember: if you marry, in a sense you marry not only the girl, but her family.

3. *Relax in his presence.* If you are conscientious and honorable, you will have nothing to hide. Don't be uptight. If you are ill at ease, he probably will be too, and wonder what's going on.

4. *Remember his power.* Jacob learned that Laban, who became his father-in-law, had plenty of influence both before and after marriage. It is not only courteous but also expedient to seek the best possible relationship with your girlfriend's father.

Don't be scared of your girlfriend's father—and don't view him as a scarecrow either.

About God: **To Do:**

Avoid Explosions at Home

"But now ye also put off all these; anger, wrath, malice, blasphemy, filthy communication out of your mouth." —Colossians 3:8

Read James 1:16-27

A young man microwaved some eggs in their shells for five minutes. While bringing them to the table, six exploded, singeing his face and severely burning his corneas.

You may have heard of other explosions at home in which a pilot light ignites fumes from freshly-spread adhesive glue or vapors from a leaking gas heater. Other devices, ranging from furnaces to barbecues to pressure cookers, may erupt.

Avoid explosions in the home that could cause physical harm to yourself and your parents. The Bible teaches good stewardship of the body. "What? Know ye not that your body is the temple of the Holy Ghost which is in you, which ye have of God, and ye are not your own?" (1 Corinthians 6:19).

But there's another type of explosion in the home that can cause much pain and damage. I'm referring to angry outbursts and temper flare-ups.

In Colossians 3:8 we read of *anger* and *wrath* that are to be put off by Christians. *Anger,* in this passage, refers to an attitude over a period of time, whereas *wrath* refers to sudden outbursts of irritation and rage. *Wrath* is the explosive type of emotion that none of our homes need.

Don't explode at your parents. When disagreeing with them, don't be disagreeable. Talk things over. Listen. Respect. Obey. Take criticism graciously and meekly. Don't yell. Don't slam the door. Don't clam up either. Especially in times of misunderstanding and differences of opinion, follow James 1:19, "Let every man be swift to hear, slow to speak, slow to wrath."

Consider these helps in overcoming wrath. Begin each day with God. Accept circumstances that can't be changed. Avoid pressure-cooker situations by not being overly busy. Pray for the person who makes you angry. Live a balanced life, trying to keep in good physical condition. Forgive those who wrong you. Avoid situations that put you under tension. In everything give thanks. Get enough sleep. If you get angry, confess your wrong to God and make restitution as far as possible to others. Respond to an angry person with a soft answer. Bear the fruit of the Spirit, each of which is incompatible with wrath. Grow up into Christ—*the more you grow up, the less you blow up.*

About God: **To Do:**

June 17

At Home With 1 Corinthians 13

"We should love one another." —1 John 3:11

Read 1 Corinthians 13

Though I win the public speaking contest at school with a speech entitled "Happy Homes" and then go home and gripe because I have to help with dishes and clean up my room, I am become as sounding brass or a tinkling cymbal.

And though in Sunday school I am able to impress my teacher and youth class with my knowledge of the deep mysteries of God, and though I have memorized 1 Corinthians 13 perfectly, and though I have much faith, and have not love at home, I am nothing.

And though I give all my allowance and summer earnings to refugees in Northern Africa, and seek to be truly on fire for God, and yet show at home the characteristics of a snapping turtle, a donkey, and a Rottweiler, it profiteth me nothing.

Love is patient with brothers and sisters, and kind to all; love is not jealous of the accomplishments of other family members; neither does it boast of itself, nor is it conceited.

Love does not misbehave but is courteous, frequently using words such as *Thanks, Please, You first, I'm sorry.* Love is unselfish and does not nab the choicest piece of meat and the biggest slice of watermelon; is not easily provoked nor resentful; does not put mistakes or wrongs of family members on file for future reference.

Love bears Father's rebukes quietly, is always trustful, always cheerful, always enduring.

Love is the greatest—the greatest need, the greatest service, the greatest challenge, and the greatest joy!

About God: **To Do:**

Verbal Encouragement

"Death and life are in the power of the tongue: and they that love it shall eat the fruit thereof." —Proverbs 18:21

Read Acts 11:22-30

I watched some ten-year-olds play softball. I heard one player shout to the batter, "You can do it!" Another would shout, "You can do it!"

Those attitudes reminded me of the Apostle Paul who repeatedly gave encouragement, commendation, and appreciation to his Christian friends. Look at the beginning of each of his epistles.

In contrast, a neighbor of mine would say of her growing son, "He's a bad one." He lived up to her expectations.

An evangelist asked a group of a thousand prison inmates, "How many of you had parents who told you that you would end up in prison some day?" Nearly everyone raised his hand.

Our words can encourage or dishearten. Encouragement means to stimulate and affirm with courage and confidence. Encouragement is something we can do for others day by day. Hebrews 3:13 says, "But exhort [encourage] one another daily, while it is called To day; lest any of you be hardened through the deceitfulness of sin."

How can we speak encouragement?

1. *Give words of appreciation and commendation.* Mention to your parents, your fellow youth, your pastor, your siblings, your fellow-workers something you appreciate about them. Who wants their work and efforts to be taken for granted? Take a lesson from God the Father who said to Jesus, "This is my beloved Son, in whom I am well pleased." Some funerals have a lot of post-mortem praise—of what good is it? Proverbs 12:25 says, "Heaviness in the heart of man maketh it stoop: but a good word maketh it glad."

   A lot more can be accomplished for good by commendation than by negative comments. Possibly the reason we tend to be so negative is that it's easier to throw a rock through a window than to put in a pane of glass.
2. *Give words of understanding.* I still remember phone calls to me in times of stress that showed people understood and cared. What an encouragement Jonathan was to his friend David when Saul was trying to kill him. "And Jonathan Saul's son arose, and went to David into the wood, and strengthened his hand in God. And he said unto him, Fear not: for the hand of Saul my father shall not find thee; and thou shalt be king over Israel" (1 Samuel 23:16, 17).

The daily reading tells of Barnabas' encouragement. Everybody needs encouragement. Everybody can give encouragement.

About God: **To Do:**

June 19

Nonverbal Encouragement

"But Barnabas took him, and brought him to the apostles, and declared unto them how he had seen the Lord in the way, and that he had spoken to him, and how he had preached boldly at Damascus in the name of Jesus." —Acts 9:27

Read Acts 4:32-37

As teenagers, our four children have given my wife and me many complimentary notes and encouraging letters. But the greatest way that they have encouraged us has been by being examples of Christian commitment.

Yesterday's daily reading told of Barnabas' encouraging words. Today's reading tells of his encouraging actions.

What kinds of actions can encourage?

1. *Gifts.* I've received gifts of money—some sizable amounts—and I have no idea who gave them. When my wife and I were at a winter Bible school where I served as a principal, she had a miscarriage. The students rallied and volunteered to take up a collection to help with the hospital expenses. The Apostle Paul was often encouraged by monetary support. Take, for example, his words after the church at Philippi sent him a gift. "But I have all, and abound: I am full, having received of Epaphroditus the things which were sent from you, an odour of a sweet smell, a sacrifice acceptable, wellpleasing to God" (Philippians 4:18).
2. *A smile.* The smile that lights the face will also warm the heart. I have heard that the most powerful thing you can do to win influence over another is to smile at him. It can act as medicine, for "a merry heart [presumably reflected in a smile] doeth good like a medicine" (Proverbs 17:22). Also, "a merry heart maketh a cheerful countenance" (Proverbs 15:13). Sometimes a smile happens in a flash, but the memory of it lasts a lifetime.
3. *A listening ear.* It is so encouraging just to unload to a friend or family member. My mom and dad weren't overly talkative, but they were good listeners. Be "swift to hear" (James 1:19).
4. *Being there.* When Paul was on his way to Rome facing imprisonment and trial, some Christians he didn't even know came to meet him once he landed in Italy, "whom when Paul saw, he thanked God, and took courage" (Acts 28:15).
5. *A touch.* We can give "the right hand of fellowship" (Galatians 2:9). We can put an arm around the shoulder of a person of the same gender. We can give a figurative pat on the back to anyone. After all, a pat on the back, though only a few vertebrae removed from a kick in the pants, is miles ahead in results. I've experienced both.

About God: **To Do:**

Honk If You Love Your Brother

"Give attendance to . . . exhortation." —1 Timothy 4:13

Read Hebrews 3:1-14

You may have seen the bumper sticker, "Honk if you love Jesus." I don't think I've ever followed this particular admonition, but I do favor a figurative honking of a different sort. Our "honking" needs to be like the honking of geese to lend encouragement to others.

Now I've never flown with a flock of geese to see close-range how they perform. But I've often observed the flying formation and heard clearly from our house and yard the loud honking of migrating geese. And I've read about geese. Consider a few lessons from geese that apply to our relation to our family and church family.

One reason geese give the familiar "Honk! Honk! Honk!" is to encourage those at the front to keep up their speed. And they do it daily. Hebrews 3:13 says, "But exhort one another daily."

Another way the geese help each other is by flying in a V-formation. As each bird flaps its long wings, it creates lift for the bird immediately following. In fact, a flock of geese can fly about seventy percent farther than each goose could fly on its own.

Similarly, Christians help each other as we keep the proper order in our homes and congregations and keep in Biblical formation. For example, I Corinthians 14:40 says, "Let all things be done decently and in order." A Christian woman should have her head covered to remind both sexes that "the head of the woman is the man" (I Corinthians 11:3). Children are told, "Obey your parents in the Lord: for this is right" (Ephesians 6:1). And Christians are instructed in Hebrews 13:17, "Obey them that have the rule over you, and submit yourselves." We have a responsibility to "warn them that are unruly" (literally, those who *break rank*) according to 1 Thessalonians 5:14.

The same verse mentions another thing geese teach us: help the weak. When a goose gets sick or is wounded by a hunter and falls out of formation, often two geese leave the formation and follow it down to help and protect it. They stay with it until it is able to fly or until it is dead. Then they launch out on their own or join another formation and try to eventually catch up with their original group. Are you ready to "comfort the feebleminded [fainthearted], support the weak, be patient toward all men"? (1 Thessalonians 5:14).

About God:

To Do:

June 21

More Encouraging Lessons From Geese

"These things speak, and exhort." —Titus 2:15

Read Hebrews 10:19-25

If a goose falls out of formation, it soon feels the drag and resistance of solitary flight and normally is quick to return to proper formation to benefit from the uplifting power of the bird ahead of it. As a Christian, I am helped by traveling with others who are headed the same direction I am. I am blessed by a sense of community, fellowship, and encouragement. That's one reason I believe that membership and keeping rank in a local congregation is vital. If we follow the example of geese, we will stay in formation with those who are headed toward our new home.

Geese also encourage each other by sharing difficult tasks. When the first goose gets tired, he rotates back in the formation and another goose flies in front, where the wind resistance is strongest. It is very helpful when various members in a congregation can serve as a trustee, be a school board member, serve on the hostess committee, be sewing circle president and take on other demanding positions.

Try to "honk" verbal encouragement to others. "Pleasant words are as an honeycomb, sweet to the soul, and health to the bones" (Proverbs 16:24). Encouraging honks have great value and beauty, for "a word fitly spoken is like apples of gold in pictures of silver" (Proverbs 25:11).

- Honk words of appreciation. I remember as a teen the encouragement I received from pastors who expressed appreciation for the spiritual interest of the youth group.
- Honk words of commendation. Take a lesson from the family of the virtuous woman: "Her children arise up, and call her blessed; her husband also, and he praiseth her" (Proverbs 31:28). One employer said, "I have never seen a man who could do real work except under the stimulus of encouragement, enthusiasm, and the approval of the people for whom he is working." God said of Jesus, "This is my beloved Son, in whom I am well pleased" (Matthew 3:17). One female, teenage lawbreaker told a policewoman who had won her confidence, "My mom and dad live like cats and dogs. They never speak encouraging words to me—only abusive, fault-finding words. I tried to go straight but it was hard to do it with no help from my parents."

Honk encouragingly if you love Jesus. It will help you to apply 1 Peter 2:17: "Love the brotherhood."

About God: **To Do:**

Basics in Relating to the Handicapped

"Ye ought to support the weak, and to remember the words of the Lord Jesus, how he said, It is more blessed to give than to receive." —Acts 20:35

Read 2 Samuel 9:1-13

We are all handicapped to some degree—socially, mentally, emotionally, physically, and spiritually. Only in heaven will we experience perfect wholeness.

However, some persons have a significantly greater degree of disability than the general populace. Consider these Scriptural principles as foundational for relating to the handicapped:

1. *Follow the Golden Rule.* "And as ye would that men should do to you, do ye also to them likewise" (Luke 6:31). Place yourself in the handicapped person's moccasins, or wheelchair, or world of emotional insecurities.
2. *Support the weak.* Paul taught it (1 Thessalonians 5:14), and exemplified it (Acts 20:35). Hitler and his philosophical relatives have disposed and do dispose of the weak, but followers of Christ have defended and do defend them.
3. *Recognize all are necessary.* "Much more those members of the body, which seem to be more feeble, are necessary" (1 Corinthians 12:22). For example, some persons with disabilities teach patience by their contented, persevering attitude; others teach patience by presenting the need for it to be demonstrated toward them.
4. *Consider Jesus' exemplary help.* To the blind, crippled, deaf, mute, the emotionally and spiritually disabled, He paid attention; He loved; He healed. First Peter 2:21 points out that Christ left "us an example, that ye should follow his steps."
5. *Remember all are one in Christ.* We could paraphrase Galatians 3:28 to read, "There is neither Jew nor Greek, there is neither bond nor free, there is neither male nor female, there is neither those with disabilities nor those with usual abilities: for ye are all one in Christ Jesus."
6. *Be patient toward all men.* "All" includes the hard of hearing, the stutterers, and the lame. A sign in a Texas country store read, "Be patient. None of us am perfect."
7. *View all of equal worth.* We may well include the mentally handicapped with "the little ones" Jesus teaches us to respect. "Take heed that ye despise not one of these little ones; for I say unto you, That in heaven their angels do always behold the face of my Father which is in heaven" (Matthew 18:10).
8. *Remember Jesus' attitude toward the innocent and weak.* "Suffer the little children to come unto me" (Mark 10:14).
9. *Realize most learning takes place slowly and gradually.* Recognize and praise even small achievements and increments of learning. Especially for the handicapped, progress is made in steps—not leaps.

About God: **To Do:**

June 23

Accepting Others

"He hath made us accepted in the beloved." —Ephesians 1:6

Read Acts 10:34-48

Isn't that a wonderful promise in Ephesians 1:6? Christ is ready to accept us penitent sinners. Should we not accept others? No matter what our religious background or church affiliation, we all need to be born again to enter into the kingdom of heaven (John 3:3). Some church people whose parents were part of a certain denomination (for example, Mennonite) develop a rather exclusive, even condescending attitude toward those who had been of another denomination or had no church affiliation.

To illustrate, here is an imaginary conversation:

"Hello. I don't think I've met you before. What's your name?" said Brother Miller after a Sunday morning service.

"Hi, I'm Chuck Duncan. I'm a visitor from a Mennonite congregation in Massachusetts."

"You said Duncan? Let's see. Is that a Mennonite name?"

"Well, perhaps there are not many Mennonites by that name. But I'm a Mennonite and that's my name so I guess that makes it a Mennonite name." Chuck smiled.

"I see. I suppose you came in from the outside?"

"I was outside of Christ, that's for sure. When I attended an Episcopalian church in my youth, I didn't really know God. Now I'm so glad that He's accepted me into His family."

"I see. Well, I'm glad God saw fit to have you join us Mennonites. I don't suppose you're married?"

"Yes, I am. A few years after joining the Mennonite church, I married a wonderful girl by the name of Martin."

"Really! Your marriage is fairly happy, I hope? Some of my brethren say that it's a rule in their home, 'Don't any of you girls think of dating an outsider.' I've always thought they had a good point. After all, who knows whether or not they will be faithful."

"We thank God for a very happy home," replied Chuck.

"Very good. Well, I want to talk to some other brethren. Someone said the hog prices may be dropping next week. I'd like to check it out with them. Duncan, you said your name is? Isn't that something. I'll have to tell my wife. So long."

That doesn't sound like a very realistic conversation, you say? I hope it doesn't seem familiar to you. I praise God for those who have decided to accept the teachings of the Bible as understood by Mennonite churches. Let us be careful and considerate in our speech and attitudes so as not to offend anyone in the brotherhood.

About God: **To Do:**

Ministering to Our Ministers

"Remember them which have the rule over you, who have spoken unto you the word of God: whose faith follow, considering the end of their conversation." —Hebrews 13:7

Read 1 Thessalonians 5:11-28

We acknowledge that our ordained men have personally helped us a great deal. That's their job, we say. That's what the term *minister* means—help and serve. But how often do we consider that we have a responsibility that's just as great and necessary to help them? "For we are labourers together with God" (1 Corinthians 3:9). The writer to the Hebrews indicates we should "consider one another to provoke unto love and to good works" (Hebrews 10:24). Briefly let us consider how we can aid and minister to our ordained men.

God wanted encouragement to be given to the leader of His people—Joshua. "But charge Joshua, and encourage him, and strengthen him" (Deuteronomy 3:28). Have you ever expressed your appreciation to your spiritual leader for his efforts to aid your spiritual growth? Or have you always thought it would sound too much like flattery? Surely there is quite a difference between flattery and a word of encouragement.

A major way of strengthening our ministry is praying on their behalf. Paul pleaded that the church at Rome would "strive together with me in your prayers to God for me" (Romans 15:30), and declared that the Corinthian church was "also helping together by prayer for us" (2 Corinthians 1:11). Can our ministers sense that we are praying always that utterance may be given unto them, that they may open their mouths boldly to make known the mystery of the gospel?

Another aspect of encouragement is giving them the love and honor their office deserves. "And we beseech you, brethren, to know them which labour among you, and are over you in the Lord, and admonish you; And to esteem them very highly in love for their work's sake" (1 Thessalonians 5:12, 13). Moreover, what greater honor can we give than to take their counsel and "obey them which have the rule over you?" Nor should we neglect to honor them with our liberal giving, for "they which wait at the altar are partakers with the altar" (1 Corinthians 9:13).

One of the best guidelines to follow in our relation to our ministry is the "Golden Rule." Mentally, put yourselves in the shoes of your pastor. Are you treating him as you would like to be treated? May God help us increase our efforts to encourage and minister to our ministers.

About God: **To Do:**

The Feeling of Guilt

"Adam and his wife hid themselves from the presence of the LORD God amongst the trees of the garden." —Genesis 3:8

Read Psalm 51

A man from Tokyo hatched a plan for getting rich. He blindly sent out a thousand form letters to Japan's richest doctors, politicians, business executives, and lawyers—none of whom he knew personally. In the letter he threatened to expose their most intimate secrets. By the time the blackmailer was caught, he had collected five million yen from 130 nervous people who had received his letter.

The topic of guilt is as old as Adam and as current as today. Guilt is a feeling of remorse or responsibility based on one's understanding of right and wrong. A person may experience true guilt (valid guilt because of sin) or false guilt (forgiven by God, but still feeling guilty).

I experienced guilt before I became a Christian. This was the work of the Holy Spirit. John 16:8-11 says, "And when he is come, he will reprove the world of sin, and of righteousness, and of judgment: of sin, because they believe not on me; of righteousness, because I go to my Father, and ye see me no more; of judgment, because the prince of this world is judged." During my life as a Christian I have also felt guilt when I have stumbled and sinned. The Holy Spirit used guilt to help me do something about my sin. Because guilt is unpleasant, it also helps me to live a life of moral responsibility.

Adam and Eve felt guilt. After their sin in the Garden of Eden, they hid themselves. They felt fear. They tried to do something about their guilt by sewing fig leaves together to cover their nakedness. The daily reading shows vividly David's experience of guilt. Achan felt guilt and hid his stolen goods. The magistrates at Philippi felt a guilty fear because they had punished uncondemned Roman citizens.

Guilt is a universal feeling. It is apparent in world religions—it is shown by penance, walking on nails, and sacrifices of atonement. It is apparent in literature like Shakespeare—Lady MacBeth tries to wash the blood of murder from her hands. It is apparent in the twenty-first century: psychiatrists keep busy trying to help people deal with guilt—often by trying to explain it away.

About God: **To Do:**

Unacceptable Ways to Face Guilt

"And as he reasoned of righteousness, temperance, and judgment to come, Felix trembled, and answered, Go thy way for this time; when I have a convenient season, I will call for thee." —Acts 24:25

Read Genesis 42:3-28

Time. A soldier had the choice of killing an enemy soldier or letting him surrender and taking him prisoner. The soldier decided to kill the enemy. This situation occurred more than once. Years later, the marine would often awaken, bathed in perspiration, haunted by the faces of those who had begged for mercy.

My wife and I once counseled a lady who, half a century before, had engaged in inappropriate behavior with a hired man. She had carried the guilt year after year. She finally chose to confess her sin instead of hiding it any longer.

In another case, a seventy-five-year-old was asked, "Do you have any regrets?"

She answered, "Yes, I should have been a better person. Kinder. More tolerant. Sometimes I wake up in the middle of the night and I remember a girlhood friend of mine who had a brain tumor and called me three times to come and see her. I was always too busy, and when she died, I was profoundly ashamed. I still remember that after fifty-six years."

Time often heals grief, but it doesn't heal guilt.

Deeds of mercy. It is common for people to think their good deeds will remove their guilt, but Galatians 2:16 says, "A man is not justified by the works of the law, but by the faith of Jesus Christ."

Distance. Because of guilt some people have moved to a different state or a different city. But guilt has a way of packing her bags too.

The daily reading reveals the guilt that stuck with the ten brothers of Joseph. "They said one to another, We are verily guilty concerning our brother, in that we saw the anguish of his soul, when he besought us, and we would not hear; therefore is this distress come upon us" (v. 21). They carried not only sacks of grain, but also a heavy burden of guilt from twenty years before. Neither time nor distance removed their guilt.

Drink. Many individuals have tried to drown their guilt in a bottle. But alcohol provides only temporary relief, and the guilt returns accompanied by other problems and sorrows.

Drugs. Although not all people on tranquilizers struggle with guilt, for many people, guilt is the root problem. But nothing is a better tranquilizer than a clear conscience.

About God: **To Do:**

June 27

More Unacceptable Ways of Facing Guilt

"When I kept silence, my bones waxed old through my roaring all the day long." —Psalm 32:3

Read 2 Samuel 11:5-27

Concealment. The story is told of a time when Sir Arthur Conan Doyle played a practical joke on twelve of his friends. He sent each of them a telegram that read, "FLEE AT ONCE . . . ALL IS DISCOVERED." Within twenty-four hours, all twelve had left the country.

Many people try to hide their guilt. The devil says, "Play it cool. Don't let any one find out. Cover your tracks."

The U.S. Treasury Department has a "Conscience Fund." It contains money sent by those who cheated Uncle Sam and who want to clear their conscience of unpaid taxes. It started in 1811 when a New York man sent in six dollars after "suffering the most painful pangs of conscience." Now the fund holds millions of dollars.

King David thought he could hide his sin of adultery with Bathsheba. He arranged for her husband to spend time with her. When that didn't work as planned, David arranged for the husband's death. But God knew (v. 27). Some people knew (v. 14). And David's conscience knew.

Noise and activity. Typically, a CD plays to and from work. The radio blares at work. The television provides noise, color, and motion. There are not many hours or even minutes of quietness and silence. Guilt dislikes stillness and silence.

Denial. Many psychologists tell patients, "There's no valid reason for guilt. It's just part of your strict upbringing."

Some people downplay the condemnation and guilt of sin by thinking of all the good things they have done. Or they could say, "What I did is not worse than what another person did."

However, when a person stands before God with sin unforgiven, there will be no excuses or rationalizing. We will have nothing to say.

Quisling was a traitor of Norway. He actively worked for Nazi Germany in World War II. When he was on trial for his life, he was quite sure he would be acquitted. His shrewd defense attorneys successfully ripped to shreds almost all the evidence against him. But then the prosecutor played a recording of the betrayer's voice on a phonograph. As the treacherous speech was heard, Quisling's head bowed lower and lower, for his own ranting voice was lauding Hitler and his perverted form of government. Finally, almost in a whisper, he muttered, "I guess I can no longer deny my guilt; it's my voice that all are hearing."

About God: **To Do:**

How to Have Guilt Removed

"Sirs, what must I do to be saved?" —Acts 16:30

Read Jonah 2, 3

1. *Repent with faith in Christ.* On the day of Pentecost, those who heard Peter's sermon felt very guilty. "They were pricked in their heart, and said unto Peter and to the rest of the apostles, Men and brethren, what shall we do?" (Acts 2:37). Peter told them, "Repent, and be baptized every one of you in the name of Jesus Christ for the remission of sins" (Acts 2:38).

Instead of guilt, there can be peace. "Therefore being justified by faith, we have peace with God through our Lord Jesus Christ" (Romans 5:1). What we each need is a peace conference with the Prince of Peace. The bumper sticker puts it succinctly, "No God, no peace; know God, know peace." You cannot have the peace of God until you know the God of peace.

2. *Confess.* The daily reading tells of Jonah's confession in prayer to God. He admits his wrong. He was then ready to do what God told him to do. The people of Nineveh demonstrated their sorrow for sin by believing God, fasting, crying mightily to God, and turning from evil. First John 1:9 gives a wonderful promise: "If we confess our sins, he is faithful and just to forgive us our sins, and to cleanse us from all unrighteousness." Confess your sins to people, also. As James 5:16 says, "Confess your faults one to another, and pray one for another, that ye may be healed."

3. *Make restitution.* Make things right as far as possible. If you broke a valuable item, saying sorry won't fix it. The prodigal son coupled his confession with a readiness to serve. Zacchaeus wanted to restore fourfold what he had cheated. If you drop a full coffee mug and it breaks on the living room floor, don't just say you are sorry. "Here, let me help clean up the mess. I'll buy you a new mug."

4. *Grasp the reality of God's forgiveness.* If you have met the conditions for the forgiveness of sins, claim His promises that you are saved, cleansed, and forgiven. You can honor God by believing Him rather than doubting Him or, in effect, calling Him a liar.

5. *Live in victory.* Don't follow a pattern of sin or naturally you will feel convicted and guilty. Although you have the potential to sin, you can be victorious by saying yes to God.

About God: **To Do:**

Reasons for False Guilt

"He that hath the Son hath life; and he that hath not the Son of God hath not life." —1 John 5:12

Read 1 John 1:7–2:10

Some individuals feel guilty for no valid reason. For example, an eighteen-year-old Christian didn't feel saved even though it was clear to me that she had met the Biblical conditions for salvation. I explained that our salvation doesn't depend on our feelings but on what Jesus has done and our response to His redemption. We looked at Bible verses with the word *"If"* in regards to assurance of salvation. (See the devotionals about *Assurance of Salvation,* November 5–11.) After she realized that she had met the conditions, she felt peace and joy.

We need to distinguish between guilt feelings and guilt. If we have met the conditions for forgiveness, the guilt is removed. But feelings of guilt and shame and regret may return. We don't need to confess the sin over and over again because the guilt is already gone. We can say, "God has pardoned my sin; I believe it whether I feel pardoned or not." Generally when Christians realize this, they feel peace.

Another reason for false guilt is what some call a supersensitive conscience. For example, you fail to show a kindness to a sibling or classmate when you had the opportunity. Or you told your parents you arrived at church at 9:25 but upon further thought you think it was 9:22, and so you conclude you may be guilty of telling an untruth. There are dozens of other types of tiny blunders or possibilities of weakness that reflect our humanness.

We can be assured that God understands our humanness. "Like as a father pitieth his children, so the LORD pitieth them that fear him. For he knoweth our frame; he remembereth that we are dust" (Psalm 103:13, 14).

Of course, it is essential that we be honest with God, that is, to walk in the light. As we do what pleases God as far as we are aware, and as we confess our sins when we become aware of them, we experience cleansing in God's eyes. First John 1:7 says, "But if we walk in the light, as he is in the light, we have fellowship one with another, and the blood of Jesus Christ his Son cleanseth us from all sin."

Praise God, Christ's blood washes you clean as you mean business with God and as you agree with Him about sin, confess it, and forsake it.

About God: **To Do:**

More Reasons for False Guilt

"But as many as received him, to them gave he power to become the sons of God, even to them that believe on his name." —John 1:12

Read Ephesians 2:1-10

A misinformed conscience can bring on guilt feelings. Let's say, for example, you buy a new camera. At home you notice the price sticker says $499 but your cash register receipt says you were charged only $449. Your conclusion? You paid less than what you should have. You return to the store to make things right. The customer service rep checks and informs you that the camera was on sale and that you paid the correct amount.

I remember a youth at Bible school whose conscience bothered him because he had been taught that the proper posture for bedtime prayer is kneeling. But if you are in the top bunk, it is quite challenging to kneel by it! I told him that although kneeling is a good posture for prayer, it is not the only posture for prayer, and that the posture of the heart is what is really important to God.

A feeling of never measuring up may produce guilt feelings too. Parents who are negative, overly-strict, and critical may produce youth who feel they don't measure up and feel bad about it. They may transfer these feelings of inadequacy and guilt to their relationship with God. Since they were seemingly never able to please their earthly father, they think they will never please the heavenly Father and find emotional rest.

But God doesn't have the failings and weaknesses of parents. We *can* please Him. Take Enoch, for example, "By faith Enoch was translated that he should not see death; and was not found, because God had translated him: for before his translation he had this testimony, that he pleased God" (Hebrews 11:5). We should not forget to do good and share with the needy, "for with such sacrifices God is well pleased" (Hebrews 13:16). By our relationship with Christ we are "accepted in the beloved" (Ephesians 1:6).

Christ loves us, understands us, and accepts us as we accept Him. It is by faith in Christ, not works, that we are saved (Ephesians 2:8, 9). We cannot earn salvation—not by longer devotions, more good deeds, extended fastings, greater generosity, stricter obedience to parents, or more expressions of nonconformity to the world. Salvation and freedom from guilt comes from accepting Christ and then following Him. There are none so good that they can save themselves and none so bad that God cannot save them.

About God: **To Do:**

Facing Regrets

"Let thine hand, I pray thee, O LORD my God, be on me, and on my father's house; but not on thy people, that they should be plagued." —1 Chronicles 21:17

Read Luke 22:31-34, 54-62

Your carelessness causes an accident, and an innocent person receives a permanent injury. A person dies to whom you feel indebted, but you no longer have the opportunity to express your appreciation. A father had intended to play lots of games with his son, to take him to the park, and to read him stories; but somehow the busy father never found much time for those activities—now the son is a teen and isn't much interested in spending time with Dad. An unmarried girl is going to have a baby. The list of possible regrets goes on. "If only I hadn't . . ." is one sort of regret. "If only I would have . . ." is another. Some regrets stem from human error, some from negligence, and others from deliberate disobedience.

The daily reading tells of Peter's remorse and heartache. Take the following lessons from him as you face regrets in your own life:

- Christ intercedes. He said to Peter, "I have prayed for thee." Christ is now at the right hand of the Father interceding for *you*. Romans 8:34 says, "Who is he that condemneth? It is Christ that died, yea rather, that is risen again, who is even at the right hand of God, who also maketh intercession for us."
- Christ understands. He told Peter that before the rooster would crow, Peter would deny Him three times.
- Christ has compassion. He looked at Peter in such a way that Peter wept regretfully. Jesus, after He rose from the dead, made a point of making sure that Peter knew about His resurrection. To the women, the angel said, "Tell his disciples and Peter" (Mark 16:7).
- Christ restores. He expressed confidence in Peter as He told him, "Feed my sheep." Clearly, Christ forgave Peter.

Therefore, as you face regrets, first accept the fact of God's forgiveness. Second, accept the reality of the situation and forgive yourself. Third, accept responsibility to serve the Lord and others—make good use of your time. Fourth, anticipate the future when there will be no sorrow.

The hardest thing may be to "forgive yourself." Focusing on regrets is a waste of energy and mental activity. The Apostle Paul, looking back at his mistakes, said, "Forgetting those things which are behind, and reaching forth unto those things which are before" (Philippians 3:13).

About God: **To Do:**

Jesus' Example of Prayer

"And he withdrew himself into the wilderness, and prayed." —Luke 5:16

Read Luke 22:39-46

Luther said, "As it is the business of tailors to make clothes and cobblers to mend shoes, so it is the business of Christians to pray." Take a few lessons from Jesus' prayer life:

- Christ prayed regularly. He went to the Mount of Olives and Gethsemane "as he was wont" and began to pray (Luke 22:39).
- Christ prayed at various times throughout the day. Sometimes He prayed in the morning (Mark 1:35). He prayed during the day (Matthew 11:25). He prayed in the evening (Mark 6:46, 47). He prayed all night (Luke 6:12).
- Christ prayed before meals. "And Jesus took the loaves; and when he had given thanks, he distributed to the disciples" (John 6:11). He prayed at the Lord's Supper. "And he took bread, and gave thanks, and brake it, and gave unto them" (Luke 22:19).
- Christ prayed in various places. He prayed on a mountain (Matthew 14:23). He prayed in the wilderness (Luke 5:16). He prayed in a park (Mark 14:32). He prayed in a house (Luke 24:30). He prayed on a cross (Luke 23:34). He prayed at a graveside (John 11:41). He prayed when He was baptized (Luke 3:21).

Sometimes Christ prayed with others, but usually He prayed alone. In a certain West African village the native Christians had no privacy for prayer in their huts. So each Christian made off to the bush behind his hut for times of prayer. After a while there was a worn track from the hut to the place of prayer. Then if it ever happened that the track became overgrown from lack of use, another Christian villager would admonish his neighbor, "Brother, there is something wrong with your prayer track."

Adoniram Judson, missionary to Burma, gave good advice about prayer. "Be resolute in prayer. Make any sacrifice to maintain it. Consider that time is short, and that business and company must not be allowed to rob thee of thy God."

About God: **To Do:**

July 3

Types of Prayer

"And Samuel said, Gather all Israel to Mizpeh, and I will pray for you unto the LORD.*"* —1 Samuel 7:5

Read Acts 12:1-19

A missionary in Africa awoke abruptly with a feeling of impending danger. She felt afraid as she gazed out the window. She awoke her husband quietly, and they looked around by the light of the moon shining through their window. Beside their bed they saw a great, deadly cobra with head reared, ready to strike. The man swiftly reached for his rifle and shot the snake through the head before it could inject its venom.

On the other side of the globe in Canada, a friend of the missionaries was sweeping the floor when she felt a strong urge to pray for the missionaries. *They must be in danger,* she thought. She prayed until she felt at peace. She believed God answered her prayer.

Later when the missionaries told her of their frightful experience, she compared the date and time of the two experiences. The peril of the missionaries and her burden to pray for them corresponded to the minute!

Intercession for others is one type of prayer. First Timothy 2:1 mentions three more types of prayer: "I exhort therefore, that, first of all, supplications, prayers, intercessions, and giving of thanks, be made for all men."

1. *Supplications.* These are prayers arising from a specific and urgent need. For example, you might pray for guidance and discernment, for forgiveness, or for help in time of danger.
2. *Prayers.* This is a general term, emphasizing the sacredness of approaching God. It includes worship and adoration, a dependence on and commitment to God, expressions of love to God, and awe when thinking of His attributes.
3. *Intercessions.* An intercession is a petition for others. It is a request offered to a superior, but with an intimacy like that of father and child. For example, you might pray for someone who is ill, for a person in need of guidance, for your Sunday school teacher, for a missionary, or for a lost person.
4. *Thanks.* Our prayers and supplications should be accompanied by thanksgiving. Philippians 4:6 says, "Be careful for nothing; but in every thing by prayer and supplication with thanksgiving let your requests be made known unto God." A thoughtful heart enjoys blessings twice—when they are received and when they are remembered.

About God: **To Do:**

Pray Through the Day

"Pray without ceasing." —1 Thessalonians 5:17

Read 1 Kings 18:21-39

Let's modernize an old story.

"Well, how did you enjoy the ministers' meeting you attended last week?" asked Mary, a young widowed mother, of her pastor and his wife who came to call on her.

"Very interesting. One of the liveliest discussions centered on the Bible command, 'Pray without ceasing.' Different ideas were presented, but no agreement was reached as to how we can actually apply this instruction from 1 Thessalonians 5:17. In fact, I'm to do research and report on what it means and how we can comply with it."

"Really?" said Mary. "It seems to me it is very easy to obey."

"Is that so?" said the pastor, surprised. "How do you understand it? Do you think it is possible to pray all the time?"

"Oh, yes, right through the day."

"But, Mary," the pastor's wife interjected, "how can you as a mother of four young children be praying all the time? You have so many things to do."

"Actually, the more things I have to do, the more I can pray," Mary stated.

"Really! How can that be? All right, tell us how you do it," said the pastor.

"Okay, I'll explain how it works for me," agreed Mary.

"When I first open my eyes I say, 'Thanks, Lord, for this day. Open the eyes of my understanding.'

"As I dress, I pray that I might be clothed with humility, wearing the robe of righteousness. Putting on shoes reminds me to have my feet shod with the preparation of the Gospel of peace.

"As I look at the clock, I pray, 'Help me to be a good steward of my time, redeeming the hours to your glory.'

"As I tiptoe downstairs and flip on the light, I pray, 'Help me to walk in the light.' If I've stumbled into something, I'm reminded to ask, 'Assist me to walk circumspectly.' As I move about doing tasks for my family I pray, 'Help me to walk in love.' "

After a moment of silence, the pastor rose to leave.

"Thanks, Mary. You've given me a lot to think about. I'm going to apply your method with a few adaptations to my rising time tomorrow. I've got an appointment shortly so I must run. But I'm really glad I was able to drop in for a few minutes. We're coming back tomorrow to see how to engage in prayer for the rest of the day."

About God: **To Do:**

Work and Pray

"Praying always with all prayer and supplication in the Spirit."
—Ephesians 6:18

Read 2 Kings 19:1-5, 14-20

"Good morning, Mary," said her pastor. "Yesterday you told us how you pray after waking up and preparing for the day."

"Did you try out some of the ideas?" asked Mary.

"Yes, and it was a blessing. Could you explain how you 'pray without ceasing' from breakfast on?"

"Here are some examples," said Mary. "When I take meat from the freezer, I pray God to preserve me from all evil until the coming of the Lord Jesus Christ. As I'm pouring the milk, I'm reminded of the sincere milk of the Word, and I'll thank God for a particular Bible promise. As I feed my young children, I think of the Scriptures, 'Open thy mouth wide and I will fill it' and I pray, 'Fill my mouth. I'm open to Your truth.'

"When vacuuming, I pray that my heart and life may be purged from all dirt and impurities.

"Whenever I adjust the thermostat, I ask God to make me a thermostat, affecting my environment rather than simply reflecting it as a thermometer.

"Ironing clothes sometimes seems like a thankless task, but it doesn't need to be a prayerless one. I often pray for the person whose clothes I am ironing. Then when I sit at my sewing machine, I pray to be like Dorcas, full of alms-deeds and good works. For stains on clothes I use a spray spot remover, which reminds me to pray for unsaved neighbors and friends. I ask that God's spot remover, the blood of Christ, may be applied to those difficult stains.

"If I'm baking bread, I'm sure you see I have lots to think about spiritually.

"Driving the car prompts several prayer requests. Turning the ignition switch, I pray that God would energize me by the power of the Holy Spirit. 'Steer me, O Lord, in the way I should go,' I ask as I drive along.

"And besides, there are many things throughout the course of the day for which to breathe a word of thanks. Of course, you understand that my prayer varies somewhat depending on the activities and duties of the day."

"Yes, I see," returned the pastor. "Well, Mary, I want to commend you for an active prayer life and thanks, too, for what you've shared. You really have me thinking about how I can apply your approach to my day's activities."

About God: **To Do:**

Hindrances to Prayer

"When ye make many prayers, I will not hear: your hands are full of blood. Wash you, make you clean; put away the evil of your doings from before mine eyes; cease to do evil." —Isaiah 1:15, 16

Read Psalm 66

When the people of Israel prayed, God didn't hear or answer their prayer. Why? "Your iniquities have separated between you and your God, and your sins have hid his face from you, that he will not hear" (Isaiah 59:2).

Clearly, *sin* is a great hindrance to answered prayer. As the daily reading points out (v. 18), if I practice sin, God won't answer prayer, even though my prayer is beautiful and eloquent. Sin cuts the line of communication. For example, when sinful Saul was being threatened by the Philistine army, he was very afraid and wanted guidance from God. "And when Saul enquired of the LORD, the LORD answered him not" (1 Samuel 28:6). Saul, instead of repenting, went deeper into sin and communicated with the familiar spirit at Endor. Instead of giving up sinning, he gave up praying.

Second, *selfishness* is a hindrance. James 4:3 says, "Ye ask, and receive not, because ye ask amiss, that ye may consume it upon your lusts." If we ask with the wrong spirit, or selfish motive, we won't receive. This doesn't mean we shouldn't ask for personal needs—health, food, finances. But remember that the chief purpose of prayer is to glorify God and advance His kingdom. There's a difference between asking God for a new job that offers more prestige and more pay, and asking God for a better work environment with more witnessing opportunities.

Often our prayers show mixed motives or a veiled concern for others. Like the girl who reportedly prayed, "Lord, please send my mother a fine son-in-law."

Third, *stinginess* hinders prayer. Proverbs 21:13 says, "Whoso stoppeth his ears at the cry of the poor, he also shall cry himself, but shall not be heard." A lack of love and generosity in the face of poverty acts as earplugs for the Lord.

In contrast 1 John 3:22 says, "And whatsoever we ask, we receive of him, because we keep his commandments, and do those things that are pleasing in his sight." This is in the context of helpfulness, of seeing a person in need of food and the necessities of life, and having compassion. George Mueller was a mighty man of prayer, but he was also a generous man of giving. What he received of God never stuck to his fingers. A Christian shows what he is by what he does with what he has.

About God: **To Do:**

More Hindrances to Prayer

"Continue in prayer, and watch in the same with thanksgiving."
—Colossians 4:2

Read James 1:1-17

- *Lack of forgiveness.* "When ye stand praying, forgive" (Mark 11:25). Forgiveness is a prerequisite for answered prayer. If you remember that you're not at peace with someone because you have done them wrong, go and make things right before your time of prayer. Jesus said, "Therefore if thou bring thy gift to the altar, and there rememberest that thy brother hath ought against thee; leave there thy gift before the altar, and go thy way; first be reconciled to thy brother, and then come and offer thy gift" (Matthew 5:23, 24). Someone put it this way, "All heaven listens when we send up a heartfelt prayer for our enemy's good."
- *Lack of family love.* There is a connection between harmony in the home and the effectiveness of prayer. A husband should show honor to his wife, viewing her as a partner "of the grace of life; that your prayers be not hindered" (1 Peter 3:7). If you use sarcasm, the silent treatment, or angry outbursts, don't be surprised if your prayers are hindered.
- *Lack of faith.* James 1:5-7 encourages praying for wisdom, "But let him ask in faith, nothing wavering." Pray in faith—if a friend gave you a check, would you wait until you cashed it to thank him? "When ye pray, believe that ye receive them, and ye shall have them" (Mark 11:24). So if you pray for rain, don't forget your umbrella.
- *Lack of understanding.* James and John did not understand God's will as they made a request of Jesus. Jesus told them, "Ye know not what ye ask."

  We aim to pray according to God's will. "And this is the confidence that we have in him, that, if we ask any thing according to his will, he heareth us: and if we know that he hear us, whatsoever we ask, we know that we have the petitions that we desired of him" (1 John 5:14, 15). Nothing lies outside the reach of prayer except that which lies outside the will of God.
- *Lack of persistence.* As Luke 18:1-8 shows, we need to persevere in prayer. The church at Jerusalem knew the power of prayer when Peter was imprisoned. "Prayer was made without ceasing of the church unto God for him" (Acts 12:5). An angel brought Peter out of prison, but it was prayer that brought the angel.

About God: **To Do:**

Four Prayer Requests

"Call unto me, and I will answer thee, and shew thee great and mighty things, which thou knowest not." —Jeremiah 33:3

Read Ephesians 3:13-21

A pastor visited an invalid confined to a wheelchair. "You are a great inspiration to me and to many others!" he said. "You're always cheerful and dynamic, though your body is often racked with pain and your limbs almost useless. How are you so contagiously cheerful?"

"I have a phone number which I constantly use!" she replied.

"A phone number?" asked the pastor. "What is it?"

The invalid replied, "It is Jeremiah 33:3."

The Apostle Paul used God's "phone number" a lot. The daily reading tells of one of his prayers made upon his knees that included four requests.

A lot of kneeling keeps a person in good standing, although it probably wasn't very convenient for a prisoner chained to a Roman guard. Kneeling for prayer is appropriate in view of the majesty and holiness of God and because an attitude of submission should accompany prayer.

Paul gives four requests, each beginning with *that*:

1. That you be strengthened by the Spirit. Not strengthened in biceps or calf muscles but *in the inner man.* Such strength is needed to resist temptation.
2. That Christ dwell in your heart. This indwelling by faith is linked to obedience. As 1 John 3:24 says, "And he that keepeth his commandments dwelleth in him, and he in him."
3. That you be rooted and grounded in love: rooted like a tree, grounded like a building on a solid foundation. Such divine love has four "dimensions": breadth, including all ages, nations, and ranks; length, from everlasting to everlasting; depth, stooping to the lowest gutter; height, rising to glory and heavenly happiness.
4. That you be filled with the fullness of God. Be open to God who wants to fill your life with blessings.

About God: **To Do:**

Value of Friends

"Iron sharpeneth iron; so a man sharpeneth the countenance of his friend." —Proverbs 27:17

Read 1 Samuel 18:28–19:7

Are you a billionaire? Our greatest wealth is not measured in terms of riches but relationships. In this sense I'm a billionaire—I estimate I have well over a thousand good friends—not that many are close friends, but they are good friends. But my greatest wealth in relationships comes from the Friend of sinners—Jesus Christ.

A friend is valuable in various ways. "Two are better than one; because they have a good reward for their labour. For if they fall, the one will lift up his fellow: but woe to him that is alone when he falleth; for he hath not another to help him up. Again, if two lie together, then they have heat: but how can one be warm alone? And if one prevail against him, two shall withstand him; and a threefold cord is not quickly broken" (Ecclesiastes 4:9-12).

First, two can do work together that an individual would find almost impossible to do (for example, moving a heavy object). Second, if one person falls into a pit, the other can help him out (this is true spiritually as well as physically). Third, two can generate heat in cold situations. Fourth, in an enemy attack, two can defeat what one could not. Fifth, the intertwining of hearts makes a person strong in the tensions and stresses of life.

The life of David shows the value of a friend. The daily reading shows the delight, assistance, support, and commendation of his friend Jonathan. Jonathan illustrates the idea that a friend is a person who goes around saying nice things behind your back (vv. 4, 5).

"Friendship doubles joys and halves griefs," said Francis Bacon centuries ago. Friends act as shock absorbers as we travel over the bumps of life's road.

A friend can stimulate good ideas, improve conduct, and deepen commitment to God like iron sharpens iron. The best kinds of friends don't sympathize with your weakness—they summon your strength.

A true friend warms you by his presence, trusts you with his confidence, speaks the truth even if it offends you, remembers you in his prayers, and walks in when the rest of the world walks out. Genuine friendship is like good health—its value is not understood until it is lost.

About God: **To Do:**

Foundations for Friendship

"Look not every man on his own things,
but every man also on the things of others." —Philippians 2:4

Read Philippians 2:17-30

A new homeowner's riding mower had broken down, and he had been working fruitlessly for two hours trying to get it back together. Suddenly, one of his neighbors appeared with a handful of tools. "Can I give some help?" he asked. In twenty minutes he had the mower functioning beautifully.

"Thanks a million," the now-happy newcomer said. "And say, what do you make with such fine tools?"

"Mostly friends," the neighbor smiled. "I'm available any time."

The good Samaritan demonstrated this formation of friendship in a very caring way. See Luke 10:30-37. We are on the wrong track when we think of friendship as something to get rather than something to give.

Both Timothy and Epaphroditis, who received Paul's words of commendation in the daily reading, were unselfish to the point of risking their lives.

A little boy and girl were riding a hobbyhorse. The boy said, "If one of us would just get off the horse, there would be more room for me."

A second foundation is respect. "Be kindly affectioned one to another with brotherly love; in honour preferring one another" (Romans 12:10). Treat your friends like family and your family like friends. To all "be courteous" (1 Peter 3:8). It's wise to pick your friends—but not to pieces.

The Golden Rule has a lot of applications to friendship. People who can hold their tongues rarely have any trouble holding their friends. If you were another person, would you like to be a friend of yours?

A third foundation is humility. How you think about yourself definitely affects how you relate to others. It is important to think soberly (Romans 12:3), not more highly or more lowly than you ought to think. First Peter 5:5 says, "Likewise, ye younger, submit yourselves unto the elder. Yea, all of you be subject one to another, and be clothed with humility: for God resisteth the proud, and giveth grace to the humble." It is good to hold your head up, but keep your nose on a friendly level. Don't boast. "Let another man praise thee, and not thine own mouth; a stranger, and not thine own lips" (Proverbs 27:2). You don't have to be a physician to understand that pride is the only disease that makes everyone sick except the one who has it.

About God: **To Do:**

July 11

Turning Strangers Into Friends

"A man that hath friends must shew himself friendly." —Proverbs 18:24

Read Ruth 2:1-17

A husband and wife were usually not very neighborly, but when they saw a moving van in front of the house across the street, they decided to change their ways. She prepared some homemade bread and together she and her husband approached the house. When someone answered the front door, she said, "Hi. We wanted to welcome you to our neighborhood. Here's some bread for you."

The woman who answered the door said, "Thank you very much for your kindness. Uh . . . this is kind of embarrassing. You see, we're not moving in. We're moving out. We've lived here eight years."

The husband and wife had a good idea, but it was a little too late. We should remember that each stranger is a potential close friend. How many friends can you name who were not strangers at one time?

The encounter of two strangers, Boaz and Ruth, described in the daily reading, illustrate some pointers for making friends:

- Say hello (or the equivalent) to the people you meet (v. 4).
- Notice people you don't know (v. 5). (However, staring at strangers is not a good way of getting to know them.)
- Use polite words. "I pray you" (v. 7) is the equivalent of "please." *Please* acknowledges the thoughtfulness of the other person. *Pardon me* recognizes the dignity of the other. *Thank you* expresses gratitude for the person's kindness. *You first* implies the worth of the other.
- Demonstrate appropriate social graces. Ruth lowered herself to the ground (v. 10). In our culture, shake hands, open the door for the other, and wait for the hostess to seat you.
- Offer a helping hand. Boaz told Ruth to help herself to the food (v. 14).
- Do deliberate acts of kindness. Boaz instructed his reapers to leave "handfuls of purpose" so that Ruth would have easy gleaning (v. 16).

The only way to have a friend is to be one. William Penn said, "A true friend advises justly, assists readily, adventures boldly, takes all patiently, defends courageously, and continues a friend unchangeable."

About God: **To Do:**

Friendliness Toward Strangers

"I was a stranger, and ye took me in." —Matthew 25:35

Read Leviticus 19:9-18, 33-37

When you meet a stranger, say *Hello, Hi, Good morning,* or the equivalent. Then introduce yourself. I say, "Hello, I'm Howard. What is your name?" Give a firm handshake—not a hand that flops like a dead fish, nor a death grip. Don't forget to take the right vitamin. I've observed that the best vitamin for developing a friendship is B1.

As the daily reading says, the people of God should show good attitudes toward strangers (v. 10). Make it easy for them. Be fair (v. 15). Don't vex them (v. 33). Love them (v. 34).

The Old Testament Law emphasizes consideration for strangers. Exodus 22:21 gives a reason. "Thou shalt neither vex a stranger, nor oppress him: for ye were strangers in the land of Egypt." If you remember being a stranger in a social context, you understand. The Israelites were told to refrain from making unfair rules for strangers: "Ye shall have one manner of law, as well for the stranger, as for one of your own country" (Leviticus 24:22). In fact, on the positive side, they were to show love, providing them with the necessities of life. "He doth execute the judgment of the fatherless and widow, and loveth the stranger, in giving him food and raiment. Love ye therefore the stranger" (Deuteronomy 10:18, 19).

Of course, caution should be used with a stranger if you are in a dangerous part of a city, alone, a female, or a child. But under normal circumstances in our community we should not vex the stranger but help, be fair, and show love.

Jesus befriended and helped many strangers. He said that welcoming and assisting a stranger is like taking Him in. The New Testament believers were repeatedly told to show hospitality. At the time of the early church, this referred primarily to traveling strangers who needed food and lodging. The natives of the island of Melita set a good example. "And the barbarous people shewed us no little kindness: for they kindled a fire, and received us every one, because of the present rain, and because of the cold" (Acts 28:2).

Athenagoras, in describing the early Christians (175 A.D.) wrote, "When they see a stranger, they take him into their homes, and they rejoice over him as a very brother. For they do not call themselves brothers after the flesh, but brothers after the spirit and in God."

About God: **To Do:**

July 13

Getting Acquainted With Friends

"The soul of Jonathan was knit with the soul of David, and Jonathan loved him as his own soul." —1 Samuel 18:1

Read Genesis 18:1-15

I've watched older children with someone they don't know. They just stand there, say nothing, and feel awkward. It's much better to start talking—even if it's only about the weather. It helps to relax the atmosphere. Don't be nosy or rude, but do ask appropriate questions. Show interest in what you think the other person is interested in. Don't talk only about yourself. The best way to form a friendship is to become interested in other people, not by trying to interest people in you.

In the daily reading Abram gives us a good example. He saw the visitors and eagerly welcomed them. He spoke courteously and made them comfortable.

Smile at the other person—it takes seventy-two muscles to frown but only fourteen to smile. Be relaxed with the other person and try to make him feel relaxed. If possible, give a compliment or at least set a non-threatening tone. Use humor if it is not forced or artificial.

Refrain from personal remarks such as, "How did you get that big scar? Your nose reminds me of a rhino. Doesn't it bother you to be getting bald so young?" Generally don't comment about an unusual name although you may think of a way to remember the name. For example, you may think, *His name is Bean—and he looks tall and skinny like a beanstalk.* Or, *he looks just the opposite of a tall and skinny bean.* Or, *he's wearing a navy shirt—I'll think of him as a navy bean.* (Although the next day he may be a brown bean, a white bean, a black bean, or a green bean.) But while you may think of unusual, even rude ways of remembering a name, don't remark about it to the person—unless it is complimentary: "You say your name is Rose. I think I'll be able to remember that—you are beautiful like a rose."

"A man that hath friends must shew himself friendly" (Proverbs 18:24). A friend is a present you give yourself by being friendly.

Even an enemy can become a friend. Abraham Lincoln was once taken to task by an associate for his attitude toward his enemies, "Why do you try to make friends of them? You should try to destroy them."

Lincoln replied gently, "Am I not destroying my enemies when I make them my friends?"

About God: **To Do:**

Avoiding Mistakes

"He that blesseth his friend with a loud voice, rising early in the morning, it shall be counted a curse to him." —Proverbs 27:14

Read Job 19:13-27

If you feel somewhat lonely and wish you had more friends, ask yourself the following questions:

- Do I prejudge people? Try to associate with those much older and younger than you. Some youth consider it to be unthinkable to be friends with more than one's own age group. I have wonderful friends who are twenty years older than me (as well as younger). Don't shy away from making friends of those of other races and ethnic backgrounds. Jesus made friends of those who were Roman, Samaritan, Syrophenician, Canaanite, and Jewish.
- Do I go by negative first impressions? First impressions are not necessarily right. Often a person is like a book—the cover isn't much to look at, but the interior is wonderful.

  Said a daughter, "Carolyn is really nice."

  Mother replied, "I thought you said she and her sister were real snobs."

  "Oh, that was before I got to know them."
- Do I make efforts to communicate? If you find someone who is shy, lonely, and withdrawn, engage the person in conversation. Help the person emerge from his shell and you will often have a good friend. Jesus could have silently waited by the well at Sychar, but instead He began to ask questions and visit with the woman at the well.
- Do I consider some people to be unworthy of my friendship? Don't reject people because of physical disabilities or economic class.
- Do I fail to listen to others? You can win more friends with your ears than with your mouth.
- Am I overly shy? Shyness can arise from not wanting to be hurt. Becoming a friend makes you vulnerable, but it's worth it.
- Do I have a critical spirit? According to the daily reading, Job's friends were uncaring and critical to the point that Job felt persecuted. Job needed to plead for pity from them. If you are constantly trying to correct your friends, you're not a friend—you're a critic.

About God: **To Do:**

July 15

Ten Rules for Deepening Friendships

"A talebearer revealeth secrets: but he that is of a faithful spirit concealeth the matter." —Proverbs 11:13

Read Romans 16:1-27

1. Be sincere. Don't flatter. Don't manipulate. Paul did not flatter his Thessalonian friends (1 Thessalonians 2:5).
2. Be open and accepting. Don't write off a friend when he makes a mistake. Real friends are those who, when you make a fool of yourself, don't think you've done a permanent job.
3. Listen. "Be swift to hear, slow to speak" (James 1:19). A white leader met with a chief of the First Nations. The white leader asked several questions but got no immediate answer. Another native explained to him, "That is what we call Indian time. He has enough respect for your questions to go away and think about them before answering." A friend is someone who listens attentively while you say "nothing."
4. Keep confidences. "Confidence in an unfaithful man in time of trouble is like a broken tooth, and a foot out of joint" (Proverbs 25:19).
5. Apologize and make things right. Confession can heal relationships (James 5:16). And every man should keep a cemetery in which to bury the faults of his friends.
6. Be there in a time of need. Onesiphorus visited Paul as a true friend. Paul tells about him. "The Lord give mercy unto the house of Onesiphorus; for he oft refreshed me, and was not ashamed of my chain: but, when he was in Rome, he sought me out very diligently, and found me. The Lord grant unto him that he may find mercy of the Lord in that day: and in how many things he ministered unto me at Ephesus, thou knowest very well" (2 Timothy 1:16-18). Truly a friend is one who is there to care.
7. Show appreciation. Don't take your friend's kindnesses for granted. As you read about literally dozens of Paul's friends named in Romans 16, you get a sense of Paul's appreciation.
8. Keep in touch. That's what Paul did as he wrote epistles. As you look over the daily reading, notice the many friends that Paul calls by name. How many friends does he mention in the passage?
9. Don't use friends. Judas tried this for financial advantage. Consider this advice: before borrowing from a friend, decide which you need more.
10. Avoid careless talk. The way to have friends is to be willing to lose some arguments.

About God: **To Do:**

Witness by Forgiveness

"Be not overcome of evil, but overcome evil with good." —Romans 12:21

Read Acts 6:8–7:2, 54-60

Once a young Armenian girl and her brother were attacked by Turks. She escaped by climbing over a wall, but not before her brother was brutally murdered before her eyes. Later on, when she was working as a nurse in the hospital, she recognized one of her patients as the very Turkish soldier who had murdered her brother. Her first feeling was revenge. He was very ill, just hovering between life and death. The slightest neglect and he would die. No one would know. His life was absolutely in her hands. But instead of revenge, she decided for Christ's sake to forgive him. She fought for his life and won, nursing him back to health.

When he was convalescing, she told him who she was. The Turkish soldier looked at her in astonishment and said, "Then why didn't you let me die when you had me in your power?"

"I couldn't," answered the girl. "I just couldn't, for I am a Christian and my own Master forgave me for His sake."

"Well," said the hardened Turk in astonishment, "if that is what it means to be a Christian, I want to be one."

You can do what that Armenian girl did. You can forgive for Christ's sake. No matter how bitterly wronged you may have been, nevertheless, for His sake you can forgive the wrong and have only goodwill toward those who have wronged you. It isn't easy, but it can be done with His help.

In less than five years, George Blaurock, a brave Anabaptist leader, baptized over one thousand new Christians. He was fiercely persecuted and imprisoned by the authorities. From prison he wrote, "The hour of the last day, to which we all must come, is at hand. Dear Lord, help us to bear the cross to the destined place, and turn Thyself to us with all grace, that we may commend our spirit into Thy hands. I sincerely pray Thee for all our enemies, O Lord, however many there may be; do not lay their sins to their charge; Lord, I entreat this according to Thy will."

Forgiveness for Christ's sake leaves a powerful witness for Christ.

About God: **To Do:**

July 17

Living Loyal Letters

"Ye are our epistle written in our hearts,
known and read of all men." —2 Corinthians 3:2

Read 2 Corinthians 3:1-18

A Christian is a special type of letter. Perhaps you have never viewed yourself as an epistle or letter, but the Bible says, "Ye are manifestly declared to be the epistle of Christ" (2 Corinthians 3:3). Some letters on my desk prompted me to ponder the nature of such a letter.

AUTHOR: The writer, type of "writing paper," and the kind (style) of penmanship is shown by 2 Corinthians 3:3, which says we are "written not with ink, but with the Spirit of the living God; not in tables of stone, but in fleshy tables of the heart."

READERS: The "letters of Christ" at Corinth were "known and read of all men." We may be largely ignorant of the extent to which our lives are read by neighbors, police, government officials, unsaved friends, and the general public. A letter is indeed confusing if it contains contradictions; our lives should be free of them.

PARTS:

(a) *Heading:* Our eternal address is the golden streets of heaven. We must be registered at that wonderful address while on this earthly pilgrimage.

(b) *Salutation:* As ambassadors of Christ, we are addressed to the spiritual needs of those who read us.

(c) *Body:* The body of a letter is the main part which carries the writer's message. Letters of Christ are to carry the message of salvation into all the world.

(d) *Closing:* "Yours truly" is an appropriate term for us for we are indebted to others. Paul wrote, "I am debtor both to the Greeks, and to the Barbarians; both to the wise, and to the unwise" (Romans 1:14). The end of an epistle of Christ is glorious, for "precious in the sight of the LORD is the death of his saints" (Psalm 116:15).

STAMP: Letters of Christ bear the image of Christ and "are changed into the same image from glory to glory, even as by the Spirit of the Lord" (2 Corinthians 3:18).

TRANSPORTATION: We will be going air mail when Jesus returns! "The dead in Christ shall rise first: then we which are alive and remain shall be caught up together with them in the clouds, to meet the Lord in the air: and so shall we ever be with the Lord" (1 Thessalonians 4:16, 17).

Let's be loyal letters of Christ, for we are the only Bible that many people read. May our entire message be consistent and convincing.

About God: **To Do:**

Victory by Dying

"Behold, I send you forth as sheep in the midst of wolves: be ye therefore wise as serpents, and harmless as doves." —Matthew 10:16

Read Acts 5:17-33

Jesus won the world's greatest victory by dying. He lovingly realized that by dying He would "destroy him that had the power of death, that is, the devil; and deliver them" (Hebrews 2:14, 15).

Our willingness to die for Christ is also the way of victory, and it delivers a powerful testimony. I was reminded of this through the experience of a Romanian pastor, Joseph Ton, during communist rule. After studying the Bible in England in the seventies, he was ready to return to Romania. He knew he faced danger upon entering the country.

He asked God about the ministry he was hoping to do in Romania and the risks involved. God seemed to bring to mind Matthew 10:16, "I send you forth as sheep in the midst of wolves." Then he thought God asked him, "What chance does one sheep surrounded by wolves have of surviving five minutes, let alone of converting the wolves? Joseph, that's how I send you: totally defenseless and without a reasonable hope of success. If you are willing to go like that, go. If you are not willing to be in that position, don't go."

Ton later gave this testimony: "After our return, as I preached uninhibitedly, harassment and arrests came. One day during interrogation, an officer threatened to kill me. Then I said, 'Sir, your supreme weapon is killing. My supreme weapon is dying. Sir, you know my sermons are all over the country on tapes now. If you kill me, I will be sprinkling them with my blood. Whoever listens to them after that will say, "I'd better listen. This man sealed it with his blood." They will speak ten times louder than before. So, go on and kill me. I win the supreme victory then.' "

The officer sent him home. "That gave me pause. For years I was a Christian who was cautious because I wanted to survive. I had accepted all the restrictions the authorities put on me because I wanted to live. Now I wanted to die, and they wouldn't oblige me. Now I could do whatever I wanted in Romania. For years I wanted to save my life, and I was losing it. Now that I wanted to lose it, I was winning it."

We thank God that Jesus died. Because He offered His life a ransom, He provides eternal life to whoever believes in Him. Let's spread the Word!

About God: **To Do:**

July 19

Witness in Music

"Sing unto him, sing psalms unto him: talk ye of all his wondrous works." —Psalm 105:2

Read Acts 16:19-34

Not all kinds of music are suitable in evangelism. But singing certainly has given a powerful witness in the history of the church. Consider this group of seven incidents in which singing is recorded in the Bible or *Martyrs Mirror.*

1. Paul and Silas sang a duet in their jail ministry, and the correctional officer and his household became Christians as told in the daily reading.
2. Two centuries later, hundreds of Christians were in a meeting place to worship when they were surrounded by soldiers who planned to burn the place. But first, anyone who would sacrifice to the god Jupiter would have freedom and even be rewarded by the Emperor. Not one came out, but "all remained together with one accord, *singing* and praising Christ as long as the smoke and vapour permitted them to use their tongues" (p. 131).
3. A mixed quartet "*sang* and rejoiced in prison, so that the enemies [who had imprisoned them] were more troubled and afraid than the prisoners" (p. 437).
4. A male quartet on the way to execution "boldly and joyfully *sang*." Then "the executioner became sad, and acted with reluctance" (p. 475).
5. An adolescent male vocalist greatly impressed King Philip with his singing. Later the boy became a Christian, and at age 18 was arrested. "On his way to death, he rejoiced greatly in the Lord, and *sang* yet as he was going into the hut of straw in which he was burnt, the last verse of the hymn composed by himself" (p. 651).
6. A chorus of 350, being condemned to death for their faith "went joyfully to meet death; while the others were being drowned and executed, the rest who were yet alive and waited for death *sang* as the executioner took them" (p. 437).
7. A female soloist, Claudine, "was beautiful of person, and a good singer, so that she moved the bystanders by her *singing*. Especially on the last day of her life, people stood before the prison to hear her sing with a joyful heart when death was announced to her" (p. 738).

May the songs we sing and the tapes of music we listen to honor our Saviour and tell of His salvation.

About God: **To Do:**

Testimony in Trials

"And if children, then heirs; heirs of God, and joint-heirs with Christ, if so be that we suffer with him, that we may be also glorified together."
—Romans 8:17

Read Acts 27:14-36

A writer for an important newspaper visited India. He met there a missionary nurse who lived among lepers and helped them. He noticed how gentle and loving she was to these poor folk. He noticed too, the open, ugly, putrefying sores she was bathing.

"I wouldn't wash the wounds of these lepers for a million dollars!" he exclaimed.

"Neither would I," answered the gallant missionary nurse, "but I gladly do it for Christ. I have no thought of any reward other than His smile of approval upon me."

No doubt Paul would not have endured the persecution and trouble he encountered for a million dollars either. Five times the Jews gave him the dreaded scourging of thirty-nine stripes. He was beaten with rods three times. He suffered shipwreck three times. He was constantly facing danger—robbers, Jews, heathen, false brethren, in cities, in the countryside, on the water, under the water. He faced fatigue, pain, hunger, thirst, nakedness, cold, and a tremendous weight of responsibility. See 2 Corinthians 11:23-28 for his testimony.

In the daily reading, we observe Paul experiencing great danger and trial. There was no lack of excitement on Paul's voyage to Rome—the ship at the mercy of the storm (and God), the soldiers' plan to kill Paul, the sailors' unsuccessful plot to escape from the ship, the angel's appearance to Paul, the shipwreck with a happy ending, and the poisonous snake which fastened itself on Paul's hand. Do not let anyone tell you that the Christian life is dull—it is one continual adventure with God. Halfhearted Christianity is unsatisfying to man and unsatisfactory to God. But the committed Christian life never lacks flavor and joy.

Furthermore, a godly person who faces trials with trust leaves a winsome witness. Two teenage girls, pictured on page 500 of *Martyrs Mirror* (notice their headship coverings), gave such a witness on their way to execution. So godly were their lives and words, so brave was their demeanor, so joyful was their attitude that the religious authorities began to have doubts as to whether they should execute the girls, though they were Anabaptists.

About God: **To Do:**

July 21

The Man Who Didn't Pass By

"Remembering without ceasing your work of faith, and labour of love, and patience of hope in our Lord Jesus Christ, in the sight of God and our Father." —1 Thessalonians 1:3

Read Luke 10:30-37

Have you ever been a good Egyptian? a good Assyrian? a good Persian? How about a good Samaritan? The latter term is familiar to us because of the noteworthy person that Jesus told about. (Canadians are reminded of him by the *Good Samaritan Act,* which doesn't hold a helpful person with good intentions liable if he makes a mistake at an accident scene. The U. S. has the same kind of law with a similar name.)

Consider the attitude of the good Samaritan, who didn't pass by. The victim he helped had fallen among thieves (v. 30). Today a thief called alcohol robs people of their health, income, and common sense. Parents can be thieves, robbing children of self-worth by constant ridicule and criticism, of innocence by sexual abuse, of faith by hypocrisy and giving offence.

The victim the good Samaritan helped was stripped of his raiment. Today, many people are stripped of hope, confidence, and dignity.

The victim was wounded. People can be wounded by words—of sarcasm, of accusations, of belittling, and of gossip. Proverbs 18:8 says, "The words of a talebearer are as wounds, and they go down into the innermost parts of the belly."

The victim was abandoned, for his assailants "departed, leaving him half dead" (v. 30). Today many people feel abandoned because people ignore them and their needs. Even in the church there can be a tendency to not get involved in the lives of "cast-offs."

Clearly, our day needs people with the attitude of the good Samaritan. He, "as he journeyed, came where he was: and when he saw him, he had compassion on him" (v. 33). Simply recognizing a person and identifying his physical or emotional or spiritual needs in a compassionate way means a lot.

Then, "he went to him, and bound up his wounds, pouring in oil and wine" (v. 34). Today Christians can provide the oil and wine of an understanding heart, encouraging words, godly counsel, and pertinent Scriptures.

The good Samaritan spent time and money to take care of the man who needed help. Helping people tends to be time-intensive and rarely is financially lucrative. But it is the right thing to do, and it testifies of God's love. One observer has concluded, "Lovingkindness has converted more sinners than either zeal, eloquence, or learning."

About God: **To Do:**

Let the Lower Lights Be Burning

"Among whom ye shine as lights in the world." —Philippians 2:15

Read Acts 26:12-23

Ever wonder what the song title means? The message of the song became more meaningful when I found out how it came to be written.

Philip P. Bliss wrote and composed the song. As a singing evangelist he travelled for a while with Moody. In a sermon Moody told of a ship captain trying to bring his boat into the Cleveland harbor on a stormy night. "The waves rolled like mountains, not a star was in the sky, and the boat rocked violently. The captain's trained eyes searched frantically for the harbor lights. In terror he realized someone had allowed those guiding lights to go out. He shouted to his crew, 'We must make the harbor, or we die.' The captain aimed his ship at the supposed opening to the harbor. He missed the channel in the darkness; the boat crashed onto the jagged rocks, and sank."

To a quiet audience, Moody concluded, "Brethren, we must keep the lower lights burning." Greatly moved, Bliss wrote the hymn by the above title to remind Christians to let their lights of testimony shine. "Some poor fainting, struggling seaman you may rescue, you may save."

In 1876 Bliss's life ended tragically at the early age of thirty-eight. The Bliss family had visited his mother in Buffalo, and he had sung a new tune called "It Is Well With My Soul." On December 26, 1876, they were on a train with 160 people. That evening the Pacific Express train was speeding across a 75-foot-high railway bridge in Ohio during a fierce snowstorm. The bridge buckled and the train tumbled into the gorge. Some died in the water; others perished in fires caused by stoves in the passenger cars. Among the ninety-two dead were Philip Bliss and his wife. One survivor reported that he saw Bliss crawl from a burning car but then return when he realized his wife was still inside.

It was discovered that their luggage had been put on another train by mistake. In it, several days later, friends found a new song that no one had heard. It must just have been written.

> I will sing of my Redeemer,
> And His heavenly love to me.
> He from death to life hath brought me,
> Son of God, with Him to be.

About God: **To Do:**

Old-Fashioned But Not Outdated

"Provide things honest in the sight of all men." —Romans 12:17

Read Genesis 43:1-23

A commentary on the times in which we live is that the noun *honesty* is often preceded by the adjective *old-fashioned.*

In 1924, *Liberty* magazine sent out one hundred letters to individuals at random throughout the United States. In each letter was enclosed a one-dollar bill with an explanation that the money was the adjustment of an error of which the addressee had complained. However, it was an error which did not really exist. Of the one hundred people who received the letter, twenty-seven returned the dollar saying there must have been a mistake.

In 1971, the magazine conducted the same test. The result? Only thirteen returned the money. If a similar test were given now, making it a twenty-dollar bill to account for inflation, how many would return the money? Would you?

I'm confident the patriarch Jacob would have returned the money. When his sons returned from buying grain in Egypt and found in their sacks the money they thought they had used to pay for the grain, Jacob said they should take it back. It may have been "an oversight" (v. 12).

Here are a few tests:

Oversight. Honesty may be tested by errors and unintentional "gifts." Take, for instance, if you made a fifteen-dollar purchase, and the sales clerk absent-mindedly handed you two twenties and a five in change for a fifty-dollar bill. Or, on a purchase of lumber from a building supply business, you receive the two-by-fours and plywood, but you don't receive a bill.

Cheating. One of my school students came to me and said, "I happened to see one of the multiple choice answers of the English exam on the desk ahead of me. I haven't done the question yet. What shall I do about it?" She wanted to be strictly honest.

Income Tax. Particularly when a person is self-employed and on his honor to declare his full income, temptations to be dishonest can be strong. We are to "Render therefore to all their dues: tribute to whom tribute is due" (Romans 13:7).

We must think honestly (Philippians 4:8), which will help us act honestly. An honest man alters his ideas to fit the truth, whereas a dishonest man alters the truth to fit his ideas. Be like the Hebrew writer who was "in all things willing to live honestly" (Hebrews 13:18). Old-fashioned honesty will never be outdated.

About God: **To Do:**

Temptations to Be Dishonest

"That which is altogether just shalt thou follow, that thou mayest live, and inherit the land which the LORD thy God giveth thee."
—Deuteronomy 16:20

Read 2 Kings 22:1-13

Exaggeration. Young people aiming to impress others may add a little to their achievements. It's not only when talking about oneself, but we may also exaggerate the mistakes of others. Rare is the person who can weigh the faults of others without putting his thumb on the scales. Fishermen have been notorious for stretching the length of their catch, but "fishers of men" should be known for close adherence to the facts.

Omission. Leaving out some information which misleads our listener is not honest. We do not need to share all the information we have, but we are obligated to say things in such a way that the truth is expressed. Consider the high school student who says that he got 92 on his last history exam but refrains from saying that the 92 refers to his total points out of 160 and not 92 percent. Or, think of the person who has a car for sale and says to the prospective buyer, "Only 43,000 miles on it," and omits mentioning that the odometer is on its second round.

Qualifications. Increasingly, some job-seekers state their qualifications, abilities, and experiences in a more favorable way than reality warrants. If you are looking for a job, put your best foot forward, but don't stumble into the pit of pretense. We should be "providing for honest things, not only in the sight of the Lord, but also in the sight of men" (2 Corinthians 8:21).

Employment. "Pssst, the boss is coming." Would such information cause you as an employee to change significantly the speed, quality, or method of your work? Colossians 3:22 instructs servants to work "not with eyeservice, as menpleasers; but in singleness [sincerity] of heart, fearing God." *Eyeservice* means "service performed under the master's eye." Be like the men of Josiah's day who dealt "faithfully."

Buying. Tony sees it advertised in the "For Sale" column. He goes to see it. As he haggles about the price, he points out its faults. He buys it for a low price. When Tony gets home he tells his brother, "Wait till you hear what I paid for it. I got it for a real steal!" Tony should read Proverbs 20:14, "It is naught, it is naught, saith the buyer: but when he is gone his way, then he boasteth." Perhaps some of our purchases are more of a steal in a literal sense than we care to admit.

About God: **To Do:**

The Truth About Lying

"Lying lips are abomination to the LORD: but they that deal truly are his delight." —Proverbs 12:22

Read John 8:31-47

The average person lies three or four times a day. This is according to David Leiberman's research. He also states in his book *Never Be Lied to Again,* that lies enter the conversation between marriage partners about ten percent of the time. Between dating couples the figures rise to thirty percent. Lieberman believes he can tell if a person is lying or telling the truth. He says if you ask a right-handed person where he has been and the person is telling the truth, he'll look up and to the left because that's the side of the brain used for recalling visual information. If the person is fabricating a lie, you'll see him look up and to the right.

I really don't know if looking left or right makes a difference or not. But I do know that looking up will make a difference—straight up to the heavenly Father who says, "Lie not one to another" (Colossians 3:9). Whether it is spouse, dating partner, or neighbor, God says, "Wherefore putting away lying, speak every man truth with his neighbour" (Ephesians 4:25).

Look up to God the Son who is "the truth" (John 14:6). He spoke the truth to His parents, saying, "I must be about my Father's business" (Luke 2:49). He spoke the truth to His friends: "I tell you the truth; It is expedient for you that I go away: for if I go not away, the Comforter will not come unto you" (John 16:7). He spoke the truth to His enemies: "But now ye seek to kill me, a man that hath told you the truth, which I have heard of God" (John 8:40).

Look up to God the Spirit. He is "the Spirit of truth" who will "guide you into all truth" (John 16:13).

Don't look down to the devil. He is the father of lies, as our daily Scripture says. He offers excuses to justify lying. Perhaps the most common attempt to justify a lie is the lie that the end justifies the means.

God's Word, which is the truth, says this about lying: "All liars shall have their part in the lake which burneth with fire and brimstone" (Revelation 21:8). Therefore tell the truth. A lie may seem to take care of the present, but it has no future.

About God: **To Do:**

Spiritual Paper Bags

"In the mean time, when there were gathered together an innumerable multitude of people, insomuch that they trode one upon another, he began to say unto his disciples first of all, Beware ye of the leaven of the Pharisees, which is hypocrisy." —Luke 12:1

Read Matthew 23:13-27

A thief in Jacksonville, Florida, had a problem that left him embarrassed and trapped. His mask consisted of a paper bag over his head with holes cut in it so he could see. During the holdup attempt, he ordered the clerk, "Give me the register!"

The clerk said, "What?"

He repeated, "Give me the register!" As the interchange continued, the bag shifted. When he shoved the bag back in place, it ripped, exposing his face. The clerk yelled, *"Bob!"* as she identified the would-be robber as a regular customer.

The figurative masks and disguises people wear are no more effective than his in concealing their identity.

Think of David. After he coveted, committed adultery with Bathsheba, and killed her husband, he thought no one could identify him as the guilty one. But when confronted by God's man, Nathan, his disguise tore and his identity was exposed.

Think of Judas. He was religious and had important responsibilities. He was an apostle and the treasurer of the group. He thought his mask was in place, but it shifted, leaving him in the dark. His attempt to shift it back failed (see Matthew 27:3-5). This thief stole his own life.

Think of King Ahab. Before his battle against Syria, he said to his ally, Jehoshaphat, "I will disguise myself, and enter into the battle; but put thou on thy robes" (1 Kings 22:30). Although this strategy endangered Jehoshaphat's life, it didn't prevent Ahab from being wounded and killed in the battle.

Think of multitudes that profess Christ but do not possess Him. Their masks of religious terminology and activity do not hide them from the Lord, who identifies them as indicated in the daily reading.

Think of yourself. Are you trying to get something that doesn't belong to you (eternal life) by pretending to be God's child? The Day of Judgment will cause all "paper bags" of pretense to rip, exposing one's real self. How much better to honestly remove the cover-up now! Be open before the Lord—about your sin, your need of forgiveness, your deception. As you trust in Jesus and take His way, you will have far more than any thief could ever steal. You can't steal eternal life, but you can receive it as a gift. But it's not for those who wear spiritual paper bags. It's for those who are honest with themselves, God, and others.

About God: **To Do:**

July 27

Don't Fudge

"A faithful witness will not lie: but a false witness will utter lies." —Proverbs 14:5

Read Exodus 32:15-29

Captain Fudge lived about three hundred years ago in England. He was the commander of a merchant ship, but he dealt in more than merchandise. He became notorious for his exaggerations and untruths about his sailing adventures. His crew members became so accustomed to his misadventures with the truth that when a sailor was thought to be lying, the rest would call him "Fudge." From this historical person comes the term *fudging*—cheating and adjusting the facts. By the 1800s, students talked about fudging. Today the term refers to inaccurate adjustments of the truth in business, on resumes, and in conversation.

The Bible condemns fudging in no uncertain terms. The Ten Commandments say, "Thou shalt not bear false witness"—no fudging. Leviticus 19:11 says, "Ye shall not steal, neither deal falsely, neither lie one to another"—no fudging. The New Testament reemphasizes the importance of truth-telling. Ephesians 4:25 says, "Wherefore putting away lying, speak every man truth with his neighbour"—no fudging.

How does America rate in the twenty-first century? Think about the frequent fudging expressed by the following statements:

"The check is in the mail." "He's not in the office at the moment." "Money cheerfully refunded." "Give me your number, and he'll call you right back." "This offer is limited to the first fifty people who call in." "I just want to take five minutes of your time." "Leave your resume and we'll keep it on file." "It's not the money; it's the principle of the thing."

Fudging has caused trouble and guilt for many years. The appeal of the first temptation was based on a lie. Satan told Eve that she wouldn't die if she ate the forbidden fruit. Cain, the first child to exercise his lungs, also tried to dodge the truth. In answer to God's question, "Where is Abel thy brother?" he said, "I know not: am I my brother's keeper?" (Genesis 4:9). He may have thought, *I don't know where his soul is.* But it is clear this murderer was guilty of fudging.

Abraham, a hero of faith, wasn't entirely truthful in every situation. When he and Sarah relocated, he told his new neighbors that Sarah was his sister. He fudged. She *was* only his half-sister, but more importantly, she was also his wife.

Aaron thought fudging was a good escape route from trouble, but how wrong he was, as our daily reading shows.

About God: **To Do:**

Finders Keepers

"If I have taken any thing from any man by false accusation, I restore him fourfold." —Luke 19:8

Read Deuteronomy 22:1-4

If you find a valuable item that someone has lost, the rhyme, "finders keepers, losers weepers" may jump into your mind. Is this a good approach? Many people seem to think keeping it is legitimate, according to an experiment done a few years ago.

Ten wallets, each containing a significant amount of money, were scattered throughout downtown Boston. Two weeks later, three wallets had been returned with the money still inside. Two were mailed back without the money, and the rest were never returned.

As the daily reading shows, Israelites were to make restitution. If the owner was unknown or lived at a distance, the person who found the lost animal or article was to keep it until the owner came for it. "Finders returners" was the commandment, not "finders keepers."

But the prevailing philosophy on lost goods is to keep it. The *New York Times* reported a discussion in a high school class in New Jersey. Students were asked about a girl who found one thousand dollars and turned it in. All fifteen class members concluded she was a fool. And the students' guidance counselor offered no opinion but this: "If I come from the position of what is right and what is wrong, then I'm not their counselor."

The basic Christian principle about lost things is honesty. The Bible says we are to "provide things honest in the sight of all men" (Romans 12:17). Christians are to "live honestly" (Hebrews 13:18), "walk honestly" (1 Thessalonians 4:12), talk honestly (2 Corinthians 4:2), work honestly (Colossians 3:22), and even think honestly (Philippians 4:8). Is it honest to keep something you found, when you know or could know the identity of the owner?

What if it is a small thing, say, a dime or quarter, which is found on a sidewalk and there is virtually no way of finding an owner? I think if there is reasonable possibility of finding the owner, it should be turned in to the authorities. However, if it is of comparatively little value, with the owner a complete mystery, it may be kept or given to charity with a clear conscience.

Don't you think the world would be a better place if the "found" ads would equal or outnumber the "lost" ads? Jesus said, "As ye would that men should do to you, do ye also to them likewise" (Luke 6:31).

About God: **To Do:**

Lying—A Lubricant?

"A false witness shall perish." —Proverbs 21:28

Read Genesis 32:1-20

Some sociologists and psychologists have written of the "benefits" of telling certain types of lies. For example, lying can serve as a "social lubricant." Lying can help us out of an embarrassing dilemma, help us avoid hurting the feelings of another, and help us ease the strain of social relations. I have decided that lying is a lubricant. It lubricates the way to misery.

Three teenage boys arrived at school late for no good reason. Their teacher asked, "Why are you late?"

Thinking that a lie would lubricate their way out of the situation, they replied, "We had a flat tire."

"All right," said the teacher, "I will give you a test first of all." She seated them apart from one another. She continued. "This test has only one question, and I'll give you 30 seconds to put down your answer. Which tire was flat?" Lying proved to be a lubricant to trouble.

So it was with Ananias and Sapphira, members of the Jerusalem Christian Fellowship. They sold land, brought *some* of the money to the apostles, and pretended they were giving all. They evidently thought their hypocrisy and lying would serve as a lubricant to a good reputation and win the esteem of the early church.

Lying is a lubricant to deception—and in the process of deceiving others, people deceive themselves. The following story, though apocryphal, makes a good point. A man was able to join the Emperor of China's orchestra although he could not play a note. Whenever the group played, he would hold his flute against his lips, not daring even to blow softly for fear he might cause a discord. He received a modest salary and was able to live in material comfort.

One day, the emperor happened to desire that each musician play for him solo. The flutist became desperate. He tried to take quick professional lessons but to no avail, for he really had no ear for music. He pretended to be sick, but the Royal Physician who attended him knew better, causing him to be increasingly apprehensive. On the day of his solo appearance, he took poison rather than "face the music."

Jacob dreaded facing the music. He had to "do a solo" before his brother as shown in the daily reading.

A good way to avoid lying is to do nothing in your relationships that needs concealment.

About God: **To Do:**

Christian Armor

"Resist the devil, and he will flee from you." —James 4:7

Read Ephesians 6:10-20

Life is not a playground but a battleground. Christians have an enemy—Satan and his demons. As our daily reading indicates, we need to stand. Our warfare is not fought from the trenches, but out in the open.

We need armor because the devil is crafty. He has deceptive schemes (wiles). He tempts us to question God's Word, to give only partial obedience, to minimize sin, and to accept error mixed with truth. Ask Joshua about prayerlessness, Uzziah about pride, Peter about overconfidence, and Demas about worldliness.

We need spiritual armor because the satanic powers are real, powerful, and superhuman. We are not spectators. We *wrestle* to overcome temptation. The devil uses the world without and the flesh within.

In Paul's time, the enemy would dip arrows in poison or inflammatory substances. These *fiery darts* were speedy, unexpected, and murderous. Christians need the shield of faith to repel temptations and trials.

A shield made of wood and covered with tough leather, measuring about four feet by two and one-half feet, was used in defense. These shields were so constructed that soldiers could interlock shields and march against the enemy like a solid wall.

What a vivid picture of Christian warfare and experience! For protection against Satan's darts of doubts, wrong thoughts, lusts, lies, and temptations, we need a shield. The shield of faith needs to be in place against the enemy of our souls. Our faith and practice needs to be interlocked with fellow soldiers for more effective defense.

About God: **To Do:**

July 31

Parts of the Armor

"Let us put on the armour of light." —Romans 13:12

Read 1 Thessalonians 5:1-11

1. *Belt of truth.* This large, heavy belt or girdle braced the soldier and held his armor in position. It also held the sword.

   Truth is a uniting force for a Christian. Hang onto God's Word. Be honest with God, yourself, and others.

2. *Breastplate of righteousness.* The breastplate was made of metal plates or chains, covering the body from neck to waist to protect the vital organs such as the heart and lungs.

   A right relationship with God leading to right living is so important. Job and Daniel wore the breastplate; Ahab and Judas didn't. Do you?

3. *Shoes of the Gospel.* The Roman soldier wore sandals with hobnails in the soles for better footing. These shoes were needed for standing and traveling.

   Christians need to keep on standing on the Gospel message. We also need to travel to share the Good News and teach all nations.

4. *Shield of faith.* Faith is essential. "This is the victory that overcometh the world, even our faith" (1 John 5:4).

5. *Helmet of salvation.* The helmet protected the head and brain. This helmet represents a mind controlled by God and a heart cleansed from sin.

6. *Sword of the Spirit.* A sword is used for both defense and offense by a soldier.

   Use the Bible. The more a soldier uses a sword, the duller it becomes. The more a Christian uses God's Sword, the sharper it is in his life.

   Jesus in His temptation near the beginning of His ministry used the Scriptures defensively ("It is written") and offensively ("Get thee hence, Satan").

   Peter used a metal sword to defend Jesus in the Garden of Gethsemane, but on Pentecost he discovered that the Sword of the Spirit does a much better job.

About God: **To Do:**

Choose Death

"For ye are dead, and your life is hid with Christ in God."
—Colossians 3:3

Read Romans 6:1-18

"You certainly have a 'dead' life," someone may tell you. A consecrated Christian can agree wholeheartedly! It's not true in the sense that the Christian life is dull, because living for Christ is exciting and following God's leading is exhilarating. However, in one sense, it is true that a Christian lives a dead life. The Bible explains, "Reckon ye also yourselves to be dead indeed unto sin" (Romans 6:11). We should follow the example of the Apostle Paul who wrote, "I am crucified with Christ," and declared he was dead "unto the world." In fact, they that are Christ's "have crucified the flesh with the affections and lusts" (Galatians 5:24).

Jesus illustrated it this way: "Except a corn of wheat fall into the ground and die, it abideth alone: but if it die, it bringeth forth much fruit. He that loveth his life shall lose it; and he that hateth his life in this world shall keep it unto life eternal" (John 12:24, 25). Clearly, it is far better in this sense to be dead when alive than alive after death to suffer the torments of eternal death.

There are specific sins to which we need to be dead. We need to be dead to dishonesty when the cashier makes an error. We need to be dead to lust as we walk down the summer streets of our towns and cities. We need to be dead to "having little time for God" in the busy months of summer and fall. We need to be dead to worry when things don't seem to go right. We need to be dead to a regular snooze in church instead of being dead to the sermon. We need to be dead to angry words when Junior tracks mud across the freshly-scrubbed floors.

We sing, "Dead to the world would I be, O Father, dead unto sin, alive unto Thee." Are we sincere in our determination as was James Calvert? He was a missionary who went to the cannibal Fiji Islands. On the way the captain of the ship on which he was traveling tried to dissuade him. "You will risk your life and those with you if you go among such savages," he warned. Calvert's exemplary reply was, "We died before we came here."

Yes, choose death to self and sin in the present in order that you may truly live now and evermore.

About God: **To Do:**

August 2

When Tempted, Listen

"Ye are of God, little children, and have overcome them: because greater is he that is in you, than he that is in the world." —1 John 4:4

Read Proverbs 7:7-23

"All one hundred chickens were killed," a friend sadly told me. He had been asked by a vacationing neighbor to feed his flock of chickens for a week.

"Dead chickens were strewn all around the floor. I felt sick. And then I saw how they died. The owner's dog had gotten loose and temptation overcame him. I don't look forward to telling the neighbor when he gets home tomorrow," my friend grimaced.

In contrast, I thought of another dog-and-chickens story told by Jack London. In his book, *White Fang,* he wrote of an animal by that name. White Fang once strayed into a hen-run and killed several hens, as his half-wolf, half-dog nature directed. The owner was very angry about his loss, but White Fang's trainer assured him, "I will guarantee that he will remain a whole afternoon in the hen-run and not kill a single chicken."

The owner agreed to the challenge, and so the test began. Whenever White Fang made a move to attack a hen, his master's voice called him back. Again and again White Fang was tempted. But whenever the old lust to kill asserted itself, his master's voice recalled him. As the animal listened to the quiet, restraining voice, the power of the temptation receded. In fact, he finally fell asleep in the middle of the hens. After he woke up, he yawned and then jumped out of the hen-run.

Christians can learn a lesson from these stories. We need to hear and heed our Master's voice. Our Owner, Jesus Christ, never goes on a vacation, but His loving voice is always within our spiritual hearing range. If we are committed to obeying that voice out of love and loyalty, we can overcome the powerful inborn urges of sin.

The heavenly Master's voice says, "Come unto me . . . take my yoke upon you, and learn of me" (Matthew 11:28, 29). He invites us into a satisfying relationship by surrender of the will in trust to Him. His care for us is much superior to a master's care for his dog. His provision and love are eternal!

As our daily reading indicates, there is great danger in listening to the voice of Miss Immorality. Rather, listen to the voice of Jesus. Look ever to Jesus; He will carry you through.

About God: **To Do:**

Hear the Master's Voice

"The Lord knoweth how to deliver the godly out of temptations."
—2 Peter 2:9

Read Hebrews 4:11-16

When asked how to deal with temptation, a little girl answered, "When Satan comes knocking at the door of my heart, I send Jesus to answer the door. When Satan sees Jesus, he says, 'Oops, I must have the wrong house.' "

When Jesus lives in your heart, you are easily within hearing distance of His voice.

The heavenly Master's voice says, "Pray." He taught His followers to entreat the heavenly Father, "Lead us not into temptation, but deliver us from evil" (Matthew 6:13). In the Garden of Gethsemane, He told His sleeping and temptation-prone disciples, "Watch and pray, that ye enter not into temptation" (Matthew 26:41). And the daily reading tells us that the Great High Priest in heaven now invites us to come boldly to obtain mercy and grace.

The Bible says that the brethren of Berea "searched the scriptures daily" (Acts 17:11). When Christ was confronted with temptations, He responded victoriously with the words, "It is written."

The Psalmist, too, knew the way to victorious Christian living, "Wherewithal shall a young man cleanse his way? By taking heed thereto according to thy word" (Psalm 119:9).

The heavenly Master's voice calls us to avoid tempting situations. In the Sermon on the Mount, He urged drastic measures to overcome the temptation of sexual lust, like plucking out the eye or cutting off a hand (Matthew 5:29, 30). We need to shut off our senses, as it were, rather than feeding sinful appetites through the senses. Turn a blind eye to pornography and the immodesty so prevalent in our society. Let your arm be as though it were cut off when facing the temptation of turning the pages of sinful books and magazines. "Enter not into the path of the wicked, and go not in the way of evil men. Avoid it, pass not by it, turn from it, and pass away" (Proverbs 4:14, 15).

The heavenly Master says, "Walk in the Spirit, and ye shall not fulfil the lust of the flesh" (Galatians 5:16). Do not violate your Spirit-instructed conscience. One's conscience can be evil (Hebrews 10:22), seared (1 Timothy 4:2), and defiled (Titus 1:15). Rather, keep it in good shape by obedience and ready confession of sin when it is violated.

Let the heavenly Master's voice guide, restrain, and keep you in the hour of temptation.

About God: **To Do:**

August 4

It Will Be Different for Me

"But thou, O man of God, flee these things." —1 Timothy 6:11

Read Matthew 26:1-5, 31-35, 69-75

A former zookeeper, Gary Richmond, wrote *A View from the Zoo* that tells of changes wild animals in captivity can go through. For example, raccoons experience a glandular change at about two years. After that, they often attack their owners.

A thirty-pound (14-kg) raccoon is a powerful animal. Therefore, Mr. Richmond told Julie, a young owner of a pet raccoon, that in a few months there could be a drastic and dangerous change.

She listened politely, then replied, "It will be different for me." Smiling, she added, "Bandit wouldn't hurt me. He just wouldn't."

Three months later, Julie underwent plastic surgery for facial lacerations received when the adult coon attacked her for no apparent reason. Bandit was released into the wild.

Likewise, sin sometimes appears harmless. People have played with it, saying, "I don't think it will hurt me. It will be different for me."

Take Judas, for instance, who played with dishonesty and treachery. With a background of getting by with thievery as treasurer of the disciples and putting on a false front at the Last Supper, he proceeded with betraying Jesus. But sin and guilt attacked him to the extent that he committed suicide.

Do we think we'll be an exception to the spiritual law, "Whatsoever a man soweth, that shall he also reap" (Galatians 6:7)? Some dabble in lotteries and think there will be no ill effects. Some have a love affair with the bottle, little expecting to face the devastation caused by alcohol. Some allow bitterness to take root in their soul, expecting to be free from its blight. Others toy with temptations and lust, thinking it will be different for them.

I heard an evangelist tell of a young man, a friend of his, who was dating. The young man called the evangelist over to his car. He noticed that the couple was sitting close together, and the girl was dressed immodestly. He later warned the boy. "That doesn't bother me," he responded. "I'm not affected by short dresses. You old guys always have your minds in the wrong place."

The evangelist shook his head. Later he learned that the couple's wedding date was advanced because they needed to get married several months earlier.

You may think you are the exception. But sin's consequences *won't* be different for you. Playing with sin is toying with judgment.

About God: **To Do:**

Termites and Transgressions

"Can a man take fire in his bosom, and his clothes not be burned?"
—Proverbs 6:27

Read Romans 2:17-29

Termites have a lot of nerve. I remember a report that termites had eaten through a stack of pamphlets entitled "Control of Termites" in the mailing room of the University of California.

I was amused until I thought of the implications for my Christian life. Would it be possible to have instructions on how to control sinful desires without using those instructions? Would it be possible to inform others without following directions myself? The Word of God presents us with the solution to the problem of transgressions, not merely termites.

I read of one famous missionary who had a definite conversion experience, was well-grounded in the Scriptures, risked his life more than once in his missionary work, had a remarkably deep understanding of spiritual truth, was used of God to write many books of the New Testament, and even had a vision of heaven. Yet it was his concern "lest that by any means, when I have preached to others, I myself should be a castaway" (1 Corinthians 9:27). We would feel that if Paul had surrendered to Satan, it would have been the height of tragedy and inconsistency. But he knew it was possible.

When I was about ten years old, I remember a visiting speaker who thundered repeatedly, "INCONSISTENCY IS SIN." Perhaps it was at the same time that I heard about the man who beat his wife in a unique and ironical way. He used a wall motto which read, "God Bless Our Home."

My fifth-grade teacher vigorously taught me the dangers of smoking cigarettes. Guess what I saw in her open purse one day—a package of cancer sticks. Imagine my shock and dismay. She evidently didn't know verse twenty-one of our daily reading, a soul-searching question for teachers, parents, and ministers.

The daily reading emphasizes the importance of being a true Jew and having a heart experience. Truly the heart of the Christian life is the heart. How sad that the Jews who possessed a knowledge of God's will and taught others (vv. 18-20) refused the Son of God! How disastrous it would be if we, personally, know of the love of God, yet fail to demonstrate that love! How ironical it is that the heathen are true to false gods, while professed Christians are often false to the true God! "Let him that thinketh he standeth take heed lest he fall" (1 Corinthians 10:12).

About God: **To Do:**

Meal Etiquette at Church

"Not forsaking the assembling of ourselves together, as the manner of some is; but exhorting one another: and so much the more, as ye see the day approaching." —Hebrews 10:25

Read Psalm 122

Proper manners are important when eating. Picture a boorish person rudely reaching across the table, jamming food into his mouth, wiping his hands on the tablecloth, and peppering you with supper and saliva as he tells you how much he appreciates the invitation to share a meal with you. How revolting! When eating a meal, you follow certain rules of etiquette and common sense. Even more important are good manners when you *eat* at God's house.

At God's house, you will be served "the sincere milk of the word, that ye may grow thereby" (1 Peter 2:2). Those who are more mature will appreciate "strong meat" (Hebrews 5:14). Basic to nutrition and vitality is the Bread of Life, Jesus.

Consider how to eat the food God wishes to share with you in a church service to help you avoid embarrassment to others, shame to yourself, and dishonor to the Divine Host.

Arrive at the appointed time. Would you feel comfortable in going to a friend's house after the other guests have arrived, slipping into an empty chair after the blessing has been asked and the appetizer already served? You certainly want to avoid making it a habit!

Go with gladness, not with a sour sense of obligation. How would a host feel if he sensed you came to his place out of duty rather than from a desire to enjoy his friendship and fellowship? One happy person, invited to God's house, declared, "I was glad when they said unto me, Let us go into the house of the LORD" (Psalm 122:1).

Dress appropriately for the occasion. Clothes worn when eating at God's house shall be clean, neat, decent, and inoffensive to the Host.

Keep your mouth closed when eating. Sometimes immature members of a family will attempt to talk and eat simultaneously. Inevitably it seems either the words don't come out clearly or the food does! We hear the Lord's invitation: "Open thy mouth wide, and I will fill it" (Psalm 81:10). So we come to His house. It is hardly mannerly to be talking to others on the church bench while feasting on the good food of the Lord. Inevitably we lose some of what the Lord has given us, and our bad manners spill over onto others, distracting them from feeding on God's provision.

About God: **To Do:**

More Manners in a Church Service

"Blessed are they that dwell in thy house:
they will be still praising thee." —Psalm 84:4

Read Psalm 24

Stay awake. If you fell asleep while your friend's wife was serving you food, your friend might think he should have shown you the guest bedroom, not the dining room table. Surely, falling asleep while eating is unusual and highly inappropriate. So it is in God's house.

Come with clean hands. Otherwise the good food may be contaminated and not benefit you. Spiritually, we need the "washing of water by the word" (Ephesians 5:26). The psalmist asked, "Who shall stand in his holy place?" He received the answer, "He that hath clean hands, and a pure heart" (Psalm 24:3, 4).

Avoid gum-chewing. You would have difficulty chewing gum and eating a meal, wouldn't you? And would you place the sticky stuff under the dining room chair? How unseemly to chew gum in God's house while partaking of the milk and meat of the Word.

Sit up. Would you consider it polite to slouch down on the dining room chair, looking bored at the fare placed before you? In God's house, be reverent and interested.

Sit where you are shown. You would surely hesitate to sit at a table without being sure you were in the proper place. Yet sometimes people in God's house boldly disregard the usher's instructions and insist on seating themselves where they choose.

Help others to be seated. Don't be among the inconsiderate ones in the place of worship who park themselves at the end of the bench and refuse to slide over graciously.

Don't spit out the food. Etiquette doesn't permit you to spit out what is disagreeable to your taste buds. Similarly, divine food should be chewed, digested, and assimilated, not rejected because you don't like the taste. Reproofs, although bitter, are needed. Don't expectorate (spit out) the warnings, admonitions, and corrections of Scripture.

Don't leave early. To leave the table at a friend's home before the meal is finished would be considered rude. In God's house, stay till the end of the service. Normally in the houses of friends and also in the house of God it is customary to remain awhile after the meal is finished for further fellowship.

Express thanks. In God's house, thank the Divine Host and His wife, the Church.

How are your manners in God's house?

About God: **To Do:**

August 8

The Church and the Great Wall of China

"I will build my church." —Matthew 16:18

Read 1 Timothy 3

The Great Wall of China is fascinating. This wall is the only man-made project visible to the human eye from space. It's 4,000 miles long—approximately seven million steps. The wall goes over 5,000-foot mountains. It stands twenty to thirty feet high and is about twenty feet wide. Every forty to sixty yards there is a forty-foot watchtower.

It is interesting to compare the Great Wall of China, which was built just over 2000 years ago, to the church, which began 2000 years ago.

The Great Wall had an important purpose. Before it was built, barbarians to the north would invade. The wall was designed to prevent the enemy from defeating and overrunning the Chinese Empire. Likewise, being a member of a brotherhood and helping to build the church is a great defense against the onslaught of evil forces. Christians do have an enemy. First Peter 5:8, 9 tells of our "adversary the devil" who attacks us and whom we should "resist stedfast in the faith." Satan has hordes of powerful forces that wish to invade and conquer the Christian life.

Constructing the Great Wall required the greatest amount of labour in history. The emperor, Chin Shih Hwang Ti, commanded every third man in China to work on the wall. Thousands upon thousands died while working on it. Their bodies were placed between the two sides of the wall and covered with dirt, making the wall "the world's largest graveyard." Building the church takes time and effort too.

It seemed that the Great Wall should provide foolproof security. It was too high to climb over, too thick to break down, and too long to go around. However, during the first 100 years of the wall's existence, China was invaded three times. How? It was not the fault of the wall. Not once did the barbarian hordes climb over it, break it down, or go around it.

So how did they get into China? The enemy understood human nature. They simply bribed a gatekeeper and then marched right in through the gate. The Chinese placed too much reliance on a wall and failed to build character in their gatekeepers.

What a lesson for the church! Without personal integrity, there will be defeat. Each member of the church is called to personal holiness, consistency, and integrity in order for the church to be victorious over the devil.

About God: **To Do:**

Unity in the Church

"Till we all come in the unity of the faith." —Ephesians 4:13

Read Psalm 133 and 134

On occasion we may hear or participate in a Bible school chorus, a street-witnessing singing group, or singing at the local nursing home. At one such time, I confess that my mind wandered from the message of the songs to some thoughts about Christians in the church. My mind focused on ways a group singing together corresponds to the brotherhood.

I noticed the efforts of the song leader as he gave clear and effective instructions to keep the group together. His example in keeping suitable timing, correct wording, and proper enunciation is crucial. So it is in the church. Jesus, the Divine Director, gives the perfect example of attitude. "Let this mind be in you, which was also in Christ Jesus" (Philippians 2:5). He gives the perfect example of actions. "Ye should follow his steps: who did no sin" (1 Peter 2:21, 22). His leadership by way of instruction is perfect too. These instructions in the Bible keep the brotherhood together.

I considered, too, that beginning a song well is important. There must be cooperation in starting together with suitable volume and tempo. The message could be weakened if one person started singing, then another half a second later, and another a second later. Some songs begin quite softly. The leader would not be pleased if one or two started singing very loudly for such a song. If several singers begin at half the speed of the group or double the normal speed, the result would be chaotic. To the Corinthian church, Paul wrote, "Now I beseech you, brethren, by the name of our Lord Jesus Christ, that ye all speak the same thing, and that there be no divisions among you; but that ye be perfectly joined together in the same mind and in the same judgment" (1 Corinthians 1:10).

Similarly, a good ending is important. Singers must follow the song leader's speed, volume, and final note emphasis of the song. I have heard some straggly, ragged endings to songs. It's not a matter of right and wrong or proper and improper, but a matter of doing it *together.* To the Ephesian church, Paul wrote that members should walk "with all lowliness and meekness, with longsuffering, forbearing one another in love; endeavouring to keep the unity of the Spirit in the bond of peace" (Ephesians 4:2, 3).

About God: **To Do:**

The Harmonious Brotherhood

"Be ye all of one mind." —1 Peter 3:8

Read Ephesians 4:1-16

A group singing well in four parts produces harmony. This harmony is not the result of all singing the same notes. Rather, harmony results from the blending of differences. This takes time, practice, and a willingness to listen to other singers. Likewise in the church, harmony stems from a blending of differences. We do not all have the same personality, emotional makeup, temperament, age, gender, or background. It takes time, effort, and listening to those around us in the church in order to produce a harmonious testimony. There needs to be unity under the lordship of Jesus Christ, yet a respect and appreciation for those who are different from us. As Paul wrote to the Galatians, "There is neither Jew nor Greek, there is neither bond nor free, there is neither male nor female: for ye are all one in Christ Jesus" (Galatians 3:28).

When we sing together, we need to follow the prescribed pattern of notes. As church members, we need to follow the prescribed pattern of behavior recorded in the Bible if order and beauty are going to be evident. The result of every man doing what is right in his own eyes is no more pleasing in a church than it is in a chorus.

The best Christian hymns combine worthwhile lyrics with an attractive tune—a combination of substance and style. If the tune is uplifting but the words are false or trite, or if the words are well-crafted and Scripturally sound but the tune is awkward or inappropriate, the song will have limited usefulness. In the Christian life we need godly doctrine mixed with godly experience. If the teaching is good but the experience doesn't correspond, or if the experience is quite good but is mixed with error, the Divine Director of the church is not pleased. Correct doctrine with godly experience is what the world needs to hear and see.

Very essential for harmonious singing is attentively watching the song leader. The Hebrew Christians were told to be "looking unto Jesus the author and finisher of our faith" (Hebrews 12:2).

As Christians, we sing for the glory of God, pointing to Jesus, and seeking a better country. So the church exists "that ye may with one mind and one mouth glorify God, even the Father of our Lord Jesus Christ" (Romans 15:6).

About God: **To Do:**

Attend Worship Services

"God is a Spirit: and they that worship him must worship him in spirit and in truth." —John 4:24

Read Psalm 26

I like the old story of a minister who went to visit a parishioner who had stopped coming to services. Although the man had attended services regularly, he no longer seemed to see the importance of corporate worship. After some weeks the minister decided to visit the absent member. It was a chilly evening, and the minister found the man at home alone, sitting before a blazing fire. Guessing the reason for the pastor's visit, the man welcomed him, led him to a big chair by the fireplace and waited.

The minister made himself comfortable and said nothing. In grave silence, he contemplated the play of the flames around the burning logs. After some minutes, he took the fire tongs, carefully picked up a brightly burning ember, and placed it to one side of the hearth. Then he sat back in his chair, still silent. The host watched all this in quiet fascination. As the lone ember's flame diminished, there was a momentary glow, but soon its fire was no more and it was cold and dead. Not a word had been spoken since the initial greetings. But as the minister rose to leave, the host said, "Thank you so much for your visit—and especially for your fiery sermon. I shall be at church next Sunday."

It is important not only to attend but also to be attentive and worshipful. There is a real danger of our worship experience being very inadequate. Look over an imaginary congregation with me.

Sister Bakseeter is making eyes at the babies around her. Brother Materialist has been trying to decide on a major business expansion. There is Brother Drowzee who can barely stay awake due to working very late the night before. Brother Eareverent is whispering again. Sister Fussey's mind has been preoccupied with the thought of dinner plans for company. Brother Impashent just looked around to see the clock. Sister Condemmer smiles secretly at how the preacher's last remark sure hit another member. And Sister Slumber should be awakened to the fact that after Eutychus slept in church, he soon fell.

Most of us have been tempted to be like the above members. It is good to come to church services. Once there, it is good to worship God in spirit and in truth.

About God: **To Do:**

August 12

Joy in Fellow Believers

"And they continued stedfastly in the apostles' doctrine and fellowship, and in breaking of bread, and in prayers." —Acts 2:42

Read Philippians 1:1-11

"The Bible knows nothing of solitary religion," said John Wesley. You cannot be a Christian and have a "lone ranger" mentality.

Paul's view of Christianity was definitely one of community. One of his greatest joys was fellowship with believers. From the daily reading you can sense the depth of his feeling for his Christian friends.

- Paul could joyfully say to the Philippians, "I have you in my mind" (see vv. 3-6). Because he was thankful, he had joy (v. 3). Because he could regularly talk to God about their needs, he had joy (v. 4). Because of their fellowship, which went all the way back to his meeting with them by the riverside (Acts 16:13-15), he had joy (v. 5). He was also happy about the good work God had begun in their lives, which he was sure God would continue (v. 6).
- Paul said, "I have you in my heart" (vv. 7, 8). Paul's love for the believers brought joy also. He, no doubt, had in mind (from Acts 16) the Philippian jailer, Lydia, riverside prayer warriors, or (from Philippians 4) Clement, Euodias, and Syntyche.

  Do you have the members of your church family in your heart? Or is it more accurate to say they get on your nerves?
- Paul could say, "I have you in my prayers." Praying purposefully also brings a sense of joy.

Here are five good prayer requests for you to pray for your friends:

1. *Love.* This important fruit of the Spirit should be both in our hearts (in knowledge) and also in our actions (in our judgment). It's good to have love in our heads, but we need it shown by our hands also.
2. *Discernment.* To approve things that are excellent and to turn from bad or partially good things takes discernment. This means testing things by the Scriptures, often with the help of parents and pastors.
3. *Sincerity.* Be honest with God and oneself. A hypocrite preaches by the yard but practices by the inch.
4. *Holiness. Without offence* means "not apt to take offence nor give offence." Paul set a good example. "Herein do I exercise myself, to have always a conscience void of offence toward God, and toward men" (Acts 24:16). Purity in the heart produces power in the life.
5. *Fruitbearing* (fruitfulness.) Right living (righteousness) is the will of God for His glory and praise.

About God: **To Do:**

Three Youth Who Resisted Peer Pressure

"Stand therefore, having your loins girt about with truth."
—Ephesians 6:14

Read Daniel 3:1-7

When a doctor performs surgery, the attending nurse must keep track of the number of hemostats and sponges used, to ensure that an incision is not closed until each item has been removed. A young nurse on her first day with this duty told the surgeon that he had used twelve sponges but she could account for only eleven. Curtly, the surgeon asserted that he had removed them all. The nurse insisted that one was still unaccounted for, but the surgeon declared that he would proceed with the suturing.

"You can't do that! Think of the patient," the nurse said, eyes blazing.

Then the doctor smiled and, lifting his foot, showed the nurse the twelfth sponge which he had deliberately dropped to the floor. "You'll do," he said approvingly. She had passed the test of backbone and integrity.

The Lord often designs tests of courage and integrity for youth. He did in years past and He still does today. Think of the bravery and consistency of the three youth called Shadrach, Meshach, and Abednego that we read about in Daniel 3. They faced the test of peer pressure—the compulsion to conform to the expectations of people around them. Captured and taken from their homeland, they faced tremendous pressure to conform. First came the invitation. "All the rulers of the provinces, were gathered together unto the dedication of the image that Nebuchadnezzar the king had set up" (v. 3). Next, came a command. "Then an herald cried aloud, To you it is commanded, O people, nations, and languages" (v. 4).

The pressure escalated to coercion. "And whoso falleth not down and worshippeth shall the same hour be cast into the midst of a burning fiery furnace" (v. 6). Perhaps these youth could see the smoke in the distance. Bend or burn was the ultimatum. In addition, there was the pull to conform by way of example—everybody was doing it. "Therefore at that time, when all the people heard the sound of the cornet, flute, harp, sackbut, psaltery, and all kinds of musick, all the people, the nations, and the languages, fell down and worshipped the golden image that Nebuchadnezzar the king had set up" (v. 7). The response to this altar call was almost unanimous.

But the three Hebrew youth stood upright for the Lord.

About God: **To Do:**

August 14

Peer Pressure and Idolatry

"Take heed to yourselves, that your heart be not deceived, and ye turn aside, and serve other gods, and worship them." —Deuteronomy 11:16

Read Daniel 3:8-18

The three youth in Babylon, transplanted from Judah, faced the test of popular idolatry. They were confronted by an idol ninety feet high and nine feet thick, worth an estimated 23 billion dollars. King Nebuchadnezzar probably wanted to exalt his god above all the deities of the nations he had conquered. (The historian Herodotus wrote of two great golden images set up in Babylon by Nebuchadnezzar.) Nearly everyone bowed low.

Today many bow down to very prominent gods. We are faced with idols costing billions of dollars to erect—the god of fashion, the god of sports, the god of mammon, the god of pornography. Some church people think they can be Christians and still bow to the gods of this world.

A Christian student in a state college had an ungodly teacher who, after he discovered he had a Christian student in his class, continually ridiculed everything Christian. Later, when attending a Christian youth rally in the college town, the student was greatly surprised to see in the choir a young man who had been a regular member of that professor's class. The Christian student was very disappointed that that singer had concealed his faith for weeks while another Christian suffered alone.

The three Hebrew youth faced the test of the world's music. When the people heard the music, they responded to it. There is a connection between worship and music, and not only at church. The popular rock music of America presently has a lot to do with worship—worship of pleasure, drugs, sex, money, fame, Satan, New Age spirits, and worship of the singers and musicians themselves.

The pressure to conform is strong because of the desire to fit in. One student said, "I listened to rock music for about four years, and it was not 'Christian rock,' because I always thought it was so hypocritical to listen to Christian rock. At least I was honest and didn't pretend to be someone I wasn't. After the first couple of times, I was already addicted to it. The reason I started was because everyone always thought I was 'goody-goody.' "

In our day, let's follow the instruction of 1 John 5:21: "Little children, keep yourselves from idols."

About God: **To Do:**

Peer Pressure and Culture

"Touch not the unclean thing; and I will receive you."
—2 Corinthians 6:17

Read Daniel 3:19-30

The three Hebrew youth who refused to bow to Nebuchadnezzar's image faced the temptation of rationalizing (in order to conform to their social environment). Consider some ways that they could have made some adjustments to fit in. They could have considered the image to be an aid to worship because it pointed upward to God. (Some churches have images and icons as "aids to worship.") Or they may have taken the approach of outwardly worshipping the idol while inwardly worshipping God (it's the heart that counts, you know). Or they may have tried to escape the situation. Or they could have rationalized that it's not a matter of faith but a matter of loyalty to government. Or they could have tried to make themselves inconspicuous, just crouching rather than standing up, or feigning sickness and getting carried out by the Babylonian paramedics.

In relating to society at large, there is pressure to be tolerant of sin and to be politically correct—for example, that a gay lifestyle is morally acceptable, that gambling is an innocent diversion, and that war is noble.

Peer pressure can be strong in the workplace—pressure to laugh at off-color jokes, to take a social drink, or to swear or use inappropriate language. The pressure to conform is felt in public education and training upgrades. As a young man I took a course on insulating houses. Although I was with a group of fifty men for only a day, I could readily sense the peer pressure.

The three Hebrew nonconformists experienced tremendous blessing for their noble, courageous stand. For one thing, God kept them safe in a remarkable way. For another, they were transformed and experienced Jesus' presence with them. As verse 25 says, "Lo, I see four men loose, walking in the midst of the fire, and they have no hurt; and the form of the fourth is like the Son of God." They literally walked with God.

Let us be willing to stand out from the crowd today. Then we, too, can experience God's blessing and presence. God is always present in any circumstance or trial when He is honored. You can be confident about tomorrow if you walk with God today.

About God: **To Do:**

August 16

The Peril of Conformity

"Wherefore come out from among them, and be ye separate, saith the Lord, and touch not the unclean thing; and I will receive you." —2 Corinthians 6:17

Read Leviticus 20:6-8, 22-26

A flock of wild geese was flying south for the winter, when one of the geese looked down and noticed a group of domestic geese by a pond on a farm. Seeing that they had plenty of grain to eat, he went down to join them. The food was so good he decided to stay with the domestic geese until spring, when his own flock would fly north again. When spring came, he heard his old flock going by and flew up to join them. The goose had grown fat, however, and flying was difficult, so he decided to spend one more season on the farm and join the wild geese on their next winter migration. The following fall, when his former flock flew southward, the goose flapped his wings a little, but kept eating his grain. By the next time they passed overhead, the now-domesticated goose didn't even notice them.

If a Christian copies those who feel at home in this world and feeds by the farmyard of sin, he will not be observant of the signs of the times. Nor will he be ready to fly or have a desire to meet the Lord in the air when He comes.

The Israelites were warned clearly when entering Canaan not to conform themselves to the abhorrent yet worldly-attractive practices of their ungodly neighbors. "Ye shall not walk in the manners of the nation, which I cast out before you: for they committed all these things, and therefore I abhorred them" (Leviticus 20:23).

The Israelites were to be nonconformed in their worship—not worshipping Baal or Ashtaroth, but only Jehovah. They were to be separate in their diets, avoiding unclean animals, birds of prey, or animals which died on their own. They were to be distinct in their clothing—a ribbon of blue was to be placed upon the fringes of their garments. They were to be different in agriculture—an ox and an ass were not to be hitched together to plow.

God instructed that there be a clear line of demarcation between His people and the people who opposed Him as seen in the daily reading.

God intends that His people today be different from secular society. Is there a definite difference between you and non-Christians? Think of your speech, goals, lifestyle, appearance, attitudes, and outlook.

About God: **To Do:**

Micaiah and Peer Pressure

"And be not conformed to this world: but be ye transformed." —Romans 12:2

Read 1 Kings 22:5-35

A friend told me a story about a spider that built a beautiful web in an old house. The spider kept his web clean and attractive so flies would visit it.

One day a fairly intelligent fly came by. Mr. Spider invited him in. The fly said, "No, I don't see other flies in your house, and I am not going in alone."

But presently he saw on the floor below a large crowd of flies dancing around on a piece of brown paper. So he decided to land.

Just then, a bee zoomed by, saying, "Don't land there. That's flypaper!" But the fly shouted back, "Don't be silly. Those flies are dancing. Everybody's doing it. That many flies can't be wrong!" Well, guess what happened! He died on the spot.

Micaiah, the prophet, did not conform to the verbal buzzing and false prophesying of four hundred prophets who were his peers. Micaiah did not have a noodle for a backbone, as shown in the daily reading.

Beware of following those who enter sin or spiritual danger. Doing what "everybody else" does is not safe. At a packing house where sheep were slaughtered, the sheep had to walk from their large pen up a narrow ramp and then turn right. In order to get the sheep to move up the ramp, a "Judas goat" was trained to lead the sheep up the ramp to their death. The goat was placed among the sheep and then walked confidently to the ramp as the nervous sheep watched. After the goat got about five feet up the ramp, he stopped and confidently looked around at the nervous sheep, who then began to follow. Near the top of the ramp the goat turned left, as a gate was opened only for him and then closed. The sheep, however, continued up the ramp and turned right, to their death.

Like sheep, unbelievers have "the understanding darkened, being alienated from the life of God through the ignorance that is in them" (Ephesians 4:18). Herdlike, the mob at Jesus' trial copied the scribes and Pharisees in clamoring for Jesus' crucifixion. At a mob scene in Ephesus in which Paul's life was at risk, "the more part knew not wherefore they were come together" (Acts 19:32).

God's smile of approval is ultimately what counts. We will not be judged by our peers at the Judgment.

About God:

To Do:

Following the Crowd

"Thou shalt not follow a multitude to do evil; neither shalt thou speak in a cause to decline after many to wrest judgment." —Exodus 23:2

Read 1 Samuel 8:4-22

At a large business, employees needed to sign in when late for work and give a reason for being tardy. Frequently one person would write his name and his reason. Subsequent late employees simply signed their names below his and jotted ditto marks under the first person's reason. A common reason for lateness, for example, was fog. One morning, however, the first person on the column wrote for his excuse the words, "Wife had twins." Below that explanation were twenty sets of ditto marks indicating that another twenty employees had the same exciting experience!

On a more somber note, on a sunny morning, September 3, 1999, a thick fog formed along a section of Ontario's busiest highway, the 401. Car followed car into the fog, its driver hoping the highway ahead was clear. It was not. A total of eighty-seven cars, trucks, and vans collided. In this veritable wrecking yard stretching over half a mile, eight people died and eighty-five were injured. Following the crowd, although in ignorance, was perilous.

Paul the Apostle followed the crowd of Jewish leaders and scribes who were persecuting the Christians. After his life was transformed by Jesus Christ, Paul wrote in 1 Timothy 1:13 about personally being "a blasphemer, and a persecutor, and injurious: but I obtained mercy, because I did it ignorantly in unbelief."

Not only do some follow the crowd ignorantly, some are manipulated and deceived into conforming. For example, one man in Utah bought several used cars and lined them up in front of his store. His business increased significantly. Because humans are conditioned to conform, we tend to find the presence of others to be an assurance that what is popular is good and right.

Many in today's culture blindly follow their peers or yield to manipulative measures that nudge them to adhere to the world's lifestyle.

About God: **To Do:**

Don't Follow the Crowd

"Set your affection on things above, not on things on the earth."
—Colossians 3:2

Read 2 Kings 17:5-20

One example of following the crowd has to do with material possessions. Your neighbor has a snowmobile—you need one too. Your coworker has a new pickup—you ought to buy (or lease) one too. Your friend has an automatic electric toe nail clipper—you owe it to yourself to get one too. The advertising world capitalizes on people's tendency to copy what other people have. As one wag said, "My neighbors are keeping me broke. They are always buying things I can't afford."

Consider, also, the matter of sexual morality. Those with a hedonistic or secular agenda promote the idea that nearly all young people engage in premarital sex and nearly all adults have affairs—and that this is normal, fine, and consequence-free. This idea is promoted by many entertainers and educators. Unfortunately, many people justify their natural carnal inclinations on the basis of what is seen in the movies, heard in music, and observed to some extent in their communities. Influential members of the entertainment industry, whose immoral lifestyles others are tempted to mimic, are like the strange woman of Proverbs 7:21-23. "With her much fair speech she caused him to yield, with the flattering of her lips she forced him. He goeth after her straightway, as an ox goeth to the slaughter, or as a fool to the correction of the stocks; till a dart strike through his liver; as a bird hasteth to the snare, and knoweth not that it is for his life."

People also follow the crowd in speech. Many tend to copy slang and questionable expressions without considering whether the words are appropriate or not. Jesus said, "Every idle word that men shall speak, they shall give account thereof in the day of judgment" (Matthew 12:36).

Finally, courting couples can easily follow sub-Christian dating practices of present or previous couples. Practices like holding hands, sitting close, and engaging in physical intimacies are easily copied by peer couples. Also, the practice of dating at an early age (before late teens) is readily followed by subsequent teens at age 16. Young men—don't rob the cradle. And be sure you are well away from the cradle yourself.

It is easier to adopt a peer's weaknesses than his qualities. Therefore, don't follow the crowd—follow the Lord.

About God: **To Do:**

No Fear

"Then said Jesus unto his disciples, If any man will come after me, let him deny himself, and take up his cross, and follow me." —Matthew 16:24

Read Luke 14:25-35

Annie Funk, Mennonite missionary to India, is best known for giving up her seat in a lifeboat of the *Titanic*. But this was just the outgrowth of a life of sacrificial living.

She made a public confession of Christ at age fourteen. Although relatively shy, she taught a Sunday school class in Berks County, Pennsylvania, where she lived. As she grew older she served the Lord in various ways, including a mission in Chattanooga, Tennessee. There she assisted in an outreach among black people.

She also was interested in foreign missions. When she was asked to serve in a mission in India, she wrote, "Several years ago I promised the Lord that if the way would open to go to the foreign field, I would do my duty. Ever since I came to know Jesus as my personal Saviour and to realize what He did for me, I longed to give the message. Now the door is open wide."

In 1906, she set sail for India. When asked about the danger of the ocean voyage, she replied, "Our heavenly Father is as near to us on sea as on land. My trust is in Him and I have no fear." The words remind me of 2 Timothy 1:7: "For God hath not given us the spirit of fear; but of power, and of love, and of a sound mind."

As she learned the language, she began teaching the Bible to village girls and women. She became known for her dedication and unselfish service. She was ready to forsake all to be Christ's disciple, as the daily reading instructs us to do.

She loved the Indians and longed for them to know Christ. About four months after arriving in India, she wrote, "These people are so very ignorant, one's heart aches for them; but they know no better, and, what is worse, they care so little. The idols which they worship represent such sinful characters that one does not wonder that these poor people live in such sin and are bound by fetters which only the power of God can break. Pray that this needy people may see their great need and long for something better. Pray also for the workers that they may have the true spirit of love and devotion and an untiring zeal for the salvation of these people."

About God: **To Do:**

Mennonite Missionary on the *Titanic*

"Greater love hath no man than this, that a man lay down his life for his friends." —John 15:13

Read John 10:9-18

After six years in India, Annie Funk received a telegram from her pastor in Pennsylvania. It told her to come home at once because her mother was very sick.

Hastily Annie packed, then climbed onto a springless oxcart, upon which she rode for 36 hours to Bombay. There she boarded the *S.S. Prussia* bound for England. Disembarking in Italy, she traveled across Europe by train while the ship traveled at a slower pace around Gibraltar.

When she reached England, she discovered that the ship she was planning to take to America was delayed at least six days due to a coal strike. Thomas Cook and Sons, who had made the travel arrangements for her, suggested that by paying extra fare she could sail second class on a brand-new ship, the *Titanic*. It was scheduled to arrive in New York in six days.

As the *Titanic* sailed out of Southampton Harbor, she sent a note back to land by the pilot boat to her friends in India. "I had to get out a few more gold pieces (to pay for passage on the *Titanic*) but I gladly did that to get home six days earlier." She had her thirty-eighth birthday on board the *Titanic*.

On April 14, 1912, the "unsinkable" *Titanic*, carrying 2,207 people but having lifeboats for only 1178, struck an iceberg. Less than three hours later, it sank.

How did Annie respond to the danger?

A British newspaper reported that she gave up her place in a lifeboat to a woman with children. When Annie's friends heard this report they said that it was just like Annie to do something like that.

During the *Titanic*'s brief voyage, Annie had gotten acquainted with a missionary mother from South India and her children. When the *Titanic* began sinking, Annie seated herself in a lifeboat. But when she saw her missionary friend and her children, she gave up her seat to them. "I'll probably find a seat in another lifeboat later," she said.

How about you? Would you have given up your seat in a lifeboat? Annie passed the supreme test of sacrificial love. She died that another might live.

About God: **To Do:**

John Troyer: Mennonite Martyr

"For I am in a strait betwixt two, having a desire to depart, and to be with Christ; which is far better." —Philippians 1:23

Read Acts 21:10-14, 27-39

John braced himself for the bullet as his wife and small children pled with the gunman, "Have mercy. Don't shoot."

The midnight gunman who had forced them from their mission house in the mountains of Guatemala assumed that they were rich Americans who had come to take advantage of the poor natives. In reality, these American missionaries were sacrificing their time, efforts, and love for the Guatemalan people.

John Troyer's intent was to serve the Lord by helping others. I knew him as a decent and spiritual young man. Although I lived in Ontario and he in Michigan, we visited back and forth a number of times in youth groups. After John married Marie, they visited me and my wife at our home. Little did I realize that I was talking with a man who would become a Mennonite missionary martyr.

Are your fellow youth willing to die for Christ? to live for Christ? Are you committed to Christ to the point of death? Are you ready to give your body a living sacrifice literally?

Another bullet came, but it missed John, then another. Maybe he wouldn't be killed after all. He and Marie had tried to explain how they were sacrificially helping the local people. They gave blankets, medicines, and clothing. They taught the people better farming methods and helped them make a better living. They gave interest-free loans to finance their crops. They told them about salvation through Jesus.

But the guerrilla leader was not persuaded. When the gunman who had been shooting at John could not or would not shoot to kill, the leader raised his gun and fired. John's body slumped to the ground and lay still, but his soul ascended to heaven.

That evening, a few hours before his martyrdom, John had testified in the church service using a favorite verse, "For to me to live is Christ and to die is gain."

As shown in the daily reading, the Apostle Paul, who wrote Philippians 1:21, was ready to risk his life to do what he believed to be God's will for him.

How about you? Let us be "faithful unto death" (Revelation 2:10).

About God: **To Do:**

Menno Simons

"For other foundation can no man lay than that is laid, which is Jesus Christ." —1 Corinthians 3:11

Read 2 Corinthians 4

Menno Simons was a man of sacrifice. He left a life of ease as a Roman Catholic priest in Holland to become an Anabaptist bishop hunted relentlessly by the authorities. Instead of wasting his time drinking and playing cards, he began to teach the Gospel, baptize new believers, write books, and give direction to churches. Menno and his wife had no home of their own for many years, but were constantly on the run to avoid capture. For twenty-five years he led souls to Christ, established churches, and wrote books to strengthen believers. He didn't lay down his life in martyrdom, but laid it down day by day for the church and its foundation, Jesus Christ.

Like the Apostle Paul, Menno was courageous, risking his life countless times. Usually he held church meetings in the late evening and traveled at night, hiding during the day to escape detection. But sometimes he felt led to boldly confront his enemies with the Gospel. According to "A Hundred Guilders for Menno," by Elmo Stoll, he walked into a village church where the priest was just completing mass. Menno witnessed to him in Latin and showed him the error of the Roman Catholic church. The priest was greatly surprised. He later became a Christian and joined the Anabaptists.

On another occasion he walked up to a notice on a church door. He saw his name in large letters and a description of himself. Then he saw the huge reward for information leading to his capture.

Menno walked in and met a startled priest. Menno witnessed to him, urging him to repent and search the Scriptures.

"Who are you and who sent you here?"

Menno bravely replied, "I am a servant of the Lord, and God sent me to speak to you about your soul." Then he turned abruptly and hurried out into the street.

Menno was a man of love. Once while visiting a congregation in Wismar, on the northern coast of Germany, he heard that a ship was stuck in the ice. The mayor of Wismar refused to help the English refugees onboard. So Menno and his followers immediately gathered food, clothing, and money and took them to the ship. They also invited the refugees to leave the ship and stay in their homes. He taught nonresistance and he lived it.

About God: **To Do:**

August 24

Teacheress But Not Traitoress

"He that is void of wisdom despiseth his neighbour: but a man of understanding holdeth his peace." —Proverbs 11:12

Read 1 Corinthians 12:12-27

"Here's a Bible. We've come to the right house," said one of the arresting officers. "And here's the teacheress. You are under arrest," they told Elizabeth.

Then they asked her, "Where is your husband, Menno Simons, the teacher?"

In reality, Elizabeth was a godly Anabaptist woman who was single. She was soon put on trial in the religious court.

First they asked her under oath to say whether she had a husband.

She said, "We ought not to swear but our words should be yea, yea and nay, nay; I have no husband."

"We've been told you are a teacher. We want to know who your friends are. We want to know who you have taught."

Elizabeth answered, "Oh, no, my lords, leave me in peace about this but interrogate me about my faith which I will gladly tell you."

"We shall make you so afraid that you will tell us."

She answered, "I hope through the grace of God to keep my tongue and not become a traitoress."

They asked her what she believed about Communion and baptism and how her beliefs compared with their Roman Catholic doctrines.

Since they couldn't convince her to relinquish her grip on Bible teachings, they brought her to the torture chamber. They applied the thumbscrews to her thumbs and forefingers so that the blood squirted out at the nails.

She said, "Oh, I cannot endure it any longer."

The persecutor said, "Confess and we will relieve your pain."

But she prayed, "Help me, O Lord. You are a helper in time of need."

They said, "Confess to us. Don't pray to God."

But she steadfastly adhered to God, and the Lord took away her pain. She said, "I no longer feel the least pain in my flesh."

So they applied the screws to her shins, one on each.

"O my lords, do not put me to shame, for never a man touched my bare body."

"We'll not treat you dishonorably," they said.

She fainted. When she revived, they asked her many more questions. But *Martyrs Mirror* tells us that "they obtained not one word from her detrimental to her brethren in the Lord."

How about your speech about your fellow church members? Do you gossip about them or speak discourteously about them? Or do you have "care one for another" as verse 25 of the daily reading says? Be loyal like Elizabeth.

About God: **To Do:**

Reaping What Was Sown

"He that despiseth his neighbour sinneth: but he that hath mercy on the poor, happy is he." —Proverbs 14:21

Read Psalm 41

"Sir," Aaron Rempel heard a man call, "please help us." Aaron was carrying some groceries home from Gnadenfeldt, a town in southern Ukraine during the Russian Revolution in 1917.

"Sir, we've been in this boxcar all day with nothing to eat. Can you help us?" Aaron saw communist soldiers of the Red Army who had been captured by the White Army of the Czar and were being shipped by boxcar to Siberia. Acting on his Christian principles, Aaron began shoving bread, cheese, and sausages through the slats to the enemy soldiers inside.

"Thank you, sir," said the man when all the food was passed through.

"God bless you," replied Aaron.

Later in the war the communist armies won victory after victory and returned to Gnadenfeldt. They rounded up the landowners, including the Mennonite farmers. Aaron Rempel was among those who were sent to Siberia.

Trying to make a living in Siberia, he began a business of buying tea from Mongolia and reselling it. But the communist government didn't approve of anyone operating a business. They thought only the state should do that, so Aaron was arrested. After the trial, the Commissar said, "Step forward to receive your sentence."

I will be executed, Aaron thought

The Commissar looked at him. "I think we have met before," he commented.

Aaron was surprised, "No, Your Honor," he replied, "we have never met."

"Yes, I think we have. Were you ever in Gnadenfeldt?"

Aaron smiled. "Why, yes, I lived there."

The Commissar continued, "Do you remember one evening when a man called to you from a boxcar, and said, 'We are so hungry. We have been in here all day with nothing to eat?' "

"Yes," Aaron said, "I remember that."

"And what did you do?"

"Why," Aaron said, "I went over to the boxcar and shoved my bread and cheeses and sausages through the slats."

"And what did you say?" the commissar asked.

Aaron paused for a moment and then replied, "I think I said, 'God bless you.' "

The Commissar said, "Yes, we have met before. I was the man who called you. You may go free. I'll sign the papers you need for your family to emigrate to another country."

Aaron's life well illustrates the truth of the first verse of the daily reading. Aaron sacrificed his groceries but received much more in return. Galatians 2:10 says, "We should remember the poor."

About God: **To Do:**

Curtis Cressman

"Looking for that blessed hope, and the glorious appearing of the great God and our Saviour Jesus Christ." —Titus 2:13

Read Matthew 25:31-46

My grandpa, Curtis Cressman, made many sacrifices. One spring he wanted to sell his heavy Western horse. A farmer liked the horse and agreed to buy it. He couldn't pay for it immediately, he said, so Curtis let him take it along without paying. The buyer used the horse for several weeks until his spring seeding was done, then brought it back and refused to pay for the horse or the use of the horse. He claimed that the horse was hard to handle (although my mom, then fourteen, had easily handled him). My mom really admired her dad's attitude of calm acceptance. He followed the teaching of Romans 12:18: "If it be possible, as much as lieth in you, live peaceably with all men."

Curtis sacrificed for the church. Ordained at age twenty-two while still single, he preached for fifty years. He gave bishop oversight to several congregations and served on numerous committees and boards without monetary remuneration.

During World War II, he visited, taught, and encouraged conscientious objectors in a camp in northern Ontario where the Trans-Canada Highway was being built.

But it was his love and sacrifice for a seven-year-old orphan (my mother) that especially impacted me. He and his wife opened their home, receiving no pay, to this naughty, hard-to-handle waif who had lived insecurely and fearfully at an orphanage. He demonstrated the teaching in our daily reading: I was a stranger and ye took me in.

After one especially trying day during which she had disobeyed, stolen, and lied, they decided to return her to the orphanage the next morning when they went to sell cheese and butter at the Kitchener market. But when my mom awoke the next morning, they had gone without her. Curtis had decided to have compassion and give her another chance. After a few years, she gave her heart to the Lord and became a godly woman known for her holiness, patience, and integrity.

The orphanage wanted Curtis to take another orphan who was on the slow side. Curtis said they couldn't afford to support another orphan, though he nevertheless agreed, with the orphanage paying for some of her clothing. Though he was not rich, he helped the poor.

As Psalm 37:21, 26 says, "The righteous sheweth mercy, and giveth . . . and his seed is blessed." Certainly as one of Curtis's descendants (seed), I have been blessed.

About God: **To Do:**

Wilt Thou Destroy Thyself?

"The integrity of the upright shall guide them: but the perverseness of transgressors shall destroy them." —Proverbs 11:3

Read Proverbs 5:1-14

The use of tobacco decreases a man's life by 13 years and a woman's by 14.5 years. The Center for Disease Control and Prevention in Atlanta also reported that smoking resulted in about 440,000 deaths a year in the United States at the turn of the century.

The problem of hurting oneself and causing physical and spiritual damage to oneself is not new. God told the people of Israel, "Thou hast destroyed thyself; but in me is thine help" (Hosea 13:9). Besides tobacco usage, how else does a person in the twenty-first century embark on such a path?

In some countries of Africa, one out of four people in the prime of life die due to AIDS. Some AIDS sufferers are innocent victims (including children and some spouses), but it is sexual impurity which brings the dreaded condition upon many. Forty million have HIV-AIDS. Tens of millions of children in Africa have been orphaned by AIDS. AIDS has taken the lives of twenty-four million people as of 2001. In North America, sexually transmitted diseases (STDs) are the symptoms of people destroying not only themselves, but also others. The Alan Guttmacher Institute claims that one out of five Americans (that is, about 60 million people) have an STD.

Drugs are destroying many people's minds and often their health. When my daughter worked in the emergency department at a local hospital, she dealt with people who came complaining of symptoms like lower-back pain and begged for pain-killing drugs. Some of these complaints were legitimate, while other individuals were assessed as being dependent on drugs and looking for a high from a narcotic.

Suicide is an irreversible way of destroying oneself. Rock culture popularizes suicides. One song says suicide is right, and if your life isn't going well, you can check out whenever you like.

Thank God, there is hope and help. God says, "You have been destroying yourself, but in me you can have help." Receive the gift of salvation "through Jesus Christ our Lord" (Romans 6:23). Salvation produces a change within that breaks the chains of sinful self-destruction. How tragic that people pay a high price for being lost when salvation is free!

About God: **To Do:**

August 28

Losing One's Brain to Alcohol

"Wine is a mocker, strong drink is raging: and whosoever is deceived thereby is not wise." —Proverbs 20:1

Read Proverbs 23:19-28

If you don't use your brain and avoid drunkenness, you could literally be losing your brain. Youth, if you want to maintain your mental capacity, think soberly about the effects of alcohol.

The link between heavy alcohol consumption and loss of gray matter has been suspected for quite some time, but now research has proven it. According to a report by Australian scientists in the *British Medical Journal,* heavy drinking shrinks the brain. In the Australian study the brains of alcoholics weighed an average of 105 grams less than those who didn't drink. Scientists examined the brains of 44 people who had died at an average age of fifty-eight. Half had been drinking heavily for thirty or forty years and their brains weighed an average of 1,315 grams compared with the normal average of 1,420 grams.

Several centuries ago, Shakespeare said, "O God, that men should put an enemy in their mouths to steal away their brains."

Several millennia ago, Solomon said, "Hear thou, my son, and be wise, . . . be not among winebibbers; . . . for the drunkard . . . shall come to poverty" (Proverbs 23:19-21). These verses warn against the high cost economically of strong drink. But they also have an application, mentally, for alcoholic consumption tends to impoverish brain cells.

Paul warns against alcohol in the context of being wise rather than being a fool. Ephesians 5:15, 17, 18 says, "See then that ye walk circumspectly, not as fools, but as wise. Wherefore be ye not unwise, but understanding what the will of the Lord is. And be not drunk with wine, wherein is excess; but be filled with the Spirit." In fact, a person loses an estimated 10,000 brain cells each time he becomes tipsy. And brain cells are irreplaceable. Skin, liver tissue, and blood cells can be replaced after damage or loss, but a brain cell which is lost cannot be replaced. In other words, every sip moves one closer to senility.

Isaiah 28:7, 8 paints a vivid picture of the effects of alcohol: "But they also have erred through wine, and through strong drink are out of the way; the priest and the prophet have erred through strong drink, they are swallowed up of wine, they are out of the way through strong drink; they err in vision, they stumble in judgment. For all tables are full of vomit and filthiness, so that there is no place clean."

About God:

To Do:

Mental Effects of Alcohol

"Let us walk honestly, as in the day; not in rioting and drunkenness, not in chambering and wantonness, not in strife and envying." —Romans 13:13

Read Proverbs 23:29-35

It's not only habitual drinkers who suffer mental impairment. In one study, trained typists were tested and their errors increased forty percent after taking only small quantities of alcohol.

But most typing errors don't cause broken bones, spinal paralysis, and death. Driving errors do. To be more precise, each year in the United States, 26,000 deaths are caused by alcohol-related accidents. (In addition, drunk drivers injure or permanently disable one million people annually.)

Alcohol also affects the memory. Tests have shown that imbibing three bottles of beer can cause a temporary loss of memory averaging thirteen percent.

The effect of alcohol on one's mental powers to think and speak is easily observed by anyone who has associated with drinking or drunken people. Solomon wrote of the babbling and contentions caused by alcoholic consumption (Proverbs 23:29) and warns the drinker, "Thine heart shall utter perverse things" (Proverbs 23:33).

The final effect of excessive booze on one's brain is death. And it's not just older people who are affected. Alcohol consumption is the second highest cause of death among teenagers.

But drunkenness causes something worse than loss of brain cells, memory, mental alertness, and life itself. According to the Bible, it also causes one to lose one's soul! Galatians 5:21 clearly says of drunkenness and reveling that "they which do such things shall not inherit the kingdom of God." This warning to avoid drinking alcohol is repeated in 1 Corinthians 6:10 and a host of other Scriptures.

In the early days of Northern Ontario's gold rush (1909), Sandy McIntyre discovered the now famous mine that bears his name. He sold it for twenty-five dollars in order to buy some liquor. Years later he still passed his time crying in the beverage room while the mine he discovered produced gold worth two hundred and thirty million dollars! That's a typical exchange for alcohol. The drinker is always the ultimate loser. But the person who drinks the "living water" that Jesus offers to each seeking soul is always the ultimate winner. This salvation, which Jesus compared to living water, is satisfying, free, and eternal.

Don't be a loser by looking to liquor. Look to the Lord. He'll keep you from the deadly stuff and give you living water.

About God: **To Do:**

Physical Effects of Alcohol

"And be not drunk with wine, wherein is excess; but be filled with the Spirit." —Ephesians 5:18

Read Isaiah 5:1-22

Just how dangerous and harmful is alcohol? The life span of alcoholics is ten to twelve years shorter than that of non-drinkers. And a host of sicknesses, accidents, and crimes follow the bottle.

In a study analyzing sickness in 130,000 alcoholics in Ontario between the ages of 20 and 70, some startling figures come to light. Although they formed only 3 percent of the population, they accounted for these percentages of death: cirrhosis of the liver, 65 percent; peptic ulcer, 23 percent; cancer of the larynx, 32 percent; stomach cancer, 19 percent; cancer of the mouth and throat, 12 percent.

Some studies indicate that there may be some health benefits of moderate consumption of wine. However, in the total picture, alcohol has a devastating effect on America's health. Total abstinence is sensible, safe, and Scriptural.

Young person, follow Daniel's example. He "purposed in his heart that he would not defile himself . . . with the wine" (Daniel 1:8). Alcohol is the number one drug problem among youth. An estimated 46 million adolescents, ages 14 through 17, experience negative consequences of alcoholic use—arrest, involvement in car accidents, impairment of health or job performance, and death.

Alcohol causes not only illness and death to oneself, but those who drink injure and kill millions of others. Take auto accidents, for instance. According to the National Safety Council (U. S.) there is a fifty-fifty chance that any one citizen (you!) will become involved in an alcohol-related accident within his or her lifetime.

One grandmother wrote after her granddaughter was killed by a drunken driver, "They say that gasoline and liquor do not mix. But we as a family have learned that they do. They mix with flesh and blood and dirt and gravel and sand and steel and stone."

Have a look at these statistics from the eighties, taken from U .S. Health and Human Services and FBI files. Alcohol was involved in 70 percent of murders, 41 percent of assaults, 50 percent of rapes, 37 percent of suicides, 45 percent of drownings, 53 percent of fire deaths, 55 percent of arrests, and caused the most admissions to mental hospitals.

Even more seriously, drunkenness leads to spiritual death. Elah, an Israelite king (1 Kings 16:8-10) was "drinking himself drunk" when his enemy, Zimri, assassinated him. If we follow his example of drunkenness, our enemy, Satan, will have the advantage and will destroy us spiritually.

About God: **To Do:**

Smoking Kills

"Let us cleanse ourselves from all filthiness of the flesh."
—2 Corinthians 7:1

Read 1 Corinthians 3:16-23

- Each year smoking kills millions worldwide.
- One person in the world dies every 10 seconds as a result of tobacco use.
- There are 1.1 billion smokers in the world.
- On the average, each cigarette costs the smoker 14.4 minutes of his life.
- Each day, about 1,000 people in the U.S. die prematurely from smoking.
- At the end of one week, a pack-a-day smoker has lost almost 2 days (42 hours) of his life.
- Typically, by the time a smoker is 55, his system has deteriorated to the extent that his body is no better than a non-smoker's at 75.
- A 2002 report says that every pack of cigarettes sold in the United States costs the country seven dollars in medical aid and lost productivity.
- A non-smoker exposed to smoke on a consistent basis suffers long-term impairment equal to one who smokes 11 cigarettes per day.
- A 1989 report stated that in the United States, 75 Americans die each year from abuse of marijuana, 2,000 from cocaine, 4,000 from heroin and morphine, and 346,000 from tobacco.

The Bible says, "Know ye not that ye are the temple of God, and that the Spirit of God dwelleth in you? If any man defile the temple of God, him shall God destroy; for the temple of God is holy, which temple ye are" (1 Corinthians 3:16, 17). God is a guest in the Christian's body. Who would want a guest to live in a filthy dwelling? The Divine Guest will not reside in an unclean life. And 2 Corinthians 7:1 says, "Having therefore these promises, dearly beloved, let us cleanse ourselves from all filthiness of the flesh and spirit, perfecting holiness in the fear of God."

The Christian should not be filled with smoke but filled with the Spirit.

About God: **To Do:**

September 1

Don't Sleep and Drive

"And there sat in a window a certain young man named Eutychus, being fallen into a deep sleep: and as Paul was long preaching, he sunk down with sleep, and fell down from the third loft, and was taken up dead." —Acts 20:9

Read Ephesians 5:14-21

Falling asleep while driving on a busy Phoenix street one autumn day was a wake-up call for Ruth Phares. "By the grace of God there were no cars around," said the fifty-two-year-old woman. "The next thing I knew I was in the next lane. And I don't know how I got there."

Nearly one in five Americans has dozed off while driving, according to the United States National Sleep Foundation 2000 Sleep in America Poll. Over fifty percent of motorists drive while drowsy. Each year an estimated 100,000 auto crashes across the United States involved drivers who were drowsy.

Three in ten drivers reported actually dozing off at the wheel, and twelve percent of that group had crashed as a result.

Most Christians in North America are motorists. How should we view driving and potential dozing? We could adapt the words of Ephesians 5:15, "See then that ye walk circumspectly" to say "drive circumspectly." *Circumspectly* means "watchfully" and "alertly." Here are some specific suggestions and observations about driving circumspectly.

Remember that the commandment, "Thou shalt not kill," applies to motorists as well as to gun owners. Trying to drive safely is an important aspect of nonresistance. Vehicle crashes are a leading cause of death among children and young adults, and a major cause of brain and spinal cord injury.

Be a good steward of the body by being a good driver. "What? Know ye not that your body is the temple of the Holy Ghost which is in you, which ye have of God, and ye are not your own? For ye are bought with a price: therefore glorify God in your body, and in your spirit, which are God's" (1 Corinthians 6:19, 20). An estimated thirteen percent of automobile deaths are caused by people who fall asleep at the wheel. This is a large number of deaths in view of an estimated 43,000 roadway fatalities.

Be considerate of other drivers on the road and of their health that could be impacted by your drooping eyelids. In the United States each year, approximately 2.6 million people are disabled by motor vehicle accidents. Ephesians 5:2 says, "Walk [or drive] in love."

About God: **To Do:**

Seven Practical Suggestions for Driver Alertness

"Let us watch and be sober." —1 Thessalonians 5:6

Read Matthew 26:36-46

1. Be alert to the effects of certain drugs and medications on drowsiness. Read labels on over-the-counter prescriptions and medicines for warnings such as "may cause drowsiness" or "avoid driving a motor vehicle." Sleepiness can be associated with medicines to treat colds, allergies, high blood pressure, and depression.

2. If possible, have someone ride with you on a trip. Even if the person is unable to give you a break by driving, just having a person to talk to can keep you more alert. When I drive alone, I tend to listen to cassette tapes with thought-provoking sermons or lectures on them. Proverbs 27:17 says, "Iron sharpeneth iron; so a man sharpeneth the countenance of his friend." A friend can also sharpen us mentally and physically when driving.

3. Be alert to times of increased danger of drowsiness—after a noon or evening meal, or when driving late at night. Peter, James, and John succumbed to sleep in the Garden of Gethsemane late one night even though "their spirits were willing" to stay awake (see Matthew 26:41). Afternoons from 1:00 to 5:00 are a time of increased drowsiness for most people—the cause being a circadian rhythm associated with the earth's rotation.

4. Counteract factors contributing to drowsiness, such as sun glare causing fatigue, boredom, or an interior car temperature on the warm side. When I begin to get drowsy, I may sing loudly, quote Scripture expressively, clap my hands vigorously, open windows wide in cool or cold weather, or stop the car and run around it speedily.

5. Stop driving at the onset of drowsiness and take a nap. If you can't nap, at least rest and also get some exercise.

6. Be aware that stimulants such as caffeine have only short-term effects on drowsiness.

7. Prepare for a trip by aiming to get adequate sleep the night before. Two friends of mine worked hard through a long day and into the evening; then at about midnight, they embarked on a 2,000-mile journey. First one youth drove and then the other. Within several hours, the driver fell asleep, resulting in a serious wreck.

The Bible tells us to be "redeeming the time" (Ephesians 5:16), but driving while dangerously drowsy is not a good use of time. If you have plans for tomorrow, drive alertly today.

About God: **To Do:**

Learn of Jesus

*"Now when they saw the boldness of Peter and John,
and perceived that they were unlearned and ignorant men, they marvelled;
and they took knowledge of them, that they had been with Jesus."* —Acts 4:13

Read Matthew 11:28–12:21

Jesus is the Master Teacher. And He wants you to be His pupil. What an invitation He gives you in the daily reading! He has matchless qualifications, for He knows all things. His teaching ability is superb—even the authorities who came to arrest Him said, "Never man spake like this man" (John 7:46). He has had thousands of years of teaching experience. And His example is perfect.

What should we learn of Him after we learn to know Him as our personal Saviour and find rest?

- *Meekness.* Jesus was meek and lowly in heart. He took unfair criticism calmly. He took abuse without retaliation. He lived humbly. He portrayed a servant attitude. He showed that meekness is not weakness, but controlled strength.
- *Burden-bearing.* The reason that His yoke is easy (fits well) and His burden is light relates to His presence to help us. When my son was young, he liked to help me carry long, heavy planks. I was glad he wanted to help. In reality, I lifted the plank close to the middle while he grasped the lighter end. So it is with Jesus. He carries the greater weight of our burdens. We are invited to cast all our care upon Him.
- *Forgiving love.* Repeatedly He forgave others—to the adulterous woman He said, "Neither do I condemn thee: go, and sin no more" (John 8:11).
- *Prayer life.* He prayed in the morning. "In the morning, rising up a great while before day, he went out, and departed into a solitary place, and there prayed" (Mark 1:35). He prayed during the day, for example, at the grave of Lazarus. See John 11:41, 42. He prayed in the evening. "And when he had sent them away, he departed into a mountain to pray. And when even was come, the ship was in the midst of the sea, and he alone on the land" (Mark 6:46, 47). He prayed during the night. "He went out into a mountain to pray, and continued all night in prayer" (Luke 6:12).
- *Compassion.* Repeatedly, the Gospels tell us He was moved with compassion. Compassion is an understanding of the troubles and hurts of others coupled with a deep desire to help.
- *Self-sacrifice.* Learn from Him to live sacrificially. Like Him, a Christian should be willing to "lay down his life for his friends" (John 15:13).

About God: **To Do:**

Learn the Bible

"But continue thou in the things which thou hast learned and hast been assured of, knowing of whom thou hast learned them." —2 Timothy 3:14

Read Deuteronomy 4:1-24

An alumnus, shown a list of current examination questions by his old political science professor, exclaimed, "Why those are the same questions you asked when I was in school!"

"Yes," said the professor, "we ask the same questions every year."

"But don't you know that students hand the questions along from one year to the next?"

"Sure," said the professor, "but in political science we change the answers."

The Bible, in contrast, has dependable, durable answers. Therefore it is worthwhile and imperative to learn its truth. As the daily reading indicates, God's people should learn God's Word that they may learn to fear God (v. 10). Deuteronomy 5:1 says, "And Moses called all Israel, and said unto them, Hear, O Israel, the statutes and judgments which I speak in your ears this day, that ye may learn them, and keep, and do them."

Children also need to learn the Bible. Deuteronomy 31:12, 13 says, "Gather the people together, men, and women, and children, and thy stranger that is within thy gates, that they may hear, and that they may learn, and fear the LORD your God, and observe to do all the words of this law: and that their children, which have not known any thing, may hear, and learn to fear the LORD your God, as long as ye live in the land whither ye go over Jordan to possess it."

It's never too late to learn Bible teaching. Isaiah 29:24 says that when people see God's work, "they that murmured shall learn doctrine."

It is a great privilege to learn Bible knowledge and application from Sunday to Sunday. Do you tune out the Sunday school teacher and the preacher, or do you listen to learn? Don't be like one college student who said, "The only thing I learned at college was how to sleep sitting up."

The Bible was written expressly for our learning. As Romans 15:4 says, "For whatsoever things were written aforetime were written for our learning, that we through patience and comfort of the scriptures might have hope."

The teachings of Scripture are meant for our protection, correction, and direction. Therefore, apply thyself wholly to the Scriptures and the Scriptures wholly to thyself.

About God: **To Do:**

September 5

Learn to Do Well

"A wise man will hear, and will increase learning." —Proverbs 1:5

Read Isaiah 1:10-20

David Livingstone, missionary to Africa said, "People talk of the sacrifice I have made in spending so much of my life in Africa. Can that be called a sacrifice which simply pays back a small part of the great debt we owe God? Is anything a sacrifice when it brings its own blessed reward in healthful activity, consciousness of doing good, peace of mind, and a bright hope of a glorious destiny hereafter? Away with such a thought. It's not sacrifice—it's a privilege."

As shown in the daily reading, it's not religious ritual that's important. It's learning to do well. As another medical missionary, Wilfred Grenfell, said, "The service we render to others is really the rent we pay for our room on this earth."

Christianity is more than talk and testimony. It is also about walk and work. Some of us have the attitude of one man who prayed, "O God, use me in an advisory capacity."

A much better concept of Christian living was expressed by a cowboy of yesterday who said something like this, "Now I'm working for Jim here. If I'd sit around, telling what a good fellow Jim is, and singing songs for him, and getting up in the night to serenade him, I'd be doing just what a lot of Christians do; but I wouldn't suit Jim, and I'd get fired mighty quick. But when I buckle on my chaps and hustle among the hills, and see that Jim's herd is all right and not suffering from lack of water or feed or getting off range and branded by cattle thieves, then I'm proving my love and serving Jim as he wants to be served."

When you stand before the Divine Judge, He will not be asking you about your academic achievements and education or even your Bible knowledge. Rather, He will be asking what you have learned and demonstrated in your spiritual life.

The question is not how much you have gotten, but how much you have given; not how many years you were comfortably retired, but how many you helped who were tired; not how much you have traveled for pleasure, but how much you have walked with the lonely; not how many degrees you have earned, but how many people you have served; not how much you have won for yourself, but what you have done for the Lord.

About God: **To Do:**

Methods of Learning

"For whatsoever things were written aforetime were written for our learning, that we through patience and comfort of the scriptures might have hope." —Romans 15:4

Read James 5:7-20

In reality, all of life is a good time to yearn to learn. There are two basic ways to learn: by observation and by experience.

A wise person studies the lives of others so he can learn from others and at their expense. After recounting the mistakes of the Israelites in the wilderness, Paul writes, "Now all these things happened unto them for ensamples: and they are written for our admonition, upon whom the ends of the world are come" (1 Corinthians 10:11).

We can learn not only from the mistakes of others but also from their good example. Our daily reading talks of learning from the patience of Job and the prayer of Elijah. James 2:22 points to the faith of Abraham. "Seest thou how faith wrought with his works, and by works was faith made perfect?"

Notice how Bible people learned by experience and how we can learn by observing them. A youth by the name of Daniel was tested severely as he stood in the court of the king of the most powerful nation on earth. The king and his subordinate, Melzar, who was over Daniel and his three godly friends, wanted to give provisions to them which were not right to partake of. Daniel learned by experience that by a courteous, reasonable request, an alternative to a wrong route could be accepted. Through it, he received blessing and promotion.

Daniel's three youthful friends learned by experience about the power of God to provide His safety and His presence as they boldly proclaimed allegiance to Him, though it meant viewing the inside of a giant toaster oven.

Experience has been described as "compulsory education." Some things we learn by experience are difficult and painful. We can reduce the pain by observing the lives of others. A wise man learns by the experience of others; an ordinary man learns by his own experience; a foolish man learns by nobody's experience. Difficulties can produce character and draw a person closer to God. It was bitter experience that put the "prod" into the prodigal son.

But experience in the will of God is rich and rewarding. Each person is invited to find out for himself the blessings of a life of obedient faith. Psalm 34:8 beckons, "O taste and see that the LORD is good: blessed is the man that trusteth in him."

About God: **To Do:**

September 7

Learned by Experience

"I waited patiently for the LORD; and he inclined unto me, and heard my cry." —Psalm 40:1

Read Genesis 45:1-15

Did you know that the expression "learned by experience" is from the Bible? It came from the lips of Laban, who said to Jacob who had lived with him for some years, "I have learned by experience that the LORD hath blessed me for thy sake" (Genesis 30:27). Because God's blessing was upon the life of Jacob, Laban indirectly benefited.

I have asked youth what they have learned by experience and read some of their insights. Some examples:

"I have learned that the more respect I give my parents, the more respect they give me," an adolescent told me.

One person said, "Planting Indian corn beside sweet corn doesn't work."

Another said, "I've learned that I can't sin without feeling guilty."

A teenager said, "I've learned not to read while baking."

Another one said, "I've learned that without my daily devotions I can't control my temper or be as kind or be like Jesus as I ought to be."

Another perceptive youth said, "I have learned that when you say, 'I'm not supposed to tell you this, but . . .' you've said too much already."

Another good lesson stated by a teenager: "I have learned that imagining God standing beside me stops me from doing things I know are wrong."

One adolescent said, "I have learned that if you want an honest answer about how you look, ask your little sister."

And from someone who recently emerged from the teenage years, "I've learned that I'm glad I grew up in a poor household. It taught me that one doesn't need a lot of money to be happy, and that there's an advantage to having to struggle a bit."

A teenager by the name of Joseph learned a lot of things by experience—the power of sibling envy, the problems of parental favoritism, the difficulty of sexual temptation, the satisfaction of being trusted by your authority, and the hardships that can result from standing for the right. But by the time he was in his thirties, Joseph could look back over his life with its numerous ups and downs, and say to his brothers, "God sent me before you to preserve a posterity in the earth, and to save your lives by a great deliverance. So now it was not you that sent me hither, but God" (Genesis 45:7, 8).

About God: **To Do:**

Adult Education

"Learn of me; for I am meek and lowly in heart." —Matthew 11:29

Read Matthew 14:22-36

A young friend told me, "I'm returning to university in a week. I love going to school. As long as I keep going to school, I don't need to pay back my student loan from the government."

A student in New York attended school until his death at age sixty-three and acquired numerous degrees. But he never held a job nor did any work. When he was a youth, a rich relative bequeathed him a comfortable living allowance as long as he remained in school so he could get a good education. This income was to cease as soon as he left school. So he went to school year after year and made what was intended to be short-term income last a lifetime.

Jesus invites us to enroll in His school for a lifetime. But there is no monetary attraction. And the courses are very practical and personal.

The Holy Spirit is the excellent registrar and is head of the Promotions Department. He impresses us with the need for Christ's instruction and influence (John 16:8-11). He promotes and glorifies the Instructor (John 16:13, 14). He enrolls us in Christ's School (1 Corinthians 12:13).

In Christ's School, you will find the Perfect Instructor who is always right, yet patient and understanding with our mistakes and lack of understanding. You will find on-the-job training—you receive divine instruction while holding a regular job or while working at home. You must sometimes take night classes as in the daily reading. One night, Peter and the rest of his class saw their Teacher walking on the sea and were taught lessons of trust and divine power, even as Peter's grade was sinking. Christ's School is adaptable to circumstances—a farm, a boat, a house, a prison, or a church. In this school, there are no fees, but the cost may be high.

The curriculum of Christ's Adult Education is broad and balanced. There are lessons on meekness and lowliness of heart. There are lessons about taking Christ's yoke. There are lessons on rest for the soul. Other lessons include prayer, forgiveness, facing difficulties with trust, generosity, sincerity, and numerous courses tailored to our individual needs.

Education with Christ is intended to be put into practice—not an avenue for financial support. Coming and learning in Christ's School means a daily following and fellowship with the Master Teacher.

About God: **To Do:**

September 9

Higher Education

"Behold, the fear of the Lord, *that is wisdom;*
and to depart from evil is understanding." — Job 28:28

Read James 3:17–4:11

Is higher education something you desire to acquire and experience?

Learning that truly represents higher education is found in God. "The wisdom that is from *above*" is higher education in its ultimate sense (James 3:17). It is good to join in the aspiration of the song writer, "Higher, higher in the school of wisdom, More of grace to know." Look at the curriculum outlined in James 3:17:

1. *Purity.* Man's wisdom may lead to sin, but God's wisdom leads to holiness and purity.

2. *Peace.* Human wisdom brings rivalry and conflict, but divine wisdom brings peace—not peace at any price, for the wisdom that is from above is *first* pure, *then* peaceable. The peace of the church is not more important than the purity of the church. Jesus is the source of true wisdom and true peace. What people around the world need is a peace conference with the Prince of Peace.

3. *Gentleness.* Human wisdom teaches me to take a tough, assertive what's-best-for-me approach. God's wisdom teaches kindness, forbearance, and unselfishness. Gentleness features moderation without sinful compromise. A gentle Christian man may be called "velvet steel."

4. *Reasonableness.* A person who is easily entreated will be approachable, willing to listen, and open to change his mind to agree with truth. He will yield to godly persuasion, not being dogmatic, stubborn, nor conceited. A Christian should not be a person who slams his mind in your face.

5. *Mercy.* The wisdom from above has the objective of compassion and forgiveness. *Full of mercy* implies being controlled by mercy. Forgiveness from others is charity; from God, grace; from oneself, wisdom.

6. *Fruitfulness.* God's program of higher education is not just academic but also very practical. Divine wisdom in the heart expresses itself in the life.

7. *Impartiality.* This calls for forgiveness and consistency in working with and relating to others. The world's wisdom teaches one to aim for the inner circle and to be exclusive. A Christian should be a friend of all, free from prejudices.

8. *Sincerity.* The Christian should live without a mask, without hypocrisy. Hypocrisy is like a pin—pointed in one direction yet headed in another.

Stay enrolled in God's school of wisdom so that you can truly experience "higher education."

About God: **To Do:**

Polycarp

"If thine enemy hunger, feed him;
if he thirst, give him drink." —Romans 12:20

Read Revelation 2:1-11

For the next several devotionals, we'll consider people who portrayed an attitude of nonresistance and peace.

Polycarp is referred to in the daily reading. He was the bishop (meaning messenger or leader) of Smyrna. Jesus said to him, "Be thou faithful unto death, and I will give thee a crown of life" (Revelation 2:10).

Polycarp was an important leader in the Early Church. His nonresistant attitude sparkled in his writing, his life, and his death. "Pray for emperors, magistrates, rulers, and for those who persecute and hate you," he wrote to the Philippians. During his life he worked to settle disputes, putting into practice the teachings of love taught by John, the apostle of love, whom he had known personally.

Prior to his martyrdom, Polycarp needed to hide from his enemies. When this aged bishop was finally found, he cordially said to his captors, "You must be hungry." With a nonresistant spirit, he told a friend, "Bring as much food and drink as the soldiers wish." Then he prayed for an hour.

Refusing to offer incense to the emperor-god, Polycarp testified, "Eighty and six years have I served Christ and He never did me wrong. How can I blaspheme my King who saved me?"

He was sentenced to be burned at the stake. After prayer and thanking God that he was "deemed worthy to die," Polycarp gave his life and entered eternal peace.

About God:

To Do:

September 11

Peter Miller

"But I say unto you, Love your enemies, bless them that curse you, do good to them that hate you, and pray for them which despitefully use you, and persecute you." —Matthew 5:44

Read Luke 22:47-62

Jesus showed a wonderful nonresistant attitude of peace, as recorded three times in the daily reading. First, to Judas, who came with hypocrisy in his heart, treachery on his tongue, and cruelty in his kiss, Jesus spoke peaceably. Jesus even called him "Friend" (Matthew 26:50).

Second, to Malchus, the high priest's servant who came to arrest Him, He restored the right ear that Peter had wrongly removed (John 18:10).

Third, to Peter who denied their friendship, He "turned and looked upon Peter" (v. 61) in such a way that Peter wept remorsefully.

Peter Miller was plagued by a most persistent and pernicious persecutor. Although you might wonder if he lived in darkness since his initials are P. M., he walked in the light. His nonresistant attitude and life show us a good approach to take in relating to an enemy.

Peter's enemy, Michael Wittman, did all he could for over 20 years to make life miserable for Peter, injuring his body, his church building, and his ministry. At length, Wittman was arrested for treason and sentenced to death. Did Peter rejoice?

Peter walked 70 miles from Ephrata to Philadelphia to talk to President George Washington, to plead for Wittman's life.

"No," Washington said, "his case is too black; I cannot give you the life of your friend."

"My *friend!* He is the bitterest enemy any man ever had."

After Peter explained, the president said, "Ah, this puts another aspect upon the matter. I could not give you the life of a *friend;* but I will freely pardon your *enemy*."

On the third day, the preacher and his persecutor walked the 70 miles home. Wittman's heart was softened. He became a Christian and Peter Miller baptized him.

About God: **To Do:**

Maximilian

"If it be possible as much as lieth in you, live peaceably with all men."
—Romans 12:18

Read Matthew 5:13-16, 38-42

Referring to Jesus' words about turning the other cheek (Matthew 5:39), Khrushchev, former premier of the communist Soviet Union said, "I cannot agree with Him when He says when you are hit on the right cheek, turn the left cheek. I believe in another principle. If I am hit on the left cheek I hit back on the right cheek so hard that the head might fall off." This statement quoted in the *New York Times* shows a typical attitude of unbelievers—try to overcome evil by doing greater evil.

Jesus' authoritative words from our daily reading, "Ye have heard . . . but I say unto you" heralded a new age. *Nonresistance,* a term taken from verse 39, "resist not [him that is] evil," is clearly God's will for His children today.

Jesus gives a series of examples to illustrate and apply the principle of nonresistance:

- Don't knock out the teeth of someone trying to punch you in the teeth. Instead of fighting back, leave yourself vulnerable to more unkindness rather than retaliating.
- For Jesus' sake be willing to be taken advantage of by unreasonable men, suffering the loss of your coat (the long inner shirt) and even your cloak (the much more valuable outer garment). Don't insist on legal rights but try to be peaceable.
- Do more than is required. Go the second mile. In Roman times, officials could insist on unpaid services. It was therefore like temporary slavery and was considered degrading. One mile was all a Roman official could demand.
- Be willing to donate or lend to another even if it means inconvenience or loss to self.

Maximilian lived in Numidia, in Northern Africa. At age 21, in 295 A.D., he was conscripted to serve in the Roman army. He believed Jesus' words of the daily reading and said, "I cannot serve as a soldier; I cannot do evil; I am a Christian."

Repeatedly, the recruiting officer, Dion, tried to persuade Maximilian to be a soldier. When they threatened to take his life if he wouldn't take the lives of others, he calmly stated, "I shall not perish, but when I shall have forsaken this world, my soul shall live with Christ my Lord." He became a martyr for his nonresistant stand, as recorded in the book *Coals of Fire.*

About God: **To Do:**

September 13

Dirk Willems

"Recompense to no man evil for evil.
Provide things honest in the sight of all men." —Romans 12:17

Read Matthew 5:43-48

Love is the best way to get rid of an enemy—by turning him into a friend. Bless those that curse you—they have enough problems already. Do good to the hateful—it often serves to make them less hateful. Pray for those who pick on you—it will certainly help you maintain a loving, forgiving spirit as well as benefiting them.

Children of God, copy the example of the heavenly Father. "Like Father, like son." He blesses both godly and ungodly with rain, water, food, sunshine, gravity, etc. Surely we should also bless and assist friend and foe.

Christians, because of divine love within, go beyond what is expected by the world. The publicans in Jesus' day who collected taxes were sometimes dishonest and failed to keep Jewish religious regulations. Unbelievers, like publicans, treat their friends well. What is distinctive about believers is their love and goodwill to friend *and* enemy.

Be perfect, that is, complete in love, with no part lacking. Just as a car needs its essential parts in order to be of service (for instance, its wheels), so Christians need that vital part, love for enemies.

Dirk Willems lived in very unpeaceful times, in an age when thousands of Mennonites were martyred. As a teenager, he became a Christian and was baptized. More than once Anabaptists held secret meetings at his house in Holland, and we know Christians were baptized there.

One incident in Dirk's life especially illustrates this verse from our daily reading, "Bless them which persecute you." The authorities wanted to execute Dirk, but first they had to catch him. One cool day they were in hot pursuit of him. Dirk tried running over some thin ice to better his chance of escape. He made it, but the thief-catcher close behind broke through. Dirk, quickly looking back, saw that the thief-catcher was in danger of drowning. What would *you* have done next?

Dirk Willems proceeded to "do good to them that hate you." Back across the ice he went and helped his persecutor out of the freezing water. Because Dirk had saved his life, the thief-catcher wanted to let him go free. But the burgomaster (the man of chief authority in the area) threatened the drenched man, ordering him not to let Dirk go. Incredibly, the rescued man seized his rescuer. Shortly after his unusual arrest, Dirk Willems died a martyr's death.

About God: **To Do:**

David Livingstone

"To speak evil of no man, to be no brawlers, but gentle, shewing all meekness unto all men." —Titus 3:2

Read James 3:12-18

As the daily reading shows, peace is linked with other desirable characteristics. It stems from wisdom. It is connected to purity, gentleness, reasonableness, mercy, good actions, fairness, and sincerity. Peace is promoted when gentleness prevails; when people are open to reason and willing to yield; when mercy flourishes; when kind actions are evident; when people are fair; when sincerity and honesty are present.

In short, peace is promoted by a consistent Christian life. The Anabaptists were described by Roman Catholic opponents in these words: "They call each other brothers and sisters; they use neither profanity nor unkind language; they use no weapons of defense. They are temperate in eating and drinking; they use no vain display of clothes. . . . They do not go to law before judicial courts, but bear everything patiently, as they say, in the Holy Spirit. . . . As concerns their outward public life they are irreproachable. No lying, deception, swearing, strife, harsh language, no intemperate eating and drinking, no outward personal display is found or is discernible among them, but only humility, patience, uprightness, meekness, honesty, temperance, and straightforwardness in such measure that one would suppose that they have the Holy Spirit of God."

David Livingstone, a famous missionary to Africa, tried to be at peace with individuals and to bring peace between races.

For instance, once when Livingstone was misjudged by a fellow missionary, he gave up his house and beloved garden with all the work and money they had cost him, to avoid a scandal in front of the heathen. To avoid a quarrel, he moved away and started afresh. The other missionary was so impressed with Livingstone's generosity that he regretted ever speaking a word against him.

Most of the time he was away from his home, traveling 29,000 miles through Africa, much of it never before seen by a white man. Why did he struggle through the jungles and deserts of Africa? To bring the Gospel of peace to the natives and expose the existence and methods of the ugly slave trade. He saw many lines of blacks chained together, forced with whips to march to the coast to be sold. In one instance, the slave drivers saw David Livingstone and fled to the jungle. Livingstone sawed through the chains to release the captives. All eighty-four freed slaves became Christians.

After thirty years of missionary work in Africa, David Livingstone died . . . on his knees.

About God: **To Do:**

Joris Wippe

"For the Son of man is not come to destroy men's lives, but to save them." —Luke 9:56

Read 1 Peter 2:13-25

Remember first grade? You learned to print neatly. To help you, your teacher probably set up alphabet cards for you to pattern your letters after.

The Greek word translated *example* in our daily reading means precisely a written copy such as is set for children, and more generally, a pattern for imitation. Christ left us "an example that ye should follow." Just as first graders at school need to look at the perfect model and then copy it, so we in the school of life need to look and look again to our Perfect Model and then imitate Him.

What specific ways are mentioned in which we should follow Jesus' example?

1. Do well and suffer patiently for it; this is what Christians are called to (v. 21).
2. Jesus did no sin. We should ask God to cleanse us from all sin and then in the power of the Spirit live in victory over temptation (v. 22).
3. Jesus spoke no deception, insincerity, or hypocrisy throughout His life, not even in His unjust trial (v. 22).
4. When His enemies hurled their insults at Him, He did not retaliate (v. 23). Instead, He prayed for them. Is this your prayer: "O to be like Thee, blessed Redeemer"?
5. When He suffered so unjustly, so cruelly, so innocently, He didn't threaten punishment. He meekly and lovingly bore it all (v. 23).
6. In His suffering He committed Himself to God. We should likewise leave everything in the hands of God (v. 23).

Joris Wippe was certainly not a hippy, although his name rhymes with hippy.

Forty-one-year-old Joris was sentenced to be drowned in a barrel for being an Anabaptist. The executioner refused to drown him. With tears in his eyes, he said, "How can I put to death this good man who has never harmed anyone? He fed my wife and children many times. I cannot do it."

For seven weeks the authorities searched in vain for someone to drown Joris. Finally a thief-catcher carried out the sentence. Before his death Joris wrote letters from prison to his wife and children which you can read on pages 584-588 in *Martyrs Mirror.* In one of them he wrote concerning our reading, "He went before us with much misery and tribulation; we must follow His footsteps."

About God: **To Do:**

Michael Sattler

"Submit yourselves to every ordinance of man for the Lord's sake: whether it be to the king, as supreme." —1 Peter 2:13

Read Romans 12:18-21; 13:1-10

Members of Christ's church return good for evil. Members of the government use force to seize and punish lawbreakers as the daily reading shows.

Christians have duties to perform in relation to the government, according to Romans 13.

Be subject means to be under the control of (v. 5). Why? First, because it is right (*for conscience sake*); second, because of wrath or punishment for wrongdoing.

Pay (v. 6). Tribute simply means taxes, of which there are many forms—sales tax, income tax, property tax, gasoline tax, export tax, etc. As in Nero's day, much tax money is spent to buy military equipment for the army and weapons for the police. Although Christians may not approve of how some tax money is spent, we must pay as Jesus taught (Matthew 17:24-27; 22:17-22).

Respect (v. 7). We should honor our judges, policemen, and government leaders with respectful speech, prayers, and obedience to laws.

Michael Sattler was well-educated and knew the original languages of the Bible. As a priest in Germany, he began studying the Bible in earnest and found peace with God. He left the monastery and married. In 1525 (the year the Mennonite denomination began), he went to Zurich, Switzerland, and united with the Swiss Brethren. He presided over a meeting which approved the Schleitheim Confession.

Michael was soon arrested for his active work for Christ. Very calmly and courageously, he explained his beliefs to a hostile court. Although the judges and officers present were rude and cruel, he referred to their responsibility under God by calling them, "ye ministers of God," and stated that if the most learned men "show us from the Holy Scriptures that we err and are in the wrong, we shall gladly be taught, and recant."

Michael was sentenced to be tortured cruelly and burned at the stake. At his martyrdom he prayed for his judges and persecutors. Soon the fire had burned a cord that bound his right hand and he raised that hand high before his brethren, an agreed-upon sign to them that he had remained steadfast, happy to die for Christ.

About God: **To Do:**

Bitterness Is a Choice

"Forbearing one another, and forgiving one another, if any man have a quarrel against any: even as Christ forgave you, so also do ye." —Colossians 3:13

Read Ephesians 4:20-32

It is clear from verse 31 of the daily reading that you can choose to be bitter or do much better and forgive. The Christian must put bitterness and its relatives away. You can hang on to bitter feelings, nurse them and feed them, and let those feelings destroy your relationship with God, or you can put them away and bury them.

A bitter person always feels justified in not forgiving. "It's not fair—I have a right to feel this way. See what he did to me. See what she said about me. See how she ignores me."

I recognize that many young people have experienced deep hurts of one sort or another. You may have seen favoritism to a sibling. You may have been passed over for a job promotion. You may have been injured by a careless or drunk driver. You may have been dumped by a special friend. You may have been falsely accused of cheating by a teacher. You may have been rejected by parents and put up for adoption. Your dad may have treated you harshly and inconsistently. You may have been abused by an acquaintance of the family.

There are numerous occurrences, big or small, that may give bitterness the opportunity to take root and grow. You may be tempted to say, "How can I help but feel upset, angry, and resentful?" The Psalmist said, "My help cometh from the LORD." Paul testified, "I am crucified with Christ: nevertheless I live; yet not I, but Christ liveth in me: and the life which I now live in the flesh I live by the faith of the Son of God, who loved me, and gave himself for me" (Galatians 2:20).

Bitterness arises from an unsurrendered self. When a Christian is wholly yielded to God's will, he can throw off hurts and resentments as a healthy skin throws off disease germs. If there is a cut or abrasion of the skin, the germs can intrude. If you have bitterness, it shows that there is an opening caused by self which is allowing resentments to fester. Let bitterness be put away by surrendering the whole situation to God.

Every Christian needs two bears: *Bear* and *Forbear*. "Bear ye one another's burdens" (Galatians 6:2); "Forbearing . . . and forgiving one another . . . even as Christ forgave you, so also do ye" (Colossians 3:13).

About God: **To Do:**

Bitterness—A Root

"But if ye have bitter envying and strife in your hearts, glory not, and lie not against the truth." —James 3:14

Read Hebrews 12:12-24

A Christian mother was facing a serious operation. More serious than the physical problem was the spiritual problem caused by a root of bitterness that had been growing in her heart against someone who had wronged her. As she thought about the possibility of dying, she said to her pastor, "Tell him I forgive him. I hold nothing against him. I ask his forgiveness for my bad attitude."

The woman chose to expose the root of bitterness spoken of in our daily reading and deal with it. Esau's life was ruined by this root because he refused to repent.

We should realize four things about the root of bitterness:

1. *It grows.* Weeds with underground stems spread and cause much backache. The weed of malice spreads and causes much heartache. The root can be fed by thought patterns of resentfulness and watered with tears of self-pity. Rather, kill it with the herbicide of forgiveness.

2. *It may not be openly apparent.* Like a root in the soil, it works underground. It may exist in a person who testifies, "I love everybody." You may deny it or fail to identify it. For example, a businessman said, "You won't catch me getting ulcers. For one thing, I just take things as they come. For another, I don't ever hold a grudge, not even against people who have done things to me that I'll never forgive." I think he should have checked with a dictionary about the meaning of *grudge*.

3. *It needs to be dealt with.* If you only deal with the weeds that spring up from the root, but fail to deal with the root, the problem will persist. When I was a boy, my family had a major problem in our garden with twitch, which is a weed with an underground stem. Unless we dug up the roots and exposed them to sun and wind, twitch kept springing up and choking out the good crops. The root of bitterness needs to be exposed by confession to let the sunshine of God's love kill it.

4. *It is not to be in God's garden.* Instead we are to "follow peace with all men."

About God: **To Do:**

September 19

Consequences of Unforgiveness

"And when ye stand praying, forgive, if ye have ought against any: that your Father also which is in heaven may forgive you your trespasses."
—Mark 11:25

Read Matthew 6:5-15

If you choose to harbor bitterness, you suffer the consequences, the most serious being that you'll not be forgiven. As shown by the daily reading, if you don't forgive others, God won't forgive you. St. Francis of Assisi said, "It is in pardoning that we are pardoned."

In addition, bitterness robs one of peace and joy. Few things are more bitter than feeling bitter. In fact, the venom of bitterness poisons you more than it does your victims. True, there is a certain perverse satisfaction in holding a grievance against the person who has hurt you, but ultimately, bitterness sours life for you. I agree with a pastor's wife who said, "Forgiveness is something good you do for yourself."

It is something like being a motorist. You approach an intersection where you have the right of way. A car approaching the intersection at right angles to you has a stop sign but does not slow down. You could say, "I have the right of way; he needs to stop," and continue into the intersection as is your right. You collide. Though you may have acted within your rights, you experience damage to your vehicle and injury to yourself.

Furthermore, bitterness can cause depression. Resentments dragged into the subconscious can wreak havoc on the emotions. Hostility plus self-pity often equals depression.

Also, bitterness begets bitterness. It can cause family feuds. It can give a destructive legacy to children. It can have a ripple effect and sour a brotherhood and destroy a congregation.

Deal with a hurt by godly first aid. Apply direct pressure of love to the wound. Wash the wound thoroughly with forgiveness to remove all revengefulness. Liberally apply the ointment of forbearance. Bandage it with a nonresistant attitude. Don't pick off the scab by rehearsing the injury and opening the wound. Take a dose of spiritual antibiotics from the Word several times daily. Keep in touch with the Great Physician.

About God: **To Do:**

Think of Christ's Forgiveness

"Lord, lay not this sin to their charge." —Acts 7:60

Read Luke 23:32-43

A woman once stayed after a church service to talk with the minister. She was downcast and despondent. "I do not suppose you can help me," she said. "For years I have been unable to pray. There is a woman who came between me and my husband, and I cannot forgive her."

The minister answered kindly, "You cannot forgive the woman for her own sake, but could you not forgive her for Christ's sake?"

At first the question did not register. Then a glimmer of hope lightened the depressed woman's face.

"Yes," she said, "you are right. I cannot forgive her for her own sake, but I can for His sake, and I will!"

Thinking of Christ's forgiveness of me and Christ's example of forgiveness while He lived on earth helps me to forgive others. As Colossians 3:13 says, "Forgiving one another, if any man have a quarrel against any: even as Christ forgave you, so also do ye."

While living in Palestine, He was not bitter to those who opposed Him and tried to hurt Him. While dying on the cross, He prayed for God to forgive. While living again in heaven, He forgives those who come to the cross.

A boy in fourth grade was mistreated by a school official because the man had a grievance with the boy's father. The boy and his parents moved from that town and years went by. The boy became an influential pastor. One day his antagonist came to the area seeking a job as superintendent of schools. The pastor knew that as soon as he told his friends on the school board about the man, the board would not hire him. The pastor, intending to get even, went to his car to go visit some board members. But then he stopped. He thought: *Here I am representing Him that was nailed to the cross, and I am carrying a grudge.* Humiliated, he went back into his house, knelt by his bedside, and prayed for God's forgiveness. He chose to have a forgiving attitude as he thought of Jesus who said, "Father, forgive them," referring to those who had wounded Him and were continuing to cause Him physical, mental, and emotional pain.

Doing good to those who hatefully mistreat you is Jesus' command. It is not natural for unregenerate man, but is normal and necessary for the follower of Jesus.

About God: **To Do:**

September 21

Tests of Forgiveness

"And if he trespass against thee seven times in a day, and seven times in a day turn again to thee, saying, I repent; thou shalt forgive him." —Luke 17:4

Read Matthew 18:21-35

A professing Christian reluctantly agreed to forgive a woman who had wronged her. "Well, I will forgive her, but I never want to have anything more to do with her," she said. Perhaps you have been inclined to have the same sentiments. However, is that the way you want God to forgive you—to have nothing more to do with you?

The daily reading warns of the dire consequences, "if ye from your hearts" don't forgive. Here are some tests of true forgiveness toward another person:

- Do I rejoice at that person's misfortune? If so, that is a sign of malice.
- Do I find fault with the offender? Here's a helpful rule to follow: if criticizing gives you pain, do it; if it gives you the slightest pleasure, keep quiet.
- Do I have feelings against the person? If I still think he ought to pay, then it's hardly forgiveness, full and free.
- Do I avoid the offender? Forgiveness ought to be like a cancelled note—burned up so that it can never be shown against the offender.
- Do I enjoy gossip about the person? It is good to remember that mansions in the sky cannot be built out of the mud thrown at others.
- Do I review the hurt, eagerly rehearsing the injury? There's no point in burying the hatchet if you are going to put up a marker on the site.

Be kind, says Ephesians 4:32. Kindness can test the depth of our forgiveness. Therefore, do good to the one who hurt you. Breathe a prayer for the offender if his name is mentioned or enters your mind. Say good things about the person who has wronged you. Say good things to the person. Love the person for what he may become.

We are most like beasts when we injure and kill. We are most like the offender when we judge and condemn. We are most like God when we show mercy and forgive.

Therefore, as an early church Christian said, "If you are suffering from a bad man's injustice, forgive him lest there be two bad men."

About God: **To Do:**

Reviewing Hurts Hurts Yourself Again

"Thinketh no evil." —1 Corinthians 13:5

Read Genesis 27:30-43

I was with a group of students on an educational tour of a local butcher shop. As the butcher was explaining and demonstrating the use of a power saw, he warned of the danger to fingers. "One butcher got a finger too close to the saw," he said. "As he was pushing a chunk of meat through the blade, it lopped a finger right off.

" 'How did it happen?' asked a friend, visiting the shop sometime later.

" 'Just like this,' said the butcher, demonstrating. And the saw *took another finger off!*"

Reviewing how the injury happened and talking to someone about it brought further injury. So it is in life with the hurts we receive from others. As we think about and mull over our hurts and grievances, we cause ourselves more trouble and harm.

It's the same principle that operates in mastering memory work. The secret is going over it again and again. Where review is combined with intense interest, learning is fast, and makes a real impact in daily living. Going over how we've been mistreated or misused by others rivets the grievance in our mind, engenders bitterness in the heart, and poisons the whole life.

Having continual mental replays of one's emotional hurts is bad for a person *physically.* Holding grudges and resentments can cause indigestion and stomach ulcers as well as other physical problems. One mother-in-law disliked her son-in-law, whom she visited annually. Each time she visited him, arthritis developed. After she returned home again, she was fine.

More serious is damage *spiritually.* Reliving the occasions when others have wounded us violates the Biblical teaching about forgiveness and love. "If any man have a quarrel against any, even as Christ forgave you, so also do ye" (Colossians 3:13).

There is no blessing in bitterness. Think of Esau. He nursed his hurt at the hands of Jacob. Genesis 27:41 tells us how Esau essentially said "in his heart," *I'll get my revenge.* His mother noted that in so doing Esau "doth comfort himself" (v. 42). A grudge offers a perverse comfort to the flesh, but contaminates the soul.

About God: **To Do:**

September 23

Forgive and Forget

"And be ye kind one to another, tenderhearted, forgiving one another, even as God for Christ's sake hath forgiven you." —Ephesians 4:32

Read Genesis 50:14-21

A friend of Clara Barton, founder of the American Red Cross, once reminded her of an especially cruel thing that had been done to her years before. But Miss Barton seemed not to recall it. "Don't you remember it?" her friend asked.

"No," came the reply, "I distinctly remember forgetting it."

How wise is the person who follows the Bible command, "Let not the sun go down upon your wrath" (Ephesians 4:26). Don't let sunset still find you nursing your anger or hurt. If you think about the offense the next day, and the next, day by day it will be harder to gain victory.

For instance, a young lady is "dumped" by her boyfriend, which causes a deep hurt. Day after day, she thinks about how he had led her to believe he really loved her. How he suddenly broke their relationship without much regard for her feelings. How he soon started dating Jessica. Regularly she nurses the resentment. It grows, damaging her spirit and her relationship with others.

Forgive and forget. That is the solution. Forgetting means not reviewing the hurt. But how? Joseph's life teaches us the method.

He consciously decided not to harbor resentment about the past but let God heal the hurt. He called his first son *Manasseh,* meaning "forgetting." "For God, said he, hath made me forget all my toil, and all my father's house" (Genesis 41:51). That is, God helped him forget his past troubles and emotional wounds.

Five more steps can be identified in Joseph's speech in Genesis 50:19-21. After Jacob's death, his brothers expected Joseph would get his revenge. They were wrong. First, Joseph recognized his humanity. "Fear not: for am I in the place of God?" Vengeance and justice would be divinely arranged. Second, he recognized God's plan for his personal life. "As for you, ye thought evil against me; but God meant it unto good." Commit all things to God rather than grudging. Third, he gave his brothers his assurance of forgiveness. "Fear ye not." Verbalizing forgiveness is important. Fourth, he acted positively. "I will nourish you, and your little ones. And he comforted them." Fifth, his words were loving and forgiving, for he "spake kindly unto them."

Let the Holy Spirit apply these principles to your life for spiritual healing and forgiveness. Don't hold your hurts and withhold forgiveness.

About God: **To Do:**

Technology and the Bible

"Elisha . . . was plowing with twelve yoke of oxen." —1 Kings 19:19

Read 2 Chronicles 26:1-15

Each day you are probably surrounded by the imprint of technology—electronics, bikes, knives, cars, clothes, hoes, clocks, books. Not much that you use comes right from nature without being shaped by technology. Technology means applications of science. It involves the use of tools, machines, materials, techniques, and sources of power.

There are various references to technology in the Bible. The development of technology has paralleled the history of man. Jabal applied technology to shelter: "He was the father of such as dwell in tents" (Genesis 4:20). His brother, Jubal, applied technology to leisure time: "He was the father of all such as handle the harp and organ" (Genesis 4:21). Tubal-cain applied technology to manufacturing: he was an "artificer in brass and iron" (Genesis 4:22).

As the Tower of Babel was built, technology was used to make building materials (Genesis 11:3). Isaac told his son Esau to take some technological tools, "thy weapons, thy quiver and thy bow" (Genesis 27:3), and find some venison. Saul had his armor. David had his slingshot. Uzziah, a teenage king, was a technological whiz, according to the daily reading. Not only did his army have shields, spears, helmets, bows, slings, and coats of mail for protecting the chest, but he also invented catapults for hurling large stones.

The New Testament refers to things like plows, fishing nets, tackling, and stocks. Occupations like tanning, carpentry, silversmithing, tentmaking, writing, and masonry all necessitated tools.

Technology has many good uses. Without it, farmers could not feed the billions of people on earth. It is used to print Bibles and Gospel literature. It enables missionaries to go into the entire world. It helps fathers have jobs to support families. Paper, pens, books, and school supplies are used in the education of children. It permits people to keep in touch with friends who are far away.

We thank God for the inventions and applications of science that help us to meet our own needs, the needs of our families, and the needs of people far away. But also we should ask God for discernment in a technological age because there are many applications of science that are put to sinful uses and are snares.

About God: **To Do:**

September 25

Principles in Identifying Snares

"Be sober, be vigilant; because your adversary the devil, as a roaring lion, walketh about, seeking whom he may devour." —1 Peter 5:8

Read Ephesians 5:1-17

Based on the daily reading, we can ask fourteen questions about whether we should buy or use a particular application of technology—tools, transportation devices, electronic inventions, etc.

1. Will it make it easier to be a "follower of God?" (v. 1) Or will it hinder my walk with Him and bring distance to our relationship?
2. Will it make it easier to resist sexual temptations (v. 3)? Or will it bring enticement to sin, in thought and deed, tempting one to "uncleanness"?
3. Will it cause me to hear inappropriate speech or see unwholesome pictures (v. 4)? "Jesting" means the use of words with double meanings, one of which is impure. Instead of filthiness and foolish talking, a Christian's life is characterized by thanksgiving.
4. Will it enhance my worship of God or make me an idolater (v. 5)?
5. Will it be a possible means of deception, bringing me in contact with "vain words" (v. 6)?
6. Will it mean fellowship with evil (v. 7)? Instead, we should give a clear testimony against evil.
7. Will it help me to walk in the light (v. 8)? Or will it cause me to walk in the twilight zone of compromise?
8. Will it cultivate the fruit of the Spirit (v. 9)? The Spirit of God is grieved if we fail to be fruitful in goodness, right living, and integrity.
9. Is it acceptable to the Lord (v. 10)? Have you sincerely prayed about it?
10. Will your use of it be a rebuke to sin (v. 11)? When people discover I don't have television, they often admit to watching shows that are unwholesome or foolish.
11. Will it act as a spiritual sleeping pill (v. 14)? Or will it increase my usefulness to the Lord?
12. Will it reveal that I am acting circumspectly (v. 15)? This means carefully looking around to see if there is danger. For example, it means that physically I look around to see if the sidewalk is icy or if there are mud puddles to avoid.
13. Will it help me to redeem the time (v. 16)? Much electronic gadgetry wastes time that could be used to edify people and glorify God.
14. Is it God's will (v. 17)? If it violates the Bible or a church or home standard, it is not.

About God: **To Do:**

Technological Traps

"For ye are bought with a price: therefore glorify God in your body, and in your spirit, which are God's." —1 Corinthians 6:20

Read Isaiah 44:1-24

One danger of technology is *physical*—wrecked cars, PTO shafts, radiation, a tendency to obesity, etc. We are to be good stewards of our bodies. Therefore, take safety precautions around machinery. Get the brakes repaired. Be careful with electricity. Balance your activities so they include adequate exercise.

Another danger is *devotional*. Does technology help you to meditate? to pray? You can talk on a cell phone with technology, but you can't talk to God through technology. Somehow technology contributes to busyness and a rat-race mentality. Logically, technology should provide more time for prayer and communion, but it rarely does.

We travel much faster than in previous centuries. In 1850, travel by land featured speeds of nine mph by stagecoach and 23 mph by clipper ship. Compare that with interstate, rail, or jet travel. But does traveling fast help us walk with God? Not necessarily. "Be still, and know that I am God" (Psalm 46:10).

Another danger is *financial*. Does technology teach contentment or covetousness—a desire for more things and money? "They that will be rich fall into temptation and a snare, and into many foolish and hurtful lusts, which drown men in destruction and perdition" (1 Timothy 6:9). The advertising industry makes sure we find out about new products and tries to convince us that we need them. Then there's the credit card trap with many people not paying off their monthly balance. Jesus gave warning about a materialistic mindset. "Take heed, and beware of covetousness: for a man's life consisteth not in the abundance of the things which he possesseth" (Luke 12:15).

Another danger is *social*. Continually relating to machines can impair human relationships. Sitting at a computer does little for social skills. Modern man educates himself with a machine (computer), acquires pleasure from a machine (television), and does work by a machine (robots). He may begin to view others as machines for his use.

Another danger is *domestic*. God placed us in a family; technology tends to displace us. The pace of life quickens and families are fragmented. Children go away evenings; some family members work shifts; the telephone interrupts; the music is on much of the time; conversation among family members decreases. If you are concerned about family togetherness, watch out.

About God: **To Do:**

September 27

Spiritual Snares

"He that glorieth, let him glory in the Lord." —1 Corinthians 1:31

Read Psalm 121

In daily life, do you think of God as your helper or technology as your helper? Do you glory in the Lord or in technology? As humans solve problems through technology, their view of God can easily be altered. There is no longer a dependence on God. Thus, for technology-lovers, God becomes a nuisance or an irrelevancy in their minds. If the borrowed axe head sinks in the water, you don't need a miracle, just an electromagnet. Technology becomes the answer, not God. Thus a perversion of Psalm 121 sounds like this: "I will lift up mine eyes unto the technologists from whence cometh my help. My help cometh from technology which is exploring heaven and earth. Technology will not suffer thy foot to be moved; behold machines will not slumber."

Even for Christians, God is diminished in the thinking of many—and our view of God is so important because it directly impacts our behavior. Technology tends to diminish God and exalt man. Sinful man has "changed the truth of God into a lie, and worshipped and served the creature more than the Creator, who is blessed for ever" (Romans 1:25).

True, technology has worthwhile uses, helping people with medical problems and printing good literature, for instance. Yet if we become less dependent on God's grace and the Holy Spirit, how much does technology help? The Laodician church had no sense of their need of God, and they were poor and blind spiritually. Technological progress can stimulate pride and self-sufficiency.

On a church level, the "electronic church" makes the local assembly seem superfluous. On Sunday, a person can just tune in to the radio, television, or Internet. There are "churches" like the First Church of Cyberspace. Biblical preaching seems dull compared with a fast-paced professional performance. Theatrics and media hype seem more exciting than prayer meeting. The electronic church does, however, have a bit of a problem distributing the emblems for Communion. It also has major problems providing fellowship, accountability, and Scriptural discipline.

About God: **To Do:**

The Media Menace

"Blessed is the man that walketh not in the counsel of the ungodly, nor standeth in the way of sinners, nor sitteth in the seat of the scornful."
—Psalm 1:1

Read Psalm 101

Many electronic media products have been developed in the past century—radios, phonographs, televisions, 8-tracks, tape players, videos, CDs, DVDs, etc. Most electronic inventions have potential for good. Unfortunately, they also have much potential for evil. Let's consider television.

Influence. A few years ago, 500 business, government, and professional leaders ranked the eighteen main influences in the U.S. by their level of impact. Television came in first ahead of the White House, the Supreme Court and Congress, and ahead of education and other media. Organized religion ranked eighteenth.

Time. The average five-year-old spends sixty-five percent of his waking hours in front of TV. By the time he graduates from high school, he will have watched 15,000-20,000 hours of TV. The average American adult spends ten years of his life watching TV. For most people, TV is the greatest single re-arranger of a person's time. Does 50,000-75,000 hours of TV viewing sound like "redeeming the time" (Ephesians 5:16)?

Violence. When the average child turns fifteen, he will have watched the violent deaths of over 13,000 people on TV.

The Bible says "evil communications corrupt good manners" (1 Corinthians 15:33). Common sense indicates that viewing violence in an entertaining way is bound to breed violence. And research confirms it.

Vulgarity and Immorality. Few TV shows are free from coarse language, cursing, and sexual innuendo. If a house built on sand will not endure (see Matthew 7:26, 27), neither will a civilization built on *dirt*.

According to the daily reading I don't think David would have set a TV in front of him (v. 2). He wanted to see the faithful of the land (v. 6), not those who deceive (v. 7).

Research shows that TV widens the range of values and behavior that people consider respectable. It does affect one's values if one sees pleasant, popular people engaging in sin, enjoying it, and not receiving any adverse effects. That is an altogether different picture than that which Bible readers get from Eve, Cain, Pharaoh, Samson, David, Jezebel, Judas, and Sapphira.

Instead of a home permeated with Scripture, many homes are simply a screen for the world to project itself. I believe TV is "not a friend to grace." Many homes and children are shaped by TV. I want mine shaped by Scripture.

About God: **To Do:**

September 29

Blessing or Woe

"These things have I spoken unto you, that my joy might remain in you, and that your joy might be full." —John 15:11

Read Psalm 132

1. Woeful are the poor who have spent all their money for machines and amusements.

2. Woeful are they which do hunger and thirst after the latest conveniences, for they shall be filled with leisure time.

3. Woeful are the inventors of evil things for they shall receive the praise of men but not of God.

4. Woeful are they who fill their eyes with TV and DVD scenes, their ears with constant music, and who use their hands and feet to play video games, for they fit right into society.

5. Woeful are they who are saturated with electronic media devices, for they shall be entertained.

6. Woeful are they whose lives are controlled by technology, for they think they can handle life by themselves just fine.

7. Woeful is the man who always buys the newest electronic gadgets and hath his quiver full of them.

8. Woeful is the man who tunes into the electronic church, for he can't edify others as he sits in his La-Z-Boy.

The advertising world would have you believe that happiness comes from the purchase and accumulation of things. The things that are advertised are usually technological devices. But real joy comes from a relationship with Jesus.

As the daily reading indicates, the saints shout for joy because they experience salvation. Don't be deceived into thinking that satisfaction and blessing come from electronic toys and lots of purchases.

About God: **To Do:**

Guidelines for Using Technology

"I therefore, the prisoner of the Lord, beseech you that ye walk worthy of the vocation wherewith ye are called." —Ephesians 4:1

Read 1 Corinthians 10:6-15

1. Be on the lookout for snares. Be alert to its present or potential danger. When I drive a vehicle, I try to practice "defensive driving." For example, if I approach an intersection where I have the right of way, I look to see if a vehicle is approaching that might not stop. Believers should practice defensive living, always on the alert. The Israelites in the wilderness, as told in the daily reading, failed to "take heed" (v. 12) and "flee" (v. 14).

2. When technological products are beneficial and their use does not violate Biblical principles, use them to the glory of God with thanksgiving.

3. Maintain your devotional life. You will soon lack discernment if you fail to keep in touch with God. Pray before purchasing.

4. Cultivate family togetherness. Talk together. Sing together. Play together. Worship together. Work together. Eat together. Many American families don't—one person is watching TV, another is using a laptop, and another is listening to a sports broadcast.

5. Keep your focus on Jesus. Even the most amazing, intriguing inventions don't compare to the wonder of God's love and the fulfillment of a close relation to Christ.

6. Appreciate the church. Forsake not the assembling of yourselves together. The preaching of the Lord is imperative for spiritual vitality and growth. Be open to the counsels of the brotherhood, especially in the area of the electronic media. Not all lawful things are expedient.

7. Appreciate God's creation. Ponder the immensity of the universe, the complexities of the microscopic world, the wonders of the human body, the beauty of plants, and the gift of animals. The skills shown by technological advances pale beside the skill of the Creator.

8. Be slow to accept, and sometimes quick to reject, innovations and inventions. "Ere you bought your last $300 of technology, did you think to pray?"

9. Focus on eternal spiritual realities, not on the material and sensory. For the kingdom of God is not electronics and vehicles, but righteousness, and peace, and joy in the Holy Ghost (see Romans 14:17).

10. Dispose of things that hinder you spiritually.

11. Keep your perspectives. All that technology brings us will be burned up some day (see 2 Peter 3:10-13).

12. Keep watching and waiting for Jesus' return. That will be far more exciting than any new technology. It will usher in an age far more glorious than the technological age.

About God: **To Do:**

Be a Manager

"As every man hath received the gift, even so minister the same one to another, as good stewards of the manifold grace of God." —1 Peter 4:10

Read 1 Chronicles 29:6-23

Do you own some things or do you own nothing? As a Christian you could answer "yes" to both questions. As a steward—one who manages the affairs of another on his behalf—you in a sense own nothing. In a legal sense you might own a car, a CD player, a baseball glove, etc. It is legitimate to think of you having ownership of things you can sell, use, or give away. The Apostle Peter, in rebuking praise-loving Ananias who had pretended to give all the money from a land sale, said, "Whiles it remained, was it not thine own?" (Acts 5:4).

However, in the ultimate sense, you should view God as the Owner and yourself as a manager of money and possessions. Psalm 24:1 says, "The earth is the LORD'S, and the fulness thereof; the world, and they that dwell therein." Psalm 50:10 says, "For every beast of the forest is mine, and the cattle upon a thousand hills." Haggai 2:8 says, "The silver is mine, and the gold is mine, saith the LORD of hosts."

Some Christians think that ten percent is the Lord's and ninety percent is their own. But really one hundred percent is the Lord's, and you are the steward of what He has entrusted to you. As the daily reading says, all things come from God (v. 14). James 1:17 points out, "Every good gift and every perfect gift is from above." Even our ability to gain wealth comes from the Lord. As Deuteronomy 8:18 says, "But thou shalt remember the LORD thy God: for it is he that giveth thee power to get wealth."

A man resented the Sunday morning sermon, because the minister claimed that the Lord is the owner of all things that we have, that we are just His workmen, stewards of His possessions. So the man invited his pastor home for dinner. After the meal the farmer took him on a tour and showed him his fields, buildings, and livestock. Then he said, "Pastor, do you mean to say I don't really own this?"

The minister was silent. Finally he said, "Ask me that question one hundred years from now."

Of course the principle of stewardship affects more than money and possessions. It applies to your body, time, talents, and the Gospel.

About God:

To Do:

Money Talks

"But lay up for yourselves treasures in heaven, where neither moth nor rust doth corrupt, and where thieves do not break through nor steal." —Matthew 6:20

Read 1 Timothy 5:1-18

Yes, money talks. It makes four speeches:

1. It may say, "*Spend me.* Take me to the mall. Buy a new pair of color-coordinated shoes to join the other sixteen pairs in the closet. Purchase a new set of luggage for the vacation in Acapulco. Next, visit the camera shop to get a camera with the very latest features. Then on to the Fashion Shoppe for still another new sweater.

"*Spend me* for your personal pleasures, ease of lifestyle, and self-indulgence. Then I will make your soul calloused and indifferent to the needs of the poor and the cry of missions. You will conclude that I am the most important thing in life. I will become your master and god—and your ruin."

2. Or it may say, "*Grip me.* Aim to accumulate me. Work for me during your employment. Dream of me in your leisure time. Count me, hoard me, and love me. Invest in the most lucrative businesses. Buy and sell profitably. Invest in the stock market. Swell the nest egg. Enjoy the wonders of compound interest. Cling to every dollar that you can from your first paycheck onward. Apply the songwriter's words to money, 'When we asunder part, it gives [me] keenest pain.'

"*Grip me* and I will dim your eyes to the beauty of nature and the needs of your fellowmen. I will cause you to neglect your children as you moonlight and multiply me. I will move your tongue to boast of your financial achievements."

3. Or it may say, "*Use me.* As the daily Scripture says, provide for the needs of your wife and your children (v. 8), your aged parents and your widowed aunt (v. 4), and pastors (vv. 17, 18). Use me to purchase food, raiment, medicine, and shelter.

"*Use me* and I will provide satisfaction for you as you meet the needs of your family."

4. Or it may say, "*Give me.* Give to the local congregation. Give to Bible schools. Give to missions. Give to relief agencies.

"*Give me*, and you shall have spiritual treasure in heaven. As the recipient receives me, he will be blessed and you shall be blessed more. I will supply medicine for the sick, food for the malnourished, clothing for the destitute, and the Gospel to the seeking. Simultaneously, I will provide joy and fulfillment for you as you give with pure motives."

About God: **To Do:**

October 3

In Support of Plastic Surgery

"Owe no man any thing, but to love one another." —Romans 13:8

Read 2 Kings 4:1-17

Some problems can be overcome by plastic surgery. A simple and inexpensive plastic surgery procedure can reduce tensions in the home, improve relationships with friends, bankers, and businessmen, enhance one's Christian testimony, and make you feel better about yourself. The operation I have in mind can be carried out right at home, preferably close to a garbage can. For this surgery, a scalpel or butcher knife may be used, but a sharp scissors is the most convenient. I have performed several such operations for myself and would be ready to perform plastic surgery for you too at any place you would choose. Of course, I would insist on having your permission to do it. Also, I would do all this for FREE. However, you can do this job yourself.

Here is how it's done. Holding the scissors in one hand, and your credit card in the other, cut the plastic into five or ten pieces. Then pitch them into the garbage.

Not everyone needs plastic surgery. Personally, I have two credit cards—a Visa card and a Sears card (used mostly for ordering merchandise by phone). I have disposed of others, using the scissors technique.

A credit card doesn't need to be a snare; it can be a service. It can be used while traveling and is especially handy in case of emergencies. It removes the need to carry very much cash in daily living. It helps to establish a credit rating, which may prove to be useful. However, it must be paid in full each month in order to be a service and not a snare.

Some of my friends and fellow church members have performed plastic surgery or something similar. Why? Credit cards may lead to impulse buying without having the funds available to pay. It is not necessarily useful, so why have it as a source of temptation? Even with paying off the minimum monthly balance, credit card debts can become a rising tide that casts a family adrift on a treacherous sea. Interest rates on credit card debts tend to be very high.

Credit cards have three dimensions: height, width, and debt. If the third dimension cannot be managed as a good steward, then the height and width should be eliminated.

About God: **To Do:**

Unusual Robberies

"Honour the L*ORD with thy substance, and with the firstfruits of all thine increase."* —Proverbs 3:9

Read Malachi 3:1-18

A goat was jailed for two days in Kenya for stealing $2.00 belonging to a fruit seller. According to a Nairobi newspaper, the *Daily Nation*, this robbery took place in Kilgoris, about 200 miles west of Nairobi. Evidently, the goat dipped its head into a bag that contained the unidentified woman's money, and fled with the cash when it was scared away. The trader chased the goat, grabbed it, and turned it over to the police. The goat was released from jail when the goat's owner refunded the money.

An even more remarkable robbery took place in Palestine about 400 B.C. Religious people robbed God. Verse 8 of the daily reading puts it this way: "Will a man rob God?"

A goat stealing from a person has a lot of gall. But a person who robs God has greater gall and temerity. And it wasn't just one person. It was everybody. As verse nine says, "Ye have robbed me, even this whole nation."

Unfortunately, it was not just in Malachi's day that God's people stole. It may well extend into our homes today. The robbery technique is the same: withholding what belongs to another.

Does the IRS or Canada Revenue Agency appreciate people who withhold tax money? Their view is shown by their investigations, audits, and stiff fines. It's important to *file* one's income tax, not *chisel* it.

Tax evasion is serious. In one case, Internal Revenue officials were somewhat suspicious about a deduction claim on a clergyman's form: $450.00 for a clerical collar. That seemed a little high, so the IRS asked him about the costly collar. The minister explained that he had made an innocent error: the $450.00 should have said $4.50. Understanding IRS men let the clergyman pay the extra tax and interest without penalty. But one auditor decided to check the returns from previous years. He discovered that the clergyman consistently had trouble with decimals. The embarrassed minister was given a hefty penalty for fraud.

Withholding money for the Lord's work surely does not please the Divine Ruler any more than it does our national rulers. The tax officials don't care if we pay income tax grudgingly or willingly, as long as we pay, but God does. 2 Corinthians 9:7 says, "Not grudgingly, or of necessity: for God loveth a cheerful giver."

Let's give to God what is *right*—not what is *left*.

About God: **To Do:**

October 5

Praying Before Purchasing

"Keep that which is committed to thy trust." —1 Timothy 6:20

Read Matthew 25:14-30

"Would you like to purchase this beautiful dining room suite? It is a super buy. Fine craftsmanship and durability. Very attractive. And it's thirty percent off till the end of the month. Shall I write up the order now?" the salesman spoke pleasantly.

"Just wait. We need some time to think this over and talk about it. We'll let you know in a day or two if we want to buy it. Thank you. You've been very helpful," said Mr. Christian.

Two good purposes are served by not making an immediate decision to purchase (under normal circumstances—delay may not always work well at an auction). My parents taught me to sleep over any major decision or purchase because a new day often gives a sense of perspective. That's one good purpose. Another good purpose served by delay is the opportunity to pray.

Even in the case of an auction, you can pray prior to attending the sale, and then at the sale you can breathe a prayer to God for guidance.

You may ask, "Should I pray before buying a pound of nails or a roast of beef?" There certainly is nothing wrong with praying about small purchases. My primary appeal is that you pray specifically about major purchases. This article presupposes that a Christian views all of life as a stewardship and all decisions and actions, great or small, are to be made in harmony with the will of God.

Why pray prior to a major purchase?

1. It promotes a sense of accountability. "Lord, is this how you would have me to use the money you have entrusted to me?"

2. It allows God to give us wisdom. As James 1:5 promises, "If any of you lack wisdom, let him ask of God, that giveth to all men liberally, and upbraideth not; and it shall be given him." How many of us have purchased something and soon regretted it? Wisdom is what we need in a day of materialistic pressures and the persuasive, pervasive ploys of advertisers.

3. It helps prevent impulse buying. Praying provides perspective and encourages us to wait on the Lord.

4. It reminds us that we are managers, not owners.

The Bible says, "Pray without ceasing." Surely that includes those expeditions to Wal-Mart.

About God: **To Do:**

How Frugal Should You Be?

*"When they were filled, he said unto his disciples,
Gather up the fragments that remain, that nothing be lost."* —John 6:12

Read Matthew 14:13-21

My teenage children looked with despair upon my frugal ways. "Why don't you throw out those scraps of lumber, Dad? When will you ever use them?"

Some people take frugality to an extreme. Take, for instance, the woman who diluted practically all the food she served. One observer said, "The ketchup looked more like runny tomato soup." Her children still remember spreading peanut butter on their saltines and watching it run through the little holes.

Men can also be frugal to a fault. One father concluded that the toothpaste manufacturers were making the tube openings larger so that consumers would use the toothpaste quicker. A daughter wrote, "So he took the cap, drilled a hole in it, and put it back on the tube. That worked two ways: less time spent removing and replacing the cap, and less toothpaste used due to the thinner ribbon."

A foreman discovered that a toilet paper roll with 75 feet of tissue removed worked as well in his car as a replacement oil filter. An employee reported, "I would see him in the parking lot changing his oil in his old Volvo, with toilet paper all over the place."

However, apart from some extremes like these, frugality is usually a virtue. Proverbs 12:27 says, "The substance of a diligent man is precious." The virtuous woman "looketh well to the ways of her household" (Proverbs 31:27). In the feeding of the 5,000 and in the feeding of the 4,000, the extra food was saved. "They took up of the broken meat that was left seven baskets full" (Matthew 15:37). It was no virtue to be wasteful.

Slothfulness is linked to wastefulness. "He also that is slothful in his work is brother to him that is a great waster" (Proverbs 18:9). Really, being frugal and economizing within reason is part of being good stewards.

But there are some areas in life where we should not be frugal and thrifty. Jesus calls His followers to give generously. He said, "Freely ye have received, freely give" (Matthew 10:8). When the heart is *converted*, the purse will be *inverted*.

Frugality and a desire to save money have their place. But remember the purpose of frugality: to save money so that we have more to meet the needs of one's family and to have to give to him that has need.

About God: **To Do:**

October 7

Give, Give, Give

"Of all that thou shalt give me I will surely give the tenth unto thee."
—Genesis 28:22

Read 2 Corinthians 9:1-15

A man complained to his pastor about the church's request for money. He fumed, "This business of Christianity is just continuous give, give, give."

The minister thought for a moment and then replied, "I want to thank you for one of the best definitions of Christianity I have ever heard."

God gives and gives and gives some more. Every good thing is a gift from God. James 1:17 says "Every good gift and every perfect gift is from above." Water, health, gravity, friends, air, food, eyesight, memory, Holy Writ, peace, and a host of other gifts come from God.

But the best gift is God's Son. "For God so loved the world, that he gave his only begotten Son, that whosoever believeth in him should not perish, but have everlasting life" (John 3:16). And after Jesus returned to heaven, He sent the Holy Spirit. "And hereby we know that he abideth in us, by the Spirit which he hath given us" (1 John 3:24).

A Christ-centered person loves to give to God. The grace of giving is a natural overflow of receiving the gift of grace.

An African convert earned money by making and selling a special kind of bean-cake. She had always been conscientious in her giving, but after she suffered a severe foot injury in an accident, her income ceased. It was many long months before she could resume her work. She eagerly awaited the day when she could sell her tasty cakes again and promised the local missionary that she would give one third of her earnings to the Lord instead of just ten percent. Her ambitious goal for the first week of business was to make a profit of three shillings. The missionary was surprised when the woman returned after only two days with one shilling as an offering for the Lord. "You surely haven't earned three shillings already," he exclaimed.

Surprised, she said, "Do you think I would give my Lord the *last* of the three? This is the first one, and it belongs to Him; the other two I make will be for me." Her heart was so filled with love for the Saviour that she found joy in honoring Him with her initial earnings.

God's people remember that all they give to God they have already received from God. We don't *own* our possessions; we *owe* them.

About God: **To Do:**

Who Says Talk Is Cheap?

"Whoso keepeth his mouth and his tongue keepeth his soul from troubles." —Proverbs 21:23

Read Matthew 12:33-37

In the central Alberta town of Olds, Patricia McDonald looked at her phone bill in shocked disbelief. The total bill for the month? $68,728.72! And to top it off, McDonald hadn't even called anyone.

She had been on a vacation to British Columbia when she lost her purse, according to my local newspaper. Although she contacted the telephone company immediately and told them to cancel her calling card, something went awry. The card was never cancelled until she got her bill. The 129-page phone bill listed hundreds of calls.

"Many of the calls were to places all over South America, others were to Central America, and some were to China and Europe," said McDonald.

The longest was a four-and-one-half-hour call to Chile.

It's not only talk on a telephone which is costly. Take, for instance, gossip. It goes far and wide, doing damage. To reckon its cost, one needs to consider its damage to reputation, its effect on the thought life of those who hear bad and inaccurate reports of another, as well as the sin put on the account of the gossiper. "Speak not evil one of another" (James 4:11). Avoid the devil's halitosis—evil talk.

Then there's the price paid by the man who speaks first and thinks afterward. "Seest thou a man that is hasty in his words? there is more hope of a fool than of him" (Proverbs 29:20). A person who constantly puts his foot in his mouth throws his whole body out of balance.

Vain words of deception are costly in terms of God's judgment. "Let no man deceive you with vain words: for because of these things cometh the wrath of God upon the children of disobedience" (Ephesians 5:6).

The cost of unwholesome talk may also be reckoned in terms of length and quality of life. "For he that will love life, and see good days, let him refrain his tongue from evil, and his lips that they speak no guile" (1 Peter 3:10).

Although Patricia McDonald did not have to pay her whopping bill, those who use idle words will always pay. Jesus said, "Every idle word that men shall speak, they shall give account thereof in the day of judgment" (Matthew 12:36).

About God:

To Do:

October 9

Put Your Head Into the Dirt

"So we thy people and sheep of thy pasture will give thee thanks for ever: we will shew forth thy praise to all generations." —Psalm 79:13

Read Psalm 100

After evaluating a group of diners, a waiter said, "Is anything all right?" I hope they weren't professed Christians, for believers are to be known for their thankful spirit and lack of grumbling. Colossians 3:15 puts it very simply: "Be ye thankful."

People of a tribe in West Africa have an unusual way of saying thank-you. Translators report that when they express thanks, they bow, put their foreheads on the ground, and say, "My head is in the dirt."

When members of another African tribe want to express gratitude, they sit for a long time in front of the hut of the person who did the favor and literally say, "I sit on the ground before you."

These Africans understand well what thanksgiving is and why it's difficult for us: at its core, thanksgiving is an act of humility. And humility doesn't come naturally to the human family with propensities to pride and presumption.

David, a man after God's own heart, often put his head in the dirt. He was grateful to those who respectfully buried the king. "Blessed be ye of the LORD, that ye have shewed this kindness unto your lord, even unto Saul, and have buried him. And now the LORD shew kindness and truth unto you: and I also will requite you this kindness, because ye have done this thing" (2 Samuel 2:5, 6).

It is noteworthy that David enjoyed a good relationship with those under him. Part of the reason for this, no doubt, was that he realized that appreciation and praise are the lubrication that makes life more enjoyable.

Too often we fail to express appreciation for what another does for us and may even have the temerity to criticize how the other has done it. A man writing at the post office desk was approached by an older fellow with a postcard in his hand. The elderly man said, "Sir, could you please address this postcard for me?"

The man gladly did so, then agreed to write a short message and sign the card for the man. Finally the younger man asked, "Is there anything else I can do for you?"

The old fellow thought about it for a moment and said, "Yes, at the end could you put, *P. S. Please excuse the sloppy handwriting.*"

Why is it that we often complain against those who do the most for us?

About God: **To Do:**

Motor Mouths

*"He that keepeth his mouth keepeth his life:
but he that openeth wide his lips shall have destruction."* —Proverbs 13:3

Read Proverbs 13:1-17

The wise man said, "Whoso keepeth his mouth and his tongue keepeth his soul from troubles" (Proverbs 21:23), and "The wicked is snared by the transgression of his lips" (Proverbs 12:13).

To illustrate: An Ontario police officer stopped a car that was weaving near Kitchener in the wee hours of the morning on Highway 401, Canada's busiest highway (and, during rush hour, Ontario's largest parking lot). As he approached the thirty-seven-year-old driver, he noticed the vehicle didn't have a rear license plate.

"That's when the traffic stop became interesting, if not humorous," reported the officer. The driver didn't do himself any favors when he opened his mouth.

The driver admitted to having "two drinks." Asked for his driver's license, he replied, "My license has just been suspended."

After being arrested for driving under suspension, the man asked the officer not to search him. When asked why not, he said, "Well, I have drugs on me."

Sure enough, the officer found some marijuana on him. Further investigation revealed that the man could not legally drive because he had unpaid fines for previous traffic violations.

Yes, there are troubles brought on by a failure to keep one's mouth while motoring. First, don't use your mouth to consume alcohol. Drivers are safer when highways are dry, and highways are safer when drivers are dry. *Cars and bars* mean *stars and scars.* No one who has kept his mouth closed to alcohol has ever been guilty of drunk driving. Therefore, don't take the first sip.

Second, don't open your mouth to hold marijuana (or any harmful drug). I read of one college student under the influence of drugs who grabbed a live kitten and ate it raw. Ultimately, drugs always give a person a raw deal.

Third, don't talk unnecessarily or excessively. This applies not only while motoring (such as talking on a cell phone) but in all areas of life. As my teenage son said, "It would not be so bad to let one's mind go blank—if one always remembered to turn off the sound." Proverbs 10:19 says, "In the multitude of words there wanteth not sin: but he that refraineth his lips is wise."

It was said of an aged minister, "The older he grew, the less he spoke, and the more he said." It seems that the only body part that is over-exercised is the lower jaw.

About God: **To Do:**

A Song of Thanksgiving

"And they sung a new song, saying, Thou art worthy to take the book, and to open the seals thereof: for thou wast slain, and hast redeemed us to God by thy blood out of every kindred, and tongue, and people, and nation." —Revelation 5:9

Read Psalm 116

Even in times of bereavement and loss, there can be thanksgiving in singing. For example, in the second century, a Greek called Aristeides was writing to a friend about Christianity and why it was gaining followers. He commented, "If any righteous man among the Christians passes from this world, they rejoice and offer thanks to God and they escort his body with songs and thanksgiving as if he were setting out from one place to another nearby."

It is appropriate to join together in thankful songs. Psalm 95:1, 2 says, "O come, let us sing unto the LORD: let us make a joyful noise to the rock of our salvation. Let us come before his presence with thanksgiving, and make a joyful noise unto him with psalms."

A young man with singing ability was stricken with cancer. His talent could well have brought him popularity and success. He was admitted to a large hospital. His sympathetic doctor said to him one day, "Young man, I am sorry to tell you this, but you will never sing again." Then he informed him that as a last chance to save his life, a glossectomy (removal of the tongue) must be performed. "You may survive the operation," said the doctor, "but one thing is certain—you will never sing again."

Looking up into the surgeon's face and smiling, the youth replied, "Doctor, I will sing again. If I never sing again on earth, I am going to sing a new song with the redeemed around the throne of God in heaven. I am going to sing unto Him who loved me and washed me from my sins in His own blood." Then he added, "I want to sing once more on earth—before you remove my tongue tomorrow morning."

The next day the youthful singer was taken into the operating room. Before the anesthetic was administered the surgeon said kindly, "Now, what about your last song?" The youth's beautiful voice filled the room as he sang, "There is a Fountain Filled With Blood" in its entirety.

Shortly after, the young man died. Because he believed in Jesus who offered His blood as a sacrifice for sin, he could join the celestial singing. Whether we know what our last song will be or not, may our song be such that we can take it to heaven with us.

About God:

To Do:

Adult Tattletales

"To speak evil of no man, to be no brawlers, but gentle, shewing all meekness unto all men." —Titus 3:2

Read James 4:8-16

"Teacher, Jimmy tried to throw grass in my face." "Sandra said a bad word, Teacher." Reports of other pupils' wrongdoings are often heard in classrooms. Teachers are glad to learn of serious offences. More often, however, students report petty grievances that they should overlook and let the teacher catch the culprit in the act. Children often have difficulty distinguishing between what should be told about and what amounts to tattling.

Adults also have difficulties in determining when to share someone's poor conduct. A lady was once discussing another person with her pastor. She was speaking critically, mentioning things this person had said and done. At length, the pastor said, "I wish you wouldn't speak evil of this person."

"But it's the truth," returned the lady.

"Of course, it is the truth," said her pastor. "If it were untrue, God would call it lying. He calls it evil speaking."

"Speak not evil one of another, brethren" (James 4:11). Paul wrote, "Let all . . . evil speaking be put away from you, with all malice" (Ephesians 4:31). Titus was instructed "to speak evil of no man," while Peter's readers were told to lay aside "all evil speakings" (1 Peter 2:1).

Evil speakers, like tattlers, want to bring attention to themselves while lowering the public esteem of the one being talked about. Perhaps evil speakers aim to cover their own faults by talking about the faults of others. But it is impossible to clean your own backyard by talking about your neighbor's!

We recognize that evil deeds must sometimes be revealed (as shown in Matthew 18, for example) in order that wrongs may be corrected. But this is different from delighting in ruining reputations by spreading evil rumors and reports. Some people have the mistaken notion that if something is true, then they are free to share it.

Someone told me three good rules which, I must admit, I haven't always been successful in following. When speaking about others ask:

1. Is it true?
2. Is it kind?
3. Is it necessary?

Running down people is a bad habit, whether you are a motorist or a talker!

There is One to whom we can freely tell all concerns about others. If we tell our friends about another's wrong or questionable behavior but don't think to confide in our heavenly Friend, what might this indicate?

About God: **To Do:**

October 13

Don't Murmur in Your Tent

"But murmured in their tents, and hearkened not unto the voice of the LORD." —Psalm 106:25

Read Psalm 106:1-27

In some homes, the only place you can find *gratitude* is in the dictionary. But Christian homes should have an abundance of thanksgiving.

Some grumbling in our homes concerns cleaning, dusting, and housekeeping. "Mom, do I have to vacuum all the rooms? How come Tommy doesn't have to help with the dusting?" Be reminded that many homes in the world have only one room, no vacuum cleaner, and few possessions to dust.

Much ingratitude in our homes concerns food. A farmer's wife in Iowa was expected to provide hearty, wholesome meals for the men who worked in the fields. Regularly they would come to dine and wolf down the food without thanking God or the woman who prepared the meal. Noticing their ingratitude, she put an unorthodox meal on the table one day to teach them a lesson. When they approached the table, they saw oats and hay. "What's going on?" they asked. "Some practical joke?"

She replied, "This is more than you deserve. During the hot days of summer, I have done my best to give you good food, but not one of you has given a word of thanks to me or to God."

Another area of grumbling concerns rules made by authorities over us. One sixteen-year-old girl, whose parents sometimes made unreasonable demands, listened while members of her youth group complained about the rules in their homes. A young man said, "I wish my folks would forget all about a curfew and let me come home whenever I please."

"I really don't think that you would like that," the girl replied. "I sometimes have difficulty accepting the demands my parents make, but actually I'm glad to know they love me enough to care. I've talked to some youth whose parents never ask where they are going or tell them when to be home. One fellow told me that it made him wonder if his parents really cared about him. He claimed he could be involved in an accident and lie in the ditch all night, but his folks wouldn't miss him until they got up for work in the morning. He said he would rather have parents who are overly strict."

Let's avoid the tendency in our tents (Psalm 106:25) to write our benefits in dust and our murmurings in marble. Don't grumble; be grateful.

About God: **To Do:**

Hypocrisy in Singing

"This people honoureth me with their lips,
but their heart is far from me." —Mark 7:6

Read Matthew 15:7-20

Have you ever finished singing a song in a worship service, closed the hymnal, and not remembered a single word of the song? I have. I am certain that our singing is more beneficial to us and more pleasing to God if we concentrate on the words and burden of the song. "I will sing with the spirit, and I will sing with the understanding also" (1 Corinthians 14:15). More serious than absent-minded singing is when what we sing does not correspond to our life. We do expect that the entire audience join in the singing and that certain phrases in songs are figurative. However, we should examine whether our songs match our life. Let's take a brief checkup.

1. Do we sing *I Love to Tell the Story* but rarely mention it?
2. Do we sing *Cast Thy Burden Upon the Lord* and then fret ourselves to frustration?
3. Do we sing *Have Thine Own Way, Lord* but prefer to take our own?
4. Do we sing *The Whole Wide World for Jesus* and never invite our next-door neighbors?
5. Do we sing *Blest Be the Tie That Binds* and then let offences sever it?
6. Do we sing *I'm Standing on the Promises of God* but fail to claim them in daily life?
7. Do we sing *Thy Word Have I Hid in My Heart* but scarcely ever commit a verse to memory?
8. Do we sing *Serve the Lord With Gladness* and gripe about what we are asked to do?
9. Do we sing *There Shall Be Showers of Blessings* but fail to come to church when it rains spiritually?
10. Do we sing *Just as Seemeth Good to Thee* but question and complain about what God allows to come into our lives?
11. Do we sing *I Love to Steal Awhile Away* but actually are indifferent to our personal devotions?
12. Do we sing *Throw Out the Lifeline* but take more pleasure in throwing out the fishing line?
13. Do we sing *Take My Life, and Let It Be* but reserve most of our energy and time for our own pursuits?
14. Do we sing *I Love to Think of My Home Above* but are so wrapped up in this life's activities that we hardly think of the heavenly home?

About God: **To Do:**

Remarkable Rain

"That I will give you the rain of your land in his due season, the first rain and the latter rain, that thou mayest gather in thy corn, and thy wine, and thine oil." —Deuteronomy 11:14

Read Psalm 104:1-13

The amount of rain, snow, and hail that falls to the earth each year is enough for each person in Canada to have 9,000 baths a day. Or, in other words, this is 380 million liters for each of the 30 million people in Canada. Although I am glad to have water to bathe in, I'm even more gratified that rain falls to produce crops. It is God that provides precipitation. As Acts 14:17 says, "Nevertheless he left not himself without witness, in that he did good, and gave us rain from heaven, and fruitful seasons, filling our hearts with food and gladness."

It is amazing how rain is formed after water evaporates. As water vapor condenses, it forms raindrops—a raindrop contains about 15 million droplets of water vapor. Ecclesiastes 1:7 says, "All the rivers run into the sea; yet the sea is not full; unto the place from whence the rivers come, thither they return again."

The Prophet Elijah prayed that it would not rain for over three years. One day after the spectacular answer to his prayer on Mount Carmel, he prayed that it would rain. As a result, 1 Kings 18:41 says, "There is sound of abundance of rain." We're not sure how much that *abundance* amounted to, but we do know that in recent times, 30.5 centimeters (12 inches) fell in Hawaii within one hour. One afternoon at Buffalo Gap, Saskatchewan, 25 centimeters (10 inches) fell between 4:30 and 5:30. Perhaps it was such torrents that fell after God shut the door of Noah's Ark. In 1950 over 98 centimeters (39 inches) fell in twenty-four hours at Yankeetown, Florida. Smethport, Pa., had over 86 centimeters (34 inches) in one day in 1942.

Some areas of the world don't have such heavy rainfalls but have a lot of drizzle. London, England, is well-known for foggy, rainy days, and in an average year over 25,000 umbrellas are left on buses and other public transit vehicles.

Rain is a wonderful gift from God. Jesus pointed out that the Father "sendeth rain on the just and on the unjust" (Matthew 5:45). We would owe a tremendous financial debt to God if we paid Him by the pound or even by the ton. One-half inch of rain on an acre weighs about 50 tons. Thank God for free rain.

About God: **To Do:**

Plentiful Plants

"Consider the lilies of the field." —Matthew 6:28

Read Psalm 104:14-35

Peaches, grapes, apples, pineapples, plums, cherries—I can't decide which fruit is my favorite. Corn, peas, beans, cauliflower, lettuce, potatoes—of these corn is my favorite. Daffodils, geraniums, tulips, roses, lilies—my wife's favorite is roses, so it's mine too. Cedar, oak, maple, pine, birch, spruce, palm—spruce has the most childhood memories for me, including climbing, picking up cones for two cents per basket, and serving as home base for Hide and Seek.

Which are your favorite fruits, vegetables, flowers, and trees? There is a tremendous variety of plants that God has made for us. Genesis 1:11, 12 tells us how plants came to be. "And God said, Let the earth bring forth grass, the herb yielding seed, and the fruit tree yielding fruit after his kind, whose seed is in itself, upon the earth: and it was so. And the earth brought forth grass, and herb yielding seed after his kind, and the tree yielding fruit, whose seed was in itself, after his kind: and God saw that it was good."

Working with plants was Adam's original work assignment. "And the LORD God took the man, and put him into the garden of Eden to dress it and to keep it" (Genesis 2:15).

We depend upon plant life for food. So God designed it. Genesis 1:29 says, "And God said, Behold, I have given you every herb bearing seed, which is upon the face of all the earth, and every tree, in the which is the fruit of a tree yielding seed; to you it shall be for meat."

But plants are useful for much more than food. Plants provide us material for shelter: wood for houses, thatch for roofs, grass for huts, bamboo for walls. Plants provide materials for clothing: cotton, flax, kapok. Plants provide oxygen we breathe, plus a multitude of other things: rubber, rope, oils, chewing gum, paper, firewood, ink, and shade, to name a few.

I'm very thankful for plants. I think the psalmist was too. He writes about God who "causeth the grass to grow for the cattle, and herb for the service of man: that he may bring forth food out of the earth" (Psalm 104:14).

With the psalmist we can conclude by singing joyfully because of God's gift of plants. "I will sing unto the LORD as long as I live: I will sing praise to my God while I have my being" (Psalm 104:33).

About God: **To Do:**

October 17

Cohesiveness of Matter

"But to us there is but one God, the Father, of whom are all things, and we in him; and one Lord Jesus Christ, by whom are all things, and we by him." —1 Corinthians 8:6

Read Colossians 1:9-19

Look at a wooden chair. What is it made of? Mostly empty space. At least according to atomic theory, matter is composed mostly of empty space since only a small portion of space is occupied by protons, neutrons, and electrons.

According to this common scientific view, matter is made of tiny, too-small-to-see bits called atoms. An atom contains protons and neutrons, which make up the core or nucleus of the atom, and electrons, which spin around the nucleus. Let's think about size. It would take 25,000,000,000,000 protons laid side by side to make one inch. Or to put it another way, the size of an electron is to a dust speck as the dust speck is to the entire earth. Or using a different comparison, on the tip of a ballpoint pen are so many atoms that if each person on earth were an atom, it would take 80,000 years until everyone had marched past a certain point.

If a hydrogen atom were one mile in diameter, its nucleus would be no bigger than a marble. The rest of the atom outside the nucleus is mostly empty space. The electrons whirl through space, completing billions of trips around the nucleus each millionth of a second. The amazing speed of the electrons makes atoms behave as though they were solid, much as a fast-moving bicycle would prevent you from putting your fingers through the spokes. If you were to somehow remove all the empty space from your body, you would fit on the head of a pin.

Who designed matter? Who understands it? Who holds all things of matter together? Today's Scripture has the answer in verses 16 and 17. "By him all things consist" means things hang together, or cohere, because of Jesus. Let us magnify Jesus and give Him preeminence.

"Who painted that mountain scene? David, you say? Oh, isn't it beautifully done! David certainly is a superb artist." If we give honor and recognition to artists, craftsmen, seamstresses, etc., we surely should give preeminent honor to the Creator of all, Jesus Christ. Not only has He created, but He also sustains the mysterious, awesome, invisible forces of nature such as gravity, magnetism, molecular attraction, etc. Without Him the universe would fall apart and fly apart and be meaningless chaos. We also need Him to give order and beauty and meaning to our lives.

About God:

To Do:

The Gift of Sunshine

"In him was life; and the life was the light of men." —John 1:4

Read Psalm 84

The sun is a wonderful gift of God. In fact, God Himself is compared to the sun in verse 11 of our daily reading: "God is a sun." How is the sun such an awesome thing that God is compared to it?

The sun is essential for life. It is estimated that if the sun would suddenly cease to exist, within three days there wouldn't be a vestige of animal or plant life on the globe. God is absolutely necessary for physical life. As Paul told the Athenians, "For in him we live, and move, and have our being" (Acts 17:28).

The sun is powerful. In one minute the sun radiates more energy than man has used since the Garden of Eden. Amazingly, at the sun's core a piece of matter the size of a grain of sand is so hot that a man standing one hundred miles (60 kilometers) away would be cooked. God is all-powerful. Look to Him with your problems for He "is able to do . . . above all that we ask or think" (Ephesians 3:20).

The sun has a cheering effect. If you are like me, you often say on a sunny day, "It's a beautiful day." Cloudiness tends to depress one's spirits. God brings cheer, joy, and comfort when He shines in one's heart. God, the Father, is the God of all comfort (see 2 Corinthians 1:3).

The sun is the source of light. As the psalmist put it—"The sun to rule by day" (Psalm 136:8). Likewise, "The LORD is my light and my salvation" (Psalm 27:1).

The sun changes one's appearance. A person who spends time in the sun becomes tanned and normally has rosy cheeks with good health. If a person lives in the beams of God's love and will, a change in appearance is noticeable: joy on the face, contentment in the eye, modesty and nonconformity overall.

The sun is faithful. It rises every morning. It yields a steady supply of heat and light. God is utterly faithful. "Great is thy faithfulness" (Lamentations 3:23).

One encyclopedia indicates the sun is expected to burn for another five billion years. Personally, I think the Lord will return much before then to take His people to heaven. "And there shall be no night there; and they need no candle, neither light of the sun; for the Lord God giveth them light" (Revelation 22:5).

About God:

To Do:

October 19

Dihydrogen Monoxide

"He that believeth on me, as the scripture hath said, out of his belly shall flow rivers of living water." —John 7:38

Read John 4:1-15

I was amused by a high school student's project at the Idaho Science Fair. His project urged people to sign a petition demanding a total elimination, or at least strict control, of the chemical dihydrogen monoxide. Why?

It can cause excessive sweating and vomiting. Accidental inhalation can kill a person. It has been found in tumors of terminal cancer patients. It can cause severe burns in its gaseous state.

Not only are there personal health issues with this dangerous chemical, but also there are concerns about it in the environment. It is a major component of acid rain. It decreases the effectiveness of automobile brakes. It contributes to erosion.

Of the fifty people the student asked to sign his petition, forty-three said, "Yes." Six were undecided. Only one said, "No," because that person knew what it was.

The Bible mentions this chemical approximately 450 times. It is mentioned first in the second verse of the Bible. It is mentioned in the fifth-to-last verse of the Bible. Jesus requested the chemical from a woman one day and He promised a reward to any person that gave the chemical to a child in the name of a disciple. This chemical is usually called H_2O or water.

Although water can be dangerous, it is also necessary for life.

Drinking sufficient water—a recommended eight glasses each day—is part of a Christian's stewardship of the body, as 1 Corinthians 6:20 says, "Glorify God in your body, and in your spirit, which are God's."

I am very thankful for water. It provides moisture for my eyes, lungs, skin, mouth, muscles, and intestines. It also cushions my nerves, lubricates my joints, and is necessary for me to hear. It carries nutrients, hormones, and enzymes all over my body, and carries wastes away. Water keeps my body temperature in balance because God gave me a built-in "air conditioner" as evidenced by sweating.

In view of how important water is to the body, it is not surprising that Jesus used it as a metaphor for vital gifts for the soul. Jesus offered living water to the Samaritan woman—salvation full and fulfilling. And heavenly health, happiness, and harmony are pictured as a "pure river of water of life, clear as crystal" (Revelation 22:1).

Water is wonderful. Drink lots of literal water for your body's welfare. Drink living water for your soul's welfare.

About God:

To Do:

Thank God for Cows

*"Better is a dinner of herbs where love is,
than a stalled ox and hatred therewith."* —Proverbs 15:17

Read Psalm 50:1-15

I must admit that I have not always appreciated dairy cows—not for the one that switched her filthy, stinging tail into my youthful face, nor the one that charged at me when I tried to move her newborn calf from the pasture to the barn, nor the one that stepped on my foot. But since my teenage years when I milked cows regularly, I have become more aware of the bovine blessings God has given us.

Cows provide us with much more than milk products—butter, cheese, ice cream, yogurt—all favorites of mine. Cattle provide us with more than meat—steaks, hamburgers, roasts, etc. There are literally hundreds of uses of cows. By-products from cows are used in a vast variety of things: paint, toothpaste, bone china, candles, shampoo, asphalt, shaving cream, explosives, rubber tires, and high gloss for magazines.

Medically, beef components, like insulin, are used to treat diabetes, and other parts have uses in treating allergies, respiratory diseases, blood clots, and hypoglycemia.

We can be glad God created cattle. "And God said, Let the earth bring forth the living creature after his kind, cattle . . . and it was so" (Genesis 1:24).

"God owns the cattle on a thousand hills" we sometimes sing. "For every beast of the forest is mine, and the cattle upon a thousand hills" (Psalm 50:10). Yet God graciously lets man use cattle in numerous ways. Consider some uses of specific parts of cattle:

- Hooves: glazes for bread and ham.
- Bones: made into gelatin used in photographic film, adhesives, marshmallows, pill coverings.
- Gallstones: used in medicines and perfumes.
- Hides: leather for furniture, belts, sports equipment, clothing.
- Beef tallow: used in such things as cough medicine, hand lotions, candles.
- Eyeballs: extracted components are used in eye surgery.

Besides the multitude of uses for cattle upon butchering, people in Third World countries use them extensively for plowing and for pulling loads. They were thus used in Bible times. For example, before Elisha was called to succeed the Prophet Elijah, he was "plowing with twelve yoke of oxen before him, and he with the twelfth" (1 Kings 19:19).

"Praise the LORD from the earth, ye . . . beasts, and all cattle; . . . let them praise the name of the LORD" (Psalm 148:7, 10, 13). Cows bring praise to God. Let us also praise the Lord for cows and for the incredible number of gifts He gives us in His Creation.

About God: **To Do:**

October 21

Like a River

"Thou shalt make them drink of the river of thy pleasures." —Psalm 36:8

Read Psalm 46

Have you ever relaxed by a river? fished in a river? boated on a river? splashed in a river?

Rivers have been a blessing to mankind in many ways besides recreation—they have provided irrigation, transportation, and power. God Himself is compared to a river. Isaiah 33:21 says, "The glorious LORD will be unto us a place of broad rivers and streams; wherein shall go no galley with oars, neither shall gallant ship pass thereby."

What does God provide for us like a place of broad rivers and streams?

1. *Safety.* Many cities were built beside a river which served as a natural fortification. The child of God has a perfect protection in his Father. Psalm 97:10 promises, "He preserveth the souls of his saints; he delivereth them out of the hand of the wicked."

2. *Satisfaction.* There's no water pollution in this river. To the thirsty soul, God fills and fulfills the basic human longing.

3. *Sustenance.* A river provides food in the form of fish and other aquatic life. In addition, irrigation from the river can multiply crop yields. The Lord is the source of our daily bread and is also our spiritual Bread.

4. *Support.* Boats are buoyed up and borne along by a river. God is underneath us to support and guide.

5. *Source of Power.* "Streampower" has great potential, whether turning a water wheel for an old mill or a huge turbine for hydroelectricity. The Lord Jesus declared, "All power is given unto me. Go ye therefore" (Matthew 28:18, 19).

6. *Spotlessness.* A river cleanses. Christ loved and gave Himself, sanctified and cleansed His followers with the washing of water by the Word "that he might present it to himself a glorious church, not having spot" (Ephesians 5:25-27).

7. *Serenity.* Have you sat by the riverside and, while enjoying its beauty, rest, and peacefulness, sung "Like a River Glorious Is God's Perfect Peace"?

Glory to our glorious Lord!

About God: **To Do:**

Purity in Thought

"Finally, brethren, whatsoever things are true, whatsoever things are honest, whatsoever things are just, whatsoever things are pure, whatsoever things are lovely, whatsoever things are of good report; if there be any virtue, and if there be any praise, think on these things." —Philippians 4:8

Read Matthew 5:1-8, 27-30

You have fifty thousand thoughts a day according to estimates. The ability to think is a wonderful gift from God. One little boy said, "Thinking is when your mouth stays shut and your head keeps talking to itself."

I enjoy thinking about thinking. I can think about things far away or things nearby, things that have happened three thousand years ago or three seconds ago, things that are true and things that are imaginary, things hundreds (or millions) of miles away, or at the end of my nose. I can think of big important ideas or of simple, ordinary things. I can think of things holy or things sinful.

Philippians 4:8 commands us to think wholesome thoughts—on pure and lovely things. This is the opposite of lustful thoughts about the opposite gender. To help think proper thoughts, believers should avoid worldly magazines, romance novels, and any music with suggestive lyrics. Also refuse to take the second look at billboards showing immodesty, people on the street who are skimpily dressed, and advertisements that use immorality to sell products. We also need to guard the pathway our thoughts may travel concerning the opposite sex. We can replace an impure thought with a wholesome one. Two thoughts cannot truly occupy the mind simultaneously. Therefore, we have the choice whether our thoughts will be clean or impure.

The daily reading gives Jesus' warning of the serious consequences of impure thought patterns. Does Jesus mean a man should literally cut off a hand or blind himself? John Coblentz, in *The Upward Call*, writes:

> Jesus has a way of putting things in eternal perspective. It would be far better to lose an eye or a hand (though they are vital members of our body) than to lose our soul for eternity. Better to go to heaven, in other words, with only one eye, or fully blinded for that matter, than to go to hell seeing with both eyes. Jesus is not prescribing literal action so much as highlighting the serious nature of sin.
>
> We can make applications, however. Are there things that cause the eye and hand to sin? Cut them off! Are there books, magazines, novels, music, or pictures that would lead the mind into lust? If Jesus calls us to lay a vital body member under the knife's edge, how much more would He call for these channels of sin to be cut off?

About God: **To Do:**

Helps for Purity

"Flee fornication. Every sin that a man doeth is without the body; but he that committeth fornication sinneth against his own body."
—1 Corinthians 6:18

Read Genesis 39:1-21

Joseph is an excellent example of a youth who lived a pure life in an immoral environment. How did he do it? Our daily reading shows the way.

First, the Lord was with him (v. 2). Clearly, he had a close relationship with God, receiving God's blessing. The nearer we are to God, the more conscious we become of the sinfulness of sin.

Second, he said, "No" to an invitation to sin (v. 8). Even if you live an upright, consistent life like Joseph, you may be propositioned by a coworker and need to give a clear refusal.

Third, he would not betray the trust that his master, Potiphar, had placed in him (v. 8). Joseph showed integrity and honor.

Fourth, he saw fornication and adultery as "great wickedness" (v. 9).

Fifth, he would not sin against God (v. 9). He feared God so much that he feared to sin. Your hatred of sin depends on your degree of love to God.

Sixth, he avoided temptation as much as he could (v. 10). Proverbs 4:14, 15 says, "Enter not into the path of the wicked, and go not in the way of evil men. Avoid it, pass not by it, turn from it, and pass away."

To illustrate: A wealthy lady needed a chauffeur. She met four applicants at her house. From her balcony she pointed to a brick wall alongside the driveway. She asked, "How close do you think you could come to that wall without scratching my car?"

The first man felt that he could drive within a foot of the wall without damaging the car. The second felt sure that he could come within six inches. The third believed that he could get within three inches. The fourth candidate said, "I do not know how close I could come to the wall without damaging your car. Instead, I would try to stay as far away from that wall as I could." This successful candidate had a different focus. He understood that true skill in driving is not based so much on the ability to steer the car to a narrow miss as on the ability to keep a wide margin of safety.

Seventh, Joseph fled from Potiphar's wife when she became insistent (v. 12). First Corinthians 6:18 says, "Flee fornication," which Joseph did literally. It is better to shun the bait than to struggle on the hook.

About God: **To Do:**

Blessings of Purity

"Blessed are the pure in heart: for they shall see God." —Matthew 5:8

Read Proverbs 4:10–5:11

A pure life is a blessed one. In the book *Keep Yourself Pure,* B. Charles Hostetter writes, "I have never yet met either a young or an old person who have looked back with regret on the fact that he had kept himself pure, have you? I have heard scores and scores of testimonies from people who with great joy thanked the Lord that they kept themselves pure and were able to present themselves as pure life partners at the marriage altar. Purity brings no regrets, leaves no remorse, and helps one to live a noble and worthwhile life. You may be slick as a whistle in avoiding venereal disease or pregnancy, but there is no defense against spiritual venereal disease, the insidious damage that comes to a man's soul when he abuses God's gift of sexual power with someone other than his true partner."

In 2000 a national survey by *Reuters News* discovered that many American teenagers who committed fornication regretted their decision to lose their virginity (53 percent of the boys and 72 percent of the girls). If you were to ask King David if impurity brings blessing, what would he say? or Amnon? or Judah? or Samson? or the Israelites of whom 1 Corinthians 10:8 speaks, "Neither let us commit fornication, as some of them committed, and fell in one day three and twenty thousand"?

A beautiful picture of living right is given in the daily reading. Verse 18 says, "But the path of the just is as the shining light, that shineth more and more unto the perfect day." In contrast, the way of the wicked is dark and is characterized by stumbling (v. 19).

It is a great blessing to avoid the effect of impurity. Verses 3 to 5 tell of four results of immorality although it looks very appealing (v. 2):

- Disappointment. The result is bitter as wormwood.
- Pain. The comparison is to the sharpness of a two-edged sword. Impurity can cause the pain physically (STDs, for example), and also spiritually because of guilt.
- Death. This is graphically illustrated by millions of deaths by AIDS, which in most cases could have been prevented by purity.
- Hell. Although sex in marriage is wholesome, honorable, and fulfilling, "whoremongers and adulterers God will judge" (Hebrews 13:4).

To be blessed now and in eternity, "Keep thyself pure" (1 Timothy 5:22).

About God: **To Do:**

A Virtuous Young Man

"And Joseph also went up from Galilee, out of the city of Nazareth, into Judaea, unto the city of David, which is called Bethlehem; (because he was of the house and lineage of David:) to be taxed with Mary his espoused wife." —Luke 2:4, 5

Read Matthew 1:18-25; 2:13-23

A Christian woman seeking God's will about courtship would do well to consider the qualities of Joseph, who was engaged to marry Mary. Look at the character traits of the man God chose to be head of the home for Jesus:

- He was sensitive and kind. When he heard that his fiancée was pregnant, he wished to spare her embarrassment as shown by the daily reading (1:19). He wanted to deal with the matter privately. Girls, you don't want to marry a man who will tell embarrassing stories about you, but rather one who will shield and protect you and your reputation.
- He was pure (1:18). If a man is not pure and clean before marriage, he is unlikely to be pure and clean after marriage.
- He was just (1:19). This means he lived right. He desired to please God. He showed integrity and honesty. Hypocrisy is very destructive in a marriage relationship.
- He was thoughtful (1:20). He was not impulsive, but gave a difficult situation some thought. In a marriage, a woman appreciates a husband who takes time to weigh matters, to meditate, to pray, and to look at things from all angles. Snap decisions made in a reactionary way often snap back painfully.
- He was obedient to God (1:24). A man's obedience to God today determines what he'll be for God tomorrow.
- He was prompt in following God's leading (1:24). A tendency to procrastinate and put things off can make for a lot of tension in a marriage.
- He was concerned for the safety of his family (2:14). How a young man will care for his family as a husband can largely be predicted by how he relates to his siblings and parents.
- He respected authority. Luke 2:4 tells us how he responded to an unhandy government law. Young lady, how does your potential boyfriend respond to parental, governmental, and church authority?
- He worked. Matthew 13:55 tells us that Jesus was known as the carpenter's Son. And Joseph had evidently taught Jesus the trade, for He also became known as the Carpenter.

About God: **To Do:**

Know the Person You Marry

"Favour is deceitful, and beauty is vain: but a woman that feareth the L*ORD, she shall be praised."* —Proverbs 31:30

Read Proverbs 12:1-16

After a singing service at a home for the aged, a resident approached me. "Are you a clergyman?" he wondered. "Would you marry me and the lady over there, the one I was sitting beside?"

"What is her name?"

"I don't know."

I said, "You don't know the name of the lady you wish to marry?" I wanted to be sure he understood my question.

"Just wait here. I'll go and ask her what her name is."

"You don't need to bother. I don't think I would be able to marry you," I told him gently, keeping back a smile.

Later, I spoke to the elderly lady in question. "Do you wish to marry the gentleman over there?"

"Oh, no. I don't really know him. Besides, I don't want to get married again."

Imagine planning to marry a person whose name you don't know! Yet how similar it may be to some young people, contemplating marriage, who don't *really* know the *name* of their prospective marriage partners.

For example, does your partner or prospective partner have the name of *Pilgrim*? In other words, by his actions and conversation, is it apparent that heaven is his home, or are his affections and loyalties to the things of this world? Evaluate his speech. Is it God-honoring, truthful, peaceable, free from filth and swearing? Observe his appearance. Is it modest, simple, clean, and free from fashion? Check out his interests. Which has priority—prayer meeting or plowing, entertainment or edification, Christian service or carnal seeking? Discern his goals.

Does your partner have the name of *Spendthrift*? Finances are a frequent source of contention in marriage. A sense of stewardship, a mutual carefulness in spending, and an ability to save will prevent a lot of tension in a marriage. Careless use of credit cards has worked havoc in many a marriage. One's yearning power must not exceed one's earning power.

Does your special friend have the name of *Faithful*? Faithfulness to the Scripture is imperative. Faithfulness in church attendance is important. Faithfulness to the expectations of parents and church leaders is essential.

Get to know the real name of your prospective marriage partner. Don't be content merely to ask the person's given name; observe his deserved name. It's not only confused senior citizens who desire matrimony without really knowing their partner's name.

About God: **To Do:**

A Godly and Pure Courtship

"Wherewithal shall a young man cleanse his way? by taking heed thereto according to thy word." —Psalm 119:9

Read 1 Thessalonians 4:1-12

To procure a wife is how some translations render the phrase of verse four from the daily reading *to possess his vessel.* Notice six principles for choosing a spouse:

1. With an intent to please God (v. 1). Earnest prayer for God's guidance is a necessity.
2. With purity (v. 3). Fornication means sexual relations prior to marriage. Godly courtship standards need to be established very soon in a relationship to make it possible to "flee fornication" (1 Corinthians 6:18).
3. With honesty (v. 6). You should not date another with no intention of marriage, misleading your special friend to believe you are serious about the possibility of marriage.
4. With the Holy Spirit's guidance (v. 8). Let Him lead you as a son or daughter of God (Romans 8:14).
5. With love (v. 9). Lust seeks to gratify self; love seeks the welfare of the other—this includes having God's smile of approval.
6. With holiness (v. 7). Love will endure if you keep it pure. The following Scriptures can help a courtship be pure:
   - Mortify (put to death) uncleanness. Colossians 3:5 says, "Mortify therefore your members which are upon the earth; fornication, uncleanness, inordinate affection, evil concupiscence, and covetousness, which is idolatry."
   - Don't be ignorant of Satan's devices (2 Corinthians 2:11). One of these is the "law of diminishing returns," that is, that the body demands increasing degrees of physical contact.
   - "Can a man take fire in his bosom, and his clothes not be burned?" (Proverbs 6:27).
   - Keep a clear conscience (Romans 14:22. 23).

About God: **To Do:**

Fulfillment in Singlehood

"I have learned, in whatsoever state I am, therewith to be content." —Philippians 4:11

Read 1 Corinthians 7:8-11, 20-39

In my youth I heard a preacher say, "Better to be single and satisfied than to be married and miserable." I know by observation how it is to be married and miserable. I know by experience what it is to be single and satisfied. And I also know what it is to be married and satisfied. The key point is seeking God's will and being in God's will.

There are some advantages to being married. For example, it's more enjoyable to eat a meal with another than by oneself. It's more fun to travel with someone. Having someone with you can give a sense of security. Loneliness is more prevalent among singles—although there is a big difference between being alone and being lonely. (Many of the loneliest people in the world are trapped in a marriage.)

There are also advantages to being single. I have many single friends who are able to travel because they are single and not tied down. They enjoy being alone when they want to be, being able to invite others over when they want, and being able to go away with others when they want.

I read of a woman who got married after many years of singlehood. It was quite a change. As a single, she could go where she wanted to, arrange her house the way she wanted it, get out of bed when she wanted, and eat what she desired. She could pray and sing to God throughout the day. She had nothing to distract her from immersing herself into church life and into God's service.

After some months of marriage, she said, "I finally adjusted to it and I love my husband; I believe it was God's will to marry. But I gave up a lot of advantages, and I often miss being single. I had so much more freedom to serve the Lord as a single than I do now."

In the daily reading Paul says in effect, "I'm glad to be single. It frees me to serve the Lord better. I recommend singlehood."

Christians should not look down on those who are single or those who are married. The important point is intimacy with Christ no matter what our marital status.

About God: **To Do:**

Relationship

"Our Father which art in heaven." —Matthew 6:9

Read John 17:1-11

I estimate that I have said the Lord's Prayer about 3,500 times. Yet it still has a lot of meaning for me. I, like the disciples, want to grow in my prayer life. Because Jesus gave the prayer in response to the request, "Lord, teach us to pray" (Luke 11:1), we could appropriately call it, "The Disciples' Prayer."

Interestingly, the disciples didn't request, as far as we know, that Jesus would teach them to preach, or heal, or teach, or counsel, or do Christian service. It was prayer they needed help with.

Jesus began, "Our Father." These words answer the philosopher's question, "Is the universe friendly?" We can approach the One who is in control of the universe; the One who is also our Father. He loves us, cares for us, and provides for us. As to an earthly father, we come to God to talk about our joys and "ouchies," to be held in the everlasting arms, to make requests, and to ask forgiveness. The term "Our Father" combines intimacy with respect.

Significantly, Jesus uses no singular pronoun but rather the plural words of *our* and *us*. This reminds us of our relation not only with God but with other children in His family. Therefore, we must not ask for ourselves what could be harmful to our brothers and sisters. This also reminds us to pray for the needs of others. Even as we address God (the vertical relationship), we are reminded of others (the horizontal relationship).

Should we use "I" or "we" in public prayer? I think either is acceptable, but there is no advantage to "I" over "we." After all, we desire to lead all in prayer.

The phrase *which art in heaven* tells us that our relation with God is founded on faith, not on our senses. As Hebrews 11:6 says, "But without faith it is impossible to please him: for he that cometh to God must believe that he is, and that he is a rewarder of them that diligently seek him."

Faith and prayer go together: Faith is like muscle; prayer is the exercise that makes it grow.

About God: **To Do:**

Reverence

"Hallowed be thy name." —Matthew 6:9

Read Habakkuk 2:20–3:6

In the tenth century an unbeliever in England by the name of Collins was out walking one day when he crossed paths with an uneducated man. Collins asked, "Where are you going?"

"To church, sir."

"What are you going to do there?"

"To worship God, sir."

"Is your God a great or a little God?" asked Collins.

"He is both, sir."

"How can He be both?"

"He is so great, sir, that the heaven of heavens cannot contain Him, and so little that He can dwell in my heart."

This really made Collins think. This concept astounds me too. God is so great, yet God is so eager to have a personal relationship with me—me, a few chemical elements and a lot of water housing a soul and spirit. Surely He deserves our awe and reverence.

Our attitude to our heavenly Father, like that of Jesus, should be one of hallowing God's name. To *hallow* means "to set apart, to sanctify, to make special." To do the opposite is to disgrace, profane, or besmirch. Of course, as we say, "Hallowed be thy name" we reverentially recognize not only His name, but also whom the name represents.

If you view God correctly, you will keep His name holy. He is perfect in character, awesome in holiness, and majestic in sovereignty. "In glory He is incomprehensible, in greatness unfathomable, in height inconceivable, in power incomparable, in wisdom unrivaled, in goodness inimitable, in kindness unutterable," said Theophilus of Antioch (second century).

God is the judge who has power of life and death over humans. "The Lord shall judge his people. It is a fearful thing to fall into the hands of the living God" (Hebrews 10:30, 31). God is approachable through Jesus, yet we dare not approach Him casually or carelessly.

If we hallow God's name, we will not use His name carelessly in expressions like, "O my God," nor flippantly like, "The man upstairs," nor sacrilegiously as in putting silly words in sacred songs.

Let us keep God's name holy in our minds and mouths—respecting and honoring, thanking and praising, and serving and glorifying Him.

About God: **To Do:**

October 31

Submission

"Thy will be done in earth, as it is in heaven." —Matthew 6:10

Read Psalm 40:1-11

Before I can seriously pray, "Thy kingdom come," I must say, "My kingdom go." I must voluntarily surrender to God's rule as King and Sovereign. As His subject, I will honor His majesty and obey His commands. My life is His throne, and I desire His kingdom to be extended into the lives of unbelievers.

The phrase "Thy kingdom come" has both present and future applications. In the present, it means that I let God rule on the throne of my heart. Regarding the future, it means that I recognize His ultimate universal reign.

As a subject of the Kingdom, I submit, praying "Thy will be done on earth." This means I have a personal responsibility to do His will. The story is told of Tommy, age five, and Susie, his seven-year-old sister, who had both misbehaved one evening. Their mother had sternly scolded them, and no one was in the "happy camper" frame of mind. The evening's conflict was still remembered as Mother read a Bible story and let the children pray.

Tommy was first. Praying right to the point, he said, "Lord, help Mommy not to be so cross. Amen."

Then Susie prayed, "And, God, help Tommy and me not to make Mommy cross."

Susie had superior insight. She and her brother could do something about answering Tommy's prayer by better conduct. As I pray, "Thy will be done," I need to do what I can in my corner of the earth to make it happen. The Psalmist prayed, "Teach me to do thy will" (Psalm 143:10).

I am intrigued by a report of the possible origin of the phrase "Let go and let God." A young man living away from home took six postcards and on them wrote in large letters L-E-T-G-O-D. He placed them on the mantelpiece in his room. One evening a gust of wind came through the window and blew the letter "D" onto the floor. As the young man read the remaining five letters, he took it as a personal message from God.

God's will is done in heaven. May it also be done on earth—in my car, my bedroom, my place of work, wherever I am on earth. As Thomas à Kempis wrote, "As thou wilt; what thou wilt; when thou wilt."

About God: **To Do:**

Petition

"Give us this day our daily bread." —Matthew 6:11

Read Exodus 16:4-6, 14-31

First, the Lord's Prayer has three requests about God:
"Hallowed be thy name"—God's person.
"Thy kingdom come"—God's program.
"Thy will be done"—God's purpose.

Second, it contains three requests in regards to ourselves:
"Give us this day our daily bread"—God's provision.
"Forgive us our debts"—God's pardon.
"Lead us not into temptation"—God's protection.

God is interested in our personal needs. This includes food for the stomach. Daily bread may well be representative of daily needs in general—water, air, clothes, shelter, and the intricate working of nerves, organs, and the brain.

The petition is for *daily* bread. The prayer does not request bread for years to come. When prayed in the morning, it requests bread for the day. When prayed in the evening, it's a request for the next day's provisions.

Notice also that it is bread—not cake or pie or dainties. We pray for the necessities, not the luxuries.

Observe also that as we pray, "Give us this day our daily bread," we are making a petition for others as well as ourselves. This should keep us from hoarding. If I have two loaves and my brother has none, it is obvious what I should do with the second loaf.

Paul told the folks at Lystra about God, who "gave us rain from heaven, and fruitful seasons, filling our hearts with *food* and gladness" (Acts 14:17). And as A. W. Tozer wrote, "With the goodness of God to desire our highest welfare, the wisdom of God to plan it, and the power of God to achieve it, what do we lack?"

About God: **To Do:**

November 2

Confession

"And forgive us our debts, as we forgive our debtors."
—Matthew 6:12

Read Psalm 103

A small boy repeating the Lord's Prayer one evening, prayed, "And forgive us our debts as we forgave those who are dead against us." He had the right idea even if his terminology was a little askew.

We all need our Father's forgiveness. "All have sinned, and come short of the glory of God" (Romans 3:23). How marvelous that God is willing to forgive each person who in faith and repentance asks for His forgiveness and salvation! As Romans 10:13 says, "For whosoever shall call upon the name of the Lord shall be saved." His forgiveness is total and permanent. "As far as the east is from the west, so far hath he removed our transgressions from us. Like as a father pitieth his children, so the LORD pitieth them that fear him" (Psalm 103:12, 13).

We also need to grant complete forgiveness to our brothers and to all who are "dead" against us. If we withhold forgiveness from another person, we stop God from forgiving us. For this reason, Augustine called this sentence of the Lord's Prayer "the terrible petition" because we are, in effect, asking God not to pardon us if we don't forgive others.

The seriousness of forgiveness of others is underlined by the fact that of the various parts of the prayer, this is the only portion that Jesus expands on. He says, "For if ye forgive men their trespasses, your heavenly Father will also forgive you: but if ye forgive not men their trespasses, neither will your Father forgive your trespasses" (Matthew 6:14, 15).

An acquaintance of John Wesley whom John knew to be harsh and proud, told him, "I never forgive."

Wesley replied, "Then, sir, I hope you never sin!"

It is imperative that we look to Jesus' example of a forgiving attitude. On the cross, He prayed, "Father, forgive them; for they know not what they do" (Luke 23:34). He is our Master and Model. Therefore, we should be forbearing of one another, and forgiving of one another, "if any man have a quarrel against any: even as Christ forgave you, so also do ye" (Colossians 3:13).

George Herbert put it concisely and correctly: "He who cannot forgive others destroys the bridge over which he himself must pass."

About God: **To Do:**

Deliverance

"Lead us not into temptation, but deliver us from evil."
—Matthew 6:13

Read 1 Corinthians 10:1-13

A mother pushed her shopping cart with her small child in it through a large grocery store. Absentmindedly, she turned down an aisle. Then it dawned on her that she was starting down the aisle containing the candy section. She wheeled the cart around and found a different aisle. Knowing her little child, she knew the candy aisle would bring him overwhelming temptation.

Our heavenly Father knows what temptations are too strong for us. It is appropriate to pray daily, "Lead us not into temptation, but deliver us from evil." I am uncertain of the exact meaning. It may mean, "Do not allow us to be led into temptation," or it could mean, "Do not let us be tested beyond our capacity to endure."

God permits us to face temptations. He also tests us. But He knows our limits. Therefore, He promises to not permit a test or temptation that we cannot overcome by His grace, as today's Bible reading tells us.

You personally have a responsibility to avoid placing yourself in temptation's path. Too many Christians succumb to sin's allure because of an attitude like that expressed by a preschooler. He was caught, up on a chair in the kitchen, eating cookies. "I just climbed up to smell them and my tooth got caught." We should walk out of the way of temptation rather than entertain it. "Enter not into the path of the wicked, and go not in the way of evil men" (Proverbs 4:14). Paul expresses the thought more forcefully: "Flee also youthful lusts" (2 Timothy 2:22).

A pastor warned his new co-pastor about the temptation to be immoral that easily comes to a person in the ministry. The handsome young co-pastor assured the experienced pastor that he always did his counseling in a group setting. "There is safety in numbers," he said.

The wise old pastor replied, "Yes, that is so, but there is more safety in Exodus." Attractive young Joseph may have tried to find safety in numbers (Genesis 39:11). But when Potiphar's wife was alone with him, he made a rapid exodus from temptation.

Paul believed that "the Lord shall deliver me from every evil work, and will preserve me" (2 Timothy 4:18). Each Christian can confidently pray "deliver us from evil" because 2 Peter 2:9 says, "The Lord knoweth how to deliver the godly out of temptations."

About God: **To Do:**

November 4

Adoration

"For thine is the kingdom, and the power, and the glory, for ever. Amen." —Matthew 6:13

Read 1 Chronicles 29:10-20

What an appropriate exclamation of worship at the close of the Lord's Prayer! It acknowledges that sovereignty, power, and glory belong to God. This beautiful doxology reminds us that the kingdom in the ultimate sense is God's; we can be part of it by His power working in us; and He deserves all the glory.

When David led the congregation in worship, he used similar but expanded terminology. "Thine, O LORD, is the greatness, and the power, and the glory, and the victory" (1 Chronicles 29:11).

Presidents, kings, prime ministers, and dictators vaunt their glory and power, but we know they will soon be a footnote on the pages of history and a curiosity in an archaeological dig.

Amen concludes the prayer. It means "so be it." We leave things in Your hands, Father. We trust You and submit to You.

May this "Model Prayer" be meaningful and practical in your experience. As an unknown author has written, "I cannot say 'our' if I live only for myself in a spiritual, watertight compartment. I cannot say 'Father' if I do not endeavor each day to act like His child. I cannot say 'who art in heaven' if I am laying up no treasure there. I cannot say 'hallowed be thy name' if I am not striving for holiness. I cannot say 'thy kingdom come' if I am not doing all in my power to hasten that wonderful day. I cannot say 'thy will be done' if I am disobedient to His Word. I cannot say 'in earth as it is in heaven' if I will not serve Him here and now. I cannot say 'give us . . . our daily bread' if I am dishonest. I cannot say 'forgive us our debts' if I harbor a grudge against anyone. I cannot say 'lead us not into temptation' if I deliberately place myself in its path. I cannot say 'deliver us from evil' if I do not put on the whole armor of God. I cannot say 'thine is the kingdom' if I do not give to the King the loyalty due Him as a faithful subject. I cannot attribute to Him 'the power' if I fear what men may do. I cannot ascribe to Him 'the glory' if I am seeking honor only for myself. I cannot say 'forever' if the horizon of my life is bounded completely by the things of time."

About God:

To Do:

If We Walk in the Light

"But if we walk in the light, as he is in the light, we have fellowship one with another, and the blood of Jesus Christ his Son cleanseth us from all sin" —1 John 1:7

Read 1 John 1:1-8

The word *if* is little, but what follows it can make a big difference.

If you pass the exam.

If you get the job.

If the lightning bolt misses you.

If she says, "I will marry you."

More important than any of these is the condition of 1 John 1:7: "But if we walk in the light, as he is in the light, we have fellowship one with another, and the blood of Jesus Christ his Son cleanseth us from all sin."

What is meant by light? Jesus said, "I am the light of the world: he that followeth me shall not walk in darkness, but shall have the light of life" (John 8:12).

It is important to walk *in* the light, not *away* from the light.

We need to love the light. Jesus clarified this with Nicodemus. "This is the condemnation, that light is come into the world, and men loved darkness rather than light, because their deeds were evil. For every one that doeth evil hateth the light, neither cometh to the light, lest his deeds should be reproved. But he that doeth truth cometh to the light, that his deeds may be made manifest, that they are wrought in God" (John 3:19-21). This shows that if we are walking in the light, we are walking in the truth.

Loving darkness means a person is doing sin. He does not want to be detected or exposed. Many evil things happen after day turns literally to night—murders, robberies, assaults, and unholy deeds.

Walking in the light means doing what is right and good, "as he is in the light." This means living after the pattern and character of Christ.

Walking in the light means living honestly before God, doing what one believes pleases Him. A person who walks in the light says, "Lord, if there is anything You want different in my life, show me and I will align my life with it." It signifies meaning business with God and not just going through the motions of religious devotion. It means being open and transparent with God and His children.

If you have come to the Light, Jesus, and sincerely are doing what you understand He wants you to do and to be, you may be assured of salvation. The promise is plain: "The blood of Jesus Christ cleanseth us from all sin."

About God: **To Do:**

November 6

If We Confess Our Sins

"If we confess our sins, he is faithful and just to forgive us our sins, and to cleanse us from all unrighteousness." —1 John 1:9

Read 1 John 1:9–2:3

Some folks say that they are not lost and don't need to be saved. For example, someone who had attended a Billy Graham crusade wrote a letter to the editor of the city newspaper. He wrote, "I am heartily sick of the type of religion that insists my soul (and everyone else's) needs saving—whatever that means. I have never felt that I was lost. Nor do I feel that I daily wallow in the mire of sin, although repetitive preaching insists that I do. . . . If in order to save my soul I must accept such a philosophy as I have recently heard preached, I prefer to remain forever damned."

To confess sin is to agree with God that I have sinned, not justifying my wrong, nor excusing it, nor denying it. Rather, I will be open, honest, and humble. If I am defensive and deny my sin, I am, in effect, making God a liar.

A person must confess and acknowledge his sin before he can be saved, being sorry about and forsaking his sin. How tremendous that God will faithfully forgive *all* of our sins and make us clean! This means I can say with assurance: "There's nothing between my soul and the Saviour. My sins are gone. 'As far as the east is from the west, so far hath he removed our transgressions from us' " (Psalm 103:12).

A man asked an old Christian woman, "Does Satan ever trouble you about your sins?"

"Oh, yes," she replied.

"What do you do?"

"Oh," said the woman, "I just send him to the east, and if he comes back, I send him to the west. I keep him going from the east to the west, and he can never find my sins."

A person needs to confess his sins after conversion. A Christian does not practice sin. God's desire is "that ye sin not. And if any man sin, we have an advocate with the Father, Jesus Christ the righteous" (1 John 2:1). Some believers claim they have such a degree of holiness that they are above temptation and sin. Such people should read 1 John 1:8: "If we say that we have no sin, we deceive ourselves, and the truth is not in us."

However, if we confess our sins we can experience cleansing and enjoy assurance of salvation and heaven.

About God: **To Do:**

If We Obey

"And hereby we do know that we know him, if we keep his commandments." —1 John 2:3

Read 1 John 2:3-6; 5:1-5

Some denominations have attempted to divorce salvation and obedience. "Just believe in Jesus; and then you are saved. If you want extra blessings, try to obey God's commands." The idea that obedience to God is optional and not essential to salvation is clearly negated by 1 John 2:4: "He that saith, I know him, and keepeth not his commandments, is a liar, and the truth is not in him." Clearly, it is not enough to raise your hand in an evangelistic crusade and say, "I believe that Jesus died for my sins," and then continue on in sin as before.

Verse 5 of the daily readings gives us the positive side of the relation of assurance and obedience.

But a person may say, "Isn't loving God the most important thing, the first and great commandment? What does obedience have to do with loving God?" Well, the Apostle of Love, John, tells about the direct link. "This is the love of [to] God, that we keep his commandments" (1 John 5:3). John records the words of Jesus, "If ye love me, keep my commandments" (John 14:15).

Someone said, "Conversion is only five percent of the Christian life. Ninety-five percent is going on in obedience to Christ." Hebrews 5:9 says, "And being made perfect, he became the author of eternal salvation unto all them that obey him."

A little boy liked to pull out of the cupboard the paper bags that his mother saved. He would then spread them around the kitchen floor and use them as a playing surface for his toy cars. This was permitted on the condition that he collect the bags and put them away when he was finished playing. One day his mother found the bags all over the kitchen and the boy in the living room where his father was playing the piano. When she told her son to pick up the bags, there was a short silence. Then his small voice said, "But I want to sing 'Jesus Loves Me.' "

His father took the opportunity to point out that it's no good singing if you're being disobedient. This passage in 1 John puts the lesson in much stronger language: "The man who says I know him, but does not do what he commands, is a liar, and the truth is not in him" (1 John 2:4, paraphrased).

About God: **To Do:**

November 8

If We Love Our Brothers

"No man hath seen God at any time. If we love one another, God dwelleth in us, and his love is perfected in us." —1 John 4:12

Read 1 John 3:10-18

Not only is love for God essential—so is love for people. It is impossible to walk in the light and have hatred toward another person. First John 2:9-11 makes this very clear: "He that saith he is in the light, and hateth his brother, is in darkness even until now. He that loveth his brother abideth in the light, and there is none occasion of stumbling in him. But he that hateth his brother is in darkness, and walketh in darkness, and knoweth not whither he goeth, because that darkness hath blinded his eyes."

God dwells in us and we mature in His love only as we have love for our brother and sister (1 John 4:12).

The daily reading gives four tests about the genuineness of our love:

1. *Do I murder?* Certainly, literal murder (as in the example of Cain) is not love. But the Apostle of Love clearly equates hatred with murder, "Whosoever hateth his brother is a murderer" (v. 15). Murder among professing Christians is not by guns and grenades but by words and attitudes. Take a checkup. Is there someone I can't stand? That I detest? despise?

2. *Do I envy?* Cain saw his brother's actions and resented him because his own deeds were bad. Envy depreciates the excellence of others. In our day, envy may reveal itself in a critical attitude. A person usually criticizes the person whom he secretly envies.

3. *Do I sacrifice?* First John 3:16 says, "Hereby perceive we the love of God, because he laid down his life for us: and we ought to lay down our lives for the brethren." Do I lay down my interests and plans in order to help, to pray, to give? The measure of my love is the measure of my sacrifice.

4. *Do I share?* As verse 17 indicates, if I see my brother has need and I can meet the need, but I say "tough luck," what kind of love is that?

On the other hand, what a wonderful basis for assurance is our love for the brotherhood. "We *know* that we have passed from death unto life, because we love the brethren. He that loveth not his brother abideth in death" (1 John 3:14).

But my love must be more than words (v. 18). People don't care how much I know until they know how much I care.

About God: **To Do:**

If Our Heart Condemns Us Not

"How much more shall the blood of Christ, who through the eternal Spirit offered himself without spot to God, purge your conscience from dead works to serve the living God?" —Hebrews 9:14

Read 1 John 3:19-24

A missionary visiting a village in Africa recognized a man to whom he had shared the Gospel. "Have you received God's Word into your heart?" asked the missionary.

"Yes, I have, and my people, too, have received it. Every night we meet for prayer. We sing our songs, 'Jesus Loves Me' and 'What Can Wash Away My Sins?' Then we ask God to protect us through the night."

"That's fine," the missionary said, and then asked, "If you should suddenly die, would you go to heaven?"

The native stood at attention. He saluted smartly and replied, "When I die, I will go to God's village. I will salute Him and say, 'Greetings, God, I am come to my house in Your village.' When God asks me what right I have to enter, I will tell Him that His Son, Jesus Christ, died for me and washed my heart clean."

Clearly, this native Christian had a clear conscience. He had confidence toward God because his heart didn't condemn him.

Think of a father-son relationship. A disobedient son can hardly come to his father with confidence and peace. However, if he has been obedient, he can enjoy a clear filial relationship. Likewise, if your conscience is clear before the heavenly Father, you have evidence that you are part of His family.

Sometimes a person feels guilty when he is not guilty. Although the person has met the conditions for the forgiveness of sin, yet the person's emotions don't correspond to the facts. In such cases we need to go by what God says in His Word. God's character and promises are more important than our emotions.

When I became a Christian, I didn't feel saved at first. Although I had genuinely repented, confessed my sin, and placed my trust in Jesus for salvation, I felt the same as I did before. It wasn't until I claimed the promises of God that my sins had been erased, that I experienced a deep peace and a clear conscience.

About God:

To Do:

If We Confess Christ and Believe

"That if thou shalt confess with thy mouth the Lord Jesus, and shalt believe in thine heart that God hath raised him from the dead, thou shalt be saved." —Romans 10:9

Read Romans 10:8-17

Some Christians think that it is improper to say, "I know Jesus has saved me and I know that I have eternal life." However, the Apostle John wrote his first epistle so that the believers who read it would have assurance of salvation. First John 5:13 says, "These things have I written unto you that believe on the name of the Son of God; that ye may know that ye have eternal life."

The key Bible verse that helped me to understand how to be saved is Romans 10:9, "That if thou shalt confess with thy mouth the Lord Jesus, and shalt believe in thine heart that God hath raised him from the dead, thou shalt be saved." To be saved, a person needs to believe that Jesus is God's Son who rose from the grave. As a result of his belief, a person needs to identify with Christ and live openly for Him.

Many promises in the Bible state that if I believe and continue to believe, I am forgiven and have eternal life. For example, John 5:24 says, "He that heareth my word, and believeth on him that sent me, hath everlasting life, and shall not come into condemnation; but is passed from death unto life." When a Philippian correctional officer asked Paul and Silas how he could be saved, the answer was clear: "Believe on the Lord Jesus Christ, and thou shalt be saved" (Acts 16:31). It is significant that the verb tense in all these verses indicates that our belief must be present tense. It doesn't say, "If you have believed," or "If you once believed," or "If you will believe." Rather, your faith must be current.

Two construction workers fell into a deep pit with steep sides. One said to the other, "Save me. Please get me out of the dirt and mud."

The other replied, "How can I? I am in the same mess as you."

Since they were both in the pit, neither one could help the other. Then they heard a voice from above calling to them to grasp a rope. A third worker had not fallen into the pit, so he was the only one who could save them. He brought help from above.

How awesome that Jesus Christ wants to save us, can save us, and will save us if we confess Him and believe Him!

About God: **To Do:**

If the Spirit Dwells in Us

"But ye are not in the flesh, but in the Spirit, if so be that the Spirit of God dwell in you. Now if any man have not the Spirit of Christ, he is none of his." —Romans 8:9

Read Romans 8:1-17

Another basis for assurance is found in 1 John 4:13: "Hereby know we that we dwell in him, and he in us, because he hath given us of his Spirit."

Many people ask, "How do I know the Holy Spirit is living in me?" I know in the same way that I know there is music on a CD, even though I don't see the music on the disk. I can know that in either of two ways. I can believe the label that says there is music, or I can play the CD and hear it. We can know the Holy Spirit indwells us by believing God who tells us in His Word, or by seeing His results in our lives when we are obedient to Him.

- It is the Spirit that convicts us and points us to Christ. John 16:8, 14 says, "And when he is come, he will reprove the world of sin, and of righteousness, and of judgment: he shall glorify me: for he shall receive of mine, and shall shew it unto you."
- It is the Spirit that regenerates. "Not by works of righteousness which we have done, but according to his mercy he saved us, by the washing of regeneration, and renewing of the Holy Ghost" (Titus 3:5).
- It is the Spirit that baptizes us into the body of Christ. First Corinthians 12:13 says, "For by one Spirit are we all baptized into one body, whether we be Jews or Gentiles, whether we be bond or free; and have been all made to drink into one Spirit."
- It is the Spirit that leads. "For as many as are led by the Spirit of God, they are the sons of God" (Romans 8:14).
- It is the Spirit that assures us that we are part of God's family. "The Spirit itself beareth witness with our spirit, that we are the children of God" (Romans 8:16).

If you have the Holy Spirit in your heart and the Holy Scriptures in your hands, you have all that you need.

About God: **To Do:**

Persecuted But Smiling

"Be ye stedfast, unmoveable." —1 Corinthians 15:58

Read Matthew 5:10-16

If your body was bruised from persecution and you were being led to the stake to be burned, would you have a smile on your face? That's what happened in 1527 in Germany just two years after the Anabaptist movement began.

"We have him now," said one officer to another. To the captured man he said, "You are under arrest, George Wagner."

The officials of the Roman Catholic state of Bavaria began to interrogate George. It soon became apparent that this young married man did not believe that a priest can forgive sins, nor that there is any saving power in water baptism, nor that Jesus' body is in the Communion bread.

They severely tortured George. The prince heard about this and felt compassion for George. He came to George in prison and pleaded with him to agree with the priests. "I will call you my friend for life," he told George. He had George's wife and child brought to him in prison.

"My wife and child are so dear to me that all the money in the country wouldn't be enough to buy them. But I cannot turn away from Jesus," said George.

The prince's servant came and made numerous promises, trying to draw George from Christ. Priests and many others came to him, but he remained steadfast in his trust in Christ. Therefore, he was sentenced to be burned at the stake.

The executioner led him to the middle of the city. George's face didn't turn pale, and his eyes did not show fear as he looked at the fire. God gave him such joy that he walked smilingly to the fire. "Today I will confess my God before all the world," he said.

The executioner bound him to a ladder in preparation for pushing him into the roaring flames. With a big smile on his face, George said good-bye to a Christian friend who was there. Thus, *Martyrs Mirror* says, he happily offered up his spirit.

It was just as Jesus said, "Blessed are they which are persecuted for righteousness' sake: for theirs is the kingdom of heaven. Rejoice, and be exceeding glad: for great is your reward in heaven: for so persecuted they the prophets which were before you" (Matthew 5:10, 12).

About God: **To Do:**

Persecuted But Faithful

"Be thou faithful unto death." —Revelation 2:10

Read Acts 7:51-60

Stephen was the first Christian martyr. A *martyr* literally means "a witness." The daily Scripture reading tells how after he had witnessed with his lips (the rest of Chapter 7), he witnessed with his life. Tens of thousands of Christians since that time have testified of Christ's grace and power and salvation by dying for their Lord.

I was in my twenties when I first heard the story of forty men whose courage continues to inspire me. It was during the second-century reign of Marcus Aurelius, who made a concentrated effort to eradicate Christianity from the Roman Empire, persecuting Christians severely. He personally decreed the punishment of forty men who refused to bow down to his image.

"Remove your clothes," he commanded. They obeyed. "Now go and stand on that frozen lake until you are ready to abandon your Nazarene-God!"

Forty men marched out onto the ice. It was cold and stormy. As they took their places, they lifted up their voices and sang to God. "Christ, forty wrestlers have come out to wrestle for Thee; to win for Thee the victory; to win from Thee the crown."

After a while, those standing by and watching noticed a disturbance among the men. One man edged away, broke into a run, entered the temple, and prostrated himself before the image of the Emperor.

The captain of the guard, who had witnessed the bravery of the men and whose heart had been touched by their teaching, tore off his helmet, threw down his spear and, disrobing himself, took up the song as he took the place of the man who had weakened. The consequences were not slow in coming, for as the dawn broke there were forty corpses on the ice.

About God: **To Do:**

November 14

Persecuted But Cheerful

"Yet the LORD will command his lovingkindness in the daytime,
and in the night his song shall be with me,
and my prayer unto the God of my life." —Psalm 42:8

Read Acts 16:13-25

Would you call a prison a pleasure garden? A young Christian student found it to be so.

Algerius had been a student in Naples, Italy, in the 1530s. When a Christian witnessed to Algerius, he listened earnestly, asked questions, and believed. Soon after he was baptized, he was thrown into prison.

His fellow Christians were, of course, concerned about how he was doing as a new Christian. He wrote to his friends an amazing letter in which he testifies of his joy in Jesus. He wrote: "In a dark hole I have found pleasure; in a place of bitterness and death, rest and hope of salvation; in the abyss or depths of hell, joy; where others weep, I have laughed; where others fear, I have found strength; who will believe this? In a state of misery I have had a very great delight; in a lonely corner I have had most glorious company, and in the severest bond, great rest. All these things my fellow brethren in Jesus Christ, the gracious hand of God has given me. . . . He comforts me; He fills me with joy; He drives from me bitterness, and renews within me strength and sweetness; He makes me well; He sustains me; He helps me up; He strengthens me. Oh, how good is the Lord, who does not suffer His servants to be tempted above that they are able. Oh, how easy, pleasant and sweet is His yoke! Is there any like God the Most High, who sustains and refreshes those that are tempted? He heals them that are bruised and wounded, and restores them altogether. . . . He gives us a cheerful mind and peaceful heart."

Although Algerius was taken to Venice in an attempt to persuade him to turn from his faith by flattery and promises, he was firm. Then he was sent to the pope in Rome, according to *Martyrs Mirror*. There, after a period of harsh imprisonment, he was put to death.

Algerius understood Jesus' words, "For what is a man profited, if he shall gain the whole world, and lose his own soul? or what shall a man give in exchange for his soul?" (Matthew 16:26).

Before Algerius died he wrote, "I shall not esteem my life more highly than my soul. I shall not exchange the future for the present."

How about you?

About God: **To Do:**

Persecuted But Singing

"He came to himself." —Luke 15:17

Read Matthew 26:69-75

Not all Anabaptists were faithful to Christ when they were persecuted. During torture, some renounced their relation to Christ. Some denied Christ but then came back to the truth. George Bauman made such a return—a wholehearted one.

Four years after Anabaptism began, Bauman was arrested and imprisoned in Germany for being an Anabaptist.

While he was in prison, the authorities put him on the rack to try to make him recant. The rack is a dreadful instrument of pain in which a prisoner is slowly stretched by his arms and legs. When the pain became extreme, Bauman broke down and agreed the Anabaptist faith was wrong. They demanded that he renounce his faith three times in the state church. Twice he went and made confession.

Before Bauman made his third confession, he came to himself. *Martyrs Mirror* tells us he thought about where he was going and what would honor God. So when he arrived at the state church the third time, he said to everyone, "You have condemned me and through pain and fear prevailed upon me to follow you; but now I renounce and revoke it all, and I am sorry that I did it."

Bauman stated that Christian discipleship as understood by the Anabaptists was the true faith. It was the way to life in Christ. "I regret that I recanted. I'm going to be a true Anabaptist and follow Christ all the way."

The priests and officials said to each other, "Why should we wait to punish him?" They arrested George and quickly sentenced him to death.

As he was led to the place of beheading, he sang joyfully. It was very muddy in the village, but, despite the mud, he walked briskly. His shoes got stuck fast in the mud, but he took no notice of it, and continued on his way barefooted. He was committed to Christ and sang for joy that God had again given him such courage and heart.

George was like Paul, who faced severe persecution but did not let it interfere with his devotion to Christ. Paul said, in Acts 20:24, "But none of these things move me, neither count I my life dear unto myself, so that I might finish my course with joy, and the ministry, which I have received of the Lord Jesus, to testify the gospel of the grace of God."

The consciousness of duty done gives us music at midnight.

About God: **To Do:**

November 16

Persecuted But Glad

"Of whom the world was not worthy." —Hebrews 11:38

Read Hebrews 11:32-40

"Maria, get out of here and don't come back until you have given up your Anabaptist notions," said Maria van Beckum's mother. So Maria ran to the home of her brother, John, and his wife, Ursula.

When the authorities heard that Maria had been driven from her home because she was an Anabaptist, they came after her. When they arrived she was in bed. She was forced to get up and go with them. Seeing the large group who had come to get her, she asked her sister-in-law to go with her. Ursula replied, "If John says it's all right, I will gladly go with you, and we will rejoice together in the Lord."

John gave his consent, and they were taken to another town to be interrogated. The questions were tricky, but they answered, "We hold to the Word of God." Since the church authorities could not support their own beliefs with Scriptures, they couldn't change the women's minds.

These two brave sisters greatly rejoiced that they were worthy to suffer for Christ. When they were led to the stake, they kept rejoicing and praising God.

When they were taken to be burned, many of the onlookers wept, but the sisters sang for joy. "We don't suffer for being a criminal, but because we adhere to Christ. We will not be separated from God."

As the fire was prepared, Maria said, "Dear sister, heaven is opened for us; for what we now suffer for a little while, we shall forever be happy with our bridegroom."

They gave each other the kiss of peace. Then they prayed that God would forgive those who had sentenced them to death.

They took Maria first. She went joyfully to the stake, praying, "To Thou, O Christ, I have given myself. I know that I shall live with Thee forever. Therefore, O God of heaven, into Thy hands do I commend my spirit."

After Maria was burned, they asked Ursula, "Will you recant?"

"No," she said, "not for death. I will not thus forsake the eternal riches." She went on, "Bid my husband, John, good night and tell him to serve God."

About God: **To Do:**

Persecuted But Loyal

"Let every one of us please his neighbour for his good to edification." —Romans 15:2

Read Judges 4:1-16

Courage was needed by Deborah, as well as faith and determination to do God's will. So it has been with women, men, and youth of all ages in the battles of life. Believers need to stand by, support, and encourage each other.

About a dozen years after the Mennonite church began, two young cousins searched the Scriptures and trusted in Christ. John and Peter lived in Flanders with their respective parents. *Martyrs Mirror* tells us they courageously desired to live according to Bible teachings. By doing much good to the poor they gained an excellent reputation. However, the state church leaders hated their godly conduct and took them from their homes to prison. There in the dungeon their faith and courage were tested. Once, when a sister of one of them brought them some fine shirts, they said, "We can't accept these shirts since we can't keep them from worms which crawl in our clothes and food."

These two young Christians supported and challenged each other. Once, due to sickness, John was released and it is thought that he could have easily obtained his freedom. Instead, he voluntarily returned to prison, desiring gladly to die with Peter for the name of Jesus. At the time of their martyrdom, Peter boldly called to John, "Fight valiantly, my dear brother; for I see the heavens open above me."

To youth today comes the challenge, "Fight valiantly." Will you bravely stand up for Jesus, standing by your Christian friends? Be an encourager. As 1 Thessalonians 5:11 says, "Wherefore comfort yourselves together, and edify one another, even as also ye do." Be loyal to Christ and to your Christian brothers and sisters. Encouragement is like peanut butter in a sandwich—the more you spread it around, the better things stick together.

About God:

To Do:

November 18

Persecuted But Persevering

"Take, my brethren, the prophets, who have spoken in the name of the Lord, for an example of suffering affliction, and of patience." —James 5:10

Read 1 Peter 4:8-19

Would you be able to show patience, love, and courtesy if you were insulted and mistreated?

Samuel Stokes, an American missionary to India, walked from village to village looking for opportunities to share the Gospel. He carried only a water bottle and a blanket, depending on God and native hospitality for his food and lodging.

In one village, the men were very antagonistic. The chief men of the village comfortably reclined and ate delicious food in front of him. Samuel needed to sit on the filthy floor.

He asked, "May I serve your sick people and teach them of Christ?" They replied very unkindly and hurled horrible insults at Samuel. With God's help, Samuel meekly said nothing.

After awhile they gave him a few stale crusts in a dirty bowl. He thanked them courteously and ate what was set before him.

Their hostility, rudeness, and inhospitality continued for another two days. He showed forbearance and the love of Christ, hoping to win them to Christ.

After three days, the head man placed his turban in front of Samuel as a token of his respect. He said to Samuel, "We had heard that Jesus' followers were commanded to love their enemies. We couldn't believe that this was true. We decided to test you when you came to our village."

As they had observed his patience and self-control, they were amazed. Now they brought their best food and eagerly listened to his teaching. Samuel was so glad he had patiently and courteously persevered.

If you retaliate and are rude, you will lose the effectiveness of your witness. Perhaps, like Samuel, the most important trip you will ever make is going the second mile. Jesus said, "And whosoever shall compel thee to go a mile, go with him twain. But I say unto you, Love your enemies, bless them that curse you, do good to them that hate you, and pray for them which despitefully use you, and persecute you" (Matthew 5:41, 44).

About God: **To Do:**

Eat Mashed Potatoes for Thanksgiving

"Enter into his gates with thanksgiving, and into his courts with praise: be thankful unto him, and bless his name." —Psalm 100:4

Read Luke 17:11-19

For some people, mashed potatoes have the power to improve memory within minutes of eating them. A University of Toronto researcher, Randall Kaplan, reported a study in 1999 of twenty healthy elderly people to whom they fed mashed potatoes or barley. The researchers found that memory was significantly improved within fifteen minutes. But they caution that it may be only the elderly and those with poor memory who have the most to gain from eating such foods.

Mashed potatoes are high in glucose. Glucose is believed to help brain function because it aids production of a chemical called a neurotransmitter, which enables one neuron to communicate with another. More research is needed, the report said.

Interesting food for thought, you say. We North Americans seem to have very weak memories when it comes to remembering the vast number of blessings from our heavenly Father. We forget to give the abundant thanks to God that He deserves since "every good gift and every perfect gift is from above, and cometh down from the Father of lights" (James 1:17). Grumbling comes more naturally than gratitude. For many people, an alarm clock is a device that causes them to rise and whine. Instead we should rise and praise as Psalm 92:1, 2 says: "It is a good thing to give thanks unto the LORD, and to sing praises unto thy name, O most High: to shew forth thy lovingkindness *in the morning,* and thy faithfulness every night."

I suspect that mashed potatoes in the stomach will not cause people to remember to give thanks. The problem is in the heart. The heart needs to be fed a diet of mashed potatoes, spiritually.

One characteristic of the last days is the fact that "men shall be . . . unthankful" (2 Timothy 3:2). A lot of people go through life standing at the complaint counter. How much better to follow 1 Thessalonians 5:18, "In every thing give thanks."

About God: **To Do:**

November 20

Learning to Be Content

"But godliness with contentment is great gain." —1 Timothy 6:6

Read Philippians 4:11-23

One hundred years ago the average American had seventy wants. Now, according to a similar survey, he has 500! This means that if we are to echo the testimony of the Apostle Paul, "I have learned . . . to be content" (Philippians 4:11), our learning will not come from our environment.

Take some good advice from a bishop of the early church. In view of his remarkable example of contentment, he was asked his secret. He said:

> It consists in nothing more than making a right use of my eyes. In whatever state I am, I first *look up* to heaven and remember that my principal business here is to get there. Then I *look down* upon the earth, and call to mind how small a place I shall occupy in it when I die and am buried. I then *look around* in the world, and observe what multitudes there are who are in many respects more unhappy than myself. Thus I learn where true happiness is placed, where all our cares must end, and what little reason I have to complain.

Watch your eyes! When you see your neighbor's new car, your cousin's beautiful complexion, or your brother-in-law's promotion, look up to heaven. See things in perspective by looking up to the riches and beauty of heaven. Gaze, too, at the Saviour who walked the dusty trails of Palestine, who was not known for His beauty (Isaiah 53:2), and wasn't interested in earthly promotion (John 6:15).

Take the old bishop's advice and look down at the ground. When your body takes up its six feet of space in the graveyard, how important is a classmate's high grades, athletic skill, or popularity?

Look around also. Even if your income is below the so-called poverty line of Canada or the United States, you are still richer than ninety percent of the world's population. We still have a far higher standard of living and comfort than the kings and dukes of the past, who lived in drafty castles with little variation of food.

Contentment is an attitude, not an accumulation. The basis of contentment is a satisfying relationship with Jesus. "Be content with such things as ye have: for he hath said, I will never leave thee, nor forsake thee" (Hebrews 13:5).

About God: **To Do:**

Thanks Be Unto God

"Praise ye the LORD. O give thanks unto the LORD; for he is good: for his mercy endureth for ever." —Psalm 106:1

Read Psalm 105:1-14

When I was seven, my parents took me on a three-day scenic vacation. I recall the excitement of traveling across part of Lake Huron by ferry to visit Manitoulin Island. The most vivid recollection and the most heart-pounding experience was the time I was standing on the deck, leaning over the rail for a better look at the deep blue-green water far below. Just then the foghorn bellowed. I jumped with fright—fortunately not over the edge—but I visualized myself, a non-swimmer, toppling into the water. I don't know how many dreams I've had since of drowning while on a boat ride. I recall being very thankful to be safe.

In another incident on a ferry on the Great Lakes, a little girl stood by the rail of the vessel, watching the water. Suddenly she lost her balance and fell overboard.

"Save my child!" screamed her frantic mother. Lying on the deck was a great Newfoundland dog which, at the command of its master, sprang into the water. Swimming to the floundering child, the dog took hold of her clothing with his teeth and steadily brought her to the side of the boat. Helpful hands lifted both child and dog onto the deck. Though still frightened, the girl threw her arms around that great dog and kissed him again and again with love and gratitude.

Should not we, who have been rescued from the waters of sin and eternal death, respond to our Saviour with affection and appreciation? "Thanks be unto God for his unspeakable gift" (2 Corinthians 9:15), the gift of salvation through Jesus "who gave himself for our sins, that he might deliver us from this present evil world" (Galatians 1:4).

In addition to being thankful for our deliverance in the past, we should be grateful for ongoing salvation and answers to prayer. A minister included in his annual report the item: "Nine people lost at sea." When the congregation expressed shock and amazement, he said, "Well, eleven people requested prayers for those going to sea, and only two asked me to give thanks for a safe return, so I assume that the other nine were lost at sea."

About God: **To Do:**

November 22

Thanks a Million

"By him therefore let us offer the sacrifice of praise to God continually, that is, the fruit of our lips giving thanks to his name." —Hebrews 13:15

Read Psalm 136

A businessman decided to make the expression, "a million thanks," more than an exaggeration. To his customers and friends he sent a book entitled *A Million Thanks.* It consisted of the word *Thanks* printed one million times.

But it is God who is truly worthy of a million thanks. Would a Christian thank the Lord a million times during his lifetime? Consider giving thanks for food. If a 73-year-old person (about the average American lifespan) gave thanks daily for 70 years, four times a day (3 meals and devotions), he has given thanks a little over one hundred thousand times throughout his lifetime. So it would be possible to thank the Lord a million times in a lifetime if gratitude were expressed ten times that often. A million thanks could well be reality for someone who regularly applies Ephesians 5:20, "Giving thanks always for all things unto God."

Many Bible characters demonstrated thankfulness. Take for example, Daniel, who said, "I thank thee, and praise thee, O thou God of my fathers, who hast given me wisdom and might, and hast made known unto me now what we desired of thee: for thou hast now made known unto us the king's matter" (Daniel 2:23).

Paul met some Christians who had walked miles to escort him to Rome, "whom when Paul saw, he thanked God, and took courage" (Acts 28:15).

The Psalmist was ready to give thanks at any hour of day or night. He said, "Seven times a day do I praise thee because of thy righteous judgments," and "At midnight I will rise to give thanks unto thee because of thy righteous judgments" (Psalm 119:164, 62).

And Jesus lived a life of gratitude. He said, "I thank thee, O Father, Lord of heaven and earth" (Matthew 11:25). Before raising Lazarus from the dead, he said, "Father, I thank thee that thou hast heard me" (John 11:41).

Our concept of thanksgiving needs to be higher than a once-a-year observance as shown by one definition: "Thanksgiving is when one species ceases to gobble and another begins." True thanksgiving needs to be year-round and much wider than a sumptuous dinner.

About God: **To Do:**

Thanks and Giving

"Every man according as he purposeth in his heart, so let him give; not grudgingly, or of necessity: for God loveth a cheerful giver."
—2 Corinthians 9:7

Read Deuteronomy 8

"What shall I render unto the LORD for all his benefits toward me?" (Psalm 116:12). Perhaps we should be asking this question by the psalmist with greater intensity and heart-searching.

Can a person be truly thankful without feeling eager to share his financial and spiritual blessings? Has our prosperity blinded us to the necessity of giving our lives, totally, in unselfish service for the Lord? Is our high standard of living more a bane than a blessing, as God warned it could be in Deuteronomy 8? It is possible to mouth words of gratitude but inwardly feel smug and self-satisfied and be slow to share. The attitude of the Pharisee who was more "proud of" than "thankful for" must be avoided. Yet I wonder if this pretense is the heart condition of a person who claims to be grateful but closes his eyes to the tremendous needs around him. Certainly thanking God and giving to God are closely linked.

An anonymous poet wrote:

> "Go break to the needy sweet charity's bread;
> For giving is living," the angel said.
> "And must I be giving again and again?"
> My peevish and pitiless answer ran.
> "Oh, no," said the angel, piercing me through,
> "Just give till the Master stops giving to you!"

If you live in a land of great surplus and wastage, it is hard to imagine the physical plight of much of the world's population. It is startling to read that if all the food in the world were equally distributed, with each person receiving equal quantities, we would all be malnourished. Yet we are faced with the far more crucial spiritual needs of those whom we meet. Will God accept a profession of thankfulness for salvation in Christ if we do little to bring others to Christ for deliverance?

We recognize that we can only make a small contribution—but let's make it! And let's make it with our total selves! The Lord wants us to *give,* not to *give up* in despair by the immensity of the task. He has promised to help those who let Him.

Let us remember both the "thanks" and the "giving" in Thanksgiving.

About God: **To Do:**

November 24

Appreciate Afflictions

"Giving thanks always for all things unto God and the Father in the name of our Lord Jesus Christ." —Ephesians 5:20

Read Psalm 94:9-23

Listen to the psalmist's testimony: "It is good for me that I have been afflicted; that I might learn thy statutes" (Psalm 119:71). On Thanksgiving Day, we customarily mention things of a more obviously positive nature—abundant food, health, homes, happiness. But afflictions? Can we sincerely thank God for the unpleasant experiences since last Thanksgiving Day?

"Giving thanks always for all things unto God" is a test I often fail. It is easier to glory about tribulations after some time has elapsed, than *in* them. "Now no chastening for the present seemeth to be joyous, but grievous: nevertheless afterward it yieldeth the peaceable fruit of righteousness unto them which are exercised thereby" (Hebrews 12:11). Someone said, "Unstoked furnaces are for little faith; the greatest compliment God can pay us is to heat the furnace to the utmost."

Strong confidence in the Lord and resignation to His will make it easier to look on the bright side of a difficult experience. I admire the attitude of Matthew Henry, who lived several centuries ago in England. One day he was robbed of his wallet. Did he complain? That night he wrote in his diary, "Let me be thankful; first, because I was never robbed before; second, although he took my purse, he did not take my life; third, although he took all I possessed, it was not much; fourth, it was I who was robbed, and not I who robbed."

Why not take the same approach next time you're facing a trial? You may need to think awhile. But it will help to make you feel better instead of bitter.

William Law put it this way: "Would you know who is the greatest saint in the world? It is not he who prays most or fasts most; it is not he who gives most alms, or is more eminent for temperance, chastity, or justice; but it is he who is always thankful to God, who wills everything that God willeth, who receives everything as an instance of God's goodness, and has a heart always ready to praise God for it."

About God: **To Do:**

How to Have Joy

"These things have I spoken unto you, that my joy might remain in you, and that your joy might be full." —John 15:11

Read John 16:19-33

If your life is lacking the Spirit's fruit of joy, consider these questions which have helped me:

1. Have I an attitude of thankfulness? A wise "gardener" said, "Thankfulness is the soil in which joy thrives." Counting our blessings instead of counting our complaints has a way of lifting spirits and putting things in perspective. Say with the psalmist, "Many, O LORD my God, are thy wonderful works which thou hast done, and thy thoughts which are to us-ward: they cannot be reckoned up in order unto thee: if I would declare and speak of them, they are more than can be numbered" (Psalm 40:5).

2. Have I learned to wait patiently on the Lord? "Commit thy way unto the LORD; trust also in him; and he shall bring it to pass. Rest in the LORD, and wait patiently for him" (Psalm 37:5, 7). If we are totally surrendered to God, we can "rejoice in tribulation" for "we know that all things work together for good to them that love God" (Romans 8:28).

3. Have I been living selfishly? Joy and satisfaction are often by-products of serving others. Not only on your birthday or on Christmas Day, but every day, joy comes from giving, not getting. Witnessing and doing the Lord's work gives lasting happiness. In spite of opposition to evangelism, "the disciples were filled with joy" (Acts 13:52).

4. Have I forgotten that Jesus is coming the second time? Life's problems decrease in size when we remember that heaven is our true home. We should use our time for the things which outlast time and frequently meditate on our glorious future.

One day, the president of Moody Bible Institute visited a home for mentally handicapped children operated by a Christian friend. He noticed the children's tiny handprints covering the window. The president remarked about them to his friend.

"Oh, those," he replied. "The children here love Jesus, and they are so eager for Him to return that they lean against the windows as they look up to the sky."

In summary, we should look on the bright side, live on the right side, serve ever on Christ's side, so that we can rejoice in eternity on God's side.

About God: **To Do:**

Manners Matter

"Be pitiful, be courteous." —1 Peter 3:8

Read Romans 12:7-16

The following story illustrates the sad state of manners today: A man gave a woman his seat on the bus—and she fainted. When she revived, she thanked him—and he fainted.

Companies in business, looking for a competitive edge for their employees, are providing courses on manners for their workers, especially those who relate to other cultures in the global marketplace. Some colleges also offer similar courses to help their graduates land jobs. Evidently, recruiters have not offered jobs to candidates who salt their food before tasting it (showing a tendency to hasty decision-making); who order filet mignon (thinking such a person would go wild on an expense account); or who begin eating a meal before the host begins.

But whether or not we are in business or looking for a job, we should all try to follow the concise command, "Be courteous." *Courtesy* comes from the word *court;* we should treat others royally and respectfully. Courtesy is a beautiful flower which carries a sweet fragrance wherever it grows.

The basis of good manners is the Golden Rule: "As ye would that men should do to you, do ye also to them likewise" (Luke 6:31).

Take eating, for instance. According to *The Complete Idiot's Guide to Etiquette,* the top seven errors in dining are:

1. Speaking with food in your mouth.
2. Holding the knife like a dagger or the fork like a cello and putting cutlery, once used, back on the table.
3. Putting purses, keys, gloves, etc., on the table.
4. Finishing your meal before or after everyone else.
5. Flapping the napkin to open it.
6. Slouching, squirming, or tilting your chair.
7. Picking or poking at your teeth.

It is not only in eating with guests that manners are important, but also with the family at home.

When eating in a restaurant, it is commonly considered polite to tip. Some Christians have established a poor reputation in this area. One waitress said she dislikes waiting on those who come to her restaurant after church on Sunday morning (Sunday dining is not a practice I would recommend) "because Christians are usually loud, they often lack good table manners, and they are stingy with the tips." Presumably if you have money to eat out, you also have money to tip for service.

About God: **To Do:**

Don't Act Like a Pig

"Charity . . . seeketh not her own." —1 Corinthians 13:4, 5

Read 1 Samuel 25:1-17

"Don't act like a pig," someone may have told you. Or perhaps you have given this blunt advice to someone else. First Peter 3:8 puts it more politely and positively, "Be courteous." In what specific ways can young people avoid acting like pigs?

Pigs are selfish and pushy, wanting the best for themselves. Their table manners (trough manners, actually) show poor meal etiquette. Moving from pigs to people, we are part of a "me-first" generation. The prevailing philosophy is "Look out for Number One," that is, self. Push others back, put them down, walk over them if it promotes the status and satisfaction of self. But Romans 12:10 reminds us to live "in honour preferring one another."

Pigs are lazy. Go to the ant, not a pig, thou sluggard. Do your share of work around the house and yard. Wash the dishes. Put things back where they belong. Mow the lawn. Weed the garden. Offer to help—don't wait to be invited to work. And keep your room tidy; don't let it become a pigpen. Habits of laziness will bring you trouble as Proverbs 15:19 pointedly declares, "The way of the slothful man is as an hedge of thorns."

Pigs have a reputation for being dirty and smelly. Is that the reputation you want? Certainly neatness and cleanliness enhance a Christian's testimony. I've heard the opinion that being clean and neat is a sign of pride; I say it's a sign of consideration for others.

Remember, too, that keeping clean *between* the ears is more important than keeping clean *behind* the ears. "Let us cleanse ourselves from all filthiness of the flesh and spirit, perfecting holiness in the fear of God" (2 Corinthians 7:1).

Pigs just grunt (when spoken to). So it is when talking with some young people. A grunt is given in return or perhaps just stony silence. Surely a "good morning" calls for more than a grunt or a stare. And a polite question calls for more than a bit of up-and-down exercise with the shoulders.

Pigs can be very mean to each other. They will pick on a weaker or injured pig. First Thessalonians 5:14 tells us to "support the weak." Be considerate of the elderly and the disadvantaged. In a different context, Paul expressed this principle: "We then that are strong ought to bear the infirmities of the weak" (Romans 15:1).

About God: **To Do:**

November 28

More Lessons From Pigs

"But if ye bite and devour one another, take heed that ye be not consumed one of another." —Galatians 5:15

Read 1 Samuel 17:18-38

Pigs don't seem to say thank you. A farmer lad ate a meal in a city restaurant. Before he began the meal, he bowed his head and gave thanks. Some other young men noticed this and began to poke fun. "Do they all do that where you come from?" they asked.

"No," he replied, "the pigs don't."

Thankfulness to God and men should be characteristic of Christians. Colossians 3:15 says, "Be ye thankful." In fact, "In every thing give thanks" (1 Thessalonians 5:18).

Pigs can be very noisy. I know. I have a neighbor who trucks hogs and transfers them from one truck to another about 100 yards from my house. Unnecessary noise around other people is rude and may very well contribute to headaches. Noise especially bothers elderly people.

Pigs bite each other. I was recently talking with a hog producer who told me of a problem he had had with some pigs chewing at each other's tails and biting them off. This brutal but common behavior weakens and sometimes kills the victim. My farmer friend discovered that the problem was closely related to diet. When he changed the feed formula, the problem virtually disappeared.

A change of diet from feeding on the faults of others and being filled with malice and envy, to feeding on the Word of God and being filled with the Holy Spirit, will eradicate the problem spoken of in Galatians 5:15, "If ye bite and devour one another, take heed that ye be not consumed one of another."

Although pigs are among the most intelligent animals, they lack courtesy. Our present generation is perhaps the best educated of any, yet good manners seem to be on the decline. Immanuel Kant had a saying, "Always treat a human being as a person, that is, an end in himself, and not merely as a means to your end."

Don't act like a pig. Act like a child of God. Be courteous.

About God: **To Do:**

A Time for Silence

"A time to keep silence, and a time to speak." —Ecclesiastes 3:7

Read Psalm 141

Be careful when and what you tell your family about your visit to the dentist, or all of you may end up in the hospital! A youth from Fort Saskatchewan traveled to Edmonton, Alberta, to get his wisdom teeth removed. On the way home the twenty-two-year-old started to tell his family about the ordeal.

The story was too graphic for his dad, who was behind the wheel of the family car. Suddenly, his dad passed out. His foot pressed down on the accelerator, and the car lurched forward, striking the car ahead of them.

The quick-thinking mother in the passenger seat grabbed the wheel, but the car swerved, jumped the curb, and hit a power pole. All four family members were taken to the hospital and treated for minor injuries.

There are other times when it is better for youth to be quiet. When you are unsure of what to say, it is wise to remain silent and think things over.

Another good time to be quiet is when you are tempted to say unkind, negative things about others. James 4:11 says, "Speak not evil one of another, brethren." We should think twice about an unkind word—and then not say it!

We should also keep mum when hearing confidential matters. A deep sense of betrayal and hurt accompanies the divulging of sensitive information. It may seem very satisfying to our fleshly nature to see eyes widen and hear the words, "Really, I didn't know that!" or "Why, that's really something. How in the world did you know that?" Be decent and faithful, for "a talebearer revealeth secrets: but he that is of a faithful spirit concealeth the matter" (Proverbs 11:13).

It is often wise to be frugal with words when you are in the wrong or someone in authority thinks you are. Anybody who thinks talk is cheap never argued with a traffic officer. As Proverbs 17:27 says, "He that hath knowledge spareth his words."

Solomon wrote, "In the multitude of words there wanteth not sin: but he that refraineth his lips is wise." For years, in my bedroom hung a plastic motto in the shape of a fish with its mouth open. (It was a gift from my brother—I'm not sure why he gave it to me!) It simply gave this pertinent observation, "Even a fish would stay out of trouble if it kept its mouth shut."

About God: **To Do:**

November 30

Giving and Receiving Advice

"My son, hear the instruction of thy father, and forsake not the law of thy mother." —Proverbs 1:8

Read Exodus 18:5-27

"Marie, listen to me! Your room looks like a disaster area! Why can't you look after your things? A sixteen-year-old girl should know by now how to hang up clothes. And your dresser . . . !" Marie's mother rolled her eyes in despair.

"Aw, Mom. I know where to find things. You're always crabbing at me about something."

"Charlotte Martin's room isn't like yours. It's spotless! Charlotte's mother gave me a quick tour of their house since they moved. I wish you could be as neat as Charlotte." Marie's mother glared at her reproachfully. "She's popular with the boys too," she added significantly.

"I don't care what that Charlotte Martin does! I'll keep my things the way I want to. And that's all there is to it." And Marie flounced out the door, slamming it for extra emphasis.

Giving and getting such advice is a common experience. I hope the above conversation isn't typical in your home.

I think you would agree that Marie's mother could have improved the way she gave her advice. And, for that matter, Marie could have received it better.

Teenagers like Marie get plenty of advice. At least they often feel they receive more than necessary. But loving parental counsel is invaluable. Whether it concerns housekeeping, hair, habits, and hours; or friends, fads, faults, and fashions, youth owe it to themselves to accept Mom and Dad's counsel. "My son, hear the instruction of thy father, and forsake not the law of thy mother" (Proverbs 1:8).

Should children give advice to parents? Yes, if it is done in a spirit of respect and helpfulness, remembering at all times, "Honour thy father and mother." This would involve advice in the form of suggestion or possible ideas, not a commanding tone of voice, "I know what's best," or "You'd better do it or else."

For instance, a son may have a suggestion as to how to improve a father's farming operation, or a daughter may advise her mother on making a salad or some aspect of housekeeping.

Parents, for their part, should listen to the ideas of their children out of respect. Parents are under no obligation to follow the advice of children, but the Bible clearly and forcefully emphasizes, "Children, obey your parents."

About God: **To Do:**

Show a Little Kindness

"She openeth her mouth with wisdom;
and in her tongue is the law of kindness." —Proverbs 31:26

Read Mark 10:13-22

One of the first Bible verses I learned was "Be ye kind," but I'll admit I haven't learned this verse very well. Is this a paradox of yours also?

Think about how much of Christ's life was spent in "merely" doing kind things: healing the sick, holding little children, helping the poor, the widows, the bereaved, the outcasts. Christ's kindness continues today. Although we may have failed to show kindness to others and others have failed to show kindness to us, yet our Father's kindness never fails. He is kind in granting some requests of ours; He is kind in withholding what would hurt us.

Kindness is an essential part of love. Kindness is welcome anywhere. It can be practiced anytime. It's needed everywhere. It's a language that the blind can see and the deaf have no trouble understanding. Even our cows, dogs, and cats can sense it. But the most important reason for showing this "love in little things" is the fact that the Bible commands it.

It is clear—perhaps so clear that we fail to emphasize and apply it. An old Scottish proverb says, "Remember, if you are not very kind, you are not very spiritual."

There are many opportunities for kindness each day: a smile, a tear, a word, a letter, a deed to one in need. Dr. William Bede McGrath, a prominent psychiatrist, says, "Ninety percent of all mental illness that comes before me could have been prevented, or could yet be cured, by simple kindness." Sometimes silence is kindest. In any event, kind words take less breath than harsh ones.

Who knows our lack of kindness better than our family? The virtuous woman is praised in Proverbs 31 because "in her tongue is the law of kindness." I am impressed with the account of a conversation between a mother and son. The boy inquired, "What do people say when they get married?" She replied, "Oh, they promise to love and be kind to each other." After a moment, the child looked up and asked innocently, "You're not always married, are you, Mother?"

Might our neighbors say likewise, "You're not always Christian, are you?"

About God: **To Do:**

Wear a Smile

"A merry heart doeth good like a medicine." —Proverbs 17:22

Read Acts 27:21-36

Where did the smiling face symbol originate? According to Harvey Ball of Massachusetts, it was he who designed it in 1963 as a part of an in-house happiness program for a company. He first drew the perky yellow face as a part of a "friendship" endeavor to ease relations between employees after two companies merged. He was paid forty-five dollars to come up with a graphic, and the company printed one hundred smiley buttons. But soon requests for tens of thousands of buttons poured in.

Although I don't see a smiling face in the Bible nor even the word *smile,* the Scriptures do teach the value of cheerfulness. Proverbs 17:22 says, "A merry heart doeth good like a medicine: but a broken spirit drieth the bones."

Wearing a smile can help not only others but also you personally to have a merry heart. According to some recent research, the act of smiling can contribute to pleasant feelings. There is apparently a relationship between facial expression and the resulting mood. In experiments, researchers found that pronouncing the word *cheese* prompted a smile and pleasant feelings.

A merry heart (cheerfulness) is a medicine to apply in three ways: First, take the medicine yourself. It will help you to be healthy in body. Not only does cheerfulness aid digestion, it also affects other body systems. Anxiety, resentment, bitterness, and negativism are harmful to one's physical health. A merry heart will also help you to be healthy in spirit. Proverbs 15:15 says, "He that is of a merry heart hath a continual feast." As you grow older, don't just smile from ear to ear but from year to year.

Second, give the medicine to others. A smile is a universal language. A smile is the shortest distance between two people. Watch an adult getting acquainted with a baby or toddler. Then you will realize that even a baby can respond to a smile.

Third, use this medicine to improve the morale of a group of people. A perception of cheerfulness and optimism is sometimes just what it takes to brighten the outlook of a gathering.

A tendency to smile is an obvious and normal part of cheerfulness. Although a smile is a curve, it can set a lot of things straight. It will also go a long way, but you have to start it on its journey. It's a powerful tool; you can even "break ice" with it. Therefore, wear a smile.

About God: **To Do:**

Put Christ First

"But seek ye first the kingdom of God, and his righteousness; and all these things shall be added unto you." —Matthew 6:33

Read Colossians 3:1-7

There is a fascinating little spider in South America that has a home under the water. It forms a bubble about itself in which, like a diving bell, it sinks to the bottom. There it remains for hours, living below, yet breathing the air of the world above. When it returns to the surface, it is perfectly dry; not the slightest moisture has penetrated the atmosphere in which it lived. The spider's experience reminds me of Colossians 3:1, 2, "If ye then be risen with Christ, seek those things which are above, where Christ sitteth on the right hand of God. Set your affection on things above, not on things on the earth." Although a Christian is surrounded by the sinful practices of the world, sin doesn't penetrate a victorious Christian's life.

Two sisters went to dances and wild parties. They repented of their sin and were converted to Christ. "There's a party on Saturday. Be sure to come. It's going to be really exciting again," someone told them.

The two new Christians said, "We cannot attend because we recently died." To be dead is to be unresponsive to stimuli.

To be dead to sin means to say "no" to it. Just as a dead collie doesn't respond to appetizing meat dangled before its nostrils, so a Christian ought not to respond to tantalizing temptations which the devil dangles.

To be *risen with Christ* means to say "yes" to the things that please God, that is, the *things which are above.* Love the Lord, not the sins and pleasures of this world. Then when Christ returns, we'll not be glued to sinful pleasures, but we will rise to be with Christ in glory, as indicated by verse four of the daily reading.

Mortify means "to put to death," or "to have no part with." All lustful impurity and sexual immorality (which involve the first four sins of verse five) as well as covetousness and a wrong desire for things which put things ahead of God (idolatry), are wrong. Such disobedience to God brings God's judgment (v. 6). They are part of the non-Christian life (v. 7).

About God: **To Do:**

December 4

Imitators of God

"For even hereunto were ye called: because Christ also suffered for us, leaving us an example, that ye should follow his steps." —1 Peter 2:21

Read Ephesians 5:1-10

Have you noticed how little children imitate their parents? Much of their early years is spent copying speech sounds, eating habits, job activities like hammering, driving tractor, and washing dishes. Christians should be followers (imitators, literally) of the heavenly Father, copying divine qualities.

For example, God is love. Therefore live in love, following Jesus' example. He lived sacrificially, in a way that pleased His Father, like a sweet fragrance.

God is righteous. Therefore have nothing to do with sexual sins and impurity. *Foolish talking* refers to obscene language, and *jesting* to words with a double meaning; that is, suggestive talk. Also don't be greedy (v. 3) but be grateful (v. 4).

God is truth. Therefore refuse deceptive words which excuse sin and deny judgment on immorality and idolatry.

Imitate God who is light by walking in the light. How can you walk in the light? Here are seven ways from the daily reading:

1. Don't have part with darkness and sin (v. 7). If you walk close enough to God, there will be no room for sin to come between you and God.
2. Don't go back to the evil engaged in before conversion (v. 8). Our sense of sin will always be in proportion to our nearness to God.
3. Bear the Spirit's fruit (v. 9). Galatians 5:22, 23 gives a more complete list. "But the fruit of the Spirit is love, joy, peace, longsuffering, gentleness, goodness, faith, meekness, temperance: against such there is no law."
4. Discern what pleases God (v. 10). Rather than saying, "I don't see what's wrong with that," test any activity by God's righteousness, God's Word, and the authorities God has placed over you.
5. Reprove deeds of darkness (v. 11). We can do this by word, by refusing to join in sinful activities, and by having no fellowship with evildoers.
6. Speak discreetly (v. 12). Don't advocate or promote sin or detailed, sensational descriptions of sin.
7. Let your life be used to convert and awaken the lost (v. 14). Once, when walking down a certain street in Chicago, D. L. Moody stepped up to a man, a perfect stranger to him, and said, "Sir, are you a Christian?"

   "You mind your own business!" was the reply.

   Moody replied, "This *is* my business."

About God: **To Do:**

Rejoice

"Rejoice evermore." —1 Thessalonians 5:16

Read Philippians 4:4-13

I like to think of the Philippian jailer reading the Philippian letter. *Ah, yes, I remember the night when Paul and Silas were in prison. Backs bleeding. Feet in stocks. Placed into the inner prison. Yet rejoicing and singing and praying. Kept some prisoners awake. But I slept till that earthquake. I thought it was all over. But then they told me how to be saved. Then I rejoiced (Acts 16:34). Yes, when Paul says, "Rejoice in the Lord always," he means it—and lives it too.*

Are you known as one who is grouchy, stubborn, unreasonable, insistent on your own way? A Christian should be known for his moderation, which means forbearance, sweet reasonableness, kindliness, yieldedness, and charitableness. Look at Jesus' example.

Look for Jesus to come again any day. Rejoice—it will be soon!

What do you think of this version of a song?

Dare to be a Daniel,
Worrying all the time,
Wondering how his life would end
And if his faith would bend.

That doesn't sound like Daniel 6:10, 11: "Now when Daniel knew that the writing was signed, . . . he kneeled upon his knees three times a day, and prayed, and gave thanks before his God, . . . making supplication before his God." Notice how Daniel followed the instruction of verse 6.

Please understand: "Be careful for nothing" is not related to how you make your bed, mow the lawn, handle valuable dishes, or ride your bike. Be careful in these things. But don't be full of care, that is, worry and anxiety.

Make good thought patterns a habit. You have little control over what pops into your mind, but you do have control over what stays there. As they say, you can't stop the birds from flying over your head, but you can stop them from building nests in your hair. Replace impure, revengeful, jealous thoughts with good ones.

Carry good thoughts through to right deeds, and God's peace will be yours. Maturity in the Christian life is not measured by what a person knows but by what he does.

About God: **To Do:**

December 6

Don't Lower Your Standards

"The just man walketh in his integrity." —Proverbs 20:7

Read Genesis 20:1-18

The bumper sticker said, "When all else fails, lower your standards." Sadly, many young people fall into that trap, lowering standards that are based on Bible principles.

For example, the exam is hard and a passing mark is important; you think and think, but the answer doesn't come; you are sure the answer is on the page of the student ahead of you—why not cheat a little?

The young lady is 24 and many of her friends are married; no young Christian man is a prospective husband; she still desires marriage—why not lower one's standards to attract a man?

Some of the most popular teens in the youth group wear mod, expensive jackets, crowd the modesty line, and violate the church's position on nonornamentation. A young person can reason, "If I want to be popular with the 'in' gang, why shouldn't I copy them?"

When that bumper sticker grabbed my attention, I was in a parking lot in Woodstock, a local city in Ontario. My wife was inside the store shopping for dress material, or some similar esoteric pursuit, so I had time to reread and ponder that popular piece of modern philosophy.

How prevalent it is today! When your moral code is given a real test, lower your standards. Go with the flow. Take it easy. Don't be boxed in by morality. Let the situation determine your ethics.

It's actually an old philosophy and practice. None of the Bible characters read the bumper sticker I did, but some of them still followed its counsel. And their lives reveal the consequences of lowering one's standards.

Abraham lied to King Abimelech, saying that his wife Sarah was his sister, when he feared he might be killed for her. Only God's merciful intervention spared the king from committing adultery, as our daily reading shows.

Saul couldn't wait for Samuel to come and offer a sacrifice, so he lowered his standards and disobeyed the Lord's command. He therefore lost his kingdom.

I recommend the more customary ending to the clause, "When all else fails." Instead of lowering your standards, "Read the directions." The Bible will direct you through the maze of moral decisions confronting young people, and it will guide you to heaven where there will be no bumper stickers advocating moral decay.

About God: **To Do:**

The Temptation to Lower Standards

"The integrity of the upright shall guide them." —Proverbs 11:3

Read Genesis 39:1-12

Young people, take warning from Bible characters with low standards.

Rebekah and Jacob thought the lower-your-standards approach looked good as they schemed, manipulated, and lied to convince blind Isaac to give the blessing to Jacob instead of to the older son, Esau, as Isaac had intended. The results of Jacob's scheming haunted him throughout his years, and his sowing of deception reaped a harvest of deception.

Aaron fell for the allure of lower standards as the pressure was on him after Moses went up Mount Sinai to receive the Ten Commandments. If I had been Aaron, I wouldn't have chosen to face my brother's wrath, God's displeasure, and gold-flavored water.

The appeal to lower standards was attractive to Peter as he stood with the anti-Jesus crowd, warming himself bodily but chilling spiritually. His way out of a tight spot was to curse, lie, and deny his best friend. For this, he wept bitterly.

And take a lesson from Joseph, a suitable hero for young people. Things looked grim, even hopeless, for him. Despised by his brothers for telling the truth, sold into slavery while obeying his father, thrown into prison for resisting sexual advances from his master's wife, he was a prime candidate to be hooked by the lower-your-standards philosophy. But his head was clear and his heart clean as he said, "How then can I . . . sin against God?" (Genesis 39:9).

Joseph had integrity, godliness, and trust in God. He took his eyes from the allurements of sin and focused his eyes on God. "The LORD was with him" (Genesis 39:23). The Lord tremendously blessed him as Joseph persevered in faith and in maintaining God's standards.

Like Joseph, don't lower your standards but lift your eyes to God for whom nothing is too hard. His grace is enough when all else fails. He will not fail. Look for the way of escape rather than lowering your moral principles and practices. As 1 Corinthians 10:13 tells us, "God is faithful, who will not suffer you to be tempted above that ye are able; but will with the temptation also make a way to escape."

Young person, you are either leaving your mark on the world, or the world is leaving its mark on you. Keep your standards of conduct high. If you want to smell like a rose, stay out of the barnyard.

About God: **To Do:**

December 8

Overdue

"The wicked borroweth, and payeth not again: but the righteous sheweth mercy, and giveth." —Psalm 37:21

Read 2 Kings 6:1-7

Eve Lettice had no anxiety about returning an overdue library book—even though it was 82 years late. While cleaning the attic she had found the overdue book *Sunshine Sketches of a Little Town* by Stephen Leacock.

The book would have brought a $7,200 fine had it not been for the library rule of a twelve-dollar maximum. The librarian said, "We're just grateful to have the book back, especially since it's a Canadian classic."

Perhaps you have some books that are overdue—books that you borrowed and it is past time you returned them. Some Christians are known to be good *bookkeepers*. The axe user of 2 Kings 6:5 was rightly concerned about the axe head that fell into the river. "Alas, master! for it was borrowed."

There may be other things that are overdue. Take, for instance, a letter of encouragement. Even a brief thinking-of-you note can bolster one's spirits.

A word of commendation may be overdue. Youth, consider your parents. "Dad, I really like the way you listen to me without jumping on my case as soon as you hear something you disagree with." Student, consider your Sunday school teacher. "Brother Jeff, I can tell you do a lot of preparation. And I also think you do a really good job of getting everyone to participate in class." Think of the church custodians. "Nate and Ruthie, we really appreciate the clean and tidy church house. Keep up the top-notch job." Consider the pastor. "Brother Louis, your sermons lately have had a lot of depth. I really feel that my family and I are being fed well."

Some quality family time may be overdue. Young people, have you arranged recently to involve yourself in some family activities instead of only having activities with your peer group?

Sacrificial giving may be overdue. Christians show what they are by what they do with what they have.

There may be other things that come to your mind that are overdue—an apology, a deed of kindness, the payment of a debt, or an unfulfilled duty.

Don't wait 82 years. The Victoria library was happy to get the overdue book back. Make some people happy today by giving to them what is overdue.

About God: **To Do:**

Do Not Stop Chain Saws With Hands

"And they all with one consent began to make excuse." —Luke 14:18

Read 1 Samuel 15:10-30

A woman from Calgary, Alberta, rode her bike at night without a front or rear light on a busy road and was struck by a car. The outcome? She successfully sued a Canadian bicycle manufacturer because the company had neglected to warn her of the dangers of riding at night without lights.

In another lawsuit, a young thief told how he was injured while trying to get into a public school. He successfully sued the school board for his fall. The school board had failed to give warning of the danger of breaking into the school via the gymnasium roof! But the warning I find most intriguing comes from a chain saw manufacturer, "Do not try to stop chain with hands."

This tendency to avoid personal responsibility goes right back to our first parents. When Adam was confronted by God because of his disobedience, he shifted the blame to Eve. "The woman whom thou gavest to be with me, she gave me of the tree, and I did eat" (Genesis 3:12). Eve then excused herself for her wrong and blamed the serpent.

And modern man has the same propensities as our first parents. Take, for instance, blaming one's parents for one's own unwise choice and its sad consequences. True, some children have endured a very poor home life. However, some children who have experienced a very insecure childhood become stable and exemplary adults. (My mother, an orphan from early childhood, is one example).

Another point to remember is that we are individuals of personal choice—we are not doomed to repeat the mistakes of our parents. Some children with abusive, alcoholic parents grow to maturity with a gentle, saintly character.

Personal responsibility is a very important concept for good mental and spiritual health. Don't blame injustices you've experienced—rise above them as Joseph did. Don't blame an unwholesome background—overcome it by wise choices as Rahab did. Don't blame your limitations on your social environment—Daniel was a captive in a foreign land, yet he had an "excellent spirit" (Daniel 6:3). Don't blame your religious background—Ruth chose to serve the true God.

Do not drink gasoline. Grab a knife by the handle, not by the blade. Do not sit on a hot barbecue. Do not use a power saw to trim your toenails. Accept personal responsibility.

About God: **To Do:**

Wonderful

"Wherefore God also hath highly exalted him, and given him a name which is above every name." —Philippians 2:9

Read Isaiah 9:1-7

Neil McDonagh of Northern Ireland grew tired of his name. So he changed it to Zebedee Zzypp. He said it was a name "to end all names." And sure enough, in the local phone book, Zebedee Zzypp is at the end.

Your name likely came about in a different way than Mr. Zzypp's. Here are a dozen names and their meanings which I personally like (probably because they represent my wife, son, and three daughters, and my father, mother, brother, and four sisters). *Barbara* means "beautiful stranger"; *Richard:* "powerful ruler"; *Esther:* "a star"; *Brenda:* "firebrand"; *Karen:* "pure"; *Gordon:* "of the cornered hill"; *Lillian:* "lily"; *Ralph:* "swift wolf"; *Catherine:* "pure one"; *Marjorie:* "a pearl"; *Doris:* "from the ocean"; *Sharon:* "a princess."

Jesus rightly merits the first name given in our daily reading (v. 6)—Wonderful! The prophecy of His birth was wonderful: a child born—Son of Man; a son given—Son of God; the government shall be upon His shoulder—Son of David.

When Jesus came, His life was wonderful from beginning to end.

- Wonderful birth. Luke 2:10-14 tells of a wonderful message. A wonderful chorus of angels gave His birth announcement.
- Wonderful boyhood. Luke 2:47 tells of the wonderful "understanding and answers" that He showed in dialogue with the theologians.
- Wonderful baptism. Luke 3:21, 22 tells us that "the heaven was opened, and the Holy Ghost descended in a bodily shape like a dove upon him, and a voice came from heaven, which said, Thou art my beloved Son; in thee I am well pleased."

All aspects of His ministry were "Wonderful." His teaching was wonderful; "never man spake like this man," said some law officers (John 7:46). His working was wonderful. He "went about doing good" (Acts 10:38). His dying was wonderful. He prayed, "Father, forgive them; for they know not what they do" (Luke 23:34). Also wonderful was His rising from the dead and His ascending to glory. Wonderful too, will be His Second Coming.

Perhaps you'd like to sing the little chorus, "Isn't He Wonderful?"

About God: **To Do:**

Counselor

"And the spirit of the LORD shall rest upon him, the spirit of wisdom and understanding, the spirit of counsel and might, the spirit of knowledge and of the fear of the LORD." —Isaiah 11:2

Read John 4:7-26

Some names are apt. In my youth I bought an auto from a mechanic called Mr. Otto. An obstetrician by the name of Dr. Nurse delivered the oldest of our daughters. In my local area I could call on Bert Flood to do my plumbing and on Robert Hammer to build a deck. Judge Fair is a local judge, and Mr. Chalk teaches school where I attended as a boy.

The name of Counselor is appropriate for Jesus. To be a good counselor takes wisdom and sympathy. Various times Jesus shed tears and He is wisdom personified. He "is made unto us wisdom" (1 Corinthians 1:30). He had an understanding mind ("he knew what was in man" says John 2:25), and He had an understanding heart which was motivated by divine love.

Consider a few examples of how He wonderfully counseled. Concerning the Samaritan woman, He engaged her in conversation by asking for a drink. He tactfully helped her see her need of living water and identified Himself as the Messiah as the answer to her questions.

He acted as a night counselor to Nicodemus, showing him the necessity, means, and results of being born again. He made house calls, as in the case of Zacchaeus, the vertically-challenged tax collector. Luke 19:5 tells us about it: "And when Jesus came to the place, he looked up, and saw him, and said unto him, Zacchaeus, make haste, and come down; for to day I must abide at thy house."

He counseled the youth. Of the rich young ruler Mark 10:21 says, "Then Jesus beholding him loved him, and said unto him, One thing thou lackest: go thy way, sell whatsoever thou hast, and give to the poor, and thou shalt have treasure in heaven: and come, take up the cross, and follow me."

Jesus is eager to listen to our hearts and give us help. He says, "Come unto me, all ye that labour and are heavy laden, and I will give you rest" (Matthew 11:28).

Confide in Him daily and receive His comfort and counsel.

About God: **To Do:**

December 12

Mighty God

"But that ye may know that the Son of man hath power on earth to forgive sins, (then saith he to the sick of the palsy,) Arise, take up thy bed, and go unto thine house." —Matthew 9:6

Read Matthew 8:14-27

I find it amazing the way many people's surnames match their occupation. When names are apt in that manner, they are called *aptonyms.* Here are a few examples:

In my local area of Ontario is a dentist called Pus, a man with the Salvation Army called Captain Pilgrim, and earth science professors called Greenhouse, Appleyard, and Cherry.

At a local university a well-known professor taught archaeology. His name was, appropriately, Lawrence Toombs.

A few years ago, Arthur E. Squirrel worked as a comptroller at Raymond's Nuts. Hence, it was unbelievable yet correct to say, "A. Squirrel works at a nut factory in Kitchener, Ontario."

Jesus was given the very appropriate name of *The Mighty God.* He created everything. "For by him were all things created, that are in heaven, and that are in earth, visible and invisible, whether they be thrones, or dominions, or principalities, or powers: all things were created by him, and for him" (Colossians 1:16). The humble Carpenter of Nazareth was also the mighty Architect of the Universe.

He sustains the universe and holds matter together. Colossians 1:17 says, "And he is before all things, and by him all things consist."

He is divine, having glory and power and position. As Hebrews 1:3 says, "Who being the brightness of his glory, and the express image of his person, and upholding all things by the word of his power, when he had by himself purged our sins, sat down on the right hand of the Majesty on high."

He controls the elements of nature such as the wind, as shown by the daily reading. He heals. No illness is beyond His ability. He is a specialist in all fields of medicine.

He saves. Hebrews 7:25 says, "Wherefore he is able also to save them to the uttermost that come unto God by him, seeing he ever liveth to make intercession for them."

As God, He will raise the dead someday. John 5:28, 29 says, "Marvel not at this: for the hour is coming, in the which all that are in the graves shall hear his voice, and shall come forth; they that have done good, unto the resurrection of life; and they that have done evil, unto the resurrection of damnation."

In summary, He said, "All power is given unto me in heaven and in earth" (Matthew 28:18) because He is the Mighty God.

About God: **To Do:**

The Everlasting Father

"I and my Father are one." —John 10:30

Read John 1:1-14

I am intrigued by the number of aptonyms in the health field. I would like to have met Ivan Doctor, an optometrist (I. Doctor for short). Aside from many doctors named Doctor, there has been one called Bonecutter, five called Bonebreak, and eighteen Butchers. Dentists have had such surnames as Filler, Chew, Gargle, Gumm, and Root. There was even a William Toothaker.

Funeral directors have also been known to carry "aptonyms"—surnames which have turned out to be amazingly apt in terms of the person's chosen vocation or interest. Consider funeral directors named Coffin, Death, and Graves, or coroners like Deadman and Slaughter.

The everlasting Father is a suitable name for Jesus. He is eternal. As Micah 5:2 foretold, "But thou, Bethlehem Ephratah, though thou be little among the thousands of Judah, yet out of thee shall he come forth unto me that is to be ruler in Israel; whose goings forth have been from of old, from everlasting."

He came from heaven. He said, "What and if ye shall see the Son of man ascend up where he was before?" (John 6:62). And in His prayer the night before He was crucified, He prayed, "And now, O Father, glorify thou me with thine own self with the glory which I had with thee before the world was" (John 17:5).

When the British queen, Victoria, lived at Balmoral Castle, she would sometimes go for a walk incognito. She would step out the side gate accompanied only by a faithful servant who followed behind.

In one instance she came on a flock of sheep being driven along the road by a boy who shouted, "Keep out of the way, stupid old woman!" The Queen smiled, but said nothing, and when her servant came along he informed the lad that she was the Queen.

"Well," said the boy, "she should dress like a queen."

Because Jesus came in humble form, some people did not recognize Him. But He is everlasting and He is one with the Father. To His critics, He said, "If I do not the works of my Father, believe me not. But if I do, though ye believe not me, believe the works: that ye may know, and believe, that the Father is in me, and I in him" (John 10:37, 38).

About God: **To Do:**

December 14

The Prince of Peace

"These things I have spoken unto you, that in me ye might have peace." —John 16:33

Read Romans 5:1-11

Some names are ironic because they do not fit the occupation of the person very well.

For example, I might have been reluctant to enter the office of two American surgeons whose nameplate on their office door read "Will Slaughter and Philip Graves."

Doctor Sugarman and Doctor Honey are both Canadian dentists. William Otto Rec worked at Chrysler Canada. Hedley Basher was a reform school official. Robin Banks did not go around robbing banks.

But there is no irony in Jesus being called the Prince of Peace. The name fits.

Before He was born, Isaiah foretold that the Messiah "shall be as an hiding place from the wind, and a covert from the tempest. And the work of righteousness shall be peace; and the effect of righteousness quietness and assurance for ever" (Isaiah 32:2, 17).

At His birth, the host of angels praised God, saying, "Glory to God in the highest, and on earth peace, good will toward men" (Luke 2:14).

On the cross, He was peacemaking. As Colossians 1:20 says, "Having made peace through the blood of his cross, by him to reconcile all things unto himself; by him, I say, whether they be things in earth, or things in heaven." Today's Bible reading says, "We have peace with God through our Lord Jesus Christ" (v. 1).

He offers peace. "Peace I leave with you, my peace I give unto you: not as the world giveth, give I unto you. Let not your heart be troubled, neither let it be afraid" (John 14:27). The expression "Merry Christmas" originally had a deeper meaning than a trite greeting. *Merry* meant "peaceful." When the Christian stays his mind on Christ, he develops a wonderful "calm-plex." Peace rules the day when Christ rules the heart.

About God: **To Do:**

The Babe

"And they came with haste, and found Mary, and Joseph, and the babe lying in a manger." —Luke 2:16

Read Luke 2:8-20

"The greatest forces in the world are not the earthquakes and the thunderbolts," said Dr. E. T. Sullivan. "The greatest forces in the world are babies." Understandably then, we are fascinated, amused, and awed by babies.

But the greatest power in the universe is not babies but "the Babe." This term for Christ was used by the angels to the shepherds on Jesus' birthday. "Ye shall find the *babe* wrapped in swaddling clothes."

I have been meditating on the implications of the term "the Babe." As a babe, He was born, yet He always existed. He developed in a womb, yet He had given birth to the world. "For by him were all things created" (Colossians 1:16).

He was laid in a manger as a helpless infant, yet He was "the mighty God" (Isaiah 9:6).

He created Mary, His mother, yet Mary was responsible for His physical life and care.

His first domicile was a stable, for Mary "laid him in a manger" (Luke 2:7); yet He was and is and shall be King of kings.

He took nourishment from Mary for survival, yet Mary knew the angels called her Baby "Christ the Lord" (Luke 2:11, 19).

There was "no room . . . in the inn" (Luke 2:7) for the Baby, yet He was worshiped by angels and deserved preeminence.

He slept as a baby (without crying, according to Martin Luther's hymn), yet He offered spiritual rest. He invited, "Come unto me, all ye that labour and are heavy laden, and I will give you rest" (Matthew 11:28).

He was wrapped in swaddling clothes instead of being clothed with the celestial splendor that He laid aside. He "made himself of no reputation, and took upon him the form of a servant" (Philippians 2:7).

His Jewish parents needed to redeem the Babe because he was Mary's firstborn (Exodus 13:1-13). They likely paid five shekels' worth to redeem the Redeemer, who now redeems us (1 Peter 1:18, 19). It seems the family was too poor to bring a lamb (Luke 2:24), but the Babe was the Lamb of God which takes away the sin of the world.

The hymnwriter of the carol, "Gentle Mary Laid Her Child," wrote, "Such a Babe in such a place, can He be the Saviour? Ask the saved of all the race, who have found His favor." This Christmas, thank God anew for the Saviour, the Babe of Bethlehem.

About God: **To Do:**

December 16

Born a King

"And Pilate wrote a title, and put it on the cross. And the writing was, JESUS OF NAZARETH THE KING OF THE JEWS." —John 19:19

Read Psalm 47

Edward had a problem. He also had a plan—an excellent plan.

His problem? As king of England in the thirteenth century, he aimed to unite England, Scotland, and Wales under his rule. As he invaded Wales, he was resisted stubbornly in battle after battle. The warriors of Wales wouldn't give in; they continued guerrilla warfare for several years.

The plan of King Edward I? He invited the Welsh leaders to a conference.

He asked them, "Will you accept and be loyal to a prince chosen by me, provided that he would meet three conditions?"

The Welsh leaders listened carefully as the king presented the conditions. First, he must be the son of a king. Second, he must have been born in their own country, Wales. Third, he must be such a man that no one could charge with any fault.

The men of Wales happily agreed, feeling sure that no such prince could be found. Immediately, King Edward named the person who had complied with all three conditions. It was his own son! Unknown to the Welsh, this son had just been born in the castle of Caernarvon, which was on Welsh soil.

Imagine the expression on the faces of the Welsh leaders as they realized there was nothing they could do but accept the young prince offered them.

This story explains why the oldest son of the British monarch is called the Prince of Wales.

The story of the Prince of Wales also illustrates three wonderful truths about the Prince of whom the wise men inquired, "Where is he that is born King of the Jews?" (Matthew 2:2).

1. Jesus is the Son of a King. "God is the king of all the earth" (Psalm 47:7). This almighty King spoke of Jesus as "my beloved Son."
2. Jesus was born in a "foreign" land. From heaven He came to earth to be born in a stable, the greatest "space mission" the world has seen. The men of Wales had to accept King Edward's son. It is essential that men on earth voluntarily accept God's Son.
3. Jesus had neither fault nor sin. Jesus challenged the unbelievers of the first century and succeeding centuries with the question, "Which of you convinceth me of sin?" (John 8:46). What a wonderful Prince, Saviour, Example, and Friend who was "tempted like as we are, yet without sin" (Hebrews 4:15).

O come let us adore Him, Christ the Lord!

About God: **To Do:**

Wise Men Who Were Shepherds

"But when the fulness of the time was come, God sent forth his Son, made of a woman, made under the law." —Galatians 4:4

Read Luke 2:8-14

One father pondered some wrong emphases at Christmastime. As Christmas approached, he called a family conference to challenge his family members to exercise self-control and discipline. "Let's not have extravagant spending this year. Let's use our time wisely."

He also encouraged them to have better relations between themselves and visiting relatives, and admonished them to have a more congenial atmosphere in their house in keeping with peace on earth, goodwill toward men. He brought his speech to a climax as he raised his voice in pitch and volume, "Let's make this the best Christmas, EVER!"

His son in second grade protested, "But, Dad, I don't see how we could improve on the first Christmas."

We'd agree! But while we can't improve on the first Christmas, we can improve our observance of it. Take four lessons from the way the shepherds related to Christ's birth as recorded in Luke 2. They may not have come from the East, but they certainly were wise men.

1. The shepherds watched and worked (v. 8). The shepherds were not lazy busybodies, waiting for the advent of the Messiah. They were humble working men who were ready in heart for a special invitation to the first appearing of "that great shepherd of the sheep" (Hebrews 13:20).

God can bless you as you work—hammering nails, providing meals and clean clothes for the family, harvesting crops, running a lathe, caring for the elderly, teaching, etc. As we wait for the Second Coming of the Messiah, let us be watching and working.

2. The shepherds listened carefully and remembered (vv. 10-14). We should listen to God's message. There are many voices in the world—from Harry Potter to Bill Gates to the Pope to the President to movie stars. These are all earthly voices. Let us listen to the heavenly message, that is, the Bible.

3. The shepherds believed and acted (v. 15). It is not enough for us to listen to advent sermons and Christmas carols. Like the shepherds, we are wise if we are responsive to God's proclamation. They heard of the Saviour so they went to Him.

4. The shepherds used communication skills (v. 15). "The shepherds said one to another." There is a lot of value in talking over spiritual endeavors with each other.

About God: **To Do:**

December 18

More Wisdom From the Shepherds

"This is a faithful saying, and worthy of all acceptation, that Christ Jesus came into the world to save sinners; of whom I am chief." —1 Timothy 1:15

Read Luke 2:15-20

The shepherds showed their wisdom in five more ways:

1. The shepherds were prompt (v. 15). "Let us now go even unto Bethlehem." Was it wise to go immediately? Was it sensible to go at night? The flock of sheep would need tending—especially after the appearance of a multitude of the heavenly host. Even if a few shepherds stayed behind, the shepherds might well lose a part of their source of livelihood. Then there would be the problem of finding the way down the dark hills and locating the proper stable. It would take time and effort. Was it wise?

Finding and following Jesus Christ will always involve sacrifice. To the world, a Christian is foolish. But the shepherds did not hesitate nor doubt the heavenly message. "They came with haste, and found" (v. 16). Wise men today follow this example. Tragically, at Christmas most of the rushing seems only to be to the stores for presents instead of to the Saviour for His abiding Presence.

2. The shepherds searched for and found Jesus. The original language suggests it took effort to find this Babe. We are to seek "the LORD while he may be found, call ye upon him while he is near" (Isaiah 55:6).

3. The shepherds witnessed (v. 17). "And when they had seen it, they made known abroad the saying which was told them concerning this child." Is our witness at Christmas that clear, vibrant, and up-to-date? Oh, that the world's attention might be turned to forgiveness instead of frivolity, to devotion instead of decoration, to penitence instead of parties! We can help them if we ourselves are ready, like the wise shepherds, to serve the Saviour without hesitation or reservation.

4. The shepherds had their priorities right (v. 20). They left their work to worship but then returned to their duties. They were not so heavenly minded that they were of no earthly good.

5. The shepherds glorified God (v. 20). Let us glorify God at Christmas as we follow the example of the wise shepherds.

About God: **To Do:**

God Gives Gifts to Us

"Therefore being justified by faith, we have peace with God through our Lord Jesus Christ." —Romans 5:1

Read 2 Peter 1:1-11

Last year a local newspaper asked for readers' suggestions for budget-wise gifts. "Books and magazine subscriptions are good ideas," responded some readers. Another suggestion especially appealed to my parsimonious nature. "In our family we have recycled gifts. These are items within a person's home that are no longer of use to the owner but are too good to throw away. We designate it to a person within the family. This has become the most exciting part of Christmas for us." One reader wrote, "I would like to receive any homemade gift. They are cheaper and they are better."

God doesn't need suggestions for His gift list for us, nor are the gifts secondhand or cheap. In His generosity and love, He has bestowed gifts of inestimable value to His children. Consider these verses He has given, telling us of His gifts relating to or resulting from the Incarnation in Bethlehem:

1. *His Son:* "For God so loved the world, that he gave his only begotten Son, that whosoever believeth in him should not perish, but have everlasting life" (John 3:16).

2. *Eternal life:* "The gift of God is eternal life through Jesus Christ our Lord" (Romans 6:23).

3. *Rest:* "Come unto me, all ye that labour and are heavy laden, and I will give you rest" (Matthew 11:28).

4. *Peace:* "Peace I leave with you, my peace I give unto you" (John 14:27).

5. *Holy Spirit:* "And hereby we know that he abideth in us, by the Spirit which he hath given us" (1 John 3:24).

6. *Promises:* "According as his divine power hath given unto us all things that pertain unto life and godliness. Whereby are given unto us exceeding great and precious promises" (2 Peter 1:3, 4).

7. *Inheritance:* "And now, brethren, I commend you to God, and to the word of his grace, which is able to build you up, and to give you an inheritance among all them which are sanctified" (Acts 20:32).

Surely Christmas Day is Thanks**giving** Day! It was a day of thanksgiving for the shepherds. After finding the Babe in the stable "the shepherds returned, glorifying and praising God for all the things that they had heard and seen" (Luke 2:20).

About God: **To Do:**

December 20

Giving Gifts to God

"And the Gentiles shall come to thy light,
and kings to the brightness of thy rising." —Isaiah 60:3

Read Matthew 2:1-12

The wise men from the East provide a worthy example of gift-giving to the Lord. First, they gave *effort*. Just how long it took them to travel to Bethlehem we don't know, but travel on a two-humped camel (if that's what they rode) from the East is far different from traveling in a four-cylinder "Pony" imported from the East. (Your local Hyundai dealer will quickly affirm this.) Their efforts carried them over the obstacles of distance, desert, and dangers to find the answer to their question, "Where is he that is born King of the Jews?" Do your attitudes and activities at Christmas show you are seeking the Lord?

Secondly, they gave Him their *worship*. Coming into the house, they fell down before their infant King. People may be worthy of our admiration, but only God is worthy of our adoration. Before they presented their gifts, they first prostrated themselves. Is your heart bowed before Jesus—humbly, loyally, unreservedly, and worshipfully?

Thirdly, they gave of their *treasures*. Gold was given in recognition of His kingship, reminding us that the King of kings stooped so low; frankincense, symbolic of prayer, was given in recognition of His divine nature as the Mediator through whom we pray; myrrh, a bitter spice, was given in recognition of His purpose in coming to give Himself a ransom for all. The gold thus reflected His royalty; the incense, His divinity; and the myrrh, His humanity. Have you given Jesus your gold (possessions), your incense (prayers and worship), and your myrrh (death to self)?

Fourthly, they gave the Lord *obedience*. Instead of returning to scheming Herod, they departed into their own country another way, as God had commanded them. Often the hardest thing to give is **in**. Are you giving obedience so that you can be guided and blessed in the journey of life?

About God: **To Do:**

Big Christmas Gifts

"And when they had seen it, they made known abroad the saying which was told them concerning this child." —Luke 2:17

Read Luke 1:39-56

If one wants to buy an expensive Christmas present, *Robb's Report* features "21 exclusive gifts for the 21st century." It includes a $30 million, 50-meter super yacht with a gymnasium and marble-floored lobby. For those preferring land transportation, consider the 485-horsepower V12 Ferrari Barchetta Pininfarina, limited edition convertible for only $285,000.

For those interested in hunting, the report suggests a twenty-one-day safari package complete with a pair of 12-gauge shotguns and a Range Rover at just over $325,000.

Less expensive possibilities include a man and woman's wardrobe of cashmere and wool from Italian manufacturer Loro Piana for $55,000 or a ski vacation for two in the French Alps for $39,400. A four-day trip for two to meet and cook with four "super chefs" costs $25,000.

I don't recommend this guidebook or the purchase of its big gifts. But I do have some suggestions for big Christmas gifts to give to each other.

There's the gift of *friendship*. Mary visited Elisabeth, both expectant mothers of promised sons, and they fellowshipped with each other for three months (Luke 1:56). There is the gift of *consideration and discretion*. Joseph gave this to Mary when he discovered that she was expecting a child before they were to be married. He was not willing to make her a public example; and so "was minded to put her away privily" (Matthew 1:19). There is the gift of *financial help*. Undoubtedly the gold from the wise men helped Jesus' family to make the trip to Egypt. There is the gift of *hospitality*. I'm not sure if the innkeeper in Bethlehem gave this gift to Mary and Joseph or not, but it is a suitable gift for the present day. There is the gift of *sharing the good news*. This gift the angels gave to the shepherds, who then shared it with the residents of Bethlehem.

Shall we give gifts (of things) to one another? Personally, I don't think it's necessary. Nor do I think it is necessarily wrong.

If you do buy gifts, here are some guidelines: Give out of a heart of love, not to impress. Give not only at Christmas. Remember to give to the poor and needy. Don't go into debt in order to give unnecessary things.

God has given to us His Son; we should give to Him.

About God: **To Do:**

Christmas Surprises

"Now the birth of Jesus Christ was on this wise: When as his mother Mary was espoused to Joseph, before they came together, she was found with child of the Holy Ghost." —Matthew 1:18

Read Luke 1:26-38

Christmas is a time of surprises. I remember my surprise and joy at age five when I received a brand-new sled so I could whiz down the hills on the farm. I remember my surprise and dismay at age nine at acquiring a pair of socks when I was expecting a game. I remember my surprise at age 22 of being presented with a hand-knit sweater from my girlfriend—it was far too big (although it would fit me well now), presumably because Barbara knit it to fit her estimation of me!

Christmas and surprises go together. So it was at the first Christmas.

Think of the surprises Mary and Joseph received. An angel, Gabriel, appeared to her (Luke 1:28), calling her blessed and highly favored. Imagine her amazement at being told she was to have a baby, and that the baby would be the Son of God!

Shocked is probably an accurate word to describe Joseph's feeling upon learning that his wife-to-be was expecting a child. No doubt his surprise at the news was only equaled by his surprise when an angel appeared to him, telling him to proceed with his plans to marry her.

Think of the surprises the shepherds received on Christmas Eve. What a dramatic change in a few minutes! First, they watched sheep in quietness, darkness, and monotony. Then they watched angels with the glory of the Lord shining around them. Not only was the angels' manner surprising but also their message: "Good news for everybody—a Saviour is born." Then there was the manger surprise. A King, the Son of God, the Messiah, placed in an animal's feeding trough? Incredible! No flashing neon lights, no loudspeaker, no live television coverage, no headlines or worldly fanfare, but the sign of a "babe wrapped in swaddling clothes, lying in a manger" (Luke 2:12).

The shepherds may well have been amazed that they were the recipients of the heavenly news—not the regal, the rich, nor the reputable; that those entrusted to care for the Son of God were so poor (swaddling bands denoted poverty); that they were invited to view the Prince not in a palace but a stable. They may also have considered that there was "no room" for the Creator of the heaven and earth. We do well to recall that the meek Carpenter of Nazareth was also the mighty Architect of the universe.

About God: **To Do:**

More Christmas Surprises

"Saying, Where is he that is born King of the Jews? for we have seen his star in the east, and are come to worship him." —Matthew 2:2

Read Isaiah 60:1-6

The pastor of a church in a small town was ordering a sign for the outdoor manger scene. The company needed to know the dimensions and wording of the sign, but the pastor wasn't sure. Since time was of the essence, the company suggested that the pastor send the information to them by way of a messenger as soon as he could. The next day a Western Union employee was shocked to see this message come across the wire: "For unto us a child is born. 8 feet long, 3 feet wide."

Think of the surprising things about the wise men. Although Christ was a Jew, was born in Judaea, ministered especially to the Jews (Matthew 15:24), yet it was Gentile kings who worshiped Him as a young child (Matthew 2:11). Although the scribes and chief priests knew where Christ should be born and knew the request of the wise men, yet those religious leaders chose not to go to Bethlehem to honor the Child Jesus. Although the travelers from the East were wise and possibly royal, yet they fell down and worshipped and gave valuable gifts to the Child. Although the wise men came from a distance, yet the local folk of Jerusalem, and presumably Bethlehem, gave Christ limited recognition. As John 1:11 says, "He came unto his own and his own received him not."

Jesus continued to surprise people: in the temple at age twelve, in His first miracle at Cana, in His arrest when "they went backward, and fell to the ground" (John 18:6). At His resurrection, He again astounded soldiers, women, disciples, and the Pharisees. Likewise, His ascension left His disciples staring (Acts 1:10, 11).

Jesus still gives wonderful surprises today. Take the testimony of Charles Gabriel who wrote, "I stand *amazed* in the presence of Jesus the Nazarene" and the challenge of Johnson Oatman who wrote, "Count your many blessings and it will *surprise* you what the Lord has done."

About God: **To Do:**

Ready for Christmas

"But when the fulness of the time was come, God sent forth his Son, made of a woman, made under the law." —Galatians 4:4

Read Hebrews 1

Here are Ten Commandments for Christmas to see if you are ready for Christmas.

I. Thou shalt meditate on the greatest gift to man, Jesus.

II. Thou shalt not place buying, selling, or any form of commercialization ahead of God.

III. Thou shalt remember to give to missions—after all, the Lord Jesus came to earth as a missionary.

IV. Remember to keep Christmas Day wholly unto the Lord, as, indeed, each day should be.

V. Honour thy father and thy mother and other family members with the best gifts—love, respect, appreciation, and fellowship.

VI. Thou shalt participate in Christian service activities sponsored by thy congregation.

VII. Thou shalt teach children, and those who look to you as an example, the proper emphasis of Christmas, focusing on God's love shown to man by sending His Son to Bethlehem.

VIII. Thou shalt ponder the truth expressed by Christmas carols old and new.

IX. Thou shalt not give grudgingly.

X. Thou shalt not covet the extravagant gift-giving of thy neighbors or relatives.

About God: **To Do:**

A Saviour Is Born

"And the angel said unto them, Fear not; for, behold, I bring you good tidings of great joy, which shall be to all people. For unto you is born this day in the city of David a Saviour, which is Christ the Lord. And this shall be a sign unto you; Ye shall find the babe wrapped in swaddling clothes, lying in a manger." —Luke 2:10-12

Read Galatians 3:22–4:7

The key point of Christmas is *a Saviour is born*. However, at Christmastime, our focus may be on such things as family gatherings and Christmas letters, shopping and gift-buying, lights and decorations, dinners and banquets, and opening presents and returning some of them. In addition, the world honors Santa Claus and engages in drunkenness, revelry, and immorality. So many people totally miss the point of the angelic telegram: the Saviour is born. As 1 Timothy 1:15 puts it, "This is a faithful saying, and worthy of all acceptation, that Christ Jesus came into the world to save sinners."

Let's consider three aspects of salvation as mentioned by the angels to the shepherds in Luke 2:10-12:

1. *Good news of great joy.* The shepherds didn't need to fear: the messengers were benign and blessed; the news was good and great; the message was impressive and inclusive of all people groups. The shepherds were ready to go to the manger.

2. *Christ the Lord is born.* The shepherds were invited to seek the Man who had "come to seek and to save that which was lost" (Luke 19:10).

3. *A babe lying in a manger.* The Saviour was once an infant needing warmth, care, milk, clothing—just as you and I did. Absolutely amazing was Christ's humanity. God so identified with human beings that He sent His Son, clothed in human flesh having lungs, bones, hormones, eyes, hands, larynx, and ears. As Galatians 4:4 says, "God sent forth his Son, made of a woman, made under the law."

Although it is a mistake to minimize His humanity, even more significant than His humanity is His divinity. It is not His humanity that makes Him unique—it is His divinity.

A girl in second grade was saying John 3:16 by memory in my daughter's classroom. She said, "For God so loved the world that he gave his only forgotten Son!" The rest of the class didn't notice, but my daughter did. This Christmas don't let Jesus be the forgotten Son of God.

About God: **To Do:**

December 26

Ready to Go Home

"In my Father's house are many mansions: if it were not so, I would have told you. I go to prepare a place for you. And if I go and prepare a place for you, I will come again, and receive you unto myself; that where I am, there ye may be also." —John 14:2, 3

Read Matthew 24:32-51

Many people like to go "home" at Christmastime.

It is possible that before another Christmas, all who are in Christ will go "home"! Remembering Christ's first coming should remind us of His Second Coming, when He will take home all those whose home is heaven.

His Second Coming is as certain as His first. Consider how His Second Coming will be like His first coming to earth.

His will be a personal return. The last chapter of the Bible says, "Behold, I come quickly" (Revelation 22:7). And 1 Thessalonians 4:16 says, "The Lord himself shall descend from heaven."

Just as Christ's coming to the Bethlehem manger was literal, so His return will be literal. The heavenly messengers said to the awestruck disciples at His ascension, "This same Jesus, which is taken up from you into heaven, shall so come in like manner as ye have seen him go into heaven" (Acts 1:11).

He will be visible. Just as truly as the shepherds and wise men saw Him, so believers shall see Him. First John 3:2 says, "When he shall appear, we shall be like him; for we shall see him as he is."

Although a few like Simeon and Anna were looking for Jesus' coming, many were not. So it is with His Second Coming: some are anticipating it, but most are unconcerned.

But there will also be major differences between His first and Second Coming. He came the first time in poverty and humiliation to a stable; the second time will be in glory and majesty. Luke 21:27 describes His "coming in a cloud with power and great glory." The first time He came with limitations, but His Second Coming will be altogether different.

In His first coming, He was known as the man of sorrows, but in His Second Coming, He shall descend from heaven with a shout. In His trial, He was made to hold a reed in mockery; at His Second Coming, He wields the scepter with authority. Before Pilate, He wore a crown of thorns, but in the future He will have the diadem of King of kings and Lord of lords.

About God:

To Do:

Ready for Christ's Return

"Be ye therefore ready also: for the Son of man cometh at an hour when ye think not." —Luke 12:40

Read 1 Thessalonians 4:9-18

The commemoration of Christ's first coming should remind us that He said, "I will come again."

What is this world coming to?

Judgment! Two women shall be washing dishes: the one shall be taken and the other left. Two people shall be cruising down the highway: one shall be taken and the other left. Two men shall be milking the cows: one shall be taken and the other left.

The tense is future but the fact is sure. Jesus is returning in bodily form to this planet. Is this the first you've thought of it today? As you meditate on Jesus' soon return, do you feel fearful uncertainty or peaceful serenity?

Regarding His sudden return, Jesus commanded, "Watch therefore." Because you may not see Him otherwise? No! "Every eye shall see Him." Watch rather, because "ye know not what hour your Lord doth come" (Matthew 24:42). Watch as if your life depended on it. It does—your eternal life.

This world is definitely coming to judgment in accord with God's eternal plan. The Righteous Judge has said so: "For the Son of man shall come in the glory of his Father with his angels; and then he shall reward every man according to his works" (Matthew 16:27). Whether we are dead or alive in the body, we must have made preparation for His triumphant return, "who shall judge the quick and the dead at his appearing and his kingdom" (2 Timothy 4:1).

How important a place does the Second Coming of the Saviour occupy in your thinking, planning, and doing? Satan desires for us to forget about Christ's return so that he can return to us with temptations more successfully. How often are we reminded of Christ's return in the New Testament? It is mentioned 318 times, or once in every 25 verses. We can't say we haven't been told.

In summary, Jesus' return is sure and soon. We need not look for the undertaker but the Uptaker! Watch and be ready. The Lord is at hand.

About God:

To Do:

December 28

Readiness to Rise

"Therefore thus will I do unto thee, O Israel: and because I will do this unto thee, prepare to meet thy God, O Israel." —Amos 4:12

Read 1 Corinthians 15:34-58

I found this account of Mike Hanzas almost too incredible to believe. Two years before he died, he began to make preparations for his death. Mike, who lived alone, bought a cemetery lot. Weekly, he visited the site where his mortal remains would be interred. He planted grass there and mowed it regularly. On Memorial Day, he placed flowers on the grave site, for he said, "I want to see flowers there now. I won't be able to see them when I'm gone."

Later Mike went into a funeral home. "I want to buy the casket which will be my new home," he said. Whenever he passed the funeral home he would go in. Standing beside the casket he would say, "That's where I'm going to live someday!"

One day Mike invited a nephew and the rest of his family to come to see him. After a hearty meal, Mike began to dispense some canned goods and personal effects among his visitors. Then he handed his nephew his will. As he did this, he dropped dead of heart failure!

Although Mike had made timely preparations for his body, the only really important funeral preparations are made by getting right with God. Death comes to all. As George Bernard Shaw said, "The statistics on death are impressive. One out of one die." Therefore all need to prepare to die and face judgment before God. "It is appointed unto men once to die, but after this the judgment" (Hebrews 9:27). It is essential to have our sins forgiven by God before we die so we do not need to face them after death.

Death does not end it all. It only opens the door and ushers us into eternity. Our body dies but our spirit lives on. And although our bodies decay, the Bible tells us of the resurrection of the body. And as the daily reading says, "The dead shall be raised incorruptible, and we shall be changed" (v. 52).

We are ready to rise if we believe in Christ. Jesus said, "Every one which seeth the Son, and believeth on him, may have everlasting life: and I will raise him up at the last day" (John 6:40).

View death and the resurrection sanely and seriously. A person's conception of *death* will steer his approach to *life*. Be ready to die so that you may rise to eternal life.

About God: **To Do:**

Are You Ready?

"But sanctify the Lord God in your hearts: and be ready always to give an answer to every man that asketh you a reason of the hope that is in you with meekness and fear." —1 Peter 3:15

Read Romans 1:7-17

- Are you ready to work? Titus reminded his flock of Christians to "be ready to every good work" (Titus 3:1). "Also learn to maintain good works for necessary uses" (Titus 3:14). Furthermore, he wanted believers to "be careful to maintain good works" (Titus 3:8).

I remember a story I read in my youth that made a deep impression on me. A Korean missionary pastor was taking an American tourist through the country. The tourist was amused to see in a field, a young man pulling a plow and an older man holding the handles.

"They must be very poor," said the tourist as he got ready to take a photo.

"Yes," said the pastor quietly. "When the church was being built, they wanted to give something. So they sold their only ox and gave the money. That is why this spring they have to plow like that."

"That must have been a real sacrifice," said the American Christian soberly, putting down his camera.

"They did not call it a sacrifice," replied the pastor. "They were glad to have an ox they could sell."

- Are you ready to give? Paul told Timothy to strictly command the rich in this world "that they do good, that they be rich in good works, ready to distribute, willing to communicate" (1 Timothy 6:18). If the poor like the Korean father and son can give, how much more responsibility lies with North Americans? The largest chapter in the Bible is Numbers 7—nearly 2000 words, all about giving. (I used to think Psalm 119 was the largest.)
- Are you ready to share the Gospel? In the daily reading, Paul was "ready to preach the gospel" (v. 15).

On an ocean liner, a passenger was lying in his cabin seriously ill. One dark night he heard a cry, "Man overboard!" He wished he could help, but he was too sick. The rescuers could not see the man in the water. Suddenly, however, a light shone out through the glass of a porthole, falling full on the struggling man. They threw him a lifebelt and rescued him. Where did the light come from? The sick man had managed to crawl out of his bunk, take a lantern down from the wall, and place it where it could shine forth.

About God: **To Do:**

Driving Into the Future

"Examine yourselves, whether ye be in the faith; prove your own selves." —2 Corinthians 13:5

Read Revelation 3:14-22

As you prepare for the New Year, give your life a tune-up to ensure your life's vehicle is functioning properly. You dare not become complacent like the Laodiceans. Check these potential trouble spots:

1. *Fuel.* There is no power or movement without the Lord. "Without me ye can do nothing" (John 15:5).
2. *Water.* Fill your radiator with God's Word. It can keep you cool under the most trying circumstances. "Great peace have they which love thy law" (Psalm 119:165).
3. *Oil.* Without the oil of the Holy Spirit, the workings of your car will grind to a halt. "Be filled with the Spirit" (Ephesians 5:18).
4. *Brakes.* Ensure that the brakes on your tongue are working, for this is a slippery one: "Keep thy tongue from evil" (Psalm 34:13).
5. *Wheels.* Align yourself in the way that God wants you to go. Steering dare not be loose on the straight and narrow way. "Narrow is the way, which leadeth unto life" (Matthew 7:14).
6. *Spark plugs.* A kind word or deed may provide the needed spark to fill a life with new energy for God. The gap must not become too great. "Be ye kind one to another" (Ephesians 4:32).
7. *Timing.* Set your timing so that you can work harmoniously with God. "Yield yourselves unto the LORD" (2 Chronicles 30:8).
8. *Horn.* Be prepared to sound a warning when danger appears. "Warn them that are unruly" (1 Thessalonians 5:14).
9. *Lights.* In a dark world see that your headlights are beaming brightly. "Ye are the light of the world" (Matthew 5:14).
10. *Tires.* Retire with full assurance of eternal life if you are in the center of the Lord's will. "I will both lay me down in peace, and sleep: for Thou, LORD, only makest me dwell in safety" (Psalm 4:8).

About God: **To Do:**

Looking Back and Forward

"Remember Lot's wife." —Luke 17:32

Read Deuteronomy 31:1-15

We are at the Deuteronomy stage of the year. In Deuteronomy, Moses looked at the past and gave advice for the future.

Should we look back? Most people would rather look backward than forward because it's easier to remember where you've been than to figure out where you're going.

There are four good Biblical reasons for looking back:

1. *To appreciate.* Psalm 111:4 says, "He hath made his wonderful works to be remembered."

2. *To see God's faithfulness.* The psalmist testified, "I have been young, and now am old; yet have I not seen the righteous forsaken, nor his seed begging bread" (Psalm 37:25). And Polycarp testified, "Eighty and six years have I served my Lord Christ and He has never done me wrong. How can I deny my King who has preserved me from all evil and so faithfully redeemed me?"

3. *To see the blessings of adversity.* Joseph, looking back with his brothers, said, "But as for you, ye thought evil against me; but God meant it unto good . . . to save much people alive" (Genesis 50:20).

4. *To learn.* Moses said of God to Israel, "And he [God] humbled thee, and suffered thee to hunger . . . that he might make thee know that man doth not live by bread only, but by every word that proceedeth out of the mouth of the LORD doth man live" (Deuteronomy 8:3).

There are four ways we should not look back:

1. *Don't focus on your failures* which discourage and retard your spiritual progress. Paul said, "Forgetting those things which are behind, and reaching forth unto those things which are before" (Philippians 3:13).

2. *Don't complain.* Jacob told Pharaoh, "The days of the years of my pilgrimage are an hundred and thirty years: few and evil have the days of the years of my life been, and have not attained unto the days of the years of the life of my fathers in the days of their pilgrimage" (Genesis 47:9).

3. *Don't live in the past.* There is no point in saying, "If only I could be an adolescent again." Don't review past hurts and injustices. Rather, redeem the time—this takes living in the present.

4. *Don't look back with indecision or compromise.* Don't look back with thoughts of turning back.

About God: **To Do:**

Themes, Devotional Titles, and Verses

	Theme	Title	Verse
January 1	Aims	Redeem the Time	Ecclesiastes 12:1
January 2		I Am Resolved	2 Timothy 2:15
January 3		Abhor Sin	Psalm 97:10
January 4		Pressing Toward Heaven	Psalm 42:2
January 5		Grow Up Into Him	2 Peter 3:18
January 6		Be a Witness	2 Corinthians 5:20
January 7		Serve One Another	Matthew 20:28
January 8	God's Guidance	God Wants to Guide You	Exodus 15:13
January 9		Ways God Has Guided	Psalm 32:8
January 10		God Guides Through the Bible	Psalm 73:24
January 11		God Guides Through Prayer	Matthew 7:8
January 12		God Guides Through His Spirit	Ephesians 6:18
January 13		God Guides Through Godly Counselors	Proverbs 11:14
January 14		God Guides Through Circumstances	2 Corinthians 2:12
January 15	Devotional Life	Devoting Oneself to Devotions	Psalm 119:145
January 16		Milk, Please	Job 23:12
January 17		Priority of Prayer	Mark 1:35
January 18		Worship	Psalm 95:6
January 19		Purposes of Prayer	Philippians 4:6
January 20		Coughing and Praying	Ephesians 6:18
January 21		Hide It in Your Heart	Psalm 119:11
January 22	Why Be Saved	We All Die	Ecclesiastes 8:8
January 23		Advantages of Living in Sin	Proverbs 13:15
January 24		There Is a Way Out	John 10:9
January 25		Present Blessings of the Christian	1 Peter 1:8
January 26		God Wants All to Be Saved	John 3:16
January 27		Reality of Hell	Psalm 9:17
January 28		Procrastination Is Dangerous	Jeremiah 8:20
January 29	How to Be Saved	Admit	Romans 3:28
January 30		Accept the Pardon	Micah 7:18
January 31		Be Cleansed by Jesus' Blood	1 John 1:7
February 1		Repent	Acts 17:30
February 2		Believe in Jesus	John 3:14
February 3		Confess	Mark 8:38
February 4		Follow Jesus	John 10:27
February 5	God's Creation: The Body	Busy Bones	Psalm 35:10
February 6		Focusing on the Eye	Isaiah 33:17
February 7		Marvels of Your Hands	Luke 24:50
February 8		Wonderfully Made: The Brain	1 Corinthians 2:16
February 9		Your Wonderful Muscles	Ephesians 6:10
February 10		Marvelous Functions of Skin	Ezekiel 37:6
February 11		More Marvelous Functions of Skin	Job 10:11

	Theme	Title	Verse
February 12	Preparing for Service	Know Christ as Saviour and Example	Acts 4:12
February 13		Know the Bible	2 Timothy 2:15
February 14		Understand and Demonstrate Humility	Philippians 2:5
February 15		Be Salt	Matthew 5:13
February 16		I'm Gonna Let it Shine	Philippians 2:15, 16
February 17		Be Consistent	Matthew 7:3
February 18		Be Willing to Die	2 Timothy 4:6
February 19	Understanding Envy	The Green Sickness	1 Corinthians 13:4
February 20		Put Away Envy	Psalm 37:1
February 21		Warning Signs of Envy	Proverbs 14:30
February 22		Envy Leads to Every Evil Work	James 3:14
February 23		Envy Puts Others Down	Titus 3:3
February 24		Envy Brings Trouble to Oneself	1 Corinthians 3:3
February 25		Envy Poisons Interpersonal Relations	Romans 13:13
February 26	Beatitudes	Have I the Right Awareness?	Matthew 5:3
February 27		Have I the Right Sorrow?	Matthew 5:4
February 28		Have I the Right Response?	Matthew 5:5
March 1		Have I the Right Appetite?	Matthew 5:6
March 2		Do I Have the Right Spirit?	Matthew 5:7
March 3		Do I Have the Right Devotion?	Matthew 5:8
March 4		Do I Have the Right Cause?	Matthew 5:9
March 5	Value of Respect for Authority	Respect Stabilizes Society	1 Peter 2:17
March 6		Respect For Authority Pleases God	John 14:31
March 7		Respect Promotes Protection	Ephesians 6:2, 3
March 8		Respect Contributes to Liberty	John 8:36
March 9		Respect Improves Relationships	John 15:14
March 10		Respect Brings Blessing	1 John 2:5
March 11		When You Disagree With Your Authority	Romans 13:7
March 12	The Bible	The Bible: Love, Use, Remember It	Hebrews 4:12
March 13		The Bible: Speak of It, Stick to It, Meditate on It	Romans 1:16
March 14		The Bible: Learn, Keep, and Respect It	Hebrews 12:6
March 15		The Bible: Read, Appreciate, and Believe It	Matthew 22:29
March 16		The Law of the Lord Is Perfect	Romans 7:12
March 17		Bible Translators	Romans 2:13
March 18		History Before It Happens	Isaiah 42:9
March 19	The First Seven Sayings of Jesus	The Business of Jesus	Luke 2:49
March 20		The Baptism of Jesus	Matthew 3:15
March 21		The Temptation of Jesus	Matthew 4:4
March 22		The Invitation of Jesus	John 1:43
March 23		The First Miracle of Jesus	John 2:4
March 24		The Night Visitor to Jesus	John 3:3
March 25		Christ's Sermon Theme: Repent	Matthew 4:17

	Theme	Title	Verse
March 26	Jesus Our Saviour	Jesus Loves Me	Ephesians 5:2
March 27		The Ganges or Calvary	John 8:36
March 28		Jesus, Saviour	Ephesians 1:7
March 29		Jesus Gave Himself for Me	John 10:11
March 30		A Man of Sorrows	Isaiah 53:4
March 31		In the Cross of Christ I Glory	Galatians 6:14
April 1		Christ Invites You	Revelation 22:17
April 2	Seven Words From the Cross	Word of Forgiveness	Luke 23:34
April 3		Word of Companionship	Luke 23:43
April 4		Word of Comfort	John 19:26, 27
April 5		Word of Suffering	Matthew 27:46
April 6		Word of Humanness	John 19:28
April 7		Word of Completion	John 19:30
April 8		Word of Commitment	Luke 23:46
April 9	Seven Sayings After the Cross	Peace Be Unto You	John 20:21
April 10		Slow of Heart to Believe	Luke 24:17
April 11		All Things Must Be Fulfilled	Luke 24:25
April 12		Be Not Faithless But Believing	John 20:27
April 13		Lovest Thou Me	John 21:16
April 14		Go and Teach All Nations	Mark 16:15
April 15		Ye Shall Receive Power	Acts 1:8
April 16	Inferiority Feelings	Dealing With Feelings of Inferiority	Romans 12:3
April 17		You Are Special: God Made You	Psalm 8:5
April 18		God Knows You and Cares For You	1 Peter 5:7
April 19		God Has a Plan for You	Jeremiah 29:11
April 20		Coping With an Inferiority Complex	1 Samuel 17:45
April 21		Four Attitudes to Avoid	1 Samuel 17:47
April 22		Thinking Soberly About Self	Romans 12:4
April 23	Work	The Blessings of Work	1 Thessalonians 4:11
April 24		Choosing a Vocation	1 Corinthians 10:31
April 25		Employee Attitudes	Colossians 3:23
April 26		Instructions for Employees	Colossians 3:22
April 27		Do Not Purloin	Exodus 20:15
April 28		Tough Days at Work	Romans 12:12
April 29		Good Job	1 Peter 2:18
April 30	Fear of God	Fear God	Deuteronomy 5:29
May 1		Don't Fear God	1 John 4:18
May 2		Cultivating a Fear of God	1 Chronicles 16:30
May 3		Commands to Fear God	Psalm 96:9
May 4		Consequences of a Lack of Fear of God	Psalm 128:1
May 5		Consequences of Fearing God	Ecclesiastes 8:12
May 6		More Good Results of Fearing the Lord	Proverbs 22:4

	Theme	Title	Verse
May 7	Appreciating Family	Appreciating a Mother's Loyalty: Mary	John 19:25
May 8		Appreciating a Mother's Care: Jochebed	Hebrews 11:23
May 9		Appreciating a Mother's Prayers: Hannah	1 Samuel 2:1
May 10		Appreciating Fathers	Luke 15:20
May 11		Appreciating Parental Discipline	Proverbs 3:1
May 12		Appreciating Siblings	Proverbs 17:17
May 13		Appreciating Grandparents	2 Timothy 1:5
May 14	Essentials for Christian Growth	Food	Jeremiah 15:16
May 15		Air	Luke 5:16
May 16		Cleanliness	John 15:3
May 17		Exercise	Philippians 3:14
May 18		Love	Philippians 1:9
May 19		Rest	Exodus 33:14
May 20		Growing in Sunlight	2 Corinthians 4:6
May 21	Missions	God's Call to Go	Matthew 28:19
May 22		Christ, the Missionary	John 20:21
May 23		Brother Andrew, A Missionary in Palestine and Greece	2 Corinthians 5:20
May 24		Jesus' Example and Exhortation	Matthew 9:38
May 25		When Good Comes From Bad	Romans 8:28
May 26		Missionaries: Misunderstood and Misused	2 Timothy 3:12
May 27		Problems and God's Presence	Isaiah 43:5
May 28	Be Filled With the Holy Spirit	Who Is the Holy Spirit?	John 14:16
May 29		How the Holy Spirit Helps Us	Romans 8:26
May 30		The Spirit of Truth	John 15:26
May 31		How to Be Filled	Ephesians 5:18
June 1		Results of Being Spirit-Filled	Romans 8:16
June 2		Fruit of the Spirit	Ephesians 5:9
June 3		Grieve Not the Spirit	Ephesians 4:30
June 4	Wonders of God's Creation	From a Frog to a Prince	Romans 12:2
June 5		Shocking Information	2 Chronicles 25:8
June 6		A Fruitful Discussion	Matthew 7:17
June 7		The Little Beasties	Psalm 62:11
June 8		A Spongy Topic	Matthew 27:48
June 9		The Head as a Hammer	Genesis 1:21
June 10		Cool Crystals	Psalm 51:7
June 11	Honoring Parents	Ten Commandments for Honoring Parents	Exodus 21:17
June 12		Beatitudes for a Happy Home	Psalm 133:1
June 13		Do You Rob Your Parents?	Deuteronomy 5:16
June 14		How to Treat Your Mother	Luke 2:51
June 15		Honor Her Parents	1 Thessalonians 5:15
June 16		Avoid Explosions at Home	Colossians 3:8
June 17		At Home With 1 Corinthians 13	1 John 3:11

	Theme	Title	Verse
June 18	Encouragement	Verbal Encouragement	Proverbs 18:21
June 19		Nonverbal Encouragement	Acts 9:27
June 20		Honk If You Love Your Brother	1 Timothy 4:13
June 21		More Encouraging Lessons From Geese	Titus 2:15
June 22		Basics in Relating to the Handicapped	Acts 20:35
June 23		Accepting Others	Ephesians 1:6
June 24		Ministering to Our Ministers	Hebrews 13:7
June 25	Guilt	The Feeling of Guilt	Genesis 3:8
June 26		Unacceptable Ways to Face Guilt	Acts 24:25
June 27		More Unacceptable Ways of Facing Guilt	Psalm 32:3
June 28		How to Have Guilt Removed	Acts 16:30
June 29		Reasons for False Guilt	1 John 5:12
June 30		More Reasons for False Guilt	John 1:12
July 1		Facing Regrets	1 Chronicles 21:17
July 2	Prayer	Jesus' Example of Prayer	Luke 5:16
July 3		Types of Prayer	1 Samuel 7:5
July 4		Pray Through the Day	1 Thessalonians 5:17
July 5		Work and Pray	Ephesians 6:18
July 6		Hindrances to Prayer	Isaiah 1:15, 16
July 7		More Hindrances to Prayer	Colossians 4:2
July 8		Four Prayer Requests	Jeremiah 33:3
July 9	Friends	Value of Friends	Proverbs 27:17
July 10		Foundations for Friendship	Philippians 2:4
July 11		Turning Strangers Into Friends	Proverbs 18:24
July 12		Friendliness Toward Strangers	Matthew 25:35
July 13		Getting Acquainted With Friends	1 Samuel 18:1
July 14		Avoiding Mistakes	Proverbs 27:14
July 15		Ten Rules for Deepening Friendships	Proverbs 11:13
July 16	Witness	Witness by Forgiveness	Romans 12:21
July 17		Living Loyal Letters	2 Corinthians 3:2
July 18		Victory by Dying	Matthew 10:16
July 19		Witness in Music	Psalm 105:2
July 20		Testimony in Trials	Romans 8:17
July 21		The Man Who Didn't Pass By	1 Thessalonians 1:3
July 22		Let the Lower Lights Be Burning	Philippians 2:15
July 23	Honesty	Old Fashioned But Not Outdated	Romans 12:17
July 24		Temptations to Be Dishonest	Deuteronomy 16:20
July 25		The Truth About Lying	Proverbs 12:22
July 26		Spiritual Paper Bags	Luke 12:1
July 27		Don't Fudge	Proverbs 14:5
July 28		Finders Keepers	Luke 19:8
July 29		Lying—A Lubricant	Proverbs 21:28

	Theme	Title	Verse
July 30	Victory	Christian Armor	James 4:7
July 31		Parts of the Armor	Romans 13:12
August 1		Choose Death	Colossians 3:3
August 2		When Tempted, Listen	1 John 4:4
August 3		Hear the Master's Voice	2 Peter 2:9
August 4		It Will Be Different for Me	1 Timothy 6:11
August 5		Termites and Transgressions	Proverbs 6:27
August 6	The Church	Meal Etiquette at Church	Hebrews 10:25
August 7		More Manners in a Church Service	Psalm 84:4
August 8		The Church and the Great Wall of China	Matthew 16:18
August 9		Unity in the Church	Ephesians 4:13
August 10		The Harmonious Brotherhood	1 Peter 3:8
August 11		Attend Worship Services	John 4:24
August 12		Joy in Fellow Believers	Acts 2:42
August 13	Peer Pressure	Three Youth Who Resisted Peer Pressure	Ephesians 6:14
August 14		Peer Pressure and Idolatry	Deuteronomy 11:16
August 15		Peer Pressure and Culture	2 Corinthians 6:17
August 16		The Peril of Conformity	2 Corinthians 6:17
August 17		Micaiah and Peer Pressure	Romans 12:2
August 18		Following the Crowd	Exodus 23:2
August 19		Don't Follow the Crowd	Colossians 3:2
August 20	Sacrificial Love	No Fear	Matthew 16:24
August 21		Mennonite Missionary on the *Titanic*	John 15:13
August 22		John Troyer: Mennonite Martyr	Philippians 1:23
August 23		Menno Simons	1 Corinthians 3:11
August 24		Teacheress But Not Traitoress	Proverbs 11:12
August 25		Reaping What Was Sown	Proverbs 14:21
August 26		Curtis Cressman	Titus 2:13
August 27	Your Body: God's Temple	Wilt Thou Destroy Thyself?	Proverbs 11:3
August 28		Losing One's Brain to Alcohol	Proverbs 20:1
August 29		Mental Effects of Alcohol	Romans 13:13
August 30		Physical Effects of Alcohol	Ephesians 5:18
August 31		Smoking Kills	2 Corinthians 7:1
September 1		Don't Sleep and Drive	Acts 20:9
September 2		Seven Practical Suggestions for Driver Alertness	1 Thessalonians 5:6
September 3	Learn	Learn of Jesus	Acts 4:13
September 4		Learn the Bible	2 Timothy 3:14
September 5		Learn to Do Well	Proverbs 1:5
September 6		Methods of Learning	Romans 15:4
September 7		Learned by Experience	Psalm 40:1
September 8		Adult Education	Matthew 11:29
September 9		Higher Education	Job 28:28

	Theme	Title	Verse
September 10	Heroes of Peace	Polycarp	Romans 12:20
September 11		Peter Miller	Matthew 5:44
September 12		Maximilian	Romans 12:18
September 13		Dirk Willems	Romans 12:17
September 14		David Livingstone	Titus 3:2
September 15		Joris Wippe	Luke 9:56
September 16		Michael Sattler	1 Peter 2:13
September 17	Bitterness and Forgiveness	Bitterness Is a Choice	Colossians 3:13
September 18		Bitterness—A Root	James 3:14
September 19		Consequences of Unforgiveness	Mark 11:25
September 20		Think of Christ's Forgiveness	Acts 7:60
September 21		Tests of Forgiveness	Luke 17:4
September 22		Reviewing Hurts Hurts Yourself Again	1 Corinthians 13:5
September 23		Forgive and Forget	Ephesians 4:32
September 24	Snares of a Technological Age	Technology and the Bible	1 Kings 19:19
September 25		Principles in Identifying Snares	1 Peter 5:8
September 26		Technological Traps	1 Corinthians 6:20
September 27		Spiritual Snares	1 Corinthians 1:31
September 28		The Media Menace	Psalm 1:1
September 29		Blessing or Woe	John 15:11
September 30		Guidelines for Using Technology	Ephesians 4:1
October 1	Stewardship	Be a Manager	1 Peter 4:10
October 2		Money Talks	Matthew 6:20
October 3		In Support of Plastic Surgery	Romans 13:8
October 4		Unusual Robberies	Proverbs 3:9
October 5		Praying Before Purchasing	1 Timothy 6:20
October 6		How Frugal Should You Be?	John 6:12
October 7		Give, Give, Give	Genesis 28:22
October 8	Speech	Who Says Talk Is Cheap?	Proverbs 21:23
October 9		Put Your Head Into the Dirt	Psalm 79:13
October 10		Motor Mouths	Proverbs 13:3
October 11		A Song of Thanksgiving	Revelation 5:9
October 12		Adult Tattletales	Titus 3:2
October 13		Don't Murmur in Your Tent	Psalm 106:25
October 14		Hypocrisy in Singing	Mark 7:6
October 15	God's Gifts in Nature	Remarkable Rain	Deuteronomy 11:14
October 16		Plentiful Plants	Matthew 6:28
October 17		Cohesiveness of Matter	1 Corinthians 8:6
October 18		The Gift of Sunshine	John 1:4
October 19		Dihydrogen Monoxide	John 7:38
October 20		Thank God for Cows	Proverbs 15:17
October 21		Like a River	Psalm 36:8

	Theme	Title	Verse
October 22	Relating to the Opposite Gender	Purity in Thought	Philippians 4:8
October 23		Helps for Purity	1 Corinthians 6:18
October 24		Blessings of Purity	Matthew 5:8
October 25		A Virtuous Young Man	Luke 2:4, 5
October 26		Know the Person You Marry	Proverbs 31:30
October 27		A Godly and Pure Courtship	Psalm 119:9
October 28		Fulfillment in Singlehood	Philippians 4:11
October 29	The Lord's Prayer	Relationship	Matthew 6:9
October 30		Reverence	Matthew 6:9
October 31		Submission	Matthew 6:10
November 1		Petition	Matthew 6:11
November 2		Confession	Matthew 6:12
November 3		Deliverance	Matthew 6:13
November 4		Adoration	Matthew 6:13
November 5	Assurance of Salvation	If We Walk in the Light	1 John 1:7
November 6		If We Confess Our Sins	1 John 1:9
November 7		If We Obey	1 John 2:3
November 8		If We Love Our Brothers	1 John 4:12
November 9		If Our Heart Condemns Us Not	Hebrews 9:14
November 10		If We Confess Christ and Believe	Romans 10:9
November 11		If the Spirit Dwells in Us	Romans 8:9
November 12	Tested But Triumphant	Persecuted But Smiling	1 Corinthians 15:58
November 13		Persecuted But Faithful	Revelation 2:10
November 14		Persecuted But Cheerful	Psalm 42:8
November 15		Persecuted But Singing	Luke 15:17
November 16		Persecuted But Glad	Hebrews 11:38
November 17		Persecuted But Loyal	Romans 15:2
November 18		Persecuted But Persevering	James 5:10
November 19	Thanksgiving	Eat Mashed Potatoes for Thanksgiving	Psalm 100:4
November 20		Learning to Be Content	1 Timothy 6:6
November 21		Thanks Be Unto God	Psalm 106:1
November 22		Thanks a Million	Hebrews 13:15
November 23		Thanks and Giving	2 Corinthians 9:7
November 24		Appreciate Afflictions	Ephesians 5:20
November 25		How to Have Joy	John 15:11
November 26	Courtesy	Manners Matter	1 Peter 3:8
November 27		Don't Act Like a Pig	1 Corinthians 13:4, 5
November 28		More Lessons From Pigs	Galatians 5:15
November 29		A Time for Silence	Ecclesiastes 3:7
November 30		Giving and Receiving Advice	Proverbs 1:8
December 1		Show a Little Kindness	Proverbs 31:26
December 2		Wear a Smile	Proverbs 17:22

	Theme	Title	Verse
December 3	Christian Living	Put Christ First	Matthew 6:33
December 4		Imitators of God	1 Peter 2:21
December 5		Rejoice	1 Thessalonians 5:16
December 6		Don't Lower Your Standards	Proverbs 20:7
December 7		The Temptation to Lower Standards	Proverbs 11:3
December 8		Overdue	Psalm 37:21
December 9		Do Not Stop Chain Saws With Hands	Luke 14:18
December 10	Names of Christ	Wonderful	Philippians 2:9
December 11		Counselor	Isaiah 11:2
December 12		Mighty God	Matthew 9:6
December 13		The Everlasting Father	John 10:30
December 14		The Prince of Peace	John 16:33
December 15		The Babe	Luke 2:16
December 16		Born a King	John 19:19
December 17	The Birth of Christ	Wise Men Who Were Shepherds	Galatians 4:4
December 18		More Wisdom From the Shepherds	1 Timothy 1:15
December 19		God Gives Gifts to Us	Romans 5:1
December 20		Giving Gifts to God	Isaiah 60:3
December 21		Big Christmas Gifts	Luke 2:17
December 22		Christmas Surprises	Matthew 1:18
December 23		More Christmas Surprises	Matthew 2:2
December 24	Ready	Ready for Christmas	Galatians 4:4
December 25		A Saviour Is Born	Luke 2:10-12
December 26		Ready to Go Home	John 14:2, 3
December 27		Ready for Christ's Return	Luke 12:40
December 28		Readiness to Rise	Amos 4:12
December 29		Are You Ready?	1 Peter 3:15
December 30		Driving Into the Future	2 Corinthians 13:5
December 31		Looking Back and Forward	Luke 17:22

Daily Readings

OLD TESTAMENT

Genesis

2:1-20	April 23
18:1-15	July 13
18:16-33	February 15
20:1-18	December 6
22:1-19	May 10
24:10-37	January 11
26:12-33	February 25
27:30-43	September 22
32:1-20	July 29
37:1-11	February 19
37:2-13, 18-34	May 12
39:1-12	December 7
39:1-21	October 23
42:3-28	June 26
43:1-23	July 23
45:1-15	September 7
50:14-21	September 23

Exodus

2:1-10	May 8
3:1-17	January 18
16:4-6, 14-31	November 1
18:5-27	November 30
20:18-26	April 30
33:12-17	January 8
32:15-29	July 27

Leviticus

10:6-8, 22-26	August 16
14:1-20	May 16
19:9-18, 33-37	July 12

Numbers

12	February 21
16:1-21	March 6

Deuteronomy

4:1-24	September 4
5:7-21	June 11
8	November 23
11:13-21	January 21
22:1-4	July 28
31:1-15	December 31

Joshua

1:1-9	March 17
7:6-15	January 9

Judges

4:1-16	November 17
6:33-40	January 14
16:1-21	February 17

Ruth

2:1-17	July 11

1 Samuel

1:9-28	May 9
8:4-22	August 18
15:10-30	December 9
17:1-37	April 20
17:18-38	November 28
17:38-51	April 21
18:28--19:7	July 9
20:1-17	January 13
26:2-25	March 10
25:1-17	November 27

2 Samuel

9:1-13	June 22
11:5-27	June 27

1 Kings

1:5-31	June 12
18:21-39	July 4
22:5-35	August 17

2 Kings

4:1-17	October 3
6:1-7	December 8
17:5-20	August 19
19:1-5, 14-20	July 5
22:1-13	July 24

1 Chronicles

29:6-23	October 1
29:10-20	November 4

2 Chronicles

26:1-15	September 24

Esther

5:7-14; 7:1-10	February 24

Job

19:13-27	July 14

Psalms

19	January 15
21	September 27
22	April 5

Theme Verse Index

OLD TESTAMENT

Christian Light Publications, Inc., is a nonprofit, conservative Mennonite publishing company providing Christ-centered, Biblical literature including books, Gospel tracts, Sunday school materials, summer Bible school materials, and a full curriculum for Christian day schools and homeschools. Though produced primarily in English, some books, tracts, and school materials are also available in Spanish.

For more information about the ministry of CLP or its publications, or for spiritual help, please contact us at:

Christian Light Publications, Inc.
P. O. Box 1212
Harrisonburg, VA 22803-1212

Telephone – 540-434-0768
Fax – 540-433-8896
E-mail – info@clp.org
www.clp.org